Mark's Gospel as
Literature and History

David Bruce Taylor

Mark's Gospel as Literature and History

SCM PRESS LTD

To the memory of

The Reverend Canon Henry York Ganderton

Formerly Headmaster of the Choir School at Durham
and my first instructor in Mark's Gospel.

0 334 00974 X

First published 1992 by
SCM Press Ltd
26–30 Tottenham Road, London N1 4BZ

Typeset by Regent Typesetting, London
Printed in Great Britain by
Mackays of Chatham, Kent

Contents

Foreword

Self-justification is assumed by politicians to be impolitic. But politicians are concerned, not with the underlying truth of a matter, but with the popular understanding of it; and even if that popular understanding is in fact a misunderstanding, that also has very little relevance to a practically-minded government. As the then Lord Halifax advised Charles II's Privy Council over the Popish Plot: We must now at least pretend to take it seriously; and the consequence of that was a whole series of public executions. Those of us who would rather be thought, if not philosophers then at least honest men, rather than politicians, do sometimes feel the need to justify ourselves – sometimes (which is perhaps most impolitic of all) even in advance of any expressed criticism.

The feature which will be found strange in the following work, I suspect, is its avoidance of any reference to other books in the same field. The modern academic fashion is for this kind of study to consist of very little else. That was already beginning to be the case when I read theology as an undergraduate some thirty years ago, largely as a consequence of the then fairly recent emphasis on the postgraduate thesis and doctorate; the present academic generation cannot conceive of a time or state of affairs when things could ever have been otherwise. The apparatus of a modern academic work, so far from merely clothing and protecting the naked babe of argument, has long since had the effect of smothering it. My own interest on the contrary is in letting the argument be heard.

My impatience with modern habits of annotation has complex origins. It so happened that I was already familiar with the Bible before I ever went up to university. It did not surprise me that the books I had to read there put things in a new and sometimes disturbing light. What they said about the Bible was often discernibly true, and in those days could still more than occasionally be well-expressed. But I quickly became aware of – and deeply dissatisfied by

– what I felt was a central lack in the accepted approach. It was then (and is even more so now) taken for granted that the Bible, rather than being a collection of books, is best seen as a collection of fragments that have been made up – often very clumsily – into books; and the task of the scholar is to break down those piles of rubble into their component parts and exhibit them almost as if they were unconnected items. As far as this goes, there is point in the aim. But it overlooks the fact, which to me is the important fact, that the existing piles of rubble are not as haphazard in their arrangement as this approach assumes; the Bible as a whole, and the various books within it, often show clear signs of a conscious plan underlying the apparent chaos. And I have always been much more interested in these long strands of coherence than in the abrupt individual grains and pebbles that go to make them up.

I early came to realize that Mark's gospel is an exceptional – I would go so far as to say a unique – illustration of this very principle. At first reading it comes across as a ragbag of tiny little incidents arranged in no particular order. In fact, as I believe I have demonstrated in the work that follows, the arrangement has been deeply pondered; the overall plan is not merely coherent, but could even be described as systematic, in a way that perhaps is exhibited in no other book of the Bible.

It was also interesting as the earliest of the gospels, and therefore by far the closest to whatever history there is in the events the gospels describe. I do not claim we can ever rediscover the real history of these events; but the historical worth of the first three gospels can still nevertheless be evaluated, and the conclusion established (which is not at first sight obvious, and which is well worth establishing) that there are genuine historical events underlying the confused and miraculous fictions we have. Mark's gospel, being the closest to those events, gives us the best view of them available to us – which is still, on the other hand, by no means a clear view.

As the title of the work itself suggests, these have been my two overriding interests throughout. It would be untrue to suggest that there has been no academic discussion of these approaches, but (at the risk of getting it broken) I am prepared to stick my neck out and suggest that academic writing on the Bible tends to have a very defective understanding of history and almost no understanding at all of literature. It does have some excuse for this, in that the Bible itself has, from our point of view, a defective understanding of history. (Historical writing about the Bible would often be improved if it started from this premise as a basic and acknowledged axiom.) It does not help, on the other hand (as a modern academic typically might wish to do) simply to strip away the miraculous or fabulous accretions and distortions in order to reveal the 'original' underlying history. Very often (as in the gospels) this underlying history cannot be coherently recreated anyway; but even if it could, the resulting 'original' historical narrative would still miss the point. Such a narrative, for instance, would have no moral, doctrinal or ideological content whatever; and Bible-reading, if it has any point at all, is about absorbing the moral ideas and doctrines with which the Bible is concerned; and these all reside, not in the original history itself, but precisely in the distorted way in which the biblical authors view it.[1]

This charge of misunderstanding literature can be illustrated from my own experience of academic comments on aspects of the the present work. To take a minor example first: on page 32 of the introduction I offer an explanation of the imagery – which has often been found to be puzzling – of Psalm 133. I am not aware of having made use of anyone else's suggestions here at all; I have, if you like, simply invented it. In that case, I have been assured, my suggestions are worthless, being – as by my own admission they are – offered without a shred of evidence to support them. I have countered with the suggestion that in interpreting imagery the only relevant 'evidence' is the inherent plausibility of the explanation offered, and the way the interpretation matches up with the imagery. No good, comes the answer; this kind of thing is mere speculation, which a properly disciplined mind is bound to set aside. This kind of crassness, I suppose, is the deserved result of our having all but banished poetry from the education syllabus.

I have encountered similar opposition (though not from the same source) to the plan of the work as a whole. As I make clear throughout, I believe I am demonstrating for the first time the plan that Mark actually devised and executed in laying out his gospel. But what *evidence* have I got for this view?, I have been asked. I point out that I have given clear labels to the various sections I claim to have discerned; and if it turns out that the content of those sections demonstrably corresponds to the labels I have given them, and also that the labels themselves seem to indicate a kind of logical progression, then this itself is the evidence that vindicates the theory.

Once again, no good. 'Unprecedented theories of this kind, without
the hard evidence to support them, are likely to be dismissed as
fanciful, and that is how I see it.' This from a body whose own idea of
evidence is often little more than providing a short-list of other
scholars who happen to agree with them[2].

This kind of open antipathy has been shown to the finished work,
but I was distantly aware of the likelihood of it long before I began. I
frankly admit that I could not have produced an academic work, or
anything like it, even if I had wanted to. But as soon as the reader
starts reading it, I am confident that my claim that I had no wish to
will be readily accepted; as will my claim that the work is all the
better for not being academically set out.

I should add that for years before I went up to university, and very
quickly again after I came down, I took it for granted that the
overriding purpose of literature – and by that I mean the whole art of
reading and writing, and not just the reading and writing of fiction –
is pleasure; and this attitude I have found incompatible with an
academic approach. For the first few years after graduating I did
from time to time grit my teeth and plough through works which
reviews had assured me were 'important'; but I usually felt that the
amount of determination and self-punishment required for this
exercise was wholly disproportionate to the fruits of it. So I decided
to concentrate on getting better acquainted with the wider traditional and accepted body of ancient literature instead, an exercise
which has been an unfailing source of pleasure and – I flatter myself –
enlightenment for the last thirty years.

I have, I dare say, included more than a few 'academic' points in
the following exposition, and perhaps I am open to deserved criticism in making no acknowledgment of their source. I admit I may
have been careless here. Since for many years I have known the text
very well and virtually carried it in my head, whenever I overheard or
casually came across an interesting observation it automatically
achieved a permanent place in my thinking by attaching itself to the
relevant part of the text. I have probably spent as much of my life in
church as any man alive apart from professed monks and nuns,
which means that in my time I have listened to numberless sermons,
not all of which by any means have been dull. A very great deal of
what follows is germinated from seeds planted by those sermons.
This is a shockingly unsystematic way of going on, but it does have
one great advantage over the card-index that an academic approach

would have required. I find that knowledge on file is rather like brandy in the bottle, in that it has stopped maturing; whereas knowledge in the head is more like brandy in the cask, in that it is maturing all the time.

I come now to the most insistent question of the age we live in: for what kind of readership am I writing? – or, as the jargon has it, what kind of 'market' do I have in mind? (Even dedicated philosophers in the modern world have learnt to talk this kind of grocer's dialect, sometimes with every appearance of sincerity.) Let me illustrate the gap I believe I have noticed in what is available. Anyone going into a religious bookshop and looking at the books on the Bible, assuming they have some prior knowledge of the subject, will effortlessly be able to sort every item into one of two piles. In one pile would be those books intended for the professional scholar or the fledgling academic student, whose style would be unreadable and whose topics would tend to be remote, abstruse and dull; and in the other pile would be those intended for the pious and devout, whose style would be just as unreadable but for a different reason, in that the claims and assumptions underlying the 'argument' would be glaringly – one could even say stupidly – unconvincing. There might also be a small pile that was intended for both; there would be no pile at all that was intended for neither.

Yet I have spent many years of my life as a regular Bible reader, and always, I think, with both profit and enjoyment. I assume furthermore that it is culturally important that there should be a literate and – not to put too fine a point on it – elitist section of the educated public with a wide and essentially non-specialist appreciation of the whole of the literary tradition, including the Bible and the classics. At this point the reader gasps with unbelief: isn't this the now 'discredited' approach of the humanist tradition? And yet we have just such a public for the classical tradition of music; and literature – though I have no wish to disparage music in anyway – is a far more essential medium for the transmission of culture than music is. In the modern world no public figure would dare to suggest that the music of the past belongs to the past, and that we must put such elitist and irrelevant pursuits behind us and concentrate solely on the practical, the useful and the marketable; we would all quite rightly be scandalized. Yet when it comes to literature, we allow them not merely to make that assumption publicly, but even to make it the stated aim of education policy, and all with hardly a word of protest.

I said above that I have read the Bible for years with profit and enjoyment. The enjoyment, I hope, will communicate itself in the work that follows, but I would like to say a few words here about what I see as the 'profit' of this exercise. When it comes to monumental literature such as the Bible is, you don't just read it through and then put it back on the shelf; you read from it repeatedly until you know it well and a jumble of little tags remembered from it are constantly running through your head. Nor is the Bible unique in this; in some degree the same applies to all great literature. The literature that makes a difference is not the literature you have simply read, but the literature you have actually *learnt* in something like this way. Any book or collection of books can become this kind of Bible; to the ancient Greeks it was Homer, to the Romans it was Homer and Virgil, to those of our own day it can even be the works of a favourite novelist – and there are probably a very great number in the modern world to whom it is the works of Shakespeare. The idea of the Bible as 'revelation' in the traditional Christian or Jewish sense does not seem to me to have much to be said for it. It *is* revelation of course in the sense that all literature is revelation; it is particular revelation in the sense that this is the literature we identify with more than any other. All Bibles in this sense are 'true' Bibles; they just are not equally true for all readers. For those who want to find a certain and eternal revelation of 'truth' this constitutes a problem; but not, I think, for the rest of us.

And what is the profit, as distinct from the pleasure, of our having *learnt* great literature in this way? The important gain, I would suggest, is those little remembered tags I spoke about that keep running through our heads. They constitute a kind of message or exhortation which comes to our rescue and offers dependable help and encouragement on those many occasions when the world around us seems to have let us down. No matter what overt claims Christians have made for the Bible in the past, we can easily see from the way they have written about it in recent centuries (particularly since the Reformation) that it also worked for them – I am almost tempted to write that it *really* worked for them – in just this way. Now that Christians by and large no longer read the Bible, they seem to anchor themselves in the platitudes of the hymn book instead. I believe they have made a very poor exchange, but they must be the ones to decide what suits them best.

This kind of message is necessarily to some extent – and often to a considerable extent – at odds with what we call 'reality', and many readers will sense a danger here of what we call religious mania. Undoubtedly there is such a thing, and it can sometimes be a dangerous thing. It is in fact quite hard to identify just what has gone wrong in religious mania. It does not seem to have much to do with the unreality of the 'message' itself. Plenty of Christians for instance – with apparent sincerity, and with no trace of incapacity for handling 'reality' – insist that the 'message' of Christianity is completely and unshakably 'true'. And on the other hand it is not rare to encounter people very like religious maniacs, but whose central ideology contains none at all of those sheer impossibilities that traditional Christianity revels in, but which is entirely concentrated on what most of us would consider to be aspects of the 'real' world: I mean such people as wholly dedicated communists, feminists, animal rights activists – perhaps indeed wholly dedicated *anything*. I suggest the answer is quite simply that two worlds are better than one: the world of experience and the world of aspiration need to be in perpetual – no, not necessarily conflict; something much milder, more like tension or contrast. Religious or ideological mania seems to result from denying the world of experience altogether: either condemning it so completely, or finding it so ungraspable, as wholly to institute the imaginary world of aspiration in its place.

There is no inherent danger then in responding even to a highly unreal imaginary world of aspiration, provided one maintains no less a response to that of reality. My own view is that an unreal vision should be deliberately chosen. Reality at its most basic is the view that we accidentally arose from primaeval sludge, and will one day inevitably return to it; but the staggering technical and cultural achievements of which we are so proud do not rest on that kind of perception at all. On the contrary, we have to insist on 'deluding' ourselves that our lives, both individually and collectively, are filled with 'significance', that we are here for a purpose and that the visible, stupendous universe is there to serve that purpose; and it is on the basis of delusions like this that we build as we have built, and marvel as we have marvelled. On a close examination it turns out that the world of reality contains no thrills for us; those all belong to the world of aspiration.

Introduction

I

The death of Jesus is normally dated about AD 35, the writing of this gospel about thirty years later. It is widely assumed that during these intervening years, if there were written records of Jesus' life, they were of a fragmentary kind, and that little importance attached to them. There seem to have been two reasons for this. The first is that a high proportion of these early Christians were probably illiterate, and for such men written records had little significance. The second – which the modern reader may find bizarre – is that no need of any permanent or durable record of Jesus' life seems initially to have been felt. The purpose of written records, after all, is to preserve information which would otherwise be lost through the passage of time; but since for these first-generation Christians the world was shortly coming to an end in any case, what need was there of records? We can trace right through the New Testament the changing course of this to us rather startling belief, from words which may very well be close to those Jesus actually used,[1] to the disappointed admission by the latest author in the New Testament that what had once been, in its most literal interpretation, the very cornerstone of Christian hope, must now be reinterpreted in what we would call a rather more spiritual sense. Compare the two following:

And he said to them, 'Truly, I say to you, there are some standing here who will not taste death before they see that the kingdom of God has come with power.' (Mark 9.1)

First of all you must understand this, that scoffers will come in the last days with scoffing, following their own passions and saying, 'Where is the promise of his coming? For ever since the fathers fell asleep, all things have continued as they were from the beginning of creation' ... But do not ignore this one fact, beloved, that with the Lord one day is as a thousand years, and a thousand years as one day ... (II Peter 3.3–4, 8)

What sort of records, then, did the early church rely on? Because, so far from thinking, as you might have concluded from the above, that what 'originally happened' scarcely mattered to them, it is clear from the record that these early local churches were intensely interested in anything anyone could tell them about the life of Jesus on earth. It would be nice to think (and has often been stated) that at any rate in the early days it largely consisted of eyewitness testimony. The gospels themselves tell us, and on this point we have no reason to doubt them, that Jesus chose from a much larger (and perhaps constantly changing) band of personal followers a nucleus of twelve 'missionaries' (the Latin derivative equivalent to the Greek 'apostles'), 'to be with him, and to be sent out to preach and have authority to cast out demons ...', (Mark 3.14–15). There is a passage in the somewhat later Acts of the Apostles which suggests that the purpose of this band of apostles was to be preachers of the gospel after Jesus' death:

> So one of the men who have accompanied us during all the time that the Lord Jesus went in and out among us, beginning from the baptism of John until the day when he was taken up from us – one of these men must become with us a witness to his resurrection. (Acts 1.21–22)

But the implication of Mark's account is that these apostles were to be extensions of Jesus' ministry during his actual life-time, and Mark describes such a mission in 6.7–13, 30–32 of his gospel.[2]

These eyewitness accounts, whether preached by twelve, or by seventy, or even by the hundred and twenty mentioned in Acts 1.15, may well have been the earliest vehicle of the Christian message, particularly within the confines of Palestine[3] itself. But long before Mark's gospel came to be written (which, remember, is probably about thirty years after Jesus' death) there were Christian communities spread over the whole of the Eastern Mediterranean, and even further afield than that. We know of two preachers – Barnabas and Paul – who were particularly active in this foreign mission, neither of whom could claim in any sense to be eyewitnesses of the gospel events. And this leads us to one of the great puzzles of the New Testament, which includes a fair number of letters from Paul to several of these local churches that he founded. Not everything ascribed to him is genuine, but we can be confident of Romans, the two letters to the Corinthians (provided we view them as collections of fragments which originally may have stood in many more letters than two) and, supremely, Galatians. This is by no means to suggest that all the rest are spurious; but in the above we have a reasonably extensive body of writing whose genuineness is pretty well unquestioned. The striking feature about all these documents is that they show no interest at all in any of the events recorded in the gospels (and amazingly this goes for all the other epistles as well, the single exception being the plainly spurious II Peter 1. 16–18). They make occasional reference to the crucifixion, frequent reference to the resurrection – but (except in the ambiguous instance of I Corinthians 15) scarcely seem to view either as historical events at all. And so far as we can tell, all these documents are *earlier* than Mark, which is our earliest gospel.

And yet the existence of Mark, and of Matthew and Luke as well, are undeniable evidence that during this period people must have been interested, indeed very keenly interested, in the events of Jesus' life. If anyone were to sit down and read these three gospels straight through, it is unlikely he would need much convincing that as historical accounts they need to be treated, shall we say, with caution. Instead of offering us a coherent narrative, all three of them seem to consist of collections of tiny little scraps. A lot of these scraps contain striking sayings, and in such cases it looks as though it is these sayings that are the reason why the story has been preserved.[4] Even more noticeably, all three gospels contain an abundance of what we call miracle stories: stories which to the modern reader will appear obviously untrue, though they may in many cases – perhaps in most – perhaps, indeed, in all – be no more than exaggerations or distortions of events which actually did occur. The gospels are not, then, straightforward and reliable accounts of the events of Jesus' life; but at the same time, the impression is unavoidable that this material contains a considerable amount of genuine reminiscence of someone who actually did exist.[5]

The modern historian can easily suggest reasons why it was that the first generation of Christians did not feel the need of written records; and he can also easily explain why, after a period of about thirty years, the need for written records began to be felt as a matter of urgency. Consider the following:

> Whoever, therefore, eats the bread or drinks the cup of the Lord in an unworthy manner will be guilty of profaning the body and blood of the Lord. Let a man examine himself, and so eat of the bread and drink of the cup. For any one who eats and drinks without discerning the body eats and drinks judgment upon himself. That is why many of you are weak and ill, and some have died. (I Cor. 11.27–30)

This was probably written about twenty years after Jesus' death, and is the conclusion of an extended passage reproving the readers for the careless and irreverent way in which they celebrate the Lord's supper. At first reading, we might be inclined to dismiss that concluding sentence as no more than an indication of a belief, common among religious enthusiasts, that offences against the deity are punished; and following often enough from that, that people who appear to have been punished must somehow have offended the deity. But in fact there is much more to it than that. Both Paul and his readers have clearly taken it for granted up to now that anyone who has been baptized into Christ can expect quite literally to live for ever – not life after death, but the actual abolition of death itself. In I Corinthians 15.15 (which may originally have belonged to quite another document than the above excerpt) he allows that people who have died will nevertheless be raised again to share in Christ's kingdom when he returns to earth; but even there he seems to suggest that most believers can expect to be still alive at the time, that their present perishable bodies will be suddenly and miraculously changed to imperishable, and they will then share in Christ's kingdom for ever without ever experiencing death. He undoubtedly meant all this to be understood quite literally as a forecast of an event which was to be expected in years rather than decades.

But by the time thirty years were up, it is likely that these weak and ill – not to mention the dead – had become very numerous, and among them would be some whose elevated sanctity could not be doubted. Not only would there be doubts about the original forecast of the end of the corruptible world, but there would also be the growing realization that the original eyewitnesses were beginning to be few and far between, and that if it was going to be a long wait after all, instead of the short wait originally calculated, some more permanent record would be needed to fill the gap.

It is this kind of impulse, it is generally supposed, that lay behind the writing of Mark's gospel. Much of the following chronology is admittedly conjectural, but we estimate that Jesus died about AD 35. Luke tells us (3.23) that Jesus was 'about thirty years of age' when he began his ministry, having told us earlier (3.1) that this was 'in the fifteenth year of the reign of Tiberius Caesar',[6] but we have no grounds for confidence that this itself is any more than Lucan guess-work, since none of the other gospels gives us any dates at all. The only thing of which we can be really confident is that Jesus died sometime while Pontius Pilate was governor of Judaea (AD 26–36).

What then are the grounds for arguing that Mark's gospel is about thirty years later than Jesus' death? The two usually put forward don't strike me as all that convincing, and I personally prefer to rely on the suggestions put forward above; but I set them out so that the reader can judge.

The first relates to the fire of Rome in AD 64, which Nero thought it politic to blame on the Christians. (We do not *know*, by the way, that Nero actually started the fire; only that he was popularly accused of it, and used this device to shift the blame.) Tradition has it that both Peter and Paul perished in the subsequent persecution, and that it was the sense of crisis created by this dramatic loss of the two great leaders of the church that brought Mark's gospel into being. The trouble with this suggestion is that it heavily relies on un-supported oral tradition, and in an overwhelming proportion of those many instances where oral tradition can be checked against the written records of the time, the oral tradition turns out to be worthless. I suspect the same would be true of this story if we had any means of checking it. We have no real reason to believe that Peter was ever at Rome at all; and though the implication of the conclusion of Acts is that Paul ended his days there, it is very odd that the author makes no mention of the connection of his death with the persecution of Christians after the fire of Rome if there had been such a connection. The natural interpretation of the passage is that after two years Paul simply died, and the likelihood is therefore that his death was in fact earlier than the fire of Rome.

The second relates to chapter 13 of Mark's gospel, which is often

referred to as the 'Marcan Apocalypse'. Here we find Jesus foretelling the fall of Jerusalem, something we have no reason to doubt
he actually did, even though the event occurred in AD 70, i.e. about
thirty-five years after his death. We have much the same material in
chapter 24 of Matthew and chapter 21 of Luke. Scholars claim to be
able to tell that chapter 13 of Mark was genuinely written before AD
70, whereas as the other two 'prophecies' have clearly been written
up later. I think the claim is true, but the grounds on which they
support it seem very flimsy. Compare Mark 13.21–23 with Matthew
24.23–28. One of the big differences is Matthew's addition of the
saying (verse 28): 'Wherever the body is, there the eagles will be
gathered together' (also found in Luke 17.31). Again, compare Mark
13.14 with Luke 21.20–21. The noticeable difference is Luke's
prophecy of 'Jerusalem surrounded by armies'. The scholars' case
seems to rest largely on these two details, which they see as *specific*
claims that Jerusalem would be destroyed by the armies of Rome, a
point on which the Marcan material is *not* specific.

APPENDIX

The earliest *evidence* we have relating to the origins of the gospel
comes from Eusebius' *Ecclesiastical History* Book III, chapter 39.
The following is virtually the whole of it – I have omitted only the
first half of the opening sentence, and only because this is the only
part that does not concern us. The passage relating to Mark's gospel
occurs towards the end of the chapter, and is of exceptional interest
as being by far the earliest surviving 'evidence' we have. However, I
take the view that it must be read with scepticism, and some
discussion of the chapter as a whole is needed to show why this is so.
The translation is by Oulton in the Loeb Edition, though I have here
and there modified the punctuation.

> ... and of Papias five treatises are extant which have also the title
> of 'Interpretation of the Oracles of the Lord'. These are also
> mentioned by Irenaeus as though his only writing, for he says in
> one place, 'To these things also Papias, the hearer of John, who
> was a companion of Polycarp and one of the ancients, bears
> witness in writing in the fourth of his books, for five books were
> composed by him'. So says Irenaeus. Yet Papias himself, accord-
> ing to the preface of his treatises, makes plain that he had in no

way been a hearer and eyewitness of the sacred apostles, but teaches that he had received the articles of the faith from those who had known them, for he speaks as follows: 'And I shall not hesitate to append to the interpretations all that I ever learnt well from the presbyters, and remember well; for of their truth I am confident. For unlike most, I did not rejoice in them who say much, but in them who teach the truth; nor in them who recount the commandments of others, but in them who repeated those given to the faith by the Lord and derived from truth itself; but if ever anyone came who had followed the presbyters, I inquired into the words of the presbyters, what Andrew or Peter or Philip or Thomas or James or John or Matthew, or any other of the Lord's disciples, had said; and what Aristion and the presbyter John, the Lord's disciples, were saying. For I did not suppose that information from books would help me so much as the word of a living and surviving voice.'

It is here worth noting that he twice counts the name of John, and reckons the first John with Peter and James and Matthew and the other apostles, clearly meaning the evangelist; but, by changing his statement, places the second with the others outside the number of the apostles, putting Aristion before him and clearly calling him a presbyter. This confirms the truth of the story of those who have said that there were two of the same name in Asia, and that there are two tombs at Ephesus, both still called John's. This calls for attention: for it is probable that the second (unless anyone prefer the former) saw the revelation which passes under the name of John. The Papias whom we are now treating confesses that he had received the words of the apostles from their followers, but says that he had actually heard Aristion and the presbyter John. He often quotes them by name and gives their traditions in his writings. Let this suffice to good purpose. But it is worthwhile to add to the words of Papias already given the other sayings of his, in which he tells certain marvels and other details which apparently reached him by tradition. It has already been mentioned that Philip the Apostle lived at Hierapolis with his daughters, but it must now be shown how Papias was with them and received a wonderful story from the daughters of Philip; for he relates the resurrection of a corpse in his time, and in another place another miracle connected with Justus surnamed Barsabas, for he drank poison but by the Lord's grace suffered no harm. Of this Justus the Acts relates that the sacred apostles set him up and prayed over him together with Matthias after the ascension of the Lord, for the choice of one to fill up their number in place of the traitor Judas: 'and they set forth two, Joseph called Barsabas, who was called Justus, and Matthias; and they prayed and said ...' The same writer adduces other accounts, as though they came to him from unwritten tradition, and some strange parables and teachings of the Saviour, and some more mythical accounts. Among them he says that there will be a millennium after the resurrection of the dead, when the kingdom of Christ will be set up in material form on this earth. I suppose that he got these notions by a perverse reading of the apostolic accounts, not realizing that they had spoken mystically and symbolically. For he was a man of very little intelligence, as is clear from his books. But he is responsible for the fact that so many Christian writers after him held the same opinion, relying on his antiquity – for instance Irenaeus, and whoever else appears to have held the same views.

In the same writing he also quotes other interpretations of the words of the Lord given by the Aristion mentioned above, and traditions of John the presbyter. To them we may direct the studious; but we are now obliged to append to the words already quoted from him a tradition about the Mark who wrote the Gospel, which he expounds as follows: And the presbyter used to say this, 'Mark became Peter's interpreter and wrote accurately all that he remembered – not indeed in order – of the things said or done by the Lord. For he had not heard the Lord, nor had he followed him, but later on, as I said, followed Peter; who used to give teaching as necessity demanded, but not making, as it were, an arrangement of the Lord's oracles, so that Mark did nothing wrong in thus writing down single points as he remembered them. For to one thing he gave attention, to leave out nothing of what he had heard, and to make no false statements in them.' This is related by Papias about Mark; and about Matthew this was said: 'Matthew collected the oracles in the Hebrew language, and each interpreted them as best he could.'

The same writer used quotations from the first Epistle of John, and likewise also from that of Peter, and has expounded another story about a woman who was accused before the Lord of many sins, which the Gospel according to the Hebrews contains. Let this suffice us in addition to the extracts made.

The interpretation of this passage is a minefield. First of all we need to sort out who everybody is. The author, Eusebius, lived approximately from 260–340, and for about the last twenty-five years of his life was Bishop of Caesarea on the coast of Palestine. His *Ecclesiastical History* is his most important work, and though by no means a masterpiece either of style, analysis or evaluation (as the reader can probably see for himself) it is valuable for its frequent reference to very early written sources of Christian history very many of which – including Papias – have not otherwise survived.

Irenaeus lived approximately from 130–200, and became Bishop of Lyons in 178; but since he claims to have heard Polycarp as a boy, it is thought that he was originally a native of Smyrna on the coast of Asia Minor. Traditionally only one work of his was known to survive, the *Adversus Haereses*, from which Eusebius is quoting. In recent times, though, a second work on the Apostolic Preaching has come to light in an Armenian translation. (Like nearly all Christians of the first two centuries – Eastern and Western – Irenaeus spoke and wrote in Greek.)

Polycarp is traditionally said to have been born about 70, though there are difficulties about this (see below). He became Bishop of Smyrna at an unknown date, and in his time he seems to have been the leading Christian bishop of Asia Minor. The tradition that he was burnt to death at the age of eighty-six during a pagan outburst of hostility to Christianity seems quite good. On the other hand, the tradition states that this was in 155 or 156, whereas Eusebius places it in the reign of Marcus Aurelius (161–180). Iranaeus specifically states that Polycarp in his youth had personal acquaintance with some of those who had known Jesus; though this is easily possible as regards actual dates, it is by no means certain that it is true (see Papias below).

Papias seems to have lived from about 60–130 and to have become Bishop of Hierapolis, an inland city of Asia Minor. Everything we know of him is contained in the above passage by Eusebius.

Omitting for the moment the names of the apostles, we are left with Aristion and John the presbyter. We know nothing of the former apart from what this passage tells us; the ascription of the 'longer ending' of Mark's gospel to him in a tenth-century Armenian manuscript is presumed to be a fanciful attempt to find work for an early Christian figure otherwise unknown. With John the presbyter we find ourselves faced with a heap of confusion. (Part of the reason why Eusebius thinks Papias is 'of very little intelligence' may well be that Eusebius himself is often confused in a way that Papias to the modern scholar does not seem to be.) There has always been a tendency, particularly among popular writers on the New Testament, to make occurrences of the same name refer as far as possible to the same person, and Eusebius is a good example of this. In the New Testament itself we have four clearly distinguishable Johns apart from John the Baptist: (*a*) the apostle, the brother of James, one of the 'Sons of Thunder'; (*b*) Mark himself was also called John (presumably 'John' to his Aramaic friends and relations, and 'Mark' to the wider Greek-speaking world); (*c*) the author of the Apocalypse or Revelation, who tells us that he 'was on the island called Patmos (presumably a prisoner) on account of the word of God and the testimony of Jesus' (1.9), and who must be clearly distinguished from (*d*) the attributed author of John's gospel and the three epistles of John.

This last John, whom we presume is the man Papias is talking about, presents us with a string of problems all of his own. The actual text of John's gospel, for instance, does not say who it is by, except that it claims to be by 'Jesus' favourite disciple' (unnamed). There are quite good grounds for arguing that the author of the gospel and that of the epistles are the same: very good grounds for connecting the author of the gospel with that of the first of the three epistles, and fairly good grounds for accepting the single authorship of all three epistles. The second and third epistles (but not the first) tell us they are written by the 'elder' or (in Greek) 'presbyter'. Where the actual name John comes from we cannot be sure. It is of course possible that the author was in fact called John; but if so (and indeed, even if not), we can be quite sure that he was not in fact one of the disciples. It is possible that originally he didn't even claim to be. I remember as a schoolboy in the fifties reading a commercially published 'gospel' called 'By an Unknown Disciple'; no one who bought the book believed, or was expected to believe, that the account was anything other than a fictional interpretation of the traditional gospel material. It is quite possible that the fourth gospel was originally written and distributed in much the same spirit.

It is tempting to suppose that Papias here gives us the evidence we otherwise lack that the author of the gospel and the epistles was indeed called John, and was this John the elder whom he claims to have known. The final assessment of the worth of Papias' testimony at the end of this appendix will be adverse; but here we should note that though the suggestion above *may* be the truth, it is equally possible that Papias is simply using an already traditional ascription to bolster his own claims. But we can now see that Eusebius was a good deal more confused than Papias seems to have been about the identity of 'John'. If we subtract John the Baptist and John Mark from our original list, we are still left with three Johns in the New Testament: (*a*) the apostle, (*b*) the author of the gospel and the three epistles and (*c*) the author of the Revelation. Eusebius' confusion derives from the fact that he sees no need of more than two: (*a*) the apostle who also wrote the gospel, and (*b*) the author of the Apocalypse, who he presumes also wrote the epistles, and whom he equates with Papias' 'John the presbyter'. And he supposes that these are the two Johns whose tombs were traditionally pointed out at Ephesus.

A second (and worse) case of mistaken identity is the reference to Philip in the second paragraph. There seems to be anything from two to four characters called Philip in the New Testament. First, each of the first three gospels gives us a list of all twelve apostles (Matthew 10.2–4; Mark 3.16–19; Luke 6.14–16); no two lists are totally the same, but Philip does appear in all three of them (as he does also in the list of eleven apostles in Acts 1.13); apart from this single mention, though, none of these three gospels makes any further reference to him. (In John's gospel, on the other hand, he has a fairly major role to play; but the conclusion I would be inclined to draw from that is that the references to Philip in John's gospel are largely fictional.) Secondly, in Act 6.5 we have a list of seven administrators (presumably non-Judaean Jews – that is the most likely meaning of 'Hellenist' in 6.1) added to the governing body of the church in Jerusalem as a result of the Hellenists' complaint that they were being discriminated against in the distribution of charity. One of these seven was called Philip. It will be obvious that this must be someone other than the apostle. In chapter 8 we find someone called Philip preaching to and converting the Samaritans, and later in the chapter preaching to and converting the Queen of Ethiopia's treasurer. We are not told which of the two this is – indeed, there is no absolute reason why it should be either of them; it is unlikely to be the apostle, however, or why should he need to send for Peter and

John to 'confirm' his converts instead of doing that himself? Finally in Acts 21.8 we have mention of 'Philip the evangelist, who was one of the seven...' who 'had four unmarried daughters who prophesied'.

This is clearly the character that Eusebius chiefly has in mind, though it is hard to avoid the impression that all of the four possible Philips are, as far as he is concerned, one and the same man. But just how many Philips are there in the New Testament? We have the coincidence, for instance, that the Philip in Acts 6.5 is one of seven administrators, while Philip in Acts 21.8 is one of seven evangelists. We do not know precisely what an 'evangelist' is in the context of Acts, but we can be fairly certain that in Paul's day the word had no connotations (as it now has for us) of a man sitting down to put pen to paper; and a fairly good case could be made for arguing that the activities of Philip in Acts chapter 8 are precisely those of an evangelist. The one great objection – why, in that case does Paul always refer to himself as an apostle, never as an evangelist? – is by no means as substantial as it seems. It is for instance very evident from Paul's own writings that some of his contemporaries were scornful of his claim to be an apostle, and not a few of them had on occasion even said so to his face (I Cor. 9.1–2; II Cor. 11.5; 12.11–13; Gal. 1.11–2.10).

Some sort of case then – but a rather slender one – could just about be made out for arguing that Philips 2–4 are one and the same man. But even this still leaves Eusebius far wide of the mark. For instance, he specifically refers to this Philip as 'Philip the Apostle', the one Philip he is most unlikely to have been. The reference to Philip's daughters makes it fairly clear also that it is the Philip of Acts 21.8 that he has in mind; for reasons which cannot be explained, though, he asserts that this Philip lived at Hierapolis (of which Papias was bishop) whereas Acts says he lived at Caesarea (Eusebius' own see). He makes these daughters (rather than Philip himself) the channel of the information Papias received from this source – necessarily, in view of the fact that Eusebius himself has stressed (in opposition to Irenaeus) that Papias says he never met any of the original apostles. The description of the 'information' that Papias received from this source does little for the modern reader's confidence in its reliability.

Let us now review the subject matter of the chapter. Eusebius knew of five books by the early second-century bishop of Hierapolis, collectively titled 'Interpretation of the Oracles of the Lord'. In the last paragraph he gives two actual quotations from the work, and both of them seem to be 'historical' comments about the origins of two of the written gospels that have actually come down to us. How far should we suppose the entire work consisted of such material, and how reliable should we suppose the material to have been?

First of all Eusebius stresses, and insists that Papias also stressed, that all the information contained is second hand. And that lands us with another huge problem, because the actual words of Papias, though capable of this interpretation, do not seem to be a totally clear declaration to that effect. The problem seems to derive from the fact that Papias apparently means something rather different by the word 'presbyter' from the way it is understood by Eusebius. Eusebius' seems to suppose that it describes first generation Christians who were not part of the original band of the disciples, but who had personally known those who were. But Papias in fact seems to be using it of the original disciples themselves, certainly including, but equally certainly not confined to, the twelve apostles. These are the words which seem to me to define what Papias means by 'presbyter': '... but if ever anyone came who had followed the presbyters, I inquired into the words of the presbyters, what Andrew or Peter or Philip or Thomas or James or John or Matthew [all these being apostles], or any other of the Lord's disciples [presumably not apostles], had said; and what Aristion and the presbyter John, the Lord's disciples, were saying.' Eusebius' understanding on the other hand seems defined by: 'The Papias whom we are now treating confesses that he had received the words of the apostles from their followers, but says he had actually heard Aristion and the presbyter John.' In the Papias passage it is unmistakably clear that Aristion and John the presbyter, though not apostles, were quite certainly 'the Lord's disciples'; and though Papias was always 'eager to hear what they were saying', it is less clear that he ever managed to hear them say it personally. But Eusebius has no doubt whatever that Papias did actually claim to have heard these last two personally. He had the book before him, as we have not; he tells us that Papias makes repeated reference to the oral teachings of Aristion and John the presbyter, and he was in a better position than we are to know whether Papias says he had heard them himself, or only through others. But what we *can* say with certainty is that if Eusebius is right on this point, he is wrong (and therefore Irenaeus is right) when he says that Papias claimed never to have met any of the original disciples. Part of the trouble seems to be that for Eusebius 'disciple' means the same as 'apostle', while for Papias (quite rightly) the first is a much wider term than the second.

On the central question, whether Papias had or had not personally heard some of Jesus' original disciples, I remain undecided. Although some of the implications that Eusebius claims to have found in Papias' writings would clearly point to the conclusion that he had, all the actual words of Papias that are quoted above are compatible with the view that he had not. But the answer either way would not affect the judgment we are forced to in considering what we know of Papias' writings, and that is that they are historically worthless: '... he relates the resurrection of a corpse in his time, and in another place another miracle connected with Justus surnamed Barsabas [see Acts 1.23], for he drank poison but by the Lord's grace suffered no harm [see Mark 16.18]'. This may accurately record the primitive teaching of the elders, but it certainly does not accurately record the facts of history.

We come now (at last) to the second last paragraph where Eusebius gives us two actual quotations from Papias about the origins of Mark's and Matthew's gospels. What he tells us about Mark it would be nice to be able to believe; and indeed, unlike what he says for instance about Justus surnamed Barsabas, here he tells us nothing that is inherently incredible. But is that enough? Unfortunately I don't think it is. What he tells us about Matthew, after all, alleges no historical impossibilities. But we have Matthew's gospel before us, and we know that what Papias tells us about its origins *cannot* be true. The work is *certainly* written by a Greek speaker, and one moreover who is consistently appalled by the low standard of Greek he found in Mark, his major source (what Papias tells us about Matthew would in fact be credible had he said it of Mark); and on the other hand, on the one occasion he tries to correct Mark's Aramaic/Hebrew (Mark 15.34 = Matt. 27.46) he gets it wrong. We know also that a very substantial portion of his non-Marcan material also came to him from written Greek sources – because of the large amount of material he includes in common with Luke, but not found in Mark, where Matthew and Luke still have a very high proportion of actual words and phrases in common with each other. In the remainder of the work (about a third of the whole) there are no unmistakable signs anywhere of an Aramaic original (one takes it for granted that by 'Hebrew' Papias can only have meant 'Aramaic');

though occasionally, once again, these can sometimes be found in Mark.

In despair some scholars have supposed that there once existed an earlier 'Matthew's gospel', and that Papias' observations relate to that and were quite possibly accurate. But since it is impossible to doubt that at the time he wrote Matthew's gospel was not only in existence but already highly regarded throughout the whole of the Christian world, it is correspondingly difficult to believe he is referring to anything other than our existing work. The Gospel according to the Hebrews[7] which Eusebius mentions in his final paragraph survives in fragments, and these fragments often do show considerable affinity with passages from Matthew; but Eusebius' testimony is unambiguous that Papias knew of both works and refers to them separately. Moreover if such a hypothesis were to be insisted on, it would at once destroy the whole value of Papias' testimony. For if there was an earlier Matthew's gospel – now lost – and this is what Papias is really talking about, who is to say that there was not also an earlier Mark's gospel; and that once again Papias gives us accurate information about the lost work, but throws no light whatever on the one we now have? The true conclusion to be drawn from Eusebius' chapter 39 is the extreme suspicion with which *all* uncorroborated oral testimony should be regarded, no matter what its source.

We are now in a position to evaluate the crucial passage from Eusebius that relates to Mark. If my evaluation of Papias is sound, it is unfortunate that the only points in it of which we can be confident are those confirmed by the gospel itself. It appears to be true that whoever wrote Mark's gospel had before him a shapeless collection of tiny little stories, and that any arrangement which the gospel displays seems to be the work of the author himself. It may well also be true that, unlike Matthew and Luke, Mark worked primarily from unwritten sources which he himself was the first to put on paper. All this is consistent with what Papias tells us, which also, it is worth pointing out again, contains nothing inherently improbable or that strains credulity. On the other hand it has to be stressed that we cannot treat the alleged connection of the author with Peter as a known fact of history. Even more, though we are justified in assuming that Papias' Mark is the John Mark of the New Testament, and that the traditional ascription of the work is also to this Mark, we would not be justified in offering Papias' testimony as evidence of the ascription; and we do not in fact have any worthwhile evidence for it. Despite which there is on the other hand no compelling reason why it should not be true.

II

The first section dealt with the history of the gospel material prior to Mark's recording it on paper, probably in the mid-sixties AD. The present section deals with the literary shape and style of the work he produced. And first of all we have to consider what scholars have come to call the synoptic problem. Anyone who has ever sat down and read all four gospels right through will be aware that there is a difference, not merely in degree but in kind, between the first three gospels and the fourth. The first three are all of them made up of tiny little bits – stories, parables, miracles, sayings, many of which could be completely detached from their surroundings without suffering any loss of meaning or coherence. The fourth gospel on the other hand consists of long stretches of debate, of explanation or of reflection; even the very few miracles that are related are all of them then made the subject of a lengthy exposition of their 'significance'. More striking even than this, we find much of the material in any one of the first three gospels repeated, often in much the same words, in one or both of the other two. But the fourth gospel has no ties of this kind with any of the other three.

We know now why this is so, though the reader will be surprised to learn that the realization dates from no earlier than the early years of the last century. Comparison of Mark's gospel with Matthew's makes it clear without question that the many points of resemblance between the two are due to the fact that Matthew has used Mark as the major source for his own work, not even bothering to retell the material afresh, but simply editing out what he considered to be (*a*) the superfluities in Mark's account and (*b*) the grammatical in-elegancies – but apart from that using much the same words. We can be quite sure that the interdependence is of Matthew on Mark and not the other way round for the following reasons: (*a*) whenever we come across material common to Matthew and Mark, it is nearly always shorter in Matthew than in Mark, though the gospel as a whole is much longer; (*b*) as the reader will see in the course of the exposition, there are occasions where the two authors disagree in the details of their wording for patently theological reasons (Mark 10.18 compared with Matt. 19.17 is the most notorious instance) and in every case it is easy to see why Matthew should have altered Mark, difficult to see why Mark should have altered Matthew.

The interdependence of Luke and Mark is just as certain, though if we did not have Matthew as well we would be less certain about the direction of it. There is a tendency in Luke also to abbreviate Mark, but it is less pronounced; there is the same tendency in Luke also to improve Mark's grammar and style. What Luke does not seem particularly interested in is correcting the theology of Mark's gospel, and the reason for this, as we shall see, may well be that Luke was not particularly alive to, or interested in, the nicer points of orthodoxy anyway: some readers will like him all the better for this. But what chiefly persuades us that Luke is later than Mark, and – like Matthew – incorporating him, is the amount of material common to Luke and Matthew which Mark does not include. The accepted symbol for labelling this material is Q, but there is considerable disagreement about what the symbol stands for. German scholars tend to claim that they invented it, and that it stands for the German word *quelle* meaning 'source'. There is a strong counterclaim by some English scholars that the symbol is an English invention and is only one of a series of four useful symbols for classifying all the material found in the first three gospels:

M = all the material found only in Matthew

L = all the material found only in Luke

P = Petrine, i.e. Mark's gospel (see Papias' comments in the appendix to the previous section – it is obviously convenient to use some other symbol than M)

Q = all the material that is common to Matthew and Luke but not found in Mark

The English explanation of the symbol is not only more plausible than the German; it is actually more useful. A great deal of New Testament scholarship has been rendered useless or misleading by the assumption that Q represents a *source* common to Matthew and

Luke. But actual examination of the Q material makes it clear that it comes from a wide variety of sources. Sometimes the verbal similarity in passages common to the two gospels makes it clear that they come from a common written source (compare Matt. 12.43–45 with Luke 11.24–26); sometimes both the similarities and the differences are equally striking, and one is at a loss to account for either (compare Matt. 4.1–11 with Luke 4.1–13, or Matt. 11.2–19 with Luke 7.18–35); sometimes it is clear that the two accounts are from different sources (compare Matt. 25.14–30 with Luke 19.11–27); and sometimes the differences are so great that one wonders how the material can be classified at all. Look at Luke 7.36–50, for instance: is this P (compare Mark 14.3–9, Matt. 26.6–13) or should we think of it as L?

Both Matthew and Luke seem to have been native and fluent Greek speakers. This does not, of course, imply that they were actual Greeks, only that Greek was their mother tongue. At the time they lived, the overwhelming cultural and literary influences were Greek in the East and Latin in the West (Roman culture being itself little more than a translation and adaptation of the Greek, flavoured with what we might call a jingoistic view of history – the Romans never forgot that although the conquerors had taken over the culture of the conquered, it was nevertheless they and not the Greeks who were the conquerors). All other languages throughout the Mediterranean world had been relegated to the status of primitive and barbarous vernaculars, unsuited to any serious literary or philosophic purpose, a point of view which continued to influence European educational practice until well into the present century.[8]

The Greek of these two gospels therefore (contrary to popular belief) is acceptable and even attractive. It is not the Greek of Attic oratory or history, any more than the English of the Authorized Version is the English of Gibbon or Macaulay – but that is indeed a very good illustration of the way the language of the gospels differs from that of Attic prose. Like the Authorized Version, the language of Matthew's and Luke's gospels is influenced by a phraseology that derives from the authors' deep immersion in an already widely-known and influential translation of the Hebrew scriptures. In the case of the Authorized Version, this was Tyndale's translation; in the case of the gospels it was the two or three hundred years old translation of the Hebrew scriptures into Greek known as the

Septuagint. The gospels are attractive to read in much the same way that the Authorized Version is attractive, and the language is suited to religious purposes in much the same way. Translation of them into a fully modern vernacular tends to destroy the archaic and awesome atmosphere they were undoubtedly intended to create. If there are differences between what Matthew and Luke were each of them trying to do – and we have already glimpsed in what has been said above that there were – it is not in the area of language or sophistication that they occur. (It looks, by the way, that they wrote at about the same time – around the 70 to 80 mark – but that at the time of writing both of them were unaware of each others' work.) It is fair to observe, for instance, that Luke's religious outlook tends towards the liberal, the lax, and the warm-hearted, whereas Matthew on the contrary has a liking for the rigid, the hierarchical, and the daunting; and these differences create the very different impressions the two gospels have on the discerning reader. But linguistically they are very much the same. It is even fairly clear that both of them were men of some education, though the bulk of the educated public of that time – as indeed of ours – would have been wide-eyed at the kind of events the two authors were clearly prepared to believe had actually happened.[9] They were undoubtedly writing for a comparatively ignorant readership; but it would be going too far to argue they were necessarily ignorant themselves, even despite their to us amazing credulity.

The Greek of Mark's gospel, on the other hand, does not convince us to anything like the same extent. Our first impression is that in this case the author was himself as ignorant as the intended 'readership'. (Bear in mind that a large proportion of the original audience could not read at all, or only with difficulty. On the other hand, the fact that the gospels were all of them written to be read aloud has no great significance, since all ancient literature was intended to be read aloud. A Roman senator 'read' a book by lolling back on a couch while an educated slave read it over to him.) It is only when we come to analyse the structure of the work, which turns out to be far more impressive than the other two, that we are forced to question whether it is really the ignorance of the author which accounts for the undoubted crudity of much of the writing: a much more likely explanation seems to be that, unlike the other two, Mark was writing in what was to him a foreign language.

How did he arrive at the plan of his narrative? We know from the

Acts of the Apostles that the earliest Christian preachers had a kind of 'potted history' of the events of Jesus' life, and that they used this as the basis of their initial approach in presenting the gospel to first-time hearers. The earliest reference to this potted history is found in the very first chapter of Acts:

> So one of the men who have accompanied us [i.e. Peter and the other 'apostles'] during all the time that the Lord Jesus went in and out among us, *beginning with the baptism of John until the day when he was taken up from us* – one of these men must become with us a witness to his resurrection. (Acts 1.21–22)

The passage in italics is the potted history. To the unpracticed eye it might look so vague and parenthetical as to be without significance; but if any reader does think that, let him compare it with Acts 10.36–43 (probably the classic instance), 11.16, and 13.23–31 (an expanded version specifically intended for potential converts from Judaism). It will be seen also that the beginning of this potted history – in all four cases – corresponds to the beginning of Mark's gospel[10] with the baptism of Jesus by John. The ending of course differs; and for the moment we must interrupt the argument while we consider as briefly as we can the very complex question of the ending of Mark's gospel.

Our earliest and best manuscripts conclude with Mark 16.8, with the words, 'and they said nothing to anyone, for they were afraid'. There is no doubt even as the text stands that Jesus has risen from the dead, but it is important to note that there is no account of any actual appearances. It was probably for this reason that from very earliest times it was felt that the original ending must have become detached from the work – a very common accident indeed with the kind of papyrus role on which the gospel will have first made its appearance. But, some readers may protest, it surely didn't circulate in just one copy; so how did it happen that *all* the copies lost their ending? The protest seems to have force until one looks at the surprisingly large number of important classical works which have come down to us with a similar defect. Suetonius' *De Vita Caesarum* now lacks what must have been the original first page: the life of Julius Caesar starts abruptly with the death of his father when he was sixteen. Juvenal's *Saturae* and Statius' *Silvae* both of them lack the conclusion of the final book. These are examples that I happen to have near me as I write; a systematic survey of the literature would provide a great many more of them. The overall evidence makes it clear that there is nothing improbable in the idea that the authentic text of Mark's gospel is incomplete. I say 'authentic' because of course chapter 16 of Mark in practically all modern Bibles goes on to verse 20. These additional twelve verses, known to scholars as the longer Marcan ending, are nevertheless extremely early, being quoted by Irenaeus (see the Appendix above) before the end of the second century as an integral part of the gospel.

It is often stated that neither Matthew nor Luke had any more complete version of Mark's gospel than we have. Myself I do not see how this can be known. Luke has clearly preferred a non-Marcan source for the whole of his passion narrative (starting with chapter 22), and I doubt if many of us would want to explain this by supposing this was because he did not have Mark's version. With regard to Matthew, although there are obvious differences between what we have in Mark chapter 16 and the 'corresponding' material in Matthew chapter 28, it seems to me impossible to overlook the fact that one of the reasons why we are convinced that Mark's gospel is incomplete is that in the existing material he twice makes Jesus tell the disciples that after his resurrection they will see him in Galilee (14.28; 16.7). Matthew's gospel ends (28.16–20) with a scene which is the perfect fulfilment of such a prediction; and my own conviction is that he is doing here just what he has been doing for most of the rest of his gospel – incorporating Mark in his own edited version. There are difficulties, though – even apart from the story of the guard of soldiers, which plays so big a part in Matthew's resurrection account, but none at all in Mark's. The real difficulty is the comparison of Mark 16.8 with Matthew 28.8. Why is it that in Mark the women are too frightened to say anything to anyone, while in Matthew they are so delighted they want to rush off immediately to tell the disciples? Did they in Mark, as they do in Matthew, actually encounter Jesus himself as soon as they have left the tomb? Only speculative answers can be given to the question; but it is there, and it is real, and it does cast doubt on my suggestion that Mark's original ending was the same as what we have in Matthew. Nevertheless, my conviction is that Matthew 28.16–20 is an edited version of the ending that he originally found in Mark.

Let us return once more to the potted history. All this discussion of the lost ending of Mark's gospel has been an attempt to show that, although as the work now stands its conclusion is different from that of the potted history, in its original form it may well have been the same. But some readers may feel that this point still has not been made. The last event in the potted history is 'the day when he [Jesus] was taken up from us' (Acts 1.22) – in other words what Christians traditionally refer to as the ascension. The account of this, as everybody knows, is given in Acts 1.6–11, and it bears no relation to what we are told even in Matthew 28.16–20. But this is less of a difficulty than the reader might think. Compare for instance the passage in Acts with the conclusion of Luke's gospel (24.50–53): even though both accounts are by the same author, there are significant discrepancies between them. The crucial verse in the gospel is 51: 'While he blessed them, he parted from them.' Unlike Acts it doesn't say how, and it is probably intentional that it doesn't. Jesus just wasn't there any longer. You could argue that this is inconsistent with 24.36–43 in which the complete physicality of Christ's risen body is emphatically stated. And yet in that very same chapter we are told (verse 31) 'And their eyes were opened and they recognized him; and he vanished out of their sight.' If my suggestion about the conclusion of the gospel is incompatible with the physicality of Christ's risen body, then so assuredly is this. Even verse 36, the opening verse of the very passage under discussion, seems to suggest that Christ's body appeared to the eleven quite suddenly, as if it had passed through solid walls. The truth is we are being misled by the terminology: Acts 1.6–11 is a description of an 'ascension', while Matthew 28.16–20 and Luke 24.50–53 are not; but all three are clearly intended to be accounts of 'the day when he was taken from us' – which, in the earliest days of Christianity, may not (indeed probably was not) thought of as an 'ascension' at all, but merely as the occasion of Jesus' last appearance to his disciples.

So much for the outer limits of the gospel which, as we have seen, were already determined for Mark by the tradition. But Papias tells us that the material as it reached the author was in no particular order; and though Papias' word alone would not convince us, when we come to look at the gospel, we can see that this is true. How then has he managed to solve the problem of presentation? The major divisions of the work seem to be three: (*a*) the public ministry 1.1–8.10); (*b*) the private preparation of the disciples for what would look to them like the catastrophe that was going to befall him (8. 11–13.37; and finally (*c*) the story of the passion, death and resurrection of Jesus told in 14.1–16.8).

This third section must obviously be in chronological order in relation to the other two, but it is almost certainly a mistake to think of the first two sections as being in chronological order in relation to each other, except in so far as there would in any case have been a greater emphasis on the public ministry in the early part of Jesus' activity, and a greater emphasis on the private instruction of the disciples in the later part. But we must still keep ourselves constantly aware that we have no reason to believe that, just because a particular incident is placed by Mark towards the end of Jesus' ministry, that was historically when the incident occurred; nor similarly that the incidents related early in the gospel necessarily took place early in Jesus' ministry. The material has clearly been arranged (and very sensibly and cleverly arranged) in a series of sections which, although at first reading they give the impression they are narrative sections and part of a narrative framework, turn out on examination to be thematic sections and part of a thematic framework. The contents page of this book is, I believe, not something that I myself have devised for the convenience of expounding Mark; I believe it to represent the actual framework the author himself had in mind when writing the gospel. That it should so cleverly give the impression that it is nevertheless a narrative work surely disposes of any likelihood that the author, despite the clumsiness of his actual writing, was therefore unintelligent or even uneducated.

The close scrutiny of this structure is something I shall be offering in the exposition itself, but two minor points are more conveniently dealt with here. First, it is often said that Mark's intention in writing was to preserve a record of the events of Jesus' life, and that he was much less interested in the teaching as such. The reason for this is the perception that Matthew and Luke, who have both of them relied on Mark to supply the basic material for their own gospels, also contain a considerable amount of material in common with each other (the Q material described above), and that much of this is sermon material. Much of it appears also, in so far as we have any means of deciding this difficult question, to be authentic. Was it not known to Mark, or did he know it and decide not to use it? The theory we are discussing seems to decide for the latter, but I personally find the suggestion incredible – helped by the observation that in fact there seems to be no lack of interest in teaching as against narrative in Mark's gospel. The whole of 4.1–34, for instance, is teaching material, as is also the

whole of 7.1–23 and 8.31–9.1; above all 10.2–45, though inter-
spersed with narrative scene-setting, is consistently a teaching section; and there are besides many smaller narratives whose point is a
doctrinal one. What we do not find in this gospel are those long
collections of uninterrupted sermon material which are a feature
above all of Matthew (see chapters 5–7; 10.5–42; 13.3–52; chapters
23–25), most of the material of which – though in less concentrated
form – can also be found in Luke, and which therefore must be
classified as Q.

Mark has just one section of such sermon material in chapter 13 –
the Marcan Apocalypse previously mentioned – and this brings me
to the second of the two minor points mentioned above. The
suggestion is often made, for reasons which are by no means clear to
me, that we here find Mark incorporating a previously existing
document. The 'feel' of the chapter is undoubtedly different from
anything else in the gospel; but as far as I am concerned that is solely
because of the subject matter, which has to do with future events
rather than with the immediate circumstances of the disciples and the
rest of Jesus' hearers. Nobody doubts that this chapter is a composite
document comprising a mosaic of short sections which originally
were completely independent of each other; there do not seem to me
to be any good grounds for arguing that the arrangement we now
have is due to anyone other than Mark himself.

A much more remarkable feature of the gospel is the striking
contrast between the way chapters 1–13 have been put together
compared with the passion narrative (chapters 14–16). Throughout
the first thirteen chapters it is fairly easy to divide the material up into
the various short sections (the scholar's term for them is *pericopae*)
which appear to have reached Mark as independent, self-sufficient
stories. The average length of these *pericopae* is six verses – many of
them are no more than three, some as short as two, and very rarely
are they more than ten. The passion and resurrection narrative on the
other hand is a continuous section of 127 verses as it stands –
probably getting on for 140 verses as Mark originally wrote it. How
do we account for this difference?

The usual suggestion, which seems to me to be sensible, is that
from very earliest times in every local Christian community there
was an annual celebration of the events of Jesus' passion, death and
resurrection. Mark's gospel incorporates the narrative of the
celebration that belonged to whatever local community he was most

familiar with.[11] Luke (unlike Matthew, who by and large follows Mark's account) may have done the same, which is why Luke's account is so different from Mark's. Even John *may* have done the same, though it may also be true that John's passion narrative was doing what the whole of the rest of John's gospel was doing: deliberately setting aside the synoptic accounts and offering an alternative which (*a*) may have included material that was either of widespread popularity or of deep personal significance to himself, but which the synoptic gospels had not included; or (*b*) he may have done this even though aware that much of this new material was historically dubious or worthless, in the belief that a mere record of events (such as he seems to have thought we find in the synoptic gospels) does not go nearly far enough as an attempt to arrive at the 'real' meaning of Jesus.

III

The third section of this introduction deals with the topic that scholars call christology – 'the study of the Person of Christ, and in particular the union in Him of the Divine and human natures' (*The Oxford Dictionary of the Christian Church*). To the modern reader who is not necessarily a Christian the big difficulty in offering any realistic discussion of such a topic will be that whereas human nature is a part of our experience, and therefore intelligible, it is not obvious that either of these things can be said of divine (or Divine) nature. Christian history began at a time when there was very little scientific curiosity about human nature either, so that both human and divine nature equally tended to be defined, not in terms of knowledge derived from observation or experience, but in terms of theories which were considered true in so far as they seemed either to be beautiful in themselves or to be likely to promote morally approved behaviour. Such aims are by no means discreditable or worthless, and are still the chief aims that religion has in mind when it continues to ponder such questions. It puts itself at a severe disadvantage, however, in still insisting that such discussions are essentially concerned with *truth*. 'Truth' nowadays is a term that has a precise meaning inseparably connected with our ideas about evidence – what is to count as evidence, how it can be arrived it, scrutinized and known, and what conclusions can properly be derived from it; and the Christian debate about christology is no way concerned with truth in that sense. It will not do for religion to insist that our present understanding of 'truth' is inadequate compared with its own much fuller and more timeless conception of it. The decisive point here is that the secular world offers us an examinable definition of what it means by truth; unless religion does the same, it has small ground of complaint if its claim to truth is disregarded.

I proceed upon the supposition, therefore, that arguments about christology are not arguments that turn on any question of truth, nor can any outcome of them claim to be a true conclusion. They may still try to uplift the mind, and to inspire it with a resolution to follow virtue; let us hope so, for if those are not the aims, it is hard to see that they have any useful aims at all. And on the other hand it should equally be borne in mind that no contemporary discussion that is concerned with a question of truth, or which hopes for a true conclusion as its outcome, allows any relevance to considerations of what elevates the mind or inspires it to follow virtue. It does not follow, therefore, just because the discussion is not concerned with any point of truth, that it serves no useful purpose.

The tradition of the Christian church is that the historic man Jesus is also the incarnation of God. For reasons set out above, there seems to me no point in asking how we know the truth of such a proposition. I could, if I had the time, the space and the expertise, show how it was that Christians came to believe in such an incarnation; but however much of all these things I had, the demonstration would still fail to show that they were *right* to believe in it. For these reasons it seems to me more sensible to think about the incarnation, not as some kind of historical event, but rather as a kind of quasi-historical but essentially *imaginative* portrait – and an unashamedly romantic portrait at that – in which it *appeals* to the artist (and hopefully to the audience also) to see Jesus in that kind of light. Traditionally-minded Christians will very likely object that one could do as much for any other religious leader. Yes, I think one could. Should that worry us?

The most famous of these portraits (which has, indeed, a good claim to be considered the original from which all others derive) is the opening of John's gospel:

> In the beginning was the Word, and the Word was with God, and the Word was God. He was in the beginning with God; all things

were made through him, and without him was not anything made that has been made. In him was life, and the life was the light of men. The light shines in the darkness, and the darkness has not overcome it.

This 'Word' (in the Greek *Logos*) was essentially a quasi-mythological figure from Greek philosophy (of no interest originally, therefore, to any but intellectuals), whose function seems to have been to explain how it was that the world of matter, which one would expect to have been a total chaos devoid of order or intelligibility,[12] in fact exemplified both these qualities to a high degree. To the Greeks this Logos not merely exemplified reason, but was itself a kind of cosmic reason, both the source of reason in man's mind and of whatever reason manifested itself in the universe of matter. The relationship of this Logos to the gods or God (Stoics, who were particularly interested in the Logos idea, also had a tendency to talk about God in the singular) was not normally of any great interest in Greek philosophy. The pagan gods (though this point can be exaggerated) tended to be used as idealizations of perfect bliss – all the sex, money and parties anyone could ever want, without having to do a hand's turn for any of it – rather than of perfect reason. In the thinking of the author of John's gospel, however, it is crucial. The man Jesus was a historical figure born (for the sake of argument) in AD 1. But the author of John's gospel clearly wishes to think of Jesus, or some part of Jesus, as having existed from eternity. (This idea most Christians would consider to be absolutely crucial to Christianity, so it needs to be said at once that the author of John's gospel is the only one of the four gospel writers for whom it has the slightest appeal.) This he achieves by viewing Jesus as an incarnation at a given moment in history of this Logos that existed eternally before the world was made, and whose active participation in its creation explains whatever rationality is to be found in the world. Were the Logos and God one and the same? The question cannot coherently be decided from the text of John's gospel, and the author probably intended that it couldn't be. One can say with certainty that the Logos of the opening paragraph is identical with the Son throughout the rest of the gospel, and similarly that God in the opening paragraph is identical with the Father throughout the rest of the gospel. But the author has clearly not made up his mind how far the two are to be considered separate and how far identical, how far the Son is to be considered as subordinate to the Father and how far equal to him.[13] This problem, which lies at the heart of the whole traditional christological debate, tends to strike the modern reader as unreal, in that it reads John's gospel as if it were a source of some kind of information whose truth could be guaranteed. If we suppose instead that the author is doing no more than suggesting what appeals to him as a 'nice idea' – and it's hard to see in what other sense we can read him – then the 'problem' does not require a solution anyway; and certainly no convincing solution has ever been given.

I pointed out above that the author of John's gospel is the only one of the four to whom the idea seems ever to have occurred of suggesting that Jesus was not simply a man born in AD 1 but was the incarnation of some kind of heavenly being who had existed from eternity. This is not to deny that all four gospels seems perfectly clear that Jesus was somehow or other God. But before I go on to explain how this can be so, I need to say something about two opposed 'heresies'[14] of early Christianity: adoptionism, or the belief that Jesus was born a human being and became the Son of God only at his baptism; and docetism (from the Greek *docein*, 'to seem'), or the belief that Jesus was in reality a totally divine being, who only seemed to be human to those around him. Let us take the second of these first, while John's gospel is still our topic – for despite the insistence of orthodoxy to the contrary, (and, it could be said, despite the insistence of the author himself, assuming that the same man who wrote the gospel also wrote the three epistles[15]) John's gospel shows unmistakable signs of being essentially a docetic work. One could go further: all of the many attempts to 'explain' how Jesus can be both God and man can be classified as being either adoptionist or docetic in tendency, and orthodoxy itself has always been inclined towards docetism. In contrast, certainly Mark's gospel, and probably Luke's also, are explicitly adoptionist works: for both of them Jesus' 'godhead' begins much later even than his birth (despite the miraculous birth and childhood Luke describes in his first two chapters). For both of them it was at Jesus' baptism that the Holy Ghost descended on him and at that moment transformed him into the anointed Son of God. Matthew gives the impression of being dissatisfied with some of the implications of Mark's christology, and (as we have seen) anxious to modify those passages where he feels it shows through, but at the same time without apparently being able to substitute any clear and coherent alternative.

This dichotomy between adoptionism and docetism is created by the dual origin of Christianity itself, which likes to portray itself (or rather did in the days when Christians were still reasonably familiar with the Old Testament) simply as a continuation of the Old Testament message. But in fact many of its more striking features, including the whole notion of an incarnation (an idea totally incompatible with Old Testament thinking) came to it from the world of Greek thought, by which it was quickly overwhelmed as more and more of the new converts came to the church from a pagan, instead of (as originally) from a Jewish, background. To put it in a nutshell, in Jewish thinking the world was corrupt because the course of history had gone wrong, and Jesus had been chosen by God to act in history and put it right; in Greek thinking the world was corrupt because it was the nature of matter to be so, and Jesus was a kind of infusion of divine nature into matter as the first stage in its cleansing and redemption. Adoptionist thinking is the result of the first view, docetic thinking of the second.

Let me show by examples how John's gospel can be seen as a docetic work. I say 'can be seen' because orthodoxy would deny that the charge of docetism can be made at all, and can give grounds for the defence. True docetism denies that Jesus had a human nature at all, insisting that although he was seen, heard and even touched by the disciples (and this relates to the *whole* of Jesus' ministry, and not just the resurrection appearances) what they experienced was simply an illusion. So far as we can tell, the question that immediately occurs to us – 'What then was the purpose of this illusion?' – does not seem to have been raised. What they were anxious to maintain was the impossibility that God could ever suffer the limitations of a human body, could ever feel hunger or the need of sleep, above all could ever under *any* circumstances feel the indignity of pain. It was these features of primitive Christianity that, even to moderately intelligent converts from paganism, seemed to offer a scandously unworthy picture of God. The Old Testament God had of course readily done all these things and felt no embarrassment; even the popular gods of paganism were all of them very much gods with a human face. But any pagan with an interest in the theoretical aspects of religion – and from an early date pagan converts contained a high proportion of these – would have imbibed with his alphabet the notion that God (as distinct from the gods) was a purely intelligent being who remained totally unaffected by *all* human passion and *all* human sensation. It was to accommodate beliefs of this kind, and to reconcile what Christians were saying about Jesus with what Greeks of this way of thinking wanted to hear, that John's gospel seems to have been written.

The author seems to think of the incarnation as being rather like a man having jumped into a huge bowl of cakemix. None of his true features are any longer discernible under the thick layer of sludge; nothing he says can easily be deciphered. Nicodemus for instance in chapter 3 misunderstands just about everything Jesus says to him. The Samaritan woman in chapter 4 spends most of the time talking at cross-purposes, though she does eventually come to realize that she is talking to no ordinary man. In chapter 5 nobody – not even the beneficiary – understands the true nature of the sign that Jesus performs in healing the man who had been ill for thirty-eight years. The crowd in chapter 6, having eaten of the loaves and fishes, are in a sense converted – but for all the wrong reasons. They want Jesus as an earthly ruler (verse 15), because it is clear he knows how to solve their material problems; but they have no understanding at all of the 'real' nourishment that Jesus offers (verses 26–27). At the end of a very long chapter in which Jesus has made every attempt (as far as the author is concerned – the modern reader is likely to have considerable sympathy with the hearers' bewilderment) to explain what this true nourishment is, some of the disciples are so non-plussed that they come to the conclusion Jesus can only be talking nonsense and wander off to look for a more comprehensible teacher (verses 60 and 66).

I could go on like this chapter by chapter, but particularly striking is the author's view of Jesus' passion and death. The other three gospels all place great emphasis on the 'agony in the garden' (Matt. 26.36–46; Mark 14.32–42; Luke – in a totally independent account from the other two – 22.39–46[16]); John's account includes no such episode. The other three gospels all agree that Jesus was no longer capable of carrying his cross to the place of execution (Matt. 27.32; Mark 15.21; Luke 23.26); John specifically denies this (19.17). Three gospels (not Luke) include the incident of Jesus being give a drink of sour wine (Matt. 27.48; Mark 15.36; John 19.28–30). In Matthew and Mark the incident seems to be a compassionate response to Jesus' obvious torment; in John it is only because Jesus asks for it, which he does only to fulfil the scripture (Ps. 69.21). All four accounts of the crucifixion are somewhat unreal in that anyone undergoing such an ordeal would not only be disinclined, but would quickly be actually incapable, of raising his voice so as to be heard. The technology of crucifixion (for want of a better word) is that the victim simply cannot bear to relieve the agony in his feet by hanging down on his wrists, and simply cannot bear to relieve the agony in his wrists by pushing up on his feet. Bear this in mind and then read John 19.25–30: the effect is grotesquely unreal. The idea that Jesus could really suffer pain was as repugnant to the author of John's gospel as it was to the most hardened and thoroughgoing docetist.

In contrast, as has already been stated, none of the first three gospels sees any need to speculate about what Jesus was before he was born. For all of them Jesus' life – bodily and spiritual – began with his birth. There is little doubt that Mark is simply following the received orthodoxy of his day in thinking of Jesus' godhead as being inaugurated by his baptism by John. (May I remind the reader also that this, after all, is the obvious implication of the 'potted history' discussed in the previous section.) Such a view has of course for centuries been condemned as heretical. If the church has nevertheless managed to read the gospel for all but two thousand years without apparently noticing the 'heresy', that is because the author takes his point of view so entirely for granted that he makes no attempt to argue it. John's views are obtrusive precisely because with every line he wrote he knew he would be raising somebody's hackles.

The two insistent claims that are made in all four gospels are that Jesus is (*a*) the Son of God, and (*b*) the Messiah. In all four gospels they are in fact the same claim. However in the synoptic gospels it is the second of these claims that is primary, while the first derives from it, whereas in the fourth gospel this order of priority is reversed. We have already begun to see what the fourth gospel means by 'the Son of God'; let us now consider what the other three mean by 'Messiah', or 'Christos'. The second of these terms is Greek, the first a slightly garbled version of a Hebrew word: both can simply be translated as 'anointed'. In Old Testament times anointing was first and foremost the ceremony by which a man was made king, and throughout the Old Testament the expression 'the Lord's anointed' without any other qualification always means the king. At some point in Israel's history it also became customary to anoint the high priest,[17] and it is in this connection that a remarkably fine poem survives which gives us the best insight we have into what ancient Israel thought actually happened at the ceremony of anointing:

Behold, how good and pleasant it is
    when brothers dwell in unity!
It is like the precious oil upon the head,
    running down upon the beard,
upon the beard of Aaron,
    running down on the collar of his robes!
It is like the dew of Hermon,
    which falls on the mountains of Zion!
For there the Lord has commanded the blessing,
    life for evermore. (Ps. 133)

This is clearly the text of an ode or anthem to be sung at the anointing of the high priest. ('Aaron' here applies to *any* high priest, just as throughout the psalms 'David' applies to any of the Davidic kings.) The 'brothers' are presumably his fellow priests standing round him in a circle and participating in the ceremony. Hermon is a mountain to the north-east of Israel, permanently snow-capped, and the 'dew' of the poem is undoubtedly the moisture running down from the melting snow bringing life to the otherwise barren plains below: so the oil running down the high priest's head brings life to those standing around him. (This of course is imagery, and not to be taken as any kind of literal 'explanation' of what 'happens' at an anointing – though undoubtedly in those days many a callow enthusiast for the high priestly office will have been carried away to insist on its 'truth'.) I am not convinced by the translation of the penultimate verse; though not a Hebrew scholar, I suspect the passage actually means something more like: 'That which falls on the mountains of Zion [i.e. the oil running down the high priest's head] is like the dew of Hermon.' The reason why something like this must be meant is that 'there' in the last verse certainly refers to Mount Zion and not to Mount Hermon.

There is no doubt that in ancient thinking the oil not merely symbolized but in a sense 'was' the spirit of God descending on the anointed head and making the anointed person if not exactly equal to God then certainly much more than human. (This is particularly well illustrated by the anointing of Saul in I Samuel chapters 9 and 10.) Take another anointing psalm, this time one that does relate to the king:

Why do the nations conspire,
    and the peoples plot in vain?

The kings of the earth set themselves,
    and the rulers take counsel together,
    against the Lord and his anointed, saying,
'Let us burst their bonds asunder,
    and cast their cords from us.'

He who sits in the heavens laughs;
    the Lord has them in derision.
Then he will speak to them in his wrath,
    and terrify them in his fury, saying,
'I have set my king
    on Zion, my holy hill.'

I will tell of the decree of the Lord:
    He said to me, 'You are my son,
    today I have begotten you.
Ask of me, and I will make the nations your heritage,
    and the ends of the earth your possession.
You shall break them with a rod of iron,
    and dash them in pieces like a potter's vessel.'

Now therefore, O kings, be wise;
    be warned, O rulers of the earth.
Serve the Lord with fear,
    with trembling kiss his feet,
lest he be angry, and you perish in the way;
    for his wrath is quickly kindled.

Blessed are all who take refuge in him. (Ps. 2)

There is a tendency among Old Testament scholars to argue that this poem belongs to a specific time in history – most probably in the ninth century BC – when the various nations which David had subdued were beginning to reassert their independence, and that the poet is reaffirming the Davidic king's right to rule over Israel's historic empire. But we cannot in fact date the poem beyond being fairly certain it was created during the Davidic monarchy – an overall period of more than four centuries – to be sung at a new king's anointing. Even if it did originally belong to the ninth century, it survived almost certainly because it remained in constant and traditional use throughout the monarchic period. That being so, it would come to have a meaning for the participants which, even if deriving originally from a particular historical context, became different from and wider than that context. It would have increasingly been interpreted as continuing to affirm the close relationship between God in heaven and his own particular king (as distinct from the kings of all the other nations) even now being anointed on Mount Zion – a relationship so close that from now on (though not until now) the king is to be thought of as God's son; and following from that, the superiority of Israel's king to all other earthly kings, his precedence over them, and his continuing mythological – as distinct from his once historic – right to rule over them.

This last idea is the crucial one, as well as being the hardest to elucidate. If the poem was in fact written in the ninth century, this 'right to rule' would originally have been understood in absolutely literal terms: David had conquered these nations and bequeathed his right to rule over them to his heirs. As time wore on, and the re-established independence of these nations had become a long-accepted fact of history, how would such an apparently unreal proclamation have been interpreted? By the end of the monarchy there would have been no one who was not acutely aware of the vast disparity between the original meaning of the ode and the changed reality of the world in which it was now being performed. Had it simply recalled a glorious past it would have been embarrassing. Its much more important function was that *it kept alive the hope of a glorious future*. And the unreality of this hope can be taken as the basis of the whole of that vast ideology surrounding the idea of the Messiah in later Jewish history. It derived from the past, and looked forward to the future; but (to the modern historian if not to the ancient) its most prominent feature was its being *hopelessly* at odds with the reality of the present. It looked to the outsider (certainly it did to the Romans) as though the imagery merely intensified the very agony it was meant to relieve. One is reminded of the cartoon of the miserable man, supported by the caption: 'I've begun to feel much better since I finally gave up hope.' As a recipe for happiness, in some circumstances this is in fact the answer.

It should be obvious from all this that it makes very little sense to ask whether Jesus 'was' the Messiah. The real question is more like: what ideas about himself did Jesus have in mind when (as he seems to have done – even if rather nervously) he encouraged the disciples to apply the title to himself. The popular notion at the time was, as popular notions usually are, rather crude. Ever since the final destruction of the monarchy roughly six hundred years before Jesus' time, Israel had been through all that time a subject people, ruled by Babylon until 536 BC, Persia until 332, Alexander the Great until 323, the Seleucids of Asia Minor and the Ptolemaids of Egypt competing with each other for sovereignty until 64 BC, and thereafter by the Romans. There had been about a century of semi-independence under the Maccabean family of priests up to the time of the Roman conquest; but this had been solely due to the weakness of the 'great powers' (Asia Minor and Egypt) in that area at the time, and it had never remotely looked feasible that Israel could have maintained its independence in opposition to a vigorous imperial power, let alone recreate what it regarded as its own destined role as the centre of a renewed empire.

Nevertheless, this hope, revived and strengthened as it had been by the comparatively recent memory of the Maccabees, was not merely alive but insanely – and there really is no other word for it – influential throughout the region of Palestine in Jesus' time. When we read in Luke 6.15 and Acts 1.13 that one of Jesus' disciples was called 'Simon the Zealot', we should understand that this Simon was committed to this very extreme form of Messianic ideology: he would be all for the demand for 'revolution *now*', without any craven calculations about the probable cost in men and resources, or the unlikelihood of eventual success. If man would only find the courage and the grit to make a start, regardless of probabilities over the outcome, God himself would provide – by miracle if need be – the strength and the resources for a swift and permanent success. But we can be quite sure that *all* the disciples were in some degree influenced in this way, and all would immediately have assumed that Jesus, if he thought of himself as Messiah, could only mean that his ambition was to lead the nation against the Romans. The first chapter of Acts suggests that this misunderstanding of Jesus' claim continued even after his death; when the disciples ask him (Acts 1.6) 'Lord, will you at this time restore the kingdom to Israel?' there seems little doubt that the author (presumed to be Luke) implies that the question should be understood in just this sense.

But we can also be sure, because all three synoptic gospels turn on the point, that Jesus' ideas about the Messiah were very different from this. Just how different will become clear in the body of the exposition. But the reader will now understand why Jesus, though he wanted the disciples to think of him as the Messiah, wanted no one outside this close inner circle to know about his claim, presumably until he had managed to convince them what the 'real' Messiah was like. It also explains why it was so easy for the Jewish authorities to persuade the Romans that Jesus was a danger to public order and must be made an example of. The political history of Palestine until AD 135, when the Emperor Hadrian finally expelled the Jews from Palestine, was littered with the corpses of Messianic claimants and their followers. There were large and catastrophic uprisings in 69 and 132, but any number also of smaller ones in the years between. The Romans no doubt thought of Jesus as just another of these claimants; it is even possible that in all sincerity so did the Jerusalem priests (who, according to the gospels, were chiefly responsible in engineering the crucifixion). Given the political situation at the time, if Jesus' claims were misunderstood, it is difficult to lay too much of the blame for that upon his hearers.

It has already been pointed out that Mark's gospel begins not with Jesus' birth but with the baptism by John, and that the likeliest reason for this is that Mark thought of Jesus' divinity (as the poet thought of the king's divinity in the psalm quoted above) as starting from that moment. Jesus was the Messiah or Anointed because his baptism by John had been the ceremony of his anointing. The reference to Psalm 2 in connection with the baptism is unmistakable in all three synoptic gospels. Even Matthew is fully aware of the implications of the event and goes out of his way to show he has misgivings about it. He alone gives us the following exchange, which he seems to have quite simply invented:

> John would have prevented him, saying 'I need to be baptized by you, and do you come to me?' But Jesus answered him, 'Let it be so now; for thus it is fitting for us to fulfill all righteousness [possibly, but not certainly, meaning that the event fulfills Old Testament prophecy – presumably the Psalm in question].' Then he consented. (Matt. 3.14–15)

In all three gospels as they now stand, the voice from heaven seems to be conflating Psalm 2.7 with Isaiah 42.1. Mark has, 'Thou art my beloved Son; with thee I am well pleased', which Matthew changes from something being said to Jesus himself to something being said to the onlookers – presumably on the grounds that it wasn't Jesus that needed to be told this. Luke is the most interesting of all. The received text gives exactly the same words to the heavenly voice as we find in Mark; but some early manuscripts have survived in which the heavenly voice says: 'Thou art my beloved Son; today I have begotten thee.' Which is the original? My own guess is that it can only be the second: it is easy to see why the above would have been altered to what we have, and very hard to see why what we have should have been altered to the above.

APPENDIX

Nothing we have said so far helps to explain a most curious feature in all four gospels, which we know was also a feature of Messianic thinking as a whole: which is that it seems to have been taken for granted that the Messiah makes himself known by working miracles. The one New Testament writer who I suspect may have noticed how peculiar this is, to have thought about it, and (in his usual round-about and intellectual fashion) tried to offer some kind of explanation, is the author of John's gospel. He seems to trace the origin of the idea (and he may well be historically accurate in doing so) to what the Old Testament tells us about Moses. Consider the following:

> Then Moses answered, 'But behold, they will not believe me or listen to my voice, for they will say, "The Lord did not appear to you"'. The Lord said to him, 'What is that in your hand?' He said, 'A rod'. And he said, 'Cast it on the ground'. So he cast it on the ground, and it became a serpent; and Moses fled from it. But the Lord said to Moses, 'Put out your hand, and take it by the tail' – so he put out his hand and caught it, and it became a rod in his hand – 'that they may believe that the Lord, the God of their fathers, the God of Abraham, the God of Isaac, and the God of Jacob, has appeared to you'. Again, the Lord said to him, 'Put your hand into your bosom'. And he put his hand into his bosom; and when he took it out, behold, his hand was leprous, as white as snow. Then God said, 'Put your hand back into your bosom'. So he put his hand back into his bosom; and when he took it out, behold, it was restored like the rest of his flesh. 'If they will not believe you', God said, 'or heed the first sign, they may believe the latter sign. If they will not believe even these two signs or heed your voice, you shall take some water from the Nile and pour it upon the dry ground; and the water which you shall take from the Nile will become blood upon the dry ground'. (Ex. 4.1–9)

Compare this with what may have been the concluding sentence of John's gospel (chapter 21 of the gospel reads like something of an appendix after this, the concluding sentence of chapter 20);

> Now Jesus did many other signs in the presence of the disciples, which are not written in this book; but these are written that you may believe that Jesus is the Christ, the Son of God, and that believing you may have life in his name. (John 20.30–31)

Readers may feel that this is rather a slender thread of coincidence on which to hang such a huge weight of conclusion. Let me then draw their attention to the concluding sign in the Exodus passage, the pouring of the waters of the Nile on the dry ground, and compare it with the following:

> So the soldiers came and broke the legs of the first, and of the other who had been crucified with him; but when they came to Jesus and saw that he was already dead, they did not break his legs. But one of the soldiers pierced his side with a spear, and at once there came out blood and water. He who saw it has borne witness – his testimony is true, and he knows that he tells the truth – that you also may believe. For these things took place that the scripture might be fulfilled, 'Not a bone of him shall be broken'. And again another scripture says, 'They shall look on him whom they have pierced'. (John 19.32–35)

The coincidence that has caught my eye is the mention of blood and water in both passages, and the common assumption (all but unintelligible to the reader) that such a manifestation somehow compels 'belief' on the part of the observer. My thesis can still undoubtedly be questioned. The relevant passage is immediately followed by two actual quotations from the Old Testament neither of which have any connection with the point I am trying to make. But it could plausibly be argued that the author, having mentioned blood and water *and immediately gone on to draw a conclusion which does not obviously follow*, assumed that for enlightened readers the point would now be clear.

To make the coincidence suggestion seem even more implausible, let me give a further example:

> 'Now is my soul troubled. And what shall I say? "Father, save me from this hour"? No, for this purpose I have come to this hour. Father, glorify thy name.' Then a voice came from heaven, 'I have

glorified it, and I will glorify it again'. The crowd standing by heard it, and said that it had thundered. Others said, 'An angel has spoken to him'. Jesus answered, 'This voice has come for your sake, not for mine ...' (John 12.27–30)

That concluding remark seems startlingly crude, until we compare it with:

> And the Lord said to Moses, 'Lo, I am coming to you in a thick cloud, that the people may hear when I speak with you, and may also believe you for ever'. (Ex. 19.9)

I would need to be writing an introduction to John's gospel rather than Mark's to be justified in pursuing the point any further. I believe I have now said enough to satisfy most readers that rather more than coincidence is involved.

Such a view could explain one of the more striking contrasts between the synoptic gospels' view of Jesus' miracles and that of the fourth gospel. In the synoptics Jesus seems to look on his miracles as something of a guilty secret – something he would rather most people didn't know about. 'See that you say nothing to anyone ...' (Mark 1.44); 'And whenever the unclean spirits beheld him, they fell down before him and cried out, "You are the Son of God". And he strictly ordered them not to make him known' (3.11–12); 'And immediately the girl got up and walked; for she was twelve years old ... And he strictly charged them that no one should know this ...' (5.42–43); 'And he charged them to tell no one ...' (7.36); 'And he sent him away to his home, saying, "Do not even enter the village"' (8.26). There is nowhere any clear explanation of this feature, but Christians have traditionally looked for one – with some plausibility – in the following:

> That evening, at sundown, they brought to him all who were sick or possessed with demons. And the whole city was gathered together about the door. And he healed many who were sick with various diseases, and cast out many demons; and he would not permit the demons to speak, because they knew him.
>
> And in the morning, a great while before day, he rose and went out to a lonely place, and there he prayed. And Simon and those who were with him followed him, and they found him and said to him, 'Every one is searching for you'. And he said to them, 'Let us go on to the next towns also; for that is why I came out'. And he

went throughout all Galilee, preaching in their synagogues and casting out demons. (Mark 1.32–38)

In other words, although Mark sees Jesus as exercising a dual ministry of teaching and healing (3.14–15), he portrays him as being embarassed by the easy success of the miracles, and as being afraid that the equally important teaching ministry will be popularly ignored if he allows any emphasis at all to be placed on them. Mark seems to assume, and to be persuading us that Jesus assumed, that belief that derives from miracles alone is all but worthless.

But in John's gospel, as in part we have already seen, the whole purpose of Jesus' miracles is to persuade people of the truth of his claims. 2.11 sets the tone for the whole of the rest of the gospel: 'This, the first of his signs, Jesus did at Cana in Galilee, *and manifested his glory*; and his disciples believed in him.' And again in verse 23 of the same chapter: 'Now when he was in Jerusalem at the Passover feast, many believed in his name *when they saw the signs which he did ...*' The woman of Samaria, though she is shown no miracle as such, is prompted to believe when she becomes aware of Jesus' extra-ordinary powers of second sight, and expects her fellow Samaritans (4.29) to take the same attitude, which in the event they do (4.39–42). The Galilean official, having brushed aside the suggestion that his request for a miracle had anything to do with testing Jesus' powers but was simply a direct request for help (4.48–49), is nevertheless induced to believe when the miracle he asks for is duly performed (4.53). The whole of chapter 5, whose implications are too complex to be worked out here, is a discussion of the connection between who Jesus claims to be and the miracles he performs (and note the double reference to Moses with which the chapter ends – 5.45–47).

In chapter 6 the author begins to develop the theme – which he increasingly emphasizes as the work proceeds – that faith created by miracles, though better than no faith at all, should also detect the deeper 'meaning' behind the perceived event (6.26); and once again the whole of the chapter is a complex meditation on this theme. It is undoubtedly this idea which underlies Jesus' professed reluctance to go up to Jerusalem in 7.1–9. His brothers in effect suggest that this is the perfect opportunity for him to 'prove' himself, while Jesus replies that that kind of proof on its own is not worth very much. In chapter 9 nobody for a moment doubts that if Jesus really has done what some people claim he has done (opened the eyes of a man born blind) then he must really be who he says he is; hence the extreme reluctance of the authorities to believe that the blind man's story is true. In 10.37–38 Jesus himself points to his miracles as being proof of his claims; while chapter 11 can be read as an extended illustration of the same theme, made explicit in 11.45–46.

This strange ambivalence, both of Jesus himself in being less than content with a belief based only on the miracle without grasping the meaning, and of the crowd in seeing the miracles and still not coming to believe, is summarized in 12.37–43, and the theme continues to be emphasized in Jesus' teaching of the disciples right up to the end (14.10–11; 15–24). There is little doubt also that the 'doubting Thomas' episode (20.24–29) is intended as some sort of concluding flourish to the theme. Throughout John's gospel Jesus insists that what he does proves that he is who he says he is. Real faith goes deeper than the miracles, but even belief that derives from miracles is acceptable as faith. This is of course exactly what he is making clear to Thomas in the incident of the hands and the side. A question he avoids, perhaps deliberately, is whether faith needs miracles at all in the first place. The words, 'Blessed are those who have not seen and yet believe' are capable of that interpretation, and it is one that is attractive to the modern sceptical reader: but the author never makes the suggestion elsewhere in the gospel, and even here he seems to take it back immediately afterwards (20.30–31 – see the quotation on page 38 above). My own view – admittedly speculative – is that, being himself a profoundly intellectual man, he gave no literal credence to any of the miracle stories he relates in his gospel; but he was aware that most of his readers would want to do so, and even seems to have tried to encourage this.

It is by no means pointless to ask what was Jesus' own attitude to miracles. Since all three synoptic gospels are agreed on the views that they put in Jesus' mouth – *and these views are also inconsistent with the implications of their narratives* – the views themselves are likely to have a historical basis. The following four excerpts are the complete synoptic evidence on this point:

> The Pharisees came and began to argue with him, seeking from him a sign from heaven, to test him. And he sighed deeply in his spirit, and said, 'Why does this generation seek a sign? Truly, I say to you, no sign shall be given to this generation'. (Mark 8.11–12)

Then some of the scribes and Pharisees said to him, 'Teacher, we wish to see a sign from you'. But he answered them, 'An evil and adulterous generation seeks for a sign; but no sign shall be given to it except the sign of the prophet Jonah. *For as Jonah was three days and three nights in the belly of the whale, so will the Son of man be three days and three nights in the heart of the earth.* The men of Nineveh will arise at the judgment with this generation and condemn it; for they repented at the preaching of Jonah, and behold, something greater than Jonah is here. The queen of the South will arise at the judgment with this generation and condemn it; for she came from the ends of the earth to hear the wisdom of Solomon, and behold, something greater than Solomon is here. (Matt. 12.38–42).

And the Pharisees and Sadducees came, and to test him they asked him to show them a sign from heaven. He answered them, ['When it is evening, you say, "It will be fair weather; for the sky is red". And in the morning, "It will be stormy today, for the sky is red and threatening". You know how to interpret the appearance of the sky, but you cannot interpret the signs of the times.] An evil and adulterous generation seeks for a sign, but no sign shall be given to it except the sign of Jonah'. (Matt. 16.1–4)

When the crowds were increasing, he began to say, 'This generation is an evil generation; it seeks a sign, but no sign shall be given to it except the sign of Jonah. For as Jonah became a sign to the men of Nineveh, so will the Son of man be to this generation. The queen of the South will arise at the judgment with the men of this generation and condemn them; for she came from the ends of the earth to hear the wisdom of Solomon, and behold, something greater than Solomon is here. The men of Nineveh will arise at the judgment with this generation and condemn it; for they repented at the preaching of Jonah, and behold, something greater than Jonah is here.' (Luke 11.29–32)

One thing that is of obvious interest is that although the substance of Jesus' attitude is given in Mark, it is clear that both Matthew and Luke are using Q rather than P material. Matthew raises the topic twice, both times to the same effect, and in neither instance does he seem to be echoing Mark's language. There are obvious differences, as well as obvious similarities, between the earlier Matthew excerpt and that from Luke. I have put one sentence in the former into italics to make it clearer that in my view the source Matthew had before him was identical with the Lucan passage and that the present differences are caused by his own deliberate alteration. These main differences are two. The Lucan order of topics is (*a*) the sign of the prophet Jonah; (*b*) the condemnation by the queen of the South; (*c*) the condemnation by the men of Nineveh. Matthew has reversed the order of these last two for the obvious reason that (*a*) and (*c*) form a better connection than (*a*) and (*b*). The fact that one can easily see why Matthew should have altered Luke, but not why Luke should have altered Matthew, implies for the critic that the Lucan order is likely to be the original. The other obvious difference is the sentence I have italicized, which has no connection with anything in Luke. My own guess is that church-minded Matthew simply couldn't resist pointing up the coincidence between Jonah's three days in the belly of the whale and the three days between Jesus' death and resurrection, and that the insertion is purely his own invention.

I ought also to comment on the square-bracketed passage in the second Matthew excerpt. Not all manuscripts contain it. It is impossible to think of any reason why, if it is authentic, any one should have wanted to cut it out, or on the other hand if it was not authentic, why anyone should have wanted to put it in. In a word, there does not seem to be any *doctrinal* controversy involved. The likeliest guess is that the passage is authentic and was left out accidentally by a scribe who had Mark's version running in his head at the time of transcribing.

All this however is incidental to the main point, which is that here we have *strong* testimony to the fact that Jesus was challenged to perform a sign (presumably that would prove he was who he said he was, though that itself causes problems – all three synoptics insist that no one outside the immediate circle of disciples was supposed to know), and that Jesus refused to do so. If the gospels we have were accurate accounts of his life, it is inconceivable that he would not simply have rattled off his miracles to date. The conclusion that the reader is forced to draw is that the testimony of the gospels to Jesus' miracles must therefore itself be suspect.

He would of course be inclined to this conclusion anyway, on the grounds of the sheer improbability of many of the stories; but the argument above will, for very many of us, clinch the matter. That Jesus had a reputation in his day as what we would call a spiritual healer does not cause the modern reader difficulty. What exactly it is that a spiritual healer does is not a question that needs to be gone into. The essential point is that if a spiritual healer really does what he says he does, then what a spiritual healer does can not be thought of as miraculous. In a word, nothing that ever actually happens can be thought of as a miracle. A miracle is – almost as it were by definition – an event which cannot happen. The gospel writers themselves share this assumption with the modern sceptic. How do we know when a gospel story is a miracle? Because it describes an event that we can tell at once (as could the authors themselves and the original readers) cannot possibly have happened. If Jesus performed 'miracles' of healing, then the accounts we have of such healings are exaggerated. And there are of course a great many other miracles that are not miracles of healing. It causes us no problem to suppose that these also are exaggerated stories of events that really happened; but we take it for granted that the exaggeration lies precisely in the transformation of a story that is not about a miracle into one that is.

Despite this, and despite the fact that Jesus himself seems to have rejected the idea that he needed – or even was able – to prove his Messiahship by his miracles, like the fourth gospel (which is probably deliberately imitating him on the point) Mark makes the recognition of Jesus' claim to be the Messiah depend on miracles. Let us go through the evidence for this. The recognition is made by Peter in Mark 8.27–30. But what prompts him to make it? The context makes this abundantly clear, as it also makes clear that Jesus himself has prompted the realization. In 8.11–13 the Pharisees ask Jesus for a sign and are refused. The following *pericope* (8.14–21) looks at first sight like a harmless sermon to beware of the religious and political authorities, the sermon having arisen quite fortuitously from a lack of provisions due to carelessness. That is how the disciples themselves at first understand it (8.16). Jesus rather cryptically tells them not to be thick: the lack of bread is neither here nor there. Don't they remember the two feeding miracles (the second of which immediately precedes the Pharisees' frustrated request)? And assuming they can remember, can't they see the significance? They can't of course – or not for the moment. They must be blind; Jesus himself offers that as the only possible explanation in 8.18. So when they fail to answer his question, the next pericope – at first sight merely a digression – tells the story of the healing of a blind man.

(The author of John's gospel seems to have grasped the point, and his own chapter 9 is a brilliant, though almost certainly quite fictional, meditation on the implications of Mark 8.22–26.) Now at last Peter, in a flash of 'insight', is able to answer Jesus' question, 'Who do you say that I am?'

But he is not just answering that particular question; he is also answering 8.21, and before that the perplexities described in 6.51–52, and before that the question the disciples themselves were asking each other in 4.41. These questions are attached to what appears at first sight to be a series of four miracles, but which turns out on closer examination to be two miracles told twice. The key passage here is 6.51–52, where the implication is that the disciples should have realized 'the answer' (but there has been no hint anywhere in the gospel so far as to what the question is) when they saw the miracle of the loaves; failing that, it is unbelievably crass of them still not to realize the answer after the walking on the water. Now as we have seen, the question is first raised by the disciples themselves as a result of the stilling of the storm at the end of chapter 4, and it will scarcely need to be pointed out to most readers that this and the walking on the water are in all likelihood two versions of one and the same miracle. The common features are the maritime setting, the rising of a storm, the increasing failure of the disciples to battle against it, the intervention of Jesus, and the passing of danger as soon as Jesus comes among them.

We have then, at the very centre of Mark's gospel, an insoluble riddle. According to Mark, Jesus' on the one hand refused to perform miracles (and the comparable material from the synoptic gospels persuades us that this response is likely to have been historical, and also makes it clear that Jesus specifically dismissed the request as irrelevant – an irrelevance that can only refer to his own claim, and his hearers' suspicion that he claimed, to be the Messiah). Yet equally Mark insists, and seems to make Jesus insist, that the truth of his claim is proved by this series of four miracles. The contradiction is glaring, and all the commentator can do is point it out. It does have a marginally reassuring corollary, though. In note 5 to this introduction (p. 367) I give a list of indications why we can be fairly sure that the figure of Jesus in the gospels derives from an actual historical person and is not simply the invention of a myth-making tradition. But this central contradiction in Mark's gospel is in some ways the most convincing indication of all. A mere forger would have to go about his work with a great deal more circumspection than we actually find Mark doing in his gospel.

IV

It will be obvious from the above that I do not accept even the possibility that a miraculous 'event' can also be a historical one. Most scholars would nowadays make the same assumption, but would tend on the whole to avoid drawing attention to it. They would prefer to point out that the question is in many ways irrelevant. The gospel writers themselves (with the possible exception, as I have suggested, of the author of John's gospel) undoubtedly did believe the miracles to be true, so that in elucidating their works it is *their* beliefs and not *ours* that must have priority. They would also add (and I have criticized this view in note 9 on page 368) that the gospels cannot be read as historical works in any case: they are statements of faith, and are intended to awaken faith in the reader rather than simply to record the events of history. But most readers – rightly as far as I am concerned – insist that what they want to know is what actually happened. This does present the scholar with a genuine problem. The author of John's gospel, though he undoubtedly understood the point, seems nevertheless to have genuinely thought that mere facts of history were far too contaminated with earthly dross to be of interest to an intellectual like himself; while the other three gospel writers seem to have had only a very hazy idea of what facts really are.

Most commentators assume that once all this has been pointed out, the reader will simply agree to let the matter drop. I myself do not share this assumption. It is true that we cannot hope to recover the 'history' of Jesus' life from the records that we have – the scholar once again is right to point this out. But the records contain a great deal of material which we *know* cannot be historical, and we must be prepared at once and openly to say so. And we have a great deal of other material that we suspect may well be history – and let it be said that this is the nearest we can ever get to establishing the 'history' underlying the gospels. The results do not add up to a biography – they do not even amount to a totally convincing portrait. (After all, Christianity could not work in the way it does unless we were able –

as undoubtedly we are – to construct for ourselves any number of portraits out of the mass of incoherent and often conflicting fragments that the gospel writers have left us). But we cannot ignore, nor indeed should we, the fact that there is an undoubted stratum of history underlying the gospel narrative, and we must make it our task as far as possible to reveal it.

At this level of brutal history we can be sure, even before the enquiry begins, that the man Jesus was born a man, died a man, worked no miracles, and never rose again. So then, are the public-house philosophers right after all? The gospels really are all lies? To adapt and invert a recent euphemism, let us describe them as being 'profuse with the truth' – that is, they include the truth so far as they know it, but their failing is to tell us much more, rather than much less, than they really know or than we can really believe. But surely doesn't this still amount to an admission that they are intended to deceive? In some ways I think we can fairly accuse the author of the fourth gospel of an intention to deceive, but not the other three. They deceive us only because they themselves were also thoroughly deceived. But even 'deceive' is probably not quite the right word. What they tell us is not strictly true; but as I pointed out at the beginning of an earlier section, just as an enquiry into truth does not at all concern itself with virtue, should it worry us if an exhortation to virtue does not primarily concern itself with truth – *provided of course that it is ready to admit that it does not*. The purpose of the gospels – this is the valid point behind the scholar's attempt to wean the reader off his simple thirst for history – the purpose of the gospels is to change the reader for the better, not simply to inform him of the facts.

What justification can there be for this? How can unreal claims, supported by improbable stories, ever have the effect of making people better? This question can in fact be answered. Let us take a look at the process of what, for want of a better term, I shall describe as formulating moral doctrine. It is customary these days to assume that there are two totally different ways of doing this, the religious and the secular. The religious way is to rely on 'given' precepts which it is believed are handed down to men directly from a heavenly source; and without that heavenly guarantee, we would have no means of knowing that these were the 'true' doctrines for the regulation of human behaviour. But the difficulty underlying such a view is obvious: we have to take on trust the basic claim (that is, we need 'faith') that such precepts do in fact derive from a guaranteed source, instead of being (as most of us suspect) arrived at in just the same way as the rest of us arrive at our own moral doctrines. In other words most of us do not believe, and the extensive coverage now-adays given in the media to the way such doctrines are arrived at undermines any inclination to believe, that there is any substance at all to the claim of a heavenly source for the doctrine, or a heavenly guarantee of its validity.

Contrasted with this, particularly in the modern world, is the secular approach to moral doctrine. The *original* claim, largely abandoned now by the majority even of the progressive-minded, is that all reliance on revelation must be set aside, and that moral doctrine is properly formulated solely on the basis of reason. What leads us increasingly to doubt this claim is the perception that on any particular moral question it is unlikely that everyone agrees, even among those for whose reasoning powers we have respect. We do have moral arguments with each other, and it is no rarity for someone to be converted from one moral view-point to an alterna-tive solely – or to all appearances solely – on the basis of argument. But very few of us any longer take it for granted that there is a reasonable view on any one moral question which only needs convincing presentation to win the general consent of all intelligent minds. The secular view nowadays increasingly concedes that there is an element in all moral doctrine which does not derive from, and is not persuaded by, any form of reasoning at all; and that civilized minds accept this and are not perturbed by it.

I myself accept the secular view once the claim to reason as the source of moral doctrine has been abandoned. But I would like to ponder this intriguing question why it is that although, as we have seen, reasoning is often relevant to moral debate, it still seems unable to resolve it. It looks to me as if there is but one technique that all of use in formulating moral doctrine, whether we think of ourselves as secular, or religious, or nothing in particular. We are all of us, I think, dissatisfied in some degree with the world as we experience it, so that all of us carry in our heads a kind of compensating 'ideal' of a different world that would be very much more to our liking. It is on the basis of this ideal that we formulate our moral doctrines, in belief that if these doctrines were applied, the existing, unsatifactory world would be transformed into something like the world of our dreams. (Woe betide us, though, and all around us, if any of us ever had our whole desire in such a matter.) Once we have a clear notion of our ideal, the business of formulating the doctrines is one that can be carried out by reasoning. But it's hard to see that reason plays any real part in creating the ideal itself. We can argue usefully with people whose ideal is not too different from our own, and convince them that the effective way to realize that ideal lies in this direction rather than that. But if the kind of world they long for is seriously different from our own, then nothing can be achieved by argument. It is in this situation that we must learn to agree to differ, and to confine our opposition to each other to methods and intensities that we hope will always fall short of actual breach of the peace. And we have to learn that our opponents are not necessarily wicked, or stupid, or blind, or stubborn, or malevolent. They simply have a different ideal world.

I should add that wicked people themselves (and undoubtedly there are such) use much the same technique for framing their wicked doctrines as moral people do for their moral ones. It is perfectly possible, and probably by no means rare, for a wicked person to be dissatisfied with the world as he experiences it because it provides too many obstacles to his wicked ambitions; and such a person, like the moral person, frames wicked doctrines which, if applied, would make the world a more wicked place. And the frustrating part of this perception is the realization that we have *no certain means* of knowing when a person whose ideal world differs from our own is a wicked person or merely a moral person who has a different vision of morality. And – even more frustrating – though we have no means of knowing this, we find in practice that we still have to take a decision on the question and then act on that decision; and we also know from experience that such decisions often turn out to be wrong.

But how does all this relate to Mark's gospel, and more particularly to all those features of it which we know can not be history, even though we also know that there must be a historical basis to the gospel narrative as a whole? It seems to me that the gospel writers generally – the first three unwittingly, the forth quite possibly with an awareness of what he was doing – were reacting to a slice of history in the same way that we react to our everyday experience: allowing an unacknowledged sense of disappointment to transform it from something real but unsatisfying into something unreal but potentially elevating; and subsequent Christian debates about the true nature of the incarnation, however unpleasant the practical features of these debates can seem to the modern historian, were a way of continuing the same process.

If that is the real explanation, now that we have seen through the device is it not time to abandon it? A vast proportion of the modern world would seem to be answering 'Yes'. Myself I think this would be at leat a pity, probably also a mistake. The useful part of religion (any religion, not just Christianity) is the way it creates a *collective* ideal and formulates *collective* doctrines in addition to the individual ideals and individual doctrines described above. I would have thought that, despite popular perception of a contradiction between them, both should have their place; just as in ancient Israel the stabilizing communal conservativism of the priests and the radical individual reformism of the prophets look to us to be interdependent, though at the time they were assumed to be mutually antagonistic. For reasons that are hard to explain – partly, I suppose, just because the religious enterprise *is* communal, perhaps also because (in most cases) it is of very long standing (I reject the idea, though, that it is because it is supernatural) religious imagery still provides the most useful, effective, and most commonly invoked frame of moral reference for society at large. The fact that it is widely and frankly disbelieved even by those making use of it in this way does not seem to me to create a difficulty. Secularism is most usefully seen as a way of interpreting the traditional images, not as an (almost certainly hopeless) attempt to replace them.

1

First Appearance

(Mark 1.1–15)

The beginning of the gospel of Jesus Christ, the Son of God. As it is written in Isaiah the prophet, 'Behold, I send my messenger before thy face, who shall prepare thy way; the voice of one crying in the wilderness: Prepare the way of the Lord, make his paths straight' – John the baptizer appeared in the wilderness, preaching a baptism of repentance for the forgiveness of sins. And there went out to him all the country of Judaea, and all the people of Jerusalem; and they were baptized by him in the river Jordan, confessing their sins. Now John was clothed with camel's hair, and had a leather girdle around his waist, and ate locusts and wild honey. And he preached, saying, 'After me comes he who is mightier than I, the thong of whose sandals I am not worthy to stoop down and untie. I have baptized you with water; but he will baptize you with the Holy Spirit'. In those days Jesus came from Nazareth of Galilee and was baptized by John in the Jordan. And when he came up out of the water, immediately he saw the heavens opened and the Spirit descending upon him like a dove; and a voice came from heaven, 'Thou art my beloved Son; with thee I am well pleased'.

The Spirit immediately drove him out into the wilderness. And he was in the wilderness forty days, tempted by Satan; and he was with the wild beasts; and the angels ministered to him.

Now after John was arrested, Jesus came into Galilee, preaching the gospel of God, and saying, 'The time is fulfilled, and the kingdom of God is at hand; repent, and believe in the gospel'. (1.1–15)

'The beginning of the gospel ...' Most readers will tend to assume that the word 'gospel' here refers to the book that is to follow; but in fact this use of the word has arisen only *as a consequence* of the work Mark wrote. What he means by the word here is the oral preaching that had been going on for the last thirty odd years. The subject of his book, therefore, is a record of the origins of that preaching.

'... of Jesus Christ, the Son of God.' As the footnote in most Bibles will make clear, the words 'the Son of God' do not appear in some of our earliest and best manuscripts. We have to decide therefore whether it was later copyists – perhaps sensing the adoptionist tone of the work as a whole and wishing to counterbalance it, or perhaps simply assuming it ought to be there – who inserted it; or on the contrary, whether it was persistent and conscious adoptionists, at a time when mainstream thinking had moved away from earlier ideas of christology, who deliberately took it out. Of the two, I think the earlier hypothesis is the more probable. What chiefly counts against the latter is the fact that the gospel contains several other references to Jesus being the Son of God which are beyond question. The most notable is the 'baptismal pronouncement' of the heavenly voice later in the above excerpt; but see also 3.11, 5.7, 15.39. It is a striking feature though, and one not easily explained, that apart from that fourth instance it is always a non-human voice – God in the first instance and demons in the other two – who hail Jesus as 'Son of God'. And even the fourth instance comes presumably from the mouth of a pagan. Neither the disciples nor Jesus' other Jewish contemporaries are ever faced with or ever make the claim. In the famous 'recognition' of Jesus by Peter in 8.29, in this gospel Peter says simply, 'You are the Christ'. (In Luke 9.20 this is expanded to 'The Christ of God' – i.e. the *exact* equivalent Old Testament phrase 'The Lord's anointed'; in Matthew 16.17 it is expanded still further into the version usually quoted – 'You are the Christ, the Son of the living God'.) If adoptionist expurgators had actually been at work on the gospel, over all one would have expected a more thorough job.

It is not being suggested, by the way, that Mark would ever have denied that Jesus was 'the Son of God'. The point is that, given the adoptionist tone of the work, he must have meant something rather different by it than what the church has traditionally understood him to mean. I say 'must have meant' advisedly. I do not pretend to be able to demonstrate just what he did mean, any more than one can be precise about what the Davidic kings meant when they made a similar claim for themselves. It is after all quite possible that he himself had no precise ideas about what he meant. And even when we consider Old Testament usage, most readers will need little persuasion that ceremonial formulas very frequently have no precise meaning; or that formulas which once had a meaning have gradually lost it as, over the centuries, those who use it have ceased ask what it means.

'As it is written ... "make his paths straight".' Some early manuscripts refer the quoted passage generally to 'the prophets' and rather than specifically to 'Isaiah the prophet' and it may well be that they accurately record what Mark actually wrote, the more precise reference being added at a later date. We must remember that the New Testament, though written by men who all knew the Old Testament very well indeed, was written without the aid of concordances or other works of reference and, perhaps more important, before the invention of the codex (the thing that we always mean when we nowadays talk about a 'book'). A 'book' to Mark meant a scroll, and checking references, even if one could remember where to look, meant laboriously unravelling the scroll until one came to the place. Obviously not many authors could be bothered – they preferred to rely on memory. Many of the garbled quotations with which the New Testament is sprinkled have their origin in nothing more sinister than this understandable laziness.

The quotation is from Isaiah 40.3 and would more correctly be translated, 'The voice of one crying, "Prepare the way of the Lord in the wilderness ..."'. The error first occurs in the Greek translation of the Old Testament known in the West as the Septuagint[1] The idea that the Old Testament ever 'prophesies' later events in the sense that Christian orthodoxy has always claimed is misleading. What certainly *is* true, though, and often important for understanding the way the gospel story is told, is that beginning with Jesus himself all the contributors to the New Testament (whether oral or scribal) held just this view, which was one of the characteristics of the Judaism of their day; and this has often greatly influenced (*a*) the way in which Jesus and the disciples saw themselves and what they were doing, (*b*) the way that later preachers and writers modified events in retelling them. Thus it is by no means rare to find events that have been 'prophesied' (as here) by what is in fact a mistranslation.

In this case, however, the error is unusually interesting. Normally where a 'prophecy' depends on the Septuagintal version of the passage rather than the original Hebrew, one concludes that the whole idea of prophecy in such incidents has been introduced later than Jesus' time; the reason being that Jesus and his contemporaries (including John the Baptist) probably knew no Greek and read their Old Testament (assuming they could read at all) in popular Aramaic translations known as Targums. But in this case it is hard to avoid the impression that John the Baptist himself had this very 'prophecy' in mind and deliberately patterned his ministry around it. It is possible therefore that some of those errors that appear in the Septuagint were popular in origin and derived from the Targums.

'John the baptizer appeared in the wilderness ...' The translation is awkward because the translators have preferred a less than convincing version of the text. What Mark wrote probably was, '... there appeared John baptizing in the wilderness'. Some later copyist, with the phrase 'John the Baptist' on the brain, seems to have added a definite article to the participle 'baptizing', and the translators have taken this to be original. The fact that he chose the wilderness as the setting for his ministry may well be due – at least in part – to the fact that he misunderstood the passage from Isaiah in the same way the Septuagint does.

'... preaching a baptism for the forgiveness of sins.' More literally of course he preached the forgiveness of sins and offered baptism as a kind of 'seal' of such forgiveness. It is sometimes suggested, particularly since the discovery of the Dead Sea Scrolls in the late 1940s, that baptism was a widespread Jewish practice in New Testament times and that Christianity simply took it over.[2] A more careful scrutiny of the evidence suggests, however, that the rite was at the time unique to John, and that the Christians took it over from him. References to 'baptism' in the Scrolls and elsewhere are more accurately interpreted simply as ritual washings. The difference is admittedly less than hard and fast. But look at the following Old Testament material: Exodus 30.17–21, Leviticus repeatedly throughout chapters 11 to 17, Numbers 19.7–13; and in the New Testament Mark 7.1–4 (where in verse 4 the Greek behind the RSV 'purify', as the footnote explains, is the very word 'baptize'). All these are descriptions of ritual washings, nor do they seem even intended to be any kind of parallel to the baptism administered by John. Two differences suggest themselves: first, these ritual washings are repeated acts, whereas baptism is administered only once; secondly, although both acts are symbolic rather than practical in character (i.e. in neither case does the intention seem to be anything to do with hygiene), the 'uncleanness' whose removal is symbolized by a ritual washing is basically a *ceremonial* uncleanness, whereas John's baptism seems intended to symbolize the removal of a *moral* guilt.

Christians still often want to be told what 'happens' at baptism. The short and truthful answer would be that baptism is what happens at baptism. What is symbolized by baptism does not 'happen' at all, in the way that the ceremony itself 'happens'. To conservative minds this is an unsatisfying view which, if accepted, drains the event of any real significance. It is this word 'real' here that is crucial. For such minds symbolism is 'true' only because whatever is symbolized by a ceremony is an event in exactly the same way that the ceremony itself is an event, and the symbolic event is causally dependent on the ceremony. To me this looks like a grotesque delusion, though it underlies both traditional Catholic thinking about the sacraments, and also a great deal of Protestant opposition to that thinking. To my mind what is symbolized by a ceremony is not an event at all; the symbolism is the inner response of those who are participating in the external ceremony. And here we encounter another misconception which seems to me to vitiate much of Christian thinking. For some reason Christians are convinced that unless that inner response is the same for all the participants, something is seriously amiss both with the ceremony and with the response to it. Indeed, the two errors are complementary: all must have the same inner response because that response is to something that 'really' happens, even though apart from 'faith' we have no means of knowing what it is that really happens.

Now 'faith' in this context (and indeed in most contexts) looks rather like a fraud word, meaning simply, 'We insist on the truth of these claims, though we have no demonstrable or examinable grounds for making them'. Provided everyone remains agreed on what 'faith' is to consist of, the practical difficulties can be contained. But when the day comes (and history shows it is never delayed for very long) that people start to disagree about faith, the resulting quarrel is inordinately fanatical for the very reason that there is no calm and rational way of deciding it; sadly also in a totally unreasonable quarrel, the least reasonable opponent is generally the victor. The history of the Christian church is perhaps the best illustration of all time of this sobering truth.

From a practical view, as well as with the desirable aim of keeping the peace, there is no reason at all why the participants in a ceremony which all are agreed is to be significant, should also have to be agreed on what that significance is to be. I say 'is to be' advisedly: for significance is something *determined* by the participants rather than something *perceived* by them. As a matter of historical fact there has been wide variation over the centuries, even among the most orthodox thinkers, as to 'what happens' in the Christian sacraments. The Catholic hierarchy (most notably) tends to hide this variability from popular awareness in the belief that to reveal it would cause uncertainty and therefore distress. But this habit of claiming certainty where there is none is itself, and always has been, the most fruitful source of distress. If historic conflicts of opinion were more openly discussed, even ordinary people would be much more easily reconciled to and unworried by inevitable (and permanent) differences in opinion. Nor are such differences any bar to 'unity': they should rather be thought of as enriching, not undermining, the common tradition of interpretation.

The ideas underlying the phrase 'repentance for the forgiveness of sins' are part of a large complex of ideas connected with John the Baptist's (and Jesus') proclamation of the coming kingdom of God, which will be dealt with more fully at the close of the chapter.

'And there went out ... in the river Jordan ...' It is an interesting, though perhaps also an idle, question just where it was that John exercised his ministry. The synoptic gospels tell us only that it was 'in the river Jordan', a river which runs the whole length of Palestine. However, since his clients come from 'the country of Judaea, and all the people of Jerusalem', the implication is that he based himself somewhere at the south end of the river, near where it flows into the Dead Sea. The fourth gospel appears to be very specific: 'This took place in Bethany beyond the Jordan, where John was baptizing' (John 1.28); 'John also was baptizing at Aenon near Salim, because there was much water there ...' (John 3.23) (That at first sight rather puzzling description of the place presumably means that the river runs unusually deep at this spot.) However, it turns out that neither of these identifications is of much use, and the places indicated on maps and shown to tourists are almost certainly examples, not so much of localities referred to in the New Testament, as of probable identifications created by it. There is for instance frequent mention of Bethany in the gospels, but in every instance apart from this it refers to a known village about two miles outside Jerusalem. This is the only reference we have to an otherwise unknown 'Bethany beyond the Jordan', and it seems likely that the place indicated on the map is not where this second Bethany actually was, but where it 'must have been'. Similarly there is in modern Israel a town called Salim, and nearby another town called Ainun, surprisingly (and also not quite believably) in the heart of what would then have been Samaria. It would not help even to look for a part of the Jordan that runs unusually deep. Such an identification might tell us what part of the Jordan it was that the author of John's gospel had in mind (assuming he had ever seen the Jordan, and did have a particular spot in mind); but that would still not necessarily be the same locality as the one the Baptist actually used. I did point out at the start that this was probably an idle question.

'... confessing their sins.' In the modern world there are two main traditions offering guidelines on how this ought to be done. Catholic practice tends to recommend that penitents should 'examine their consciences', mentally compile a list of actual misdeeds, and relate these item by item to a 'confessor' who must be an ordained priest, supposedly having a divinely given power to absolve sins. The protestant tradition (which on this subject I think I prefer) lays less emphasis on individual sins and more on a general awareness of sinfulness, less emphasis on the role of the confessor – who in any case need not be any kind of expert, but simply a valued friend whose advice and encouragement is expected to prove helpful – and more on the unlimited readiness of God himself to offer forgiveness to those who sincerely ask for it. What both traditions have in common is the view that the sinner is inwardly afflicted and must be offered inward healing. Luke's gospel (only) has a most interesting passage which seems to be a description of those who came to John for baptism actually in the process of 'confessing their sins':

> And the multitudes asked him, 'What then shall we do?' And he answered them, 'He who has two coats, let him share with him who has none; and he who has food, let him do likewise'. Tax collectors also came to be baptized, and said to him, 'Teacher, what shall we do?' And he said to them, 'Collect no more than is appointed you.' Soldiers also asked him, 'And we, what shall we do?' And he said to them, 'Rob no one by violence or by false accusation, and be content with your wages.' (Luke 3.10–14)

It is very noticeable that, in contrast to subsequent Christian tradition over many centuries, none of these people seem troubled by any

kind of inner anguish. What they are looking for is not an inner
feeling of forgiveness, but an easily grasped and easily followed
regulation of their outward behaviour – to use the Old Testament
word, righteousness. The guilty conscience, emphasized in all Christian teaching, does not seem to be equally characteristic of Old
Testament religion. We are told, in connection with one of David's
milder pranks against Saul, that 'David's heart smote him' (I Sam.
24.5); that is, he felt guilty about it. The phrase sticks in the mind
precisely because it is in fact very hard to find a parallel elsewhere in
the Old Testament. Christians traditionally identify seven peni-
tential psalms: 6, 32, 38, 51, 102, 130 and 143. But of these 6, 38,
102 and possibly 143 can be discarded; if you examine them closely,
the poet is complaining not that he feels guilty, but that he feels put
upon. Virtue for Old Testament authors is the same as righteousness,
which is essentially concerned with a man's external relations, either
with God or with his fellow men. Even man's relations with God
typically have more to do with outward acts than with inner
attitudes – a feature of Old Testament thought that has more to be
said for it than Christians have traditionally allowed.

The call of the solitary life in the wilderness has had a powerful
fascination both for later Judaism and for Christianity: in both
traditions if one wants to meet God, that is where one goes to find
him. In earlier times Moses had found God (or rather God had
revealed himself to Moses) in the wilderness of Horeb (Ex. 3. 1–6);
Israel's original demand from Pharaoh is that they be allowed to go
out into the wilderness to worship God (Ex. 5.1; 7.16; 8.25–28;
10.7–11); above all, the Law had been declared to Israel in the
wilderness of Sinai[3] (Ex. 19 right through to Num. 10.10). It was in
the wilderness that Israel had been close to God (Deut. 1.31; 2.7 –
and the whole of ch. 8 is a classic exposition of the relationship
between God and Israel: close and totally unencumbered during the
hardships of the wilderness, but in danger of being obscured by the
life of ease and plenty in cultivated land). This kind of thinking
pervades the Old Testament, and in Jesus' time (as we know from the
Dead Sea scrolls, which are the remains of the library of such a
community) often manifested itself in the colonization of parts of the
desert to the east of Judaea, both by individuals and by communities
of eremites or desert-dwellers. I would not personally enthuse about
this form of religiosity under any of its guises, but it can fairly be
pointed out that the typically Christian tradition of the solitary life

has a noticeably morbid streak running through it which is much less present (though not entirely absent) in what we know of Jewish forms. And it is undoubtedly the cult of the guilty conscience that makes the difference. Although the Christian love affair with guilt seems to be almost as old as the religion itself, Jesus himself in all four gospels shows hardly a trace of it – hence the plausibility with which Christains can claim that he was 'sinless'. In extreme contrast, in the writings of one whom many consider to be the *real* founder of Christianity as it has come down to us – namely Paul – it has become a hideous and pervasive blight; and through him the whole of the tradition, Catholic as well as Protestant, has become thoroughly infected by it. Once again, the Protestant tradition seems to have a slight edge on the Catholic in this area: Protestantism, though no less keenly appreciative of the pangs of conscience, acknowledges the morbid streak in the Christian tradition of ascetism and for this reason tends to view it with suspicion.

'Now John was clothed ... locusts and wild honey.' As Jesus himself points out later in the gospel (9.11–13), John the Baptist was the 'fulfilment' of Old Testament prophecy that Elijah would return to earth to prepare the way for the coming of God's Messiah. Everything we know about John indicates that, at any rate as regards the identification with Elijah, he himself thought the same; so that his appearance and habits were intended to remind those who encountered him that this was his role. The description of John's appearance is lifted straight from the Old Testament:

> He said to them, 'What kind of man was he who came to meet you and told you these things?' They answered him, '*He wore a garment of haircloth, with a girdle of leather about his loins*'. And he said, 'It is Elijah the Tishbite'. (II Kings 1.7–8)

The point about his diet of locusts and wild honey was that he lived in the desert off whatever he could find there. Apart from the general association in the mind of Judaism between the desert and closeness to God (see above), one of the more famous episodes in the life of Elijah was his sojourn in the desert related in I Kings 19. Mark's description of Jesus' own sojourn in the desert after his baptism (see below) is clearly modelled on it.

'And he preached ... "he will baptize you with the Holy Spirit".' Although we can accept as historic fact the New Testament suggestion that John thought of himself as a second Elijah in fulfilment of

Old Testament prophecy, it is much less certain – it is indeed highly unlikely – that he thought of himself as Jesus' forerunner in particular, or the Messiah's forerunner in general. The following is the passage he would chiefly have had in mind:[4]

> Remember the law of my servant Moses, the statutes and ordinances that I commanded him at Horeb for all Israel. Behold, I will send you Elijah the prophet before the great and terrible day of the Lord comes. And he will turn the hearts of the fathers to their children, and the hearts of children to their fathers, lest I come and smite the land with a curse. (Mal 4.4–6)

Readers will at once – and relevantly – be reminded of the 'transfiguration' recounted in Mark 9.2–8, the passage immediately preceding the discussion of whether Elijah is 'to come', and if so, whether John the Baptist is to be thought of as Elijah. To Moses was traditionally ascribed the giving of the Law, the most sacred part of the Jewish Bible. Elijah was the first, and therefore to many the greatest of the prophets, even though – unlike all the other prophets – the surviving literature is interested not at all in what he said but only in what he did. The juxtaposition of the two of them is clearly a visual image for the Law and the Prophets, the usual description in the gospels for what we now call the Old Testament, but which was then – to Jesus himself and all his followers – quiet simply the Bible. The point being made by the transfiguration is that Jesus is the fulfilment of promises made by God in this Bible, and it is this assumption which underlies what at first appears to be the complete non-sequitur of Mark 9.11–13.

All this, however, is what *Christians* made of Malachi 4.4–6 and of John the Baptist. The Christian reader is intended to assume, and always has assumed, that this 'one who is mightier than I' is Jesus. But what about John the Baptist himself? Assuming the words are actually part of John's teaching – as I am prepared to accept they probably are – he will have meant something very different by them. The 'one who is mightier than I' in John's thinking (as indeed in Malachi's) will have been God himself, whose imminent visitation of the world John thought of himself as proclaiming. We have some reason to think that this hijacking of the Baptist's preaching by the increasing Christian community was resented by the apparently declining group of the Baptist's followers. The best evidence for this is hidden in the pages of John's gospel:

And this is the testimony of John, when the Jews sent priests and
Levites from Jerusalem to ask him, 'Who are you?' He confessed,
he did not deny but confessed, 'I am not the Christ.' (John
1.19–20)

The modern reader very reasonably asks, 'Whoever said you *were*
the Christ? And how does your saying you aren't amount to a
confession of anything?' The answer is, of course, that the author of
the gospel is deliberately undermining the claims, presumably still
being made in his day in the locality in which he wrote, of followers
of the Baptist. In the same gospel 3.25–36 is an even more elaborate
(and more unfair and unkind) exercise on the same theme.

But what can the Baptist have meant (assuming once again that he
said it) by 'I have baptized you with water; but he will baptize you
with the Holy Spirit?' John seems to have thought of his baptism as a
preparatory cleansing; baptism with the Holy Spirit – when God
(and not Jesus, or even the Messiah) eventually appeared on earth –
would be the real thing. The Q version of the saying adds 'and with
fire' (see Matt. 3.11; Luke 3.16). Without that addition we would
assume that the Old Testament reference was Joel 2.28–29 (3.1–2 in
the Hebrew version), which we know from Acts 2.17–18 was a
favourite text with early Christians to prove that their disconcerting
habit of going into a frenzy and uttering unintelligible speech (i.e.
what the New Testament calls 'speaking with tongues' – see note 1 of
the final chapter) was the fulfilment of Old Testament prophecy.
Mark's shorter version of the saying is probably influenced by just
this phenomenon, with which of course he would have been daily
familiar. But the Q version makes it clear that what John was really
thinking of was Malachi – in particular 3.2–3, but the whole of
chapters 3 and 4 (ch. 3 in the Hebrew version) are relevant. The
reader will find a fuller discussion of this idea towards the end of the
chapter.

'In those days ... by John in the Jordan.' The really interesting
point here is simply the word Nazareth, the question being whether
the place ever really existed until the New Testament created it. No
one, for instance, denies that we have no earlier reference to it than
the gospels. But the really persuasive evidence tends to be hidden
from anyone who cannot read the New Testament in Greek. There
are four references in Mark's gospel besides the present one to 'Jesus
of Nazareth' (1.24; 10.47; 14.67 and 16.6). In each case Mark's

Greek for 'of Nazareth' transliterates as *Nazarenos*. That by itself causes no problems. But for some reason, on the two occasions when Matthew wishes to talk of 'Jesus of Nazareth' (2.23 and 26.71), he rejects the form *Nazarenos* and substitutes *Nazoraios*, an important feature which is concealed in the English versions. He can scarcely have invented the form he uses, and in both instances it is inconvenient for his purposes. In 2.23 the passage reads: 'And he went and dwelt in a city called Nazareth, that what was spoken by the prophets might be fulfilled, "He shall be called a Nazoraean" [my transliteration].' Even apart from the fact that nowhere do the prophets tell us that 'he shall be called a Nazoranaean' (there is no such passage anywhere in the Old Testament), he must surely have noticed that Mark's *Nazarene* was much closer to *Nazareth* than his own *Nazoraean*; and in 26.71 he has deliberately altered what Mark actually wrote. He must therefore have been *strongly* convinced that *Nazoraean* was the correct form – and in fact he was right, though he clearly had no idea why he was right.

Luke uses the term three times: 4.34; 18.37; 24.19. The first and third are *Nazarenos*, the middle reference has *Nazoraios*; since all three passages are P material, it looks as though he was in practice more familiar with the *Nazoraios* form, had made a decision to adopt the form he found in Mark, and that 18.37 is a careless slip. In John's gospel the term is found three times only in the Passion Narrative (18.5; 18.7 and 19.19), every time *Nazoraios*, though 1.45–6 is proof that he too thought it meant 'from Nazareth'. Acts, though we have good reason to believe it is written by the same author as Luke's gospel, also reverts to *Nazoraios* (2.22; 3.6; 4.10; 6.14; 22.8; 24.5 – 'the sect of the *Nazoraeans*' – and 26.9). There is a single instance (10.38) where Jesus is described literally as 'Jesus from Nazareth'; there are no instances of *Nazarenos*. If we did not have the 10.38 reference, we would assume (I think once again correctly) that the sources Luke used for Acts made no connection between *Nazoraios* and any sort of locality.

We can in fact make a very good guess what *Nazoraios* means, and the guess we make also helps to explain why Matthew should have thought there was an Old Testament prophecy explaining the term. It is worth reading the whole of Isaiah chapter 49 in this connection (it is actually well-worth reading the whole of Isaiah chapters 40 to 66) but the particular passage that concerns us is this:

It is too light a thing that you should be my servant

> to raise up the tribes of Jacob and to restore the
> > preserved of Israel;
> I will give you as a light to the nations,
> that my salvation may reach to the end of the earth
> > (Isa. 49.6)

The particular word that interests us is 'preserved' in line three, where the Hebrew word is *n'zorey*; there is little doubt not only that this word underlies the New Testament term *Nazoraios* but that this actual reference does. The idea of the 'preserved' of Israel, that minority of the nation who have remained closely faithful to God while the majority (as the majority of all nations always will) have gone on their easy, backsliding way, is frequently found in the Old Testament, most strikingly in the following:

> And behold, there came a voice to him, and said, 'What are you doing here, Elijah?' He said, 'I have been very jealous for the Lord, the God of hosts; for the people of Israel have forsaken thy covenant, thrown down thy altars, and slain thy prophets with the sword; and I, even I only, am left; and they seek my life to take it away'. And the Lord said to him, 'Go, return on your way to the wilderness of Damascus; and when you arrive, you shall anoint Hazael to be King over Israel; and Elisha the son of Shaphat of Abelmeholah you shall anoint to be prophet in your place. And him who escapes from the sword of Hazael shall Jehu slay; and him who escapes from the sword of Jehu shall Elisha slay. Yet I will leave seven thousand in Israel, all the knees that have not bowed to Baal, and every mouth that has not kissed him.' (I Kings 19.13b–18)

The fact that the explanation of this passage is to modern ears exceedingly unedifying does nothing to diminish its importance for understanding the significance of *Nazoraios*. Let's start with the expression 'God of hosts', which means quite simply – with no romantic connotations of 'angelic hosts' or 'heavenly hosts' or 'spiritual forces'– which means quite simple 'God of armies'. Its occurrence in the Old Testament is so frequent that it can often be dismissed simply as a conventional epithet; but not here. Armies – that is to say earthly, everyday, brutal, murdering armies – have everything to do with the way God is going to effect his will. Elijah complains that he is the only individual left who is still faithful to God, but the conclusion of the passage implies that he is wrong about that, and that there are seven thousand others like him. What about the rest? The answer is that the nation is about to be overwhelmed by disaster: first in the resurgence of Israel's traditional enemy Syria (which is to begin with Hazael's murder of King Benhadad and his own usurpation of the throne – see II Kings 8.7–15); secondly in the revolution and bloodshed initiated by Jehu's murder of King Joram – see II Kings 9.14–10.28; thirdly by the fact that this slaughter is itself to be instigated by Elisha's incitement of Jehu to sieze the throne – see II Kings 9.1–13. No one needs to be told that the total loss of life will be absolutely appalling. What God is telling Elijah in the above passage is that those who are killed will die because they have forsaken him, and those who survive (seven thousand in all) will live because they have remained faithful. Fashions in moral thinking, though undoubtedly more durable than most other fashions, do mercifully change over time.

As I say, this is one prominent instance – and apparently the earliest – of the kind of thing that is meant by 'the preserved of Israel', an idea occurring frequently in the Old Testament in all sorts of contexts. The important and unvarying features are that they are a minority of the nation who have remained faithful; the nation as a whole is threatened with destruction, but this faithful remnant will survive and be the nucleus of a restored nation which will from now on be wholly faithful to God. And the point of the passage from Isaiah is that this idea of 'the preserved of Israel'is itself inadequate. The reason why I suggested it is worth reading the whole of Isaiah chapters 40 to 66 is that repeatedly throughout this section, in a way that is not matched elsewhere in the Old Testament, the author takes up ideas that have evolved out of Israel's history – and up to now have been thought of as belonging exclusively to that history – and reinterprets them in a way that makes them part of world history. I suppose a hostile view could interpret the result as cultural imperialism. If on the other hand one is well-disposed, one can equally see the poems as a very early and inspiring vision of universalism – which is undoubtedly the author's intention. So here, 'the preserved of Israel' are to be preserved not merely to be the basis of a new and faithful nation of Israel, but to be the means of bringing the whole world to closeness and fidelity to God.

This is almost certainly the significance that *Nazoraios* had in the sources that lie behind the New Testament documents. It is of course possible that there was also a village called Nazareth from which

Jesus came; so that by coincidence he could be called both *Nazoraios* in the sense defined above, and also (*pace* Mark) *Nazarenos* in the sense that he came from Nazareth. But this would be a large coincidence. A more convincing theory is that 'Nazareth'is simply the brain-child of someone who had not the slightest idea what *Nazoraios* meant (the term would, after all, be unintelligible outside Hebrew/Aramaic circles), and invented a place called Nazareth to get round the difficulty.

So where *did* Jesus come from? On the evidence of Mark's gospel there is no doubt that during the period of his Galilaean mission he was centred on Capernaum and may even have owned a house there.[5] And on the other hand all references to a connection between Jesus and Bethlehem can almost certainly be dismissed as fabrication made on the basis of Old Testament 'prophecy'.

'And when he came up ... "with thee I am well pleased".' Mark seems to think of the descent of the Spirit as a visionary moment experienced only by Jesus himself. Matthew and Luke, despite the high degree of verbal identity between their accounts and that of Mark, both seem in fact to derive the baptism incident, as they do the rest of their John the Baptist material, from a Q source. They both agree (Matt. 3.16; Luke 3.22) that the opening of the heavens was an external event, presumably therefore witnessed by all. Some copies of Matthew add 'to him' after 'the heavens were opened', and I am inclined to think this is authentic – an instance of Matthew conscien-ciously trying to reconcile what he read in Mark with what he read in his other source.

Few things are harder to account for than this very early and subsequently very persistent portrayal in Christian imagery of the Holy Spirit as a dove. It occurs in all four gospels (Matt. 3.16; Mark 1.10; Luke 3.22; John 1.32), but nowhere else in the New Testa-ment, not even in Acts (2.1–4). Subsequently in Christian art, as most readers will not need to be told, the imagery has become all but obligatory. But there does not seem to be anything in the Old Testament, or in surviving Jewish literature between the testaments, that will explain the imagery. Suggestions of scholars that the dove traditionally symbolized Israel get us no further. Instances can be found, but not many, nor particularly well-known. And even if it were otherwise, the fact that the dove traditionally symbolizes Israel would offer no sort of explanation why it here symbolizes the Holy Spirit.

The voice from heaven and what it says have already been discussed sufficiently in the Introduction.

'The Spirit immediately drove him out ... and the angels ministered to him.' The idea that the Spirit 'drove him out' into the wilderness is striking – too much so for Matthew and Luke, both of whom have the less graphic phrase that 'Jesus was led [up] by the Spirit' (Matt. 4.1; Luke 4.1); either once again because they preferred a Q source to Mark, or else because they felt Mark sounded as if he thought Jesus were suddenly possessed. But there can be little doubt (see the third section of the Introduction) that Mark actually intended it to sound like that. The sojourn in the wilderness itself is deliberately modelled on that of Elijah in I Kings 19.4–18, as is made clear by the references to 'forty days' (19.8) and 'the angels ministered to him' (19.5–7). Matthew adds the improbable detail – in no way implied by Mark – that 'he fasted forty days and forty nights' (Matt. 4.2). Luke goes one better (or worse): 'he ate nothing in those days' (Luke 4.2). It looks once again as though this is a Q suggestion. One could argue that it is a genuine misunderstanding of the Elijah passage, where the text reads: 'And he arose, and ate and drank, and went in the strength of that food forty days and forty nights ...' Mark seems to interpret this as meaning that for forty days and forty nights (note that on the first day the angel visits Elijah twice) the angel kept returning with food for Elijah, and that is what he lived on throughout that period. The Q interpretation, on the other hand, is that after that second and final meal, Elijah went the next forty days and forty nights without eating anything further.

In what way was he tempted by Satan? We tend to assume we know the answer to this because Matthew and Luke have told us (Matt. 4.1–11; Luke 4.1–13); but I hope that by now the reader is beginning to appreciate that Mark did not always and necessarily mean the same thing as they did. However, in this instance I am inclined to accept that the ideas at the back of Mark's mind were much the same as what the other two evangelists have put on paper. In which case there are three main temptations: to win adherents by working miracles, particularly of a kind that actually make things easier for people (Matt. 4.3–4; Luke 4.3–4; John 6.15); to 'prove' who he was by a display of invulnerability (Matt. 4.5–7; Luke 4.9–12); to exploit purely political hopes of deliverance (Matt. 4.8–10; Luke 4.5–8). We need not read these accounts as true, historical descriptions of what 'actually happened' in the wilderness;

it is quite likely that the gospel writers themselves did not intend us to do so (note Luke 4.5 'And the devil took him up, and showed him all the kingdoms of the world *in a moment of time ...*') But regardless of their status as history, as an imaginative description of the very beginning of Jesus' ministry they can be accepted as perceptive and appropriate.

'Now after John was arrested, Jesus came into Galilee ...' The comparative chronology of Jesus and John the Baptist is all but impossible to establish. We have no dates at all for Jesus – if we discount (as I think we should) the information of Luke 3.1 and 3.23 – apart from the fact that he was executed some time between AD 26 and 36 (the dates of Pilate's governorship of Judaea). We have an account of John the Baptist from a source external to the New Testament in Josephus' *Antiquities* (see pages 164–7), but what Josephus tells us is as approximate as regards dates as the New Testament is. Should we deduce from the present passage that Jesus was baptized by John, then immediately disappeared into the wilderness, during which time John was arrested? I doubt it. A much lengthier period seems implied, although that is the only conclusion we can safely come to.

Matthew (11.2–19) and Luke (7.18–35) imply that John was still alive, though confined in prison, in the early part of Jesus' ministry. In itself the idea presents no difficulty; but how do we reconcile it with the quite well-attested idea that Jesus was widely thought of as 'John the Baptist risen from the dead',[6] which would seem to imply some kind of gap between the death of John and the first appearance of Jesus? It should be noted also that this implies that Jesus' public ministry was considerably longer than the three years that the tradition usually estimates. We seem to have to allow for the following stages: (*a*) Jesus is baptized by John, who (if Matthew and Luke – see above – are to be believed) has no idea of Jesus' identity at the time; (*b*) sometime later John is arrested; (*c*) while he is in prison Jesus' growing fame comes to his ears, and he sends his own disciples to report on Jesus' mission; (*d*) John is executed, and only then does Jesus begin to emerge as a well-known wandering preacher; (*e*) it is only now that he becomes of any interest to Herod, who begins to want to put him out of the way for much the same reasons as he put John out of the way.

'... preaching the gospel of God, and saying "... believe in the gospel".' The gospel, of course, is the announcement 'The time is

fulfilled, and the kingdom of God is at hand.' Matthew suggests, and
I think I believe him, that the core of Jesus' message and that of John
the Baptist were the same: 'Repent, for the kingdom of heaven is at
hand' (Matthew. 3.2; 4.17). What did either of them mean by 'the
kingdom of heaven' and in what sense did they believe it was 'at
hand'. The earliest author in the Old Testament with whom we can
connect the idea is the prophet Amos:

> Woe to you who desire the day of the Lord!
>   Why would you have the day of the Lord?
>   It is darkness, and not light;
> as if a man fled from a lion,
>   and a bear met him;
> or went into the house and leaned with his hand against
>   the wall,
>   and a serpent bit him.
> Is not the day of the Lord darkness, and not light,
>   and gloom with no brightness in it? (Amos 5.18–20)

We can tell, not only from this passage but from the book as a whole,
that this notion of 'the day of the Lord' was a popular, somewhat
jingoistic belief which the prophet was determined to reinterpret in a
moral sense. Like the idea of the Messiah, it seems to derive from the
awareness of a sense of decline that the nation clearly felt as they saw
David's vast empire (for the time and locality) being whittled away.
Thus the book opens with denunciations, each in turn, of: Syria, the
Philistines, Tyre, Edom, the Ammonites and Moab. With the exception of Tyre, which had been an ally rather than a subject of David,
all these nations had been part of the Davidic empire, and by Amos'
time (about 750 BC) all had become not merely independent from,
but actually something of a threat to, Israel. 'The day of the Lord' in
the popular mind was the day on which all that was going to be put
right again; and the first chapter of Amos, and the first three verses of
the second, exploit and reinterpret that belief. For Amos the day of
the Lord was indeed the day on which these nations would be
punished for their 'misdeeds' (i.e. in the popular mind, rebelling
against Israel). But Amos then goes on (2.4–16) to denounce the two
Israelite nations in exactly the same terms, and to threaten them with
exactly the same fate; his point being that the rebellion for which all
these nations will be punished is not rebellion against Israel but
rebellion against God; and of this crime Judah and Israel are just as
guilty as their neighbours.

The next passage we need to look at is from Haggai:

> The word of the Lord came a second time to Haggai on the twenty fourth day of the month, 'Speak to Zerubbabel, governor of Judah, saying, I am about to shake the heavens and the earth, and to overthrow the throne of kingdoms; I am about to destroy the strength of the kingdoms of the nations, and overthrow the chariots and their riders; and the horses and their riders shall go down every one by the sword of his fellow. On that day, says the Lord of hosts, I will take you, O Zerubbabel my servant, the son of Shealtiel, says the Lord, and make you like a signet ring; for I have chosen you, says the Lord of hosts'. (Hag. 2.20–23)

The evidence indicates that this passage should be dated about 521 BC, the year in which Darius I came to the throne of Persia after overthrowing a usurper. His early years were spent putting down revolts in Persia, Babylon and other eastern provinces, and it seems highly probable that these are the disturbances referred to by the prophet. We know little about Zerubbabel, but the little we do know suggests that he was a descendant of the Davidic royal house who had also been appointed by the Persians as governor of the restored Judaic state. A single and rather out-of-the-way reference in Chronicles tells us: 'The descendants of Jehoiakim: Jeconiah his son, Zedekiah his son; and the sons of Jeconiah, the captive: Shealtiel his son, Malchiram, Pedaiah, Shenazzar, Jekamiah, Hoshama, and Nedabiah; and the sons of Pedaiah: Zerubbabel and Shimei' (I Chron. 3.16–19a). The information is nowhere corroborated, and in some details is known to be inaccurate – Zedekiah for instance was Jehoiakim's brother, not his grandson. But I think we can accept that Zerubbabel was a direct descendant of the last but one Davidic king (Zedekiah, the last, had no descendants, all his children having been executed in his presence as a punishment for his rebellion – II Kings 25.7); presumably therefore the legitimate pretender to the throne, should the throne ever be restored.

What Haggai seems to be telling him is that the series of upheavals with which the Persian empire is convulsed are the beginning of a series of events which are the direct activity of God in history, and which will culminate in Zerubbabel's restoration to his ancestral right. This example makes particularly clear the extent to which this expectation of the day of the Lord is simultaneously mythological *and* historical in character. It is mythological in that no actual events of history ever can, or ever will, 'disprove' it; it is historical in that the actual events of history are continually being examined and inter- preted in the light of it, and in that it frequently influences the way those who hold this expectation react to events – very often with disastrous results. The Haggai prophecy is itself almost certainly an instance of this. We hear nothing more of Zerubbabel beyond this date, and it is plausibly suggested that this is because once Darius had secured his position, he removed Zerubbabel from being governor on the grounds of the dangerous focus for disturbing influences that he constituted. With Zerubbabel disappears any real hope of a restoration of the Davidic monarchy. Thereafter the Messianic hope is no longer attached to an identifiable individual, while the position of being the focal point of national identity is more and more usurped by the High Priesthood.

I drew attention earlier to the fascination, perhaps even to the point of obsession, that the ideas of Malachi chapter 3 (and 4) seem to have had for John the Baptist; and this passage is the next that we need to consider:

> Behold, I send my messenger to prepare the way before me, and the Lord whom you seek will suddenly come to his temple; the messenger of the covenant in whom you delight, behold, he is coming, says the Lord of hosts. But who can endure the day of his coming, and who can stand when he appears?
>
> For he is like a refiner's fire and like fuller's soap; he will sit as a refiner and purifier of silver, and he will purify the sons of Levi and refine them like gold and silver, till they present right offerings to the Lord. Then the offerings of Judah and Jerusalem will be pleasing to the Lord as in the days of old and as in former years.
>
> Then I will draw near to you for judgment; I will be a swift witness against the sorcerers, against the adulterers, against those who swear falsely, against those who oppress the hireling in his wages, the widow and the orphan, against those who thrust aside the sojourner, and do not fear me, says the Lord of hosts.
>
> For I the Lord do not change; therefore you, O sons of Jacob, are not consumed. From the days of your fathers you have turned aside from my statutes and have not kept them. Return to me, and I will return to you, says the Lord of hosts. But you say, 'How shall we return?' Will man rob God? Yet you are robbing me. But you say, 'How are we robbing thee?' In your tithes and offerings. You

are cursed with a curse, for you are robbing me, the whole nation of you. Bring the full tithes into the storehouse, that there may be food in my house; and thereby put me to the test, says the Lord of hosts, if I will not open the windows of heaven for you and pour down for you an overflowing blessing. I will rebuke the devourer for you, so that it will not destroy the fruits of your soil; and your vine in the field shall not fail to bear, says the Lord of hosts. Then all nations will call you blessed, for you will be a land of delight, says the Lord of hosts.

Your words have been stout against me, says the Lord. Yet you say, 'How have we spoken against thee?' You have said, 'It is vain to serve God. What is the good of our keeping his charge of or walking as in mourning before the Lord of hosts? Henceforth we deem the arrogant blessed; evildoers not only prosper, but when they put God to the test they escape.'

Then those who feared the Lord spoke with one another; the Lord heeded and heard them, and a book of remembrance was written before him of those who feared the Lord and thought on his name. They shall be mine, says the Lord of hosts, my special possession on the day when I act, and I will spare them as a man spares his son who serves him. Then once more you shall distinguish between the righteous and the wicked, between one who serves God and one who does not serve him.

For behold, the day comes, burning like an oven, when all the arrogant and all evildoers will be stubble; the day that comes shall burn them up, says the Lord of hosts, so that it will leave them neither root nor branch. But for you who fear my name the sun of righteousness shall rise, with healing in its wings. You shall go forth leaping like calves from the stall. And you shall tread down the wicked, for they will be ashes under the soles of your feet, on the day when I act, says the Lord of hosts.

Remember the law of my servant Moses, the statutes and ordinances that I commanded him at Horeb for all Israel. Behold, I will send you Elijah the prophet before the great and terrible day of the Lord comes. And he will turn the hearts of fathers to their children and the hearts of children to their fathers, lest I come and smite the land with a curse. (Mal. 3.1–4.6, or in the Hebrew 3.1–24)

The text *seems* to belong (and we cannot be more precise than that) to that lengthy period during which Israel was part of the Persian empire (536–330 BC). At any rate there is an earlier mention of a governor (1.8) who is clearly not himself an Israelite, while mention of (and condemnation of) divorcing wives (2.13–16) reminds us of the discreditable episode recounted in Ezra chapter 10, which can be roughly dated towards the middle years of the fifth century. It should be noted also that the word *Malachi* in Hebrew means literally 'my messenger', and when we come to compare this with the contents of the book, a suspicion arises that the name refers not to the author of the book but to its subject matter. All this however is by the way. More to the purpose is the fact that John seems pretty clearly to have identified himself with this messenger, and to have thought of himself as the 'fulfilment' of the 'prophecy' set forth in these chapters. Whoever wrote the chapters, of course, is unlikely to have thought of them as a prophecy in this sense at all. In so far as he had any intention of prophesying, it would have been in the belief that the events he was foretelling were immediately to be expected. As the reader can now appreciate, everyone in either Testament who announces the coming perfect world does so in the belief that what he prophecies is going to come about in the most *immediate* future. No amount of repeated disappointment ever shakes this ineradicable idea. The passage from II Peter quoted on page 1 of the introduction is therefore something of a minor revolution in the history of Judaeo-Christianity.

If we are right in supposing that John closely identified himself with the themes of the above passage, the big reason why he is likely to have done so is that Malachi is the only book of the Old Testament which manages to announce God's approaching judgment *without connecting it with any overtly political themes*. And it looks as if this was the essential difference between John's mission and that of Jesus. The ideas that they had in common were (*a*) that the kingdom of God was imminent; (*b*) that their own appearance on earth (i.e. both of them seem to have made this claim on behalf of themselves) was the sign of this. The difference between them seems to be one of what I suppose we could call controlling imagery: that is, the particular passage or passages of scripture which seemed to each of them, as we should say to epitomize, as they would have said to prophesy, this appearance. As we shall see in the course of the gospel, the controlling imagery in Jesus' case seems to vary in accordance with the particular aspect of his ministry that most occupies him at the time.

As regards the present topic (the imminent appearance of God to judge the world) it looks as though it comes from Daniel chapter 7, which is too long to be quoted here in full. The chapter falls neatly into two halves, the first half (1–14) recounting a 'vision' (the word here describing what is clearly no more than a literary device), while the second half gives the explanation of that vision (which saves me the trouble of having to explain it here). What the reader needs to know is that, although the author of the book tries to give the impression that he is writing in the middle of the sixth century BC, we know that he is in fact writing just before 167 BC; so that his apparently miraculous foreknowledge of events that would be happening long after his death disappears under scrutiny. Jesus of course did not know this, but we shall see that his interpretation of the passage would not have been much affected if he had done.

The particular section that concerns us is:

> I saw in the night visions, and behold, with the clouds of heaven there came one like the son of man; and he came to the Ancient of Days and was presented before him. And to him was given dominion and glory and kingdom, that all peoples, nations and languages should serve him; his dominion is an everlasting dominion, which shall not pass away, and his kingdom one that shall not be destroyed. (Dan. 7.13–14)

Notice first of all the phrase 'one like the son of man'. Readers will not need to be told that by far the commonest self-description that Jesus uses, at any rate in the synoptic gospels, is 'Son of man'. Commentators have often professed to be puzzled by this, pointing out that in the Old Testament (particularly in the prophecy of Ezekiel, who also frequently applies the phrase to himself) the words describe quite simply a member of the human race. As far as it goes, this is true: it is even true of the above passage. The author means nothing more than that after a series of 'beasts' (signifying a series of world empires), the final victory is won by a 'man' (signifying the final victory of Israel). But having used the phrase in this way, he has – at any rate for Jesus – transformed it. The 'Son of man' for Jesus is not simply an emblem of mankind, but of a particular man – somewhat more than a man because of his gigantic destiny: he has been appointed by God to win the final victory over the whole world (but by means that are totally different from those that any world power has ever used up to now), and to sit beside him and reign over that world, now eternally restored to its original perfection. And this man, Jesus 'realizes', is himself.

APPENDIX

Many readers will be inclined to question whether we should not regard Jesus and John the Baptist as quite simply mad. There are after all people in our own culture who are convinced they are Napoleon or Wagner or some great figure from the past, and we have no hesitation in confining them to institutions. Their misgivings will be strengthened by the knowledge that Mark has been sufficiently tactless to record that Jesus' family *did* think he was mad, and *did* try to put him under restraint (3.21), an important fact of history (as most of us would think) that the other three evangelists have thought it unnecessary to preserve. The madness theory therefore cannot totally be dismissed; on the other hand, whatever element of truth there may be in it, it cannot be accepted as the whole of the explanation.

There can be no doubt that both John and Jesus were driven by powerful obsessions which, neither in their own day nor in ours, can be regarded as simply normal. But whether such obsessions are classified as insanity depends very largely on the cultural context within which they manifest themselves. In this area of madness (and perhaps in all) we need to remind ourselves that madness is as much a normative as a medical diagnosis. By this I mean that one of the most important factors in determining what is to count as madness is the generally accepted idea of how people *ought* to behave; and I don't suppose I need to point out that this generally accepted idea varies enormously in content in different cultures, and within the same culture at different periods of its history. It is simply a *fact* that exactly the same kind of behaviour, and exactly the same kind of obsession, can in one society be regarded as harmless eccentricity, in another as powerful and uplifting vision, and in a third as dangerous and atrocious madness.

Add to this that in *any* society great achievements are usually the result of some kind of powerful obsession. Most of us, I dare say, indulge in daydreams which we would blush to communicate to any other person. Most of us simply enjoy them on our own and do nothing more about them. But there are others who are gripped by just these kinds of daydreams, but far more fiercely, and who therefore carry them forward into action. Often they fail in their attempts and are dismissed with scorn; occasionally they succeed and are the focal point of admiration; the difference between failure and success in these endeavours is often merely accident, though observers usually offer an 'explanation' for it.

Undoubtedly within the context of a culture like ours both Jesus and John would be classified as mad; but within the context of their own they were thought of as powerful visionaries. Jesus' family may have thought that he was mad – as Jesus himself pointed out, how could they be expected to take him seriously, having known him from boyhood (Mark 6.4) – and his opponents among the religious leaders may have suggested that he was demon-possessed (Mark 3.22); but large numbers of people took him absolutely seriously. And no matter what the doctors say, in most societies this is as an absolute guarantee of sanity.

There is, however, another figure in the gospel story whose opinion on this point we should perhaps consult. When Jesus stood before Pilate, although none of the gospels suggests it – in fact they rather suggest the opposite – we need not doubt that Pilate thought he was mad. But then we can be pretty confident that Pilate, like the Romans generally, thought the whole of the culture was mad. When Pilate went out to the Pavement to discuss the case with the chief priests and scribes, we can shrewdly guess that he had no great opinion of their sanity either. Judaism as a whole presented educated Romans with a severe problem. Even when, like Cicero, they largely discounted the claims of religion to produce any real 'results' in such matters as answers to prayer, they still had a high idea of its importance as a means of social cohesion and restraint. The prevailing attitude of the times will never be more brilliantly summarized than it has been in Gibbon's famous paragraph:

> The policy of the emperors and the senate, as far as it concerned religion, was happily seconded by the reflections of the enlightened, and by the habits of the superstitious, part of their subjects. The various modes of worship which prevailed in the Roman world were all considered by the people as equally true, by the philosopher as equally false, and by the magistrate as equally useful. And thus toleration produced not only mutual indulgence but even religious concord.

In such a situation the only problem that arose in any particular locality was the problem of which religion, and why. And the Roman answer was simple: the ancestral religion. Religion was not something that you believed, or needed to believe; it was something you inherited.

In Judaea therefore there was no question but that ancestral Judaism was, as the Romans called it, *religio licita*. There was no question but that everything should be done to encourage it and nothing should be done to obstruct it. On the other hand the Romans knew – and were deeply repelled by the knowledge – that Jews regarded their own religion as true and all others as false, their own God as the real God and all others as at best idolatrous illusions (I Cor. 8.4), but often as beings that did exist but were really malevolent demons (I Cor. 10.20). This made no difference to their usual policy of upholding the traditional religion of the locality, but at the same time they made no secret of their utter contempt for the religion they were upholding. This could create an agonizing dilemma for anyone of Jewish descent. If he adhered to his ancestral religion, he was likely to be despised for doing so; if he abandonded it, he was equally despised for that.

2

'A Day in the Life of ...'

(Mark 1.16–39)

And passing along by the Sea of Galilee, he saw Simon and Andrew the brother of Simon casting a net in the sea; for they were fishermen. And Jesus said to them, 'Follow me and I will make you become fishers of men'. And immediately they left their nets and followed him. And going on a little farther, he saw James the son of Zebedee and John his brother, who were in their boat mending the nets. And immediately he called them; and they left their father Zebedee in the boat with the hired servants, and followed him.

And they went into Capernaum; and immediately on the sabbath he entered the synagogue and taught. And they were astonished at his teaching, for he taught them as one who had authority, and not as the scribes. And immediately there was in their synagogue a man with an unclean spirit; and he cried out, 'What have you to do with us, Jesus of Nazareth? Have you come to destroy us? I know who you are, the Holy One of God'. But Jesus rebuked him, saying, 'Be silent, and come out of him!' And the unclean spirit, convulsing him and crying with a loud voice, came out of him. And they were all amazed, so that they questioned among themselves, saying, 'What is this? A new teaching! With authority he commands even the unclean spirits, and they obey him'. And at once his fame spread everywhere throughout all the surrounding region of Galilee.

And immediately he left the synagogue, and entered the house of Simon and Andrew, with James and John. Now Simon's mother-in-law lay sick with a fever, and immediately they told him of her. And he came and took her by the hand and lifted her up, and the fever left her; and she served them.

That evening, at sundown, they brought to him all who were sick or possessed with demons. And the whole city was gathered together about the door. And he healed many who were sick with various diseases, and cast out many demons; and he would not permit the demons to speak, because they knew him.

And in the morning, a great while before day, he rose and went out to a lonely place, and there he prayed. And Simon and those who were with him pursued him, and they found him and said to him, 'Every one is searching for you'. And he said to them, 'Let us go on to the next towns, that I may preach there also; for that is why I came out'. And he went throughout all Galilee, preaching in their synagogues and casting out demons. (1.16–39)

It is very noticeable that after the first paragraph, once Jesus and the four disciples have arrived in Capernaum, all the rest of the narrative takes place in the course of one day. (No, some may argue, it doesn't: it takes place on two days. But look at Genesis 1.5 – 'And there was evening and there was morning, one day'; see also verses 8, 13, 19, 23 and 31.) The opening paragraph itself, however, cannot belong to this day's events but must be earlier – how much earlier is not indicated. We know this because we find both pairs of brothers actually at work, while the day the rest of the passage describes is the sabbath.

Is any particular point being made by this complex – unparalleled until we come to the passion story (chapters 14 to 16) – of incidents having a purely narrative connection with each other? Answers to the question must be largely guesswork, but two reasonably worthwhile guesses suggest themselves. The first is that the material actually came to Mark as the story of one day. (If one wants to be *really* fanciful, one can imagine Peter saying to Mark, 'I clearly remember my very first day as a disciple ...') The second, which I think I like less, is that Mark himself has constructed a typical 'day in the life of' out of material left over from his other sections, and used it as a kind of preface to them.

'And passing along ... for they were fishermen.' All accounts agree that Simon was the earliest of the disciples to be called, and suggest (though details of the narrative itself throw strong doubt on the suggestion[1]) that throughout the ministry he was the obvious leader of the band. They also agree that Andrew was his brother. All four gospels take it for granted that there was a 'core' band of twelve apostles, and all but John actually give us their names. Yet apart from these two pairs of brothers with which Mark's gospel opens, none of the other eight plays any real part in any of the synoptic gospels. And even within this immediate circle, are we to think of Andrew as being in it, or out of it? If he is in it, why is he excluded from witnessing the raising of Jairus' daughter (Mark 5.37), and from the transfiguration (9.2), and should we conclude that there had been some kind of rift between him and the others quite early in the ministry? But then he suddenly reappears – and again as one of the inmost circle – in 13.3 apparently during the very last stages of the Jerusalem ministry. On the other hand this is the *only* other mention of him (the passage has no parallel in Matthew and Luke) in any of the synoptic gospels.

'And Jesus said ... fishers of men.' One of the great advantages that religion has over other techniques of social motivation and control is its capacity to invest utterly simple images with an ineradicable and eternal force that exerts an equal power over society's most ordinary and most sophisticated members. Regardless of beliefs, it is hard to see how any cohesive form of society will ever be able to dispense with it. Like Voltaire's God, if it did not exist we would have to invent it. This phrase 'fishers of men' is a perfect instance of this power. Not only is it still universally familiar, even in a supposedly secular age, but the mere utterance of it automatically animates a whole series of mental images, reaching simultaneously far back into the past and far forward into the future, which quite involuntarily evoke a response from the hearer. It may be only *mildly* hostile, or only *mildly* sympathetic: but I find it hard to believe the response is ever purely indifferent. The New Testament writers themselves were already conscious of the peculiar power of this image, as we can tell from the gospels of Luke and John, in the first of which the saying has been transformed into a story (Luke 5.1–11 – Luke does not record the saying as such, though he must certainly have been familiar with it from Mark's gospel), while in the second it has been further transformed from a story into an allegory of the entire operation of the church that Jesus leaves behind on earth (John 21.1–14 – but the whole of the chapter is a unified narrative which expands the theme).

'And immediately they left their nets and followed him.' Just how immediate, I wonder, is 'immediately'? I've heard many a sermon in my time which took it for granted that 'immediately' meant just that: that Jesus' power was so electric that the disciples responded to his call almost before they'd had time to think about it. On the other hand it is recognized that 'immediately' is a kind of reflex word in Mark's vocabulary, so often used that perhaps he was not always aware of using it, and therefore did not always mean anything particularly by it. In the Greek text the word *euthys* occurs no less than forty times altogether (eleven in chapter 1 alone) compared with twenty and seventeen times respectively in the much longer gospels of Matthew and Luke. Even in those gospels a high proportion of the incidence is probably due to Mark's prior suggestion; John's gospel uses the word only six times. The traditional suggestion (see above) is not really credible, and I think we should not place too much emphasis here on 'immediately'.

'And going on a little farther ... and followed him.' We take it for granted (or rather the tradition does) that the original disciples were all of them poor and ignorant men; but both these epithets, though no doubt true in a comparative sense, can be questioned in an absolute one. Let's take 'ignorant' first. In a famous passage of Acts (4.13) we are told: 'Now when they [the priests and scribes] saw the boldness of Peter and John, and perceived that they were uneducated, common men ...' To put it a little more starkly (which the Greek in fact does), they were illiterate and working-class; and 'illiterate' (*agrammatoi*) should be understood – pardon the etymological confusion – quite literally. On the other hand Jesus himself, whose social origins can hardly have been brilliant, cannot be thought of as illiterate on the evidence we have. The only instance of him actually reading (Luke 4.16–20) can easily be dismissed: the passage, as we noted, is found only in Luke and is his version of Mark 6.1–6 = Matthew 13.53–58 where there is no mention of reading. But it is hard to see how he can have been gripped to the extent he was by obsessions derived from the Old Testament (in particular Daniel chapter 7 and some of the later chapters of Isaiah) if he could not in fact read the Old Testament for himself – not impossible, admittedly, but certainly hard. There are those would want to add the fact that he is quite often addressed as 'Rabbi' in the gospels, which is inconceivable had he been illiterate.[2]

But what particularly makes us doubt, not merely whether Jesus himself can have been illiterate, but even whether all the original disciples can have been is the all-pervasive thread of Old Testament allusion underlying both the gospel narrative as whole, but also a host of smaller incidents which, if we did not have the evangelists to point it out, we would never have dreamed of connecting with the Old Testament at all. This way of thinking is so insistent in all three synoptic authors, even in material that is peculiar to each of them, that it is clearly not the personal contribution of any one of them, but an inherent characteristic of the tradition *as a whole and from its earliest inception.*[3] The earliest preservers, shapers and repeaters of the gospel material, though they seem one and all to have been uninterested in putting anything down on paper, clearly included a considerable proportion of regular Old Testament *readers* who allowed that reading to determine their whole way of thinking. Some of us may be inclined to dismiss the process as profoundly unintelligent; but this does not alter the fact that it was unquestionably literate. Paul's interest in the new movement points in the same direction: would a man like him have been remotely prepared to join a body that was wholly illiterate? Yet Paul's conversion to Christianity is likely to have happened within about ten years of Jesus' death.

In the same way, how poor should we think the original disciples were? Comparatively poor, no doubt – though there may have been exceptions to that (see Luke 8.3, where the wife of Herod's steward cannot have been total riffraff; but also the 'many others' mentioned must all of them have been at least in comfortable circumstances). However poor Peter may have been when Jesus met him, there seems no reason to doubt that he was practising a trade, and therefore certainly not destitute. We also know that he was married and living in his own family house – see 1.29–31 below. In the present passage Zebedee, the father of James and John, is doing sufficiently well to pay for extra (i.e. non-family) help. Jesus himself seems to have lived pretty much as a beggar and to have encouraged his followers to do the same. But whenever he talks about the first step to discipleship – and most readers will not need to be told he does this very frequently – it is always in terms of *renunciation*: he doesn't say, 'If you have nothing, why not come and join me', but 'If you want to come join me, you must first give it all away'.

'And they went ... the synagogue and taught.' No explanation is given why Jesus, supposedly a native of 'Nazareth', now enters Capernaum and seems to spend a great deal of his subsequent ministry in the town. I have difficulty also (though admittedly I know little about the inner workings of the average Galilaean synagogue in the first century AD) in accepting that Jesus, as a complete newcomer to the locality, would be invited to teach in the synagogue at his first appearance there. The implication to me is that Jesus is already well-known, and that he must have been living in the town for some time.

'And they were astonished ... and not as the scribes.' One cannot be precise in suggesting what the differences were between Jesus' style of teaching and that of the recognized religious leaders. But it is not difficult to offer highly plausible guesses. He was first of all interesting, whereas they tended to be dull. He had an astonishing gift (as the parables scattered through all three synoptic gospels make clear) of vividly illustrating his meaning, in contrast to their laborious attempts to explain it. He appealed to daily experience shared by himself and his hearers, whereas they tended to refer to documents that they were familiar with but their audiences were not. Need one add that they were trained professionals, while he was an enthusiastic amateur?

'And immediately ... the surrounding region of Galilee.' There are two healings that take place in a synagogue in Mark's gospel – this one and 3.1–6. The big difference between the two stories is that the second one ends with the Pharisees immediately holding counsel with the Herodians against him, 'how to destroy him', whereas the only reaction recorded here is the entirely favourable one of the crowd. Unclean spirits[4] seem as a matter of course to know who Jesus is (3.11 and 5.6–7), but on the other hand are the only beings he encounters who have this faculty. This is no doubt because, although they *are* unclean, they are still entirely real (to the age and culture in which Jesus lived) – as is their chief Beelzebul (3.23). But God is more powerful, and that is why unclean spirits are invariably afraid of Jesus. Mark seems to think of Jesus as possessed in very much the same way as the people he healed were, except that in his case it was by a benign and all-powerful, instead of a malignant and not all-powerful, spirit. It is for that very reason that suggestions like those of the scribes in 3.22 ('He is possessed by Beelzebul, and by the prince of demons he casts out the demons') were particularly hard to refute, and therefore particularly resented.

Mark places significant emphasis on the violent convulsions of those cured of demon possession not only here, but in 5.13 and particularly 9.26. Once again it is noticeable (see note 4, p. 374 below) that Matthew ignores the phenomenon. Admittedly there is only one instance where a direct comparison can be made (Mark 9.26 = Matt. 17.18), where what looks like a significant omission could simply be no more than a desire to compress, and to leave out merely colourful detail. But it is at least equally possible that Matthew is embarassed, and without creating too much upheaval is trying to filter out the howling dervish characteristics that undoubtedly cling to Mark's portrayal of Jesus. It hardly needs to be said that the features of Mark's gospel which Matthew seems to have found embarassing are precisely those where the modern reader will be most convinced of Mark's closeness to history.

'And they were all amazed ... "and they obey him".' It's difficult to see why the crowd should be quite so amazed as Mark makes them appear. Difficult because, as the gospels themselves remind us (Matt. 12.27 = Luke 11.19) exorcism was not a rare thing in that part of the world in those days. Is this, I wonder, one of those few occasions when we catch Mark tinkering with the record? As the reader will now be aware, Matthew's reputation for fair and honest reporting has been blown sky-high by the unfortunate survival of one of his major sources, namely Mark's gospel. Mark himself gives the impression of being a thoroughly honest man, but this may be in part because none of the sources he used has actually survived, and had they done so we would have much more to accuse him of. Let us compare the three versions of the Beelzebul passage referred to above:

> Then a blind and dumb demoniac was brought to him, and he healed him, so that the dumb man spoke and saw. And all the people were amazed, and said, 'Can this be the Son of David?' But when the Pharisees heard it they said, 'It is only by Beelzebul, the prince of demons, that this man casts out demons'. Knowing their thoughts, he said to them, 'Every kingdom divided against itself is laid waste, and no city or house divided against itself will stand; and if Satan casts out Satan, he is divided against himself; how then will his kingdom stand? *And if I cast out demons by Beelzebul, by whom do your sons cast them out? Therefore they shall be your judges.* But if it is by the Spirit of God that I cast out demons, then the kingdom of God has come upon you. Or how can one enter a strong man's house and plunder his goods, unless he first binds the strong man? Then indeed he may plunder his house.' (Matt. 12.22–32)

> ... and the crowd came together again, so that they could not even eat. And when his family heard it, they went out to seize him,

for people were saying, 'He is beside himself'. And the scribes who came down from Jerusalem said, 'He is possessed by Beelzebul, and by the prince of demons he casts out the demons.' And he called them to him, and said to them in parables, 'How can Satan cast out Satan? If a kingdom is divided against itself, that kingdom cannot stand. And if a house is divided against itself, that house will not be able to stand. And if Satan has risen up against himself and is divided, he cannot stand, but is coming to an end. But no one can enter a strong man's house and plunder his goods, unless he first binds the strong man; then indeed he may plunder his house.' (Mark 3.22–27)

Now he was casting out a demon that was dumb; when the demon had gone out, the dumb man spoke, and the people marvelled. But some of them said, 'He casts out demons by Beelzebul, the prince of demons'; while others, to test him, sought from him a sign from heaven. But he, knowing their thoughts, said to them, 'Every kingdom divided against itself is laid waste, and a divided household falls. And if Satan also is divided against himself, how will his kingdom stand? For you say that I cast out demons by Beelzebul. *And if I cast out demons by Beelzebul, by whom do your sons cast them out? Therefore they shall be your judges.* But if it is by the finger of God that I cast out demons, then the kingdom of God has come upon you. When a strong man, fully armed, guards his own palace, his goods are in peace; but when one stronger than he assails him and overcomes him, he takes away his armour in which he trusted, and divides his spoil.' (Luke 11.14–23)

As the reader can see, to try and sort out individual words and phrases into categories of M, L, P and Q would be unbelievably complex; but it is also clear that Matthew and Luke have enough features in common that are not found in Mark to make it plausible to classify their versions as Q rather than P. The fact therefore that both their versions include – in exactly the same words – the saying in italics, which Mark does not include, need not be significant. On the other hand I cannot entirely rid my mind of the suspicion that Mark's source also contained it, and that he has deliberately suppressed it in order to give the (untrue) impression that Jesus' powers of exorcism were unique.

'And at once his fame ... region of Galilee.' In the early part of the gospel this becomes something very like a Marcan catch-phrase; it appears again at the end of the present section (1.39), and subsequently at 3.7–12 (a very expanded version), 6.6b (a very compressed version), and 6.56. If the reader compares these references with those for the various sections of the work listed on my contents page, it can be seen that in every instance apart from the present one they are the concluding verses of one of these sections. I believe this to be Mark's actual intention, and have divided up the work for comment on the basis of that belief. On the other hand, two points could be held to count against it. The first is that this first instance of the catch-phrase does not seem to be the end of a section; the second is that by no means all the sections end with it. It is a point, however, that the reader will be perfectly capable of judging.

'And immediately he left the synagogue ... and she served them.' We need not doubt that in Mark's own eyes this and the preceding story are both of them equally works of healing. To the modern reader on the other hand there will be a temptation to classify this as the first of a whole series of healing miracles, many of which (though perhaps not this one) he will find it impossible to accept as history. The previous story is an exorcism: that is, for the hard-nosed it involves simply the workings of the mind and thus creates no difficulties for belief. Granted that the man possessed really believed he was possessed, and that both he and Jesus genuinely shared that belief and the belief that Jesus could release him, there is no reason why such stories of exorcism should not be substantially true in the form we have them. But when it comes to the healing of physical ailments, belief becomes a more difficult matter. There is not too much difficulty nowadays in accepting the possibility of 'spiritual healing' in general, and the present story could well be accepted as an instance of that. But we undoubtedly come across any number of healing miracles in Mark which, if we take all the details literally, simply defy belief.

It is likely though that in the present instance not many readers will want to insist that the story cannot be true. Perhaps not a totally instantaneous cure, even though the text does claim that. But if we modify it to, 'She was up within the hour and making a meal for them' (that being the significance of 'she served them'), then we have something pretty close to the text that most people will also have little difficulty in believing.

'That evening at sundown ... because they knew him.' They

waited until sundown because up till then it was still the sabbath. The Jewish sabbath begins at sundown and ends at the following sundown. In the course of the gospel (specifically the concluding story of chapter 2 and the opening story of chapter 3) it is made clear that all kinds of 'work' (including works of healing) were prohibited on the sabbath. Some readers may be inclined to wonder why all this is not explained here, since the detail has an important bearing on the story and is not immediately obvious. The likeliest answer is that to the readership that Mark originally had in mind it *was* immediately obvious. (On the other hand, it is to be noted that in 15.42 Mark feels it necessary to explain that 'the day of Preparation is the day before the sabbath'.) They are much more likely to have been puzzled – as I am – that he should describe Jesus' disregard of the tradition without making any comment or offering any explanation; this too he reserves for the later stories referred to above.

It is difficult for the modern reader to appreciate just how shocking Jesus' disregard for the sabbath must have been to his contemporaries, and therefore just how remarkably uncluttered his moral vision must also have been. It is obvious to us that the traditional sabbath regulations and restrictions were essentially a ceremonial[5] practice; the point, we would like to think, being not that any useful *moral* purpose was served, or even that anybody thought so, but that by the simple fact of a common observance of a common tradition a sense of unity and cohesion was created. We have the Old Testament before us, however, to undeceive us. Jeremiah is normally thought of as an unusually clear-sighted man who, unlike most of his contemporaries, realized the sheer *inevitability* of the Babylonian empire, and who therefore taught that rebellion was so absolutely doomed to failure that the mere contemplation of it was not just foolish but actually immoral: God would *punish* such criminal recklessness (chapter 27). Yet even a man like that can put forward the following ideas in all seriousness:

> Thus said the Lord to me: 'Go and stand in the Benjamin Gate, by which the kings of Judah enter and by which they go out, and in all the gates of Jerusalem, and say: "Hear the word of the Lord, you kings of Judah, and all Judah, and all the inhabitants of Jerusalem, who enter by these gates. Thus says the Lord: Take heed for the sake of your lives, and do not bear a burden on the sabbath day or bring it in by the gates of Jerusalem. And do not carry a burden out

of your houses on the sabbath day or do any work, but keep the sabbath day holy, as I commanded your fathers. Yet they did not listen or incline their ear, but stiffened their neck, that they might not hear and receive instruction.

But if you listen to me, says the Lord, and bring in no burden by the gates of this city on the sabbath day, but keep the sabbath day holy and do no work on it, then there shall enter by the gates of this city kings who sit on the throne of David, riding in chariots and on horses, they and their princes, the men of Judah and the inhabitants of Jerusalem; and this city shall be inhabited for ever. And people shall come from the cities of Judah and the places round about Jerusalem, from the land of Benjamin, from the Shephelah, from the hill country, and from the Negeb, bringing burnt offerings and sacrifices, cereal offerings and frankincense, and bringing thank offerings to the house of the Lord. But if you do not listen to me, to keep the sabbath day holy, and not to bear a burden and enter by the gates of Jerusalem on the sabbath day, then I will kindle a fire in its gates, and it shall devour the palaces of Jerusalem and shall not be quenched."' (Jer. 17.19–27)

Clearly a very great deal – the whole future of the city and the monarchy – here depends on the true observance of the sabbath: not surprisingly the prophet makes no attempt to explain how or why. But we can now begin to appreciate the enormous *moral* emphasis that was placed on sabbath day observance, both under the original monarchy, and even more so in Jesus' time when a new Davidic empire, however insanely, was agonizingly awaited as the only hope of deliverance for the nation. We even find it suggested in Rabbinic literature, no doubt under the direct influence of the Jeremiah passage above, that the appearance of the Messiah actually depends on the proper observance of the sabbath. It may in fact be just this idea which lies behind Jesus' own attitude. After all, he actually *was* the Messiah – but a completely different Messiah from anything that was popularly expected. So his working *did* depend on the proper observance of the sabbath – but once again a very different kind of sabbath from that of popular observance.

'And in the morning ... "why I came out".' It is clear that Jesus, like religious people generally, found great benefit from periods of solitude, and may even have found them necessary to him at times when large decisions were to be made. The most notable of these periods was of course the forty days in the wilderness (i.e. in modern parlance 'six weeks or so' – we need not think of it as an exact measurement of time) that followed after his baptism by John. Mark gives us this information here, I suspect, in order to imply that Jesus was *in the habit* (hence the title I have given this chapter) of getting up in the early hours and wandering off into the countryside to pray. Such a hypothesis gets round an obvious difficulty that arises if we take the passage as plain narrative: how on earth would Simon Peter have known where to look for him? And knowing how enormous a task such a search would be for one person to carry out (which is what the text implies), why on earth would he have undertaken it in the first place?

Matthew omits this incident altogether (Luke however includes a version of it in 4.42–43). No doubt he thought – not unreasonably – that any points it makes had already been covered in his own much fuller account of the temptation. The implication of Mark's text, after all, is that Jesus very well knew that 'Everyone is searching for you', and that this was very much the subject of his prayer. If so, the point is much the same as that underlying Matthew's third temptation (4.8–10).

'And he went ... and casting out demons.' Apart from the repetition of this formula at key points throughout the earlier chapters of the work (to which I have drawn attention above) it is quite important to notice the juxtaposition here of the two ideas of 'preaching ... and casting out demons'. This dual nature of Jesus' ministry, mentioned here almost as an aside, is in fact an important thread running right through the gospel narrative, and looks to my eyes to have provided Mark with his structural themes for those passages that I have suggested are chapters 5 and 6 of his work.

3

Jesus and the Pharisees

(Mark 1.40–3.12)

There are a number of parables in Matthew and Luke on the theme
of God's rejection of the established religion of Israel and its leaders,
and his replacing them with outsiders – all kinds of outsiders, both
social (publicans and sinners) and ethnic (*ethnici* being the Greek for
the Latin *gentiles* and the Hebrew *goyim*). I would like to think (and
do in fact believe) that much of this (in particular Matthew's
distasteful diatribe in chapter 23) has much more to do with post-
resurrection anti-Jewish bile on the part of the Christian community
than with any actual words of Jesus himself; on the other hand, some
degree of historicity of the theme in Jesus' own thinking cannot be
doubted. One sees no reason to doubt, for instance, the substantial
authenticity of Matthew 21.28–32(M), 33–43(P), 22.1–10(M) (the
inappropriateness of the sequel in verses 11–14 is probably due to
the conflation of two originally separate parables, both on the theme
of a wedding feast, during the oral stage of the tradition). Luke, to
whom the idea particularly appeals, has a great deal more of such
material: 7.29, 7.36–50, 10.29–37, 13.28–29, the whole of chapter
15, 17.11–19, 18.9–14, 19.2–10, all of this without parallel in the
other gospels. One suspects that quite a lot of it, perhaps most of it, is
not authentic;[1] but enough is still left to validate the theme.[2]

Apart from the single parable of the vineyard (Mark 12. 1–12 =
Matt. 21.33–46) Mark contains none of this material; but there is
little doubt in my mind that this and the following chapter are his
own exposition of the theme, while the evidence of Matthew and
Luke convinces me that Mark did not invent the idea, but that it was
embedded in the tradition from earliest times.

One small point about translation. Above, when I described the
social outcasts of Jesus' day, I used the traditional – almost prover-

bial – English phrase 'publicans and sinners'. This is hard, I suppose,
on the licensed victualling trade, since 'publican' in the New Testament means something entirely different from what it means in
everyday language. (I suspect, however, first that the everyday
meaning of 'publican' started life as a witticism derived from the
New Testament anyway, secondly that most publicans do not in fact
mind in the least.) The Greek term *telonae* is consistently translated
in the Vulgate as *publicani*,[3] a term which the early English versions,
instead of trying to translate, simply borrowed. The RSV, which
provides the English text for this commentary, translates *telonae*
consistently (and accurately) as 'tax collector'; but it seems to me a
mistake, when a word has become part of the language, to allow
scholars to rake over the flower bed like that; so that in every case I
have restored the traditional 'publicans'.

> And a leper came to him beseeching him, and kneeling said to him,
> 'If you will, you can make me clean'. Moved with pity, he
> stretched out his hand and touched him, and said to him, 'I will; be
> clean'. And immediately the leprosy left him, and he was made
> clean. And he sternly charged him, and sent him away at once, and
> said to him, 'See that you say nothing to anyone; but go, show
> yourself to the priest, and offer for your cleansing what Moses
> commanded, for a proof to the people'. But he went out and began
> to talk freely about it, and to spread the news, so that Jesus could
> no longer openly enter a town, but was out in the country; and
> people came to him from every quarter. (1.40–45)

I pointed out earlier that Matthew seemed to have a deliberate policy
of filtering out the more primitive characteristics that often show
through in Mark's portrayal of Jesus. This story provides an excellent illustration of the point — somewhat obscured, though, by the
misleading tone of the English translation in the crucial part of the
text: 'And he sternly charged him, and sent him away at once.' The
Greek actually says: 'And having raged at him, he immediately
pushed him out.' Why on earth, you may ask, should Jesus react like
that; and aren't the translators simply expressing the real meaning of
Mark, which he himself only got wrong because of his imperfect
mastery of Greek? But what the English here implies is correctly
rendered in the original Greek at 3.12, 5.43, 7.36, 8.30, and 9.9. I am
as puzzled as the reader and the translators as to why Mark says

what he does say; but I have no doubt that he actually meant to say it. Matthew's retelling of the story – using a high proportion of Mark's actual words – simply omits the sentence altogether.

Mark begins the section with this story because the leper, much more even than the publican or the sinner, was the extreme example of the social outcast of Jesus' day. Within the inevitable limits imposed by any social structure the publican and the sinner can be said to have chosen their own destiny; but the leper, though purely the victim of circumstance, was held in even greater abhorrence. Just what leprosy was thought to be in those days is unclear, even though we have a very full description of it in chapters 13 and 14 of Leviticus. The only thing we can be sure of is that though it would certainly have included what we now define as leprosy, it also included a lot more besides, including a great deal (such as reactivated scars, 'leprosy' in clothes and buildings) that we would nowadays consider to be no real danger to anyone. The condition of being a leper is briefly described thus:

> The leper who has the disease shall wear torn clothes and let the hair of his head hang loose, and he shall cover his lip and cry, 'Unclean, unclean'. He shall remain unclean as long as he has the disease; he is unclean; he shall dwell alone in a habitation outside the camp. (Lev. 13.45–46)

On the stipulation that he shall 'let the hair of his head hang loose', Josephus (a Jerusalem priest only a generation after Jesus' time) mordently comments, 'as though dead'. The same idea is found in the Old Testament itself:

> And the anger of the Lord was kindled against them, and he departed; and when the cloud removed from over the tent, behold, Miriam was leprous, as white as snow. And Aaron turned towards Miriam, and behold, she was leprous. And Aaron said to Moses, 'Oh, my lord, do not punish us because we have done foolishly and sinned. Let her not be as one dead, of whom the flesh is half consumed when he comes out of his mother's womb.' (Num 12.9–12)

The hardest condition of all was that of isolation from the community – not only beyond the reach of proper care, but in enforced contact with others who might have something very much worse than one's own complaint. If one didn't in fact have what we call leprosy, one stood a very good chance of catching it once one had been pronounced a leper.

Jesus' reaction here is probably to be thought of as ambivalent (similar perhaps to his ambivalent attitude to the Syrophoenician woman in 7.24–30): so far from rejecting traditional orthodoxy on the subject of leprosy (or paganism), I think we should assume that up to now he had unquestioningly accepted it. It was when actually confronted by a leper (or a pagan) who had need of his help that his good-nature got the better of his orthodoxy, and regardless of what he had always been told to believe, he gave the help he was asked for. His attitude to the sabbath probably had the same basis; the difference being that whereas he only rarely came in contact with either lepers or pagans, the distress caused by a too rigid observance of sabbath regulations had been familiar to him from boyhood, so that his attitude to that seems to have been immediate and very deeply felt.

For the first time in Mark's gospel – but by no means the last – we are hard up against the problem of credibility. The problem is presented not so much by the cure itself as by the claim that it was immediate. We can see two reasons why this immediacy presented no problem to Mark himself. Firstly to him Jesus' powers were of course miraculous, and the immediacy of the cure was simply part of the miracle. But secondly, as we noted above, although the modern reader would like to make a distinction between a purely psychological healing such as that of the man possessed in 1.23–27, and the curing of a physical ailment such as the fever of Peter's mother-in-law in 1.30–31, Mark does not seem to have made any such distinction at all. For him *all* the ailments that Jesus encounters are caused by demon possession, and *all* the healing miracles are examples of casting out demons. That is why, at the end of the previous chapter, I paraphrased 'preaching in their synagogues and casting out demons' as describing a dual ministry of teaching and healing. In this gospel 'casting out demons' and 'healing' are one and the same thing;[4] and it is chiefly for this reason that the idea of an *immediate* cure causes no problems of credibility for its author.

This by no means solves the problem though for the modern reader. Is it possible that a man was cured of leprosy – or of any of the conditions described as such in Leviticus 13 – on the instant? Are we to suppose that the disease was psychologically caused, so that the symptoms disappeared all but immediately? But if we make the suggestion here (which in any case does not convince me), must we then make the desperate assumption that *all the diseases Jesus ever encountered* were diseases of the mind rather than the body? What of the very next story, the paralytic in 2.3–12? The man with the withered hand in 3.1–5; the woman with the flow of blood in 5.25–34; the deaf and dumb man in 7.32–36; the blind man in 8.22–26? Are all of these, and presumably many more, to be thought of as psychological diseases? Such a hypothesis clearly is as incredible as the phenomena it was originally intended to explain. Nor do I think we can hope for any explanation other than the humdrum supposition that Jesus' powers of healing, though perhaps genuine enough and greatly admired by the Galilaean crowds, have been greatly exaggerated in all three synoptic gospels. In John's gospel the problem is side-stepped rather than resolved. The spiritual allegories that the miracles stories have there become present no problem of belief to the unsophisticated reader because he sees no difficulty in believing anyway, while the sophisticated reader can sense the allegory, and thus feels released from any need to believe; and this dual response seems to be the one deliberately being aimed at by the author.

> And when he returned to Capernaum after some days, it was reported that he was at home. And many were gathered together, so that there was no longer room for them, not even about the door; and he was preaching the word to them. And they came bringing to him a paralytic carried by four men. And when they could not get near him because of the crowd, they removed the roof above him; and when they had made an opening, they let down the pallet on which the paralytic lay. And when Jesus saw their faith, he said to the paralytic, 'My son, your sins are forgiven'. Now some of the scribes were sitting there, questioning in their hearts, 'Why does this man speak thus? It is blasphemy! Who can forgive sins but God alone?' And immediately Jesus, perceiving in his spirit that they thus questioned within themselves, said to them, 'Why do you question thus in your hearts? Which is easier, to say to the paralytic, "Your sins are forgiven", or to say, "Rise, take up your pallet and walk"? But that you may know that the Son of man has authority on earth to forgive sins' – he said to the paralytic – 'I say to you, rise, take up your pallet and go home'. And he rose, and immediately took up the pallet and

went out before them all; so that they were all amazed and glorified God, saying, 'We never saw anything like this!' (2.1–12)

Having concluded the previous passage with the words, 'so that Jesus could no longer openly enter a town ...' the next thing Mark tells us is that he returned to Capernaum. There is undoubted naivety here, but presumably we are meant to infer something like 'there were times when Jesus could no longer ...' Nor is this the only occasion when a plain indicative in Mark is best understood in a frequentative or iterative sense.

The main point of the story – the first point which needs comment – appears in verse 5 where Jesus says to the paralytic, 'My son, your sins are forgiven'. Is this at last a passage which specifically refutes the idea that Mark takes an adoptionist view of Jesus? Isn't Jesus' claim here to have power to forgive sins (whose historicity, by the way, I have no wish to challenge) a *cast-iron-proof* that the traditional view of Jesus' nature and his relationship with God is essentially the same as the one Jesus himself held, and as Mark relates? I cannot *disprove* the claim; but I can show that the passage is consistent with the adoptionist christology that I have claimed for the gospel as a whole. Beyond that point the reader must judge the question for himself.

It seems to me that the power Jesus here claims to forgive sins is essentially the same as his power to perform any other kind of exorcism; and the idea makes better sense of the passage than the traditional one, which explains along the following lines: 'If I have the miraculous power which enables me to heal this man, that proves that I am no ordinary man but the Son of God, and therefore able to forgive sins also.' But I suggest the real meaning is as follows: 'I am possessed by the spirit of God, therefore I have irresistible power over all malign spirits. This man is in the state he is in because he is in the power of malign spirits. They got that power over him because of the sins he has committed.[5] My power to forgive his sins and my power to heal his body are one and the same power, and the processes are one and the same process. I could not do the one if I could not do the other. I could of course say, "Your sins are forgiven", and leave it at that, and no one would know whether they were forgiven or not. In that sense it would be easy to say it. But if I now heal his body, you will have visible proof that I have the power over malign spirits that I say I have.'

He went out again beside the sea; and all the crowd gathered about him, and he taught them. And as he passed on, he saw Levi the son of Alphaeus sitting at the tax office, and he said to him, 'Follow me'. And he rose and followed him.

And as he sat at table in his house, many publicans and sinners were sitting with Jesus and his disciples; for there were many who followed him. And the scribes of the Pharisees, when they saw that he was eating with sinners and publicans, said to his disciples, 'Why does he eat with publicans and sinners?' And when Jesus heard it, he said to them, 'Those who are well have no need of a physician, but those who are sick; I came not to call the righteous, but sinners'. (2.13–17)

It is clear from all three synoptic gospels that Jesus preached a lot of his sermons beside the sea, and later in the gospel Mark explains why this was so and how it was done:

And he told his disciples to have a boat ready for him because of the crowd, lest they should crush him; for he had healed many, so that all who had diseases pressed upon him to touch him. (3.9–10)

Again he began to teach beside the sea. And a very large crowd gathered about him, so that he got into a boat and sat in it on the sea; and the whole crowd was beside the sea on the land. (4.1)

One thought that does occur, however, is that he must have had extraordinary lung power to be able to make himself heard in such circumstances.

'And as he passed on ...' Readers often assume (and are often encouraged to assume) that Levi was some kind of customs officer specifically connected with the maritime trade. It should first be pointed out that though we talk about the 'Sea' of Galilee, this is in fact a lake, and by no means a very large lake either. The only commercial activity connected with it seems to have been fishing. No doubt the fisherman had to pay taxes like everybody else, and it *may* have been Levi's particular job to see to this. But we can't be sure of that from the text before us.

As is well-known, the man described as Levi here (and in Luke 5.27) is called Matthew in Matthew 9.9, and Matthew's gospel seems to be ascribed to 'Matthew' purely on the strength of this detail (the real identity of the author of the first gospel being of course unknown). The reason for the change seems to be that Mark gives a list of the twelve apostles in 3.16–19, and that Levi's name does not appear among them. On what principal the name Matthew has been chosen out of seven possibles (i.e. excluding Peter, Andrew, James, John, and Judas Iscariot) is not clear. It is not necessary though to suppose there is any inconsistency here in Mark: we have no reason to believe he thought of Levi as specifically one of the twelve, as distinct from the very much larger body who could also be called disciples (see Acts 1.15). In that case, though, why does he go out of his way to describe Levi's call, when apart from him he doesn't even describe the call of any of the twelve apostles except the first four? The answer is of course that Jesus is just about to enjoy his first – probably rather riotous – party with publicans and sinners, and the call of Levi sets the scene for this subsequent debauch. Mark makes a point of telling us about Levi's call because, considering who he was and how he made a living, it was so very *shocking*.

'And as he sat at table …' Christian exegesis traditionally maintains that Jesus' attitude to publicans and sinners was different from that of the acknowledged religious leaders of his day in that they looked on both professions as so utterly degraded that it was incompatible even with respectability, let alone with sanctity, to have any contact with such people for whatever purpose; whereas Jesus on the contrary had compassion on these 'degraded' creatures, and went out of his way to befriend and thus to reform them. This is certainly the view that the gospels themselves promote; and yet I find it impossible to believe. In the first place, although the religious leaders of those days (like the religious leaders of any day and any religion) undoubtedly looked down on such people as spivs and tarts, we have no reason to believe, nor is it likely, that they avoided all contact with them; it is very much more probable that their attitude to them was the very one that in the gospels is credited to Jesus, namely one of solicitous concern for their redemption from a life of sin and shame. That these leaders are scandalized when they see Jesus sitting down to dinner with such people seems only too likely, and I am inclined to accept that this open and intense disapprobation is historical. But the only hypothesis that convinces me is that Jesus plainly did *not* think of his lowlife companions as particularly degraded or very much in need of redemption at all. He took them as he found them and laughed with them instead of preaching at them; and it was this that so scandalized the religious leaders.

I make no attempt to conceal the fact that this interpretation is plainly contradicted by the text: 'Those who are well have no need of a physician, but those who are sick; I came not to call the righteous, but sinners.' How can I possibly claim to know better than that? I suppose I could argue that the words, though authentic, are being used as what philosophers call an *argumentum ad hominem*: an argument used not so much to vindicate the position of the person who uses it as to expose the contradiction in the position of his opponents. But let me also try and give some *evidence* in support of the interpretation I offer. First:

'... A man had two sons; and he went to the first and said, "Son, go and work in the vineyard today". And he answered, "I will not"; but afterward he repented and went. And he went to the second and said the same; and he answered, "I go, sir", but did not go. Which of the two did the will of his father?' They said, 'The first'. Jesus said to them, 'Truly, I say to you, the publicans and the harlots go into the kingdom of God before you. For John came to you in the way of righteousness, and you did not believe him, but the publicans and the harlots believed him; and even when you saw it, you did not afterward repent and believe him.' (Matt. 21.28–32)

The passage is found only in Matthew but looks to me to have a very good claim to be considered authentic. And what are the implications? Not that the religious leaders have no need of a physician but precisely the opposite: that it is the religious leaders that have need of repentance, while the publicans and harlots are already very much closer to righteousness. It seems to me that is the attitude that is most likely to have caused offence.

The second passage on the contrary is found only in Luke, and seems to have no claim at all to be considered authentic; but it is useful here in that it offers almost a caricature of the traditional interpretation of Jesus' attitude:

He entered Jericho and was passing through. And there was a man named Zacchaeus; he was a chief publican, and rich. And he sought to see who Jesus was, but could not on account of the crowd, because he was small of stature. So he ran on ahead and climbed up into a sycamore tree to see him, for he was to pass that way. And when Jesus came to the place, he looked up and said to him, 'Zacchaeus, make haste and come down; for I must stay at your house today'. So he made haste and came down, and received him joyfully. And when they saw it they all murmured, 'He has gone in to be the guest of a man who is a sinner'. And Zacchaeus stood and said to the Lord, 'Behold, Lord, the half of my goods I give to the poor; and if I have defrauded any one of anything, I restore it fourfold'. And Jesus said to him, 'Today salvation has come to this house, since he also is a son of Abraham. For the Son of man came to seek and to save the lost'. (Luke 19.1–10)

The story is riddled with improbabilities, the most obvious of which is that Jesus passes under a sycamore tree, sees someone sitting up in the branches and immediately knows who he is, what his occupation is, and why he is sitting there. But there are also more subtle improbabilities. Any rich man will tell you that a man who gives half his goods to the poor (presumably half his income rather than half his actual wealth, but even that is being more than generous), and whose guilt feelings prompt him to pay out four times over for every piece of sharp practice – such a man is never going to be rich. And then if Jesus accepts everything that Zacchaeus tells him as being simply the truth, could any response be more inappropriate than to claim he has come 'to seek and to save the lost'? If a man like Zacchaeus is lost, Lord, who then *can* be saved!

Now John's disciples and the Pharisees were fasting; and people came and said to him, 'Why do John's disciples and the disciples of the Pharisees fast, but your disciples do not fast?' And Jesus said to them, 'Can the wedding guests fast while the bridegroom is with them? As long as they have the bridegroom with them, they cannot fast. The days will come when the bridegroom is taken away from them, and then they will fast in that day. No one sews a piece of unshrunk cloth on an old garment; if he does, the patch tears away from it, the new from the old, and a worse tear is made. And no one puts new wine into old wineskins; if he does, the wine will burst the skins, and the wine is lost, and so are the skins; but new wine is for fresh skins.' (2.18–22)

To compare the opening of this story with Matthew's and Luke's version is instructive. Matthew has: 'Then the disciples of John came to him, saying, "Why do we and the Pharisees fast, but your disciples do not fast?"' And Luke: 'And they said to him, "The disciple of John fast often and offer prayers, and so do the disciples of the Pharisees, but yours eat and drink?"' All three versions have significant differences, and yet we have no real reason to suppose that Matthew and Luke derive from any other source than Mark. The obvious point on which Matthew and Luke agree with each other against Mark is that Mark ties the discussion to a specific occasion, whereas the other two both seem to want to expand the discussion into something non-specific.

We can probably take it as fact that whereas the disciples of John made a habit of observing the customary religious fasts, the disciples of Jesus were conspicuous in their carelessness about such matters. This ties in well with Jesus' equally conspicuous carelessness on the subject of sabbath observance, and is quite likely to be authentic. We can easily imagine him concluding that since the practice of fasting served no very clear moral purpose, it mattered very little whether one observed such fasts or not. A New Testament author (quite possibly, but by no means certainly Paul) makes a very shrewd comment on all such features of ecclesiastical discipline:

> If with Christ you died to the elemental spirits of the universe, why do you live as if you still belonged to the world? Why do you submit to regulations, 'Do not handle, Do not taste, Do not touch' (referring to things which all perish as they are used), according to human precepts and doctrines. These have indeed an appearance of wisdom in promoting rigour of devotion and self-abasement and severity to the body, but they are of no value in checking the indulgence of the flesh. (Col. 2.20–23)

– and the footnote offers an alternative translation to that conclusion: 'but they are of no value, serving only to indulge the flesh'. Whichever alternative we take, we are likely to accept the suggestion that so far from being a path to spirituality, the meticulous observance of church rules is often a means of fastening the attention on matters that are petty, worldly, pointless and far from spiritual. To that extent the modern reader is likely to be impressed by Jesus' apparent sense of proportion.

However, verse 20 gets badly in the way of such an interpretation: 'The days will come when the bridegroom is taken away from them, and then they will fast in that day.' In other words, this free and easy attitude applies only so long as Jesus is still with the disciples; once he is gone and the disciples are left behind, then they will behave with exactly the same rigour as John's disciples and those of the Pharisees. One must of course be very careful about suspecting passages simply because they are inconvenient. One cannot deny the possibility that the whole passage is close to what Jesus actually said, in which case the suggestion made above will have had no place in his thinking. But if that *is* the case, it's hard to see what his thinking can have been. It is for this reason that the suggestion has been made that verse 20 has been inserted into the saying after Jesus' death, and that its purpose is to justify the gradual development of the original free-and-easy band of Jesus' road-followers into a disciplined and increasingly rigid religious community just like any other. The reader must judge to what extent this may be plausible.

'No one sews a piece of unshrunk cloth ... new wine is for fresh skins.' Mark presents these two sayings as part of Jesus' answer to those who criticized his attitude to fasting, and the context in which he places them suits them well enough. But it is in fact quite likely that as they came to him they had no connection at all with the fasting controversy and that Mark himself is responsible for the connection. We must bear in mind that sayings which occur in the early part of Mark's gospel may very well belong historically to late in Jesus' ministry (and vice versa), and are placed where they are because they seem to him to be appropriate to the theme he is handling at the moment; also that sayings which are strung together (as here) as part of a continuous speech may originally have reached Mark having no connection with each other at all. The point is important because, as we shall see below, it sometimes looks as if Mark occasionally misunderstood a saying and distorted its meaning by placing it in a less than appropriate context.

The effectiveness of the sayings as illustrations of the general theme of the passage – the incompatibility of the old with the new, and the rejection of the old in favour of the new – is not in doubt, even to a generation for which patching (except as a means of adorning the clothes of the carefree young) has become pretty well a thing of the past. Similarly, although it is quite likely that no one who reads this book will have any direct experience of wine-skins, I doubt if they will on those grounds find the saying on that topic hard to grasp. I suspect, however, that Mark has missed, and thus helped to conceal, the original meaning in particular of the second illustration.

Let me first deal with an item of evidence which strongly supports

Mark's interpretation, and therefore strongly questions the view I am about to put forward. If we turn to the parallel passage in Luke (5.33–39) we note that Luke adds a further saying, not found in Mark, at the end of the passage: 'And no one after drinking old wine desires new; for he says, "The old is good".' Mark understood both his sayings, we decided, as recommending the rejection of the old in favour of the new, and up to this point in Luke there is nothing that implies that Luke himself understood them in any other sense. Yet this final saying makes exactly the opposite point: where there is conflict between the old and the new, it is the old that has the preference. Did Jesus actually use the words, and is this what he meant by them? The answer to both questions I am confident is No. My own suggestion would be that the unconverted Jewish community was regularly taunted by the Christians with this saying and had come up with a counter-saying of their own in reply; and it is this counter-saying that Luke here records.[6] But the implication of this is that Mark is not personally responsible for the meaning he has given this saying, but that it was widely-known throughout the Christian churches and always had the meaning which it has here in Mark's gospel.

Against this let me put forward my own guess as to what Jesus himself may have meant by it. Jesus regarded himself as a prophet (Mark 6.4); he may have regarded himself as more than a prophet (Mark 8.27–30), but he certainly regarded himself as a prophet as well. John the Baptist, for whom he clearly had the profoundest admiration, also regarded himself as a prophet, and was so regarded by Jesus – who praised the readiness of ordinary people to accept his claim and denounced the reluctance of the religious leaders to do so. This, I suspect, is what the saying was originally about. In orthodox eyes prophecy was extinct, and had been so for all but half a millennium. Prophets had claimed the right to set the priestly tradition aside and speak directly to the people in God's name; they had claimed the right to denounce everything the tradition regarded as holy as being in fact a sham which, far from manifesting, actually concealed the true holiness of God from the eyes of the people. Even in the heyday of prophecy, although the person of the prophet was supposed to be inviolate, Jeremiah not once but several times came near to losing his life, both at the hands of the priests who treated his denunciation of the temple as blasphemy (Jer. 26) and at the hands of the army and the politicians who treated his denunciation of resistance to the Babylonians (it must be admitted not unreasonably) as treason (38.1–6). It is obvious that once such an inconvenient tradition has died out, no political or religious leader with any sense of responsibility will be anything but reluctant to allow its revival. It is for this reason that throughout the gospels we find both Herod and the priests united in their distrust of and opposition to both Jesus and John the Baptist: so much so that John's death is eventually engineered by Herod, and Jesus' death by the priests at the hands of the Roman governor. (The tradition has its own apologetic reasons for wanting to exonerate Pilate and incriminate the Jews, but I suspect that the gospel portrayal is close to the real history of the event in any case.) By the 'new wine' of this saying I am convinced Jesus originally meant prophecy, whose potent freshness and immediacy was tearing to shreds the withered and worn usages of traditional religion that were trying to hold it in.

One sabbath he was going through the grainfields; and as they made their way, his disciples began to pluck heads of grain. And the Pharisees said to him, 'Look, why are they doing what is not lawful on the sabbath?' And he said to them, 'Have you never read what David did, when he was in need and was hungry, he and those who were with him: how he entered the house of God, when Abiathar was high priest, and ate the bread of the Presence, which it is not lawful for any but the priests to eat, and also gave it to those who were with him?' And he said to them, 'The sabbath was made for man, not man for the sabbath; so the Son of man is lord even of the sabbath'.

And he entered the synagogue, and a man was there who had a withered hand. And they watched him to see whether he would heal him on the sabbath, so that they might accuse him. And he said to the man who had the withered hand, 'Come here'. And he said to them, 'Is it lawful on the sabbath to do good or to do harm, to save life or to kill?' But they were silent. And he looked around at them with anger, grieved at their hardness of heart, and said to the man, 'Stretch out your hand'. He stretched it out, and his hand was restored. The Pharisees went out and immediately held counsel with the Herodians against him, how to destroy him. (2.23–3.6)

Mark has already made clear to us in another story about a healing in a synagogue (1.21–28) that Jesus had little regard for the regulations and prohibitions that attached to traditional sabbath observance. It is on this question of sabbath observance that Jesus seems to have been most persistently at variance with the orthodoxy of his day, and also on this question that he seems to have given most offence. How much offence is made clear by the conclusion of the above passage: it was Jesus' unconcealed disregard of these rules that apparently instigated meetings between the religious and political leaders to assess the gravity of the threat that he posed to stability, and the most suitable means of eliminating the danger.

This may to some ears sound a little fanciful – for two reasons. The first is that we are still in the opening stages of Jesus' ministry, which tradition supposes to have been at least two or three years, and as we have seen could well have been very much longer. Is it credible on the one hand that powerful factions could have been determined at such an early stage to bring about Jesus' downfall, and on the other that it should have taken them so long to succeed? It is here that insistence on the thematic, rather than the narrative, structure of Mark's gospel as a whole seems particularly relevant. Just because Mark gives us this information in the early verses of only his third chapter, it in no way follows that it belongs to the early part of Jesus' ministry. It belongs to a discussion of Jesus' attitude to the sabbath, and Mark himself probably had little idea about what period of the ministry it actually belonged to.

And that brings us to the second reason for perplexity. We have three largely independent and very full accounts of Jesus' trial and execution (Mark/Matthew, Luke and John), and in none of them is there any mention of resentment in connection with disregard of the sabbath. Herod is mentioned in one of them (Luke 23.6–12) as having heard of Jesus, but his only interest in seeing him seems to be the satisfaction of curiosity. In flat contradiction to the implications of the present passage he there seems to agree with Pilate that Jesus presents a negligible threat to stability and could be quietly released were it not for the unaccountable insistence of the Jerusalem priests that he should be put to death. And that reminds us that in the event it was neither the Pharisees nor the Herodians that were responsible for Jesus' execution, but the Sadducees. A fuller discussion of these parties, and to what extent they were involved in Jesus' life and death, will be found in the appendix.

'One sabbath he was going through the grainfields ...' A modern farmer if he came across the disciples doing what is here described would raise a cry of tresspass and damage to property. An ancient farmer would have had no complaint:

> When you go into your neighbour's vineyard, you may eat your fill of grapes, as many as you wish, but you shall not put any in your vessel. When you go into your neighbour's standing grain, you may pluck the ears with your hand, but you shall not put a sickle to your neighbour's standing grain. (Deut. 23.24–25)

From that point of view then the disciples were doing nothing that they were not strictly entitled to do. The point was they were doing it on the sabbath. The Lucan account (6.1–5) is slightly more detailed: 'his disciples plucked and ate some ears of grain, *rubbing them in their hands*.' Luke wants to make clear that there were two offences: plucking the grain was 'reaping', rubbing it in their hands to separate the grain from the husk was 'threshing'.

'Have you never read what David did, when he was in need ...' That is the point that seems to have so offended Jesus. Simply as a ritual, sabbath observance was harmless – like eating fish on Fridays. That sort of thing appeals to that sort of person – what of it? The trouble is that there is a tendency for these rituals to be invested with an undue and ever-increasing importance. Tangible good was never the purpose of them in the first place, but once they get a hold tangible harm is often the consequence. The point that to Jesus insists on is *need*; what meets man's need is good, what prevents that need from being met is bad. The sabbath has long ago developed into a hindrance and not a help to human need.

Fairness compels one to add that either Jesus' himself or the subsequent tradition shows a certain carelessness in Old Testament quotation. If we look up the passage here alluded to (I Sam. 21.1–6), we shall find that although David himself was to some extent in need, any mention of followers is a lie on David's part to make his urgency seem greater than the priest (*not* the high priest, whose office did not exist for at least another three centuries) would have judged it to be; and the priest in question was not Abiathar, but his father Ahimelech, who was subsequently murdered by Saul – along with all his family except Abiathar – as a direct result of this incident (I Sam. 22.11–19); and David had reason at the time to expect that this would be the consequence (I Sam. 22.22). The original event is distinctly less morally improving than its quotation here implies.

'The sabbath was made for man, not man for the sabbath' is clear enough and merely reiterates in another form what was said above about human need and ritual observance. But what of the other saying: 'so the Son of man is lord even of the sabbath'? What Mark means by it is clear enough, as is also his obvious feeling of being very daring in making the claim. (Both Matthew and Luke omit the word 'even'; they take it for granted that Jesus has a status that Mark feels some of his readers may have misgivings about.) Jesus has the powers that he here claims in exactly the same way, Mark probably felt, that he had the power to forgive sins in 2.1–12. But the modern reader has some excuse for a nagging feeling that the former incident is much closer to history than this present saying; because there Jesus, within the conventions of his time, can offer some sort of 'proof' of his claim, and does so. Here he can't: the claim is made to stand or fall entirely on his own say so. It is because of this nagging feeling that there has been a strong desire on the part of a number of scholars either to doubt that Jesus ever said it, or that if he did, he meant something very different by it than the way Mark clearly understands it.

One must be very careful about suggesting that because an action or saying attributed to Jesus is out of tune with modern presuppositions, therefore he cannot have done or said it. And this is as good a place as any for reminding the reader of what has always been a disfiguring tendency in the whole field of scripture interpretation: 'I strongly feel that this is right; therefore this must be what the Bible really means.' 'I strongly feel that this is wrong; therefore the Bible *properly interpreted* condemns it, even though it may not seem to.'[7] I think we can reject out of hand the solution favoured by some that the expression 'Son of man' here – and possibly throughout the gospel – is not one that is making any kind of special claim for Jesus, but merely describes him as a member of the human race. (As we have noted, this is what the expression *always* means in the Old Testament). On this interpretation, 'The Son of man is lord even of the sabbath' would mean much the same as the saying that precedes it: Man is entitled to make whatever use of the sabbath best meets his needs. The difficulty in accepting this interpretation of the epithet, setting aside for the moment the question what Jesus may have meant by it, is that Mark has virtually defined his own understanding of it for us in the passion narrative:

Again the high priest asked him, 'Are you the Christ, the Son of the Blessed?' And Jesus said, 'I am; and you will see the Son of man seated at the right hand of Power, and coming with the clouds of heaven'. (Mark 14.61b–62)

If this is what 'Son of man' means to Mark in chapter 14, it seems absurd to suggest that he means anything else but that anywhere in the gospel. But is that what Jesus meant? The only realistic answer we can make is that on this point we have no good reason to doubt Mark's testimony, and that the misgivings of those who do so seem to derive from other considerations than those of historical probability.

The other resource for those who find the saying difficult is to suppose that Jesus never said it. Even bearing in mind the admonition above about insisting the bible always agrees with you, this idea does have possibilities. 'The sabbath was made for man, not man for the sabbath', is not only a neat and satisfying observation but a *self-sufficient* one. The addition of what follows spoils that neatness by going on to say more than is necessary, and by introducing new ideas. Even if Jesus did actually say it, I have no doubt that he did not say it on the same occasion. Despite the obvious dangers, I am tempted by the supposition that the saying is not authentic, but an example of the tradition inflating Jesus' original claims for himself once he himself is no longer around to contradict.

'Again he entered ... who had a withered hand.' Just what kind of affliction this withered hand could be is not at all clear – particularly when we are asked to believe that the cure of the ailment was immediate. 'And they watched him ... so that they might accuse him.' Several features about this event (assuming it corresponds to anything that actually happened) point to its having occurred late in Jesus' ministry, or outside the area of Galilee, or both. There are representatives of two highly influential bodies present in the synagogue – perhaps deliberately planted to collect evidence against Jesus. Not only is Jesus' reputation as a healer established, therefore, but equally so is his reputation as a disregarder of the sabbath. People like the Pharisees and Herodians do not take these kind of precautions on the basis of vague rumours about scarcely heard-of activists in distant parts. Jesus is evidently aware of all the implications of the circumstance, and his challenging tone is no doubt due to this. The question, 'Is it lawful on the sabbath to good or to do harm, to save life or to kill?', is intended to put them in the wrong by showing how unreasonable their views on the sabbath are. Their silence indicates that they refuse to be drawn but have not changed their minds, which is why Jesus reacts with anger. Not to be intimidated, therefore, he does what they expected him to do, and deliberately gives them the handle against him he knows they were looking for.

> Jesus withdrew with his disciples to the sea, and a great multitude from Galilee followed; also from Judaea and Jerusalem and Idum and from beyond the Jordan, and from about Tyre and Sidon, a great multitude, hearing all that he did, came to him. And he told his disciples to have a boat ready for him because of the crowd, lest they should crush him; for he had healed many, so that all who had diseases pressed upon him to touch him. And whenever the unclean spirits beheld him, they fell down before him and cried out. 'You are the Son of God'. And he strictly ordered them not to make him known. (3.7–12)

This, the longest of the 'end of chapter summaries' we discussed earlier, contains several curious points, beginning with the opening statement that 'Jesus withdrew with his disciples to the sea'. Chapter 2 opened with Jesus returning to Capernaum, which happens to be by the sea, and Mark has said nothing to indicate any change of locality since then. On the other hand we suggested above that the healing of the man with the withered hand may well have taken place outside Galilee. In Mark's gospel as it stands, Jesus ministry takes place, if not solely in Galilee, then solely in the northern areas of the country until a single final visit to Jerusalem beginning with 10.32, and this structure is imitated by both Matthew and Luke. In John's gospel on the other hand Jesus makes repeated visits to Jerusalem throughout the ministry (John 2.13; 5.1; 7.1–10 in addition to the Palm Sunday entry in chapter 12), and this is likely to be true to history even though John's reasons for adopting this structure are not historic. The Jerusalem material given in chapters 11 to 13 of Mark may well belong to several visits, and Mark himself may have been perfectly well aware that it did; he adopts the structure that he does only because it better suits his thematic approach to presenting the material. So in this instance I suggest that the healing of the man with the withered hand may well belong to one of these visits to the south, where representatives of influential bodies were likely to be thicker on the ground, and where the question of stability was much more to the fore of everybody's thinking. It may well be this passage that actually suggested to John a feature of which he makes considerable play in his gospel: that not only did Jesus make several visits to the south, but that he was also in physical danger there, and that his retreats to the north were in order to avoid such threats (4.1–3; 5.18; 7.1, 19–20 and 25; 8.37 and 40; 11.8).

The crowd that followed him comes from every surrounding region: his fellow Galilaeans, Jerusalem in the south, Idumaea (Edom of the Old Testament) a non-Judaic region to the extreme south east, all the non-Judaic territories to the east of Jordan, as also the non-Judaic coastal region to the north of Galilee (i.e. from about Tyre and Sidon).

All other details in this passage have already been covered previously.

APPENDIX

In the course of Mark's gospel we come across the names of four distinct religious/political groups: the Pharisees (often), the Herodians (3.6;12.13), the Zealots (Simon the Cananaean in Mark 3.18 and Matthew 10.4 is described as Simon the Zealot in Luke 6.15 and Acts 1.13, and this equivalence is usually accepted), and the Sadducees (12.18). I have briefly outlined the aspirations of the Zealots on page 35 of the introduction. Before I go on to say a little more about them, as well as the other three groups, it will be as well first of all to defend my description of all four of them as 'religious/ political' groups. At a simplistic level of interpretation it is obvious that two of them (the Zealots and the Herodians) are definitely political, and two of them (the Pharisees and the Sadducees) definitely religious. At a slightly less simplistic level, the Zealots are much more involved in a religious dimension than the Herodians are, and the Sadducees in a political dimension than the Pharisees are. On the other hand, the Herodians do not at all think that religious considerations are irrelevant to their aims, nor do the Pharisees think that of political considerations. At this point the modern commentator is conventionally expected to point out that this was a society in which religious and political considerations were hopelessly interwoven; so that the reader, brought up in a secular society in which the separation of the two is taken for granted, cannot avoid the feeling that this is a situation that is all but unintelligible. I think, however, that I can do better than that.

Political and religious aspirations have this in common, that both are directed towards creating cohesion among groups of people who wish to define themselves in terms of their close involvement with each other and their separateness from others who do not belong to the group. Political aspirations are primarily directed towards the maintenance of territory, and the safety and prosperity of those within that territory; religious aspirations primarily towards the sense of unity that is experienced as a profound and primary satisfaction when the group affirms a common system of beliefs, and gives expression to that system by means of shared ceremonies, slogans, emblems and stories.

Some readers may well find this view hopelessly old-fashioned. A huge proportion of any modern society for instance seems to make no religious responses whatever, and if it did these would not be concerned primarily with ceremonies, slogans, emblems and stories at all (that, they would say, is religiosity rather than religion), but with the beliefs themselves – beliefs about the real originator of the world we live in, our real relation to that originator, the real purpose of our lives within that world, (for some the real nature of our destiny after this life,) the real nature of morality and so on. And it is because these readers are satisfied that there is no *real* answer to any of these questions, and indeed that it scarcely makes sense to ask them in the first place, that they dismiss religion as an outmoded error of the past, dependent on the illusory notion that man is the central feature of the universe, that it was created solely for his benefit and his are the only purposes it serves. And on the other hand they would point out that politics itself is as much concerned with ceremonies, slogans, emblems and stories as it is with the maintenance of territory, and the safety and prosperity of those within that territory. Politics itself has in a sense a religious dimension, which no politician of experience would dream of undervaluing.

That last point needs, of course, no debate. Indeed I myself am so impressed with it that I doubt, not merely whether we actually do separate religion and politics, but whether we actually can. We like to think of religion as a private matter between ourselves and our consciences, and to an extent it is. But in that sense our religion is a private matter even in relation to whatever religious body we may happen to belong to. The aims that religious bodies themselves pursue, on the other hand, are not a private matter at all. The eccentricities of small religious bodies can be practically ignored except by those that belong to them; but the eccentricities of large religious bodies are of relevance to everyone, whether they are members of that body or not. The separation of politics and religion is usually taken to mean that no matter what doctrines, pronouncements, regulations or attitudes a religious body tries to impose upon its members, the state demands that membership of the religious body must be voluntary, and that this imposition must be confined solely to members; thus the state has no right of interference between the religious body and its members, nor has the religious body any right to try and impose itself beyond the limits of its volunatry members. Practically and on the whole the idea works well, but it seems to me neither necessary nor desirable that we should view all this as some kind of unchallengeable axiom. Any question, after all, that concerns any large number of people is a political question – I do not see how else a political question can be defined. To give a few practical examples, there is no fundamental moral reason why a government – particularly in countries that are severely beset by problems of over-population – should not impose requirements on catholics which are inconsistent with those that the church wishes to impose. It may be practically unwise, but it is not obviously immoral; nor, if the situation became sufficiently desperate, would it necessarily be immoral even to introduce measures that come close to being a form of religious persecution. Similarly it may be unwise but would not necessarily be immoral for governments to declare the ceremonial religious slaughter of animals illegal, or to remove the dispensation Sikh's at present enjoy from wearing crash-helmets on motorbikes.

Religious questions commonly do have a political dimension therefore, and the political order has an undoubted right to interfere even on specifically religious questions. But do political questions similarly have a specifically religious dimension? We agreed above that in its use of ceremonies, slogans, emblems and stories it had points of resemblance to religion; but I think the resemblance goes very much deeper than these mere superficialities. Let me return to the passage above where I listed what most people would think of as genuinely religious beliefs – beliefs about the real originator of the world we live in and so on. I suggested that most of us reject this kind of belief because it is obvious to us that it derives from a wholly illusory view of man's position and significance in the universe. My personal inclination, which some readers may at first sight find perverse, is to agree that such is the source from which these beliefs derive, but to doubt whether that is such a fatal flaw in religious claims as most of us have been brought up to suppose. It is for instance clear to me that *any* form of improving doctrine can *only* be derived from an illusory view of man's position and significance in the universe. And it is fortunately the case that modern politics supplies us with a towering example of just such a doctrine – first, which derives from an illusory view of man, and secondly (and perhaps even more surprisingly in a supposedly secular world) is increasingly considered to be morally *obligatory*; so much so that nations which fall short of orthodoxy on the point are more and more faced with the threat of punishment. I mean, of course, the doctrine of human rights.

Whether there really are such things as human rights does not seem to me to be the proper question to ask. We are perfectly entitled to decide that *from now on there are going to be* human rights should we wish to do so, and I suggest that is basically what we have done. In that sense, it could be argued, no error or illusion is involved. The idea admittedly promotes a vulgar error which is inseparable from any popular doctrine, and perhaps always has been and always will be: people are apt to suppose that doctrines, like facts, must be either true or false, and that 'belief in a doctrine' is the same thing as 'believing a doctrine is true'. A more accurate view is that no doctrine is ever either true or false. We frame doctrines with a view to influencing behaviour in order to bring about a situation which we desire. We regard a doctrine as *valid* if (*a*) we ourselves desire the situation it seems intended to create, and (*b*) if we believe it to be aptly and effectively designed to bring about that situation. If we regard it as invalid, it may either be because we do not desire the situation, or because even though we do, we do not believe the doctrine is an effective means of getting us there. With this proviso, it may be thought, we have given a clean bill of health to a belief such as that in human rights; many are under an illusion about the nature of the doctrine, but this is not a criticism of the doctrine as such.

But how do we square such an attitude to human rights with our belief that 'religion' and 'politics' ought to be separate? If it is abhorrent that any religious doctrine should be made compulsory, but perfectly all right that political ones should become so, what purpose does the separation serve? Can we be sure that there has *been* any such separation made in the first place? Are we not likely to move towards a situation where 'This doctrine is religious' simply means that we regard it as being voluntary, while 'This doctrine is political' means that it is to be regarded as compulsory. And such a development, which already seems to be taking place, is a short route back to the very situation we promised ourselves we were escaping from: that of there being compulsory beliefs, imposed by a political authority that is not merely intolerant of criticism and opposition, but is actually determined to punish them. As yet there is available the mitigating plea that no one has suggested for instance that people who do not believe in human rights should be tortured and burnt. But for how long? After all, it took a thousand years or so for Christianity to get round to that way of thinking.

Let no one suppose therefore that we have achieved some kind of superiority over the Pharisees and Sadducees, the Zealots and the Herodians; or that they belong to a remote and unintelligible past with which the modern reader cannot hope to come to terms. We can and should try to think of them as pretty much like ourselves. We can take it for granted for instance that though they professed worthy aims, their real intentions would often scarcely have stood up to scrutiny; that though professing to serve others, in many cases they really hoped to advance themselves. We can take all this for granted of them because we take it all for granted of ourselves. So let us begin this survey with the realization that, however striking the superficial differences may be, none of these people are all that different from what we are perfectly familiar with, nor is our boasted secularization any bar to our understanding their supposedly non-secular outlook.

The biggest acting part in all three synoptic gospels after that of Jesus himself is that of the Pharisees. (They play a comparable part in the fourth gospel also, but in that gospel an even greater part is played by 'the Jews'. The precise nature of the distinction in that gospel between the Jews in general and the Pharisees in particular is never made clear.) We get the impression from the gospels therefore, which we know from other sources is correct, that the Pharisees were the most prominent leaders in the Palestine of Jesus' day. So far as we can tell, they have their origin in the struggles for independence from Seleucid domination which broke out in 167 BC and are described in

I Maccabees (and also underly the book of Daniel). It is tempting to derive the origin of the Sadducees also from this period, and we are probably right to see both parties playing much the same opposing roles in relation to the Seleucids as we find them playing in the gospels in relation to the Romans. In the earlier period it was the ambition of the Seleucid king (Antiochus Epiphanes) to replace ancestral Judaism with the newer Hellenism (the classical and post-classical cultural traditions of Greece) that was as much accepted as the cultural norm in the eastern mediterranean of his day as 'Westernism' is accepted as the cultural norm among us. This involved not merely replacing the Mosaic law and ceremonies with pagan mythology and practice but, perhaps even more important, imposing the kind of civic and intellectual life that was as much the vehicle as the product of paganism. All the books we are likely to read on the subject will assure us that Antiochus was a wicked man, his aims were wicked aims, and his sympathizers among the Jews were wicked apostates. The truth on the first two points is that Antiochus was a politician, and his aims were political aims; on the third point, how automatically would we be prepared to condemn a Muslim for instance who had doubts as to whether Islamic fundamentalism were altogether a good thing or Westernism altogether a bad? These two situations are very closely comparable.

The incident that precipitated the crisis of 167 BC was the erection of 'the abomination of desolation' (the image of Olympian Zeus erected above the altar of burnt offering in the Jerusalem temple), the sending round of commissioners to the towns and villages of Palestine to enforce sacrifice to the new gods, and the murder by the priest Mattathias of one of these commissioners (together with an over-eager apostate) in the town of Modin (see I Macc. 1.54–2.30). Mattathias' supporters were those who refused to have anything to do with the new policy, and who were determined to resist to the death any change whatever to the traditional religion and the traditional way of life. At the time they described themselves as Hasidim ('righteous ones'). These Hasidim, so far as we can tell, are the origin of the Pharisees of the New Testament. By contrast there were those who thought that there was something to be said after all for a certain amount of new influence to loosen up the hardened arteries of traditional Judaism. We need not suppose they were in favour of *replacing* Judaism with Hellenism altogether; essentially their aim seems to have been to admit the influence of Hellenism into the Jewish tradition and to see what would emerge of its own accord from the mix. My personal preference is very much in favour of these mild-mannered libertarians, as against the zealous martyrs prepared to offer their very lives in support of their own grisly brand of conviction politics. And it is these comparatively easy-going, gentlemanly souls that appear to be the origin of the Sadducees.

In Jesus' day there were virtually two totally different kinds of religion in operation. The most sacred building in all Judaism – not merely in Palestine itself but for the Jewish communities which had grown up in every part of the mediterranean world – was the Jerusalem temple. The existing edifice had been built by Herod in the closing years of the first century BC, and was therefore not all that old; but it had every right to consider itself as the direct successor to the temple that Solomon had built getting on for a thousand years earlier. In Solomon's day, and for many centuries after that, the Jerusalem temple – though undoubtedly the most prestigious – was just one among many religious institutions dotted all over (as it then was) Canaan. In the very last years of the monarchy, towards the end of the seventh century BC, all these other temples/shrines/sanctuaries had been suppressed by King Josiah, and from then on the Jerusalem temple was the only legitimate temple in the land. It so happened that within a generation Jerusalem itself was sacked by the Babylonians, and the temple also was destroyed (586 BC). We have evidence, though, that although the building itself was destroyed, the site of the building never ceased to be a holy place and to be used as such from the day that the Babylonians left the land in charge of Gedaliah (Jer. 41.4–5). Fifty years later, when the Persians gave permission (and even put up some of the funds) for the restoration of the institutions of Judaism, there never seems to have been any doubt that there was still to be only one temple, and that was the temple at Jerusalem.

It will be obvious that as a provision for the ordinary religious needs of a people now scattered across the whole of the known world, this single institution was wholly inadequate, not to say (for many of them) largely irrelevant. As a result of the original suppression of local sanctuaries in the seventh century there had quickly grown up what could almost be described as another kind of religion, no longer centred on the yearly festivals and the animal sacrifices that accompanied them, but on weekly meetings for the purpose of hearing, thinking about and discussing the sacred writings, which probably then for the first time began to be widely circulated and to have relevance beyond the priestly caste that up to now had created, transmitted and amplified them. This was the religion of the synagogue.

One is here tempted into easy contrasts which are largely true but must be used with a certain caution nevertheless. The religion of the temple tended to be that of the Sadducees, the religion of the synagogue that of the Pharisees. (But it needs to be pointed out again that the Maccabees, around whom the Hasidim formed themselves in 167, were a *priestly* family.) Pharisees tended to be Pharisees by conviction, while Sadducees were more likely to be Sadducees by inheritance. It seems certain, though, that even in Jesus' day some of the priests thought of themselves as Pharisees rather than Sadducees; nor have we any compelling reason to doubt the truth of Acts 6.7 '... and the number of the disciples multiplied greatly in Jerusalem, and a great many of the priests were obedient to the faith'. Fifty years ago an English readership would easily have comprehended a comparison drawn between the Sadducees and the Church of England clergy on the one hand, and the Pharisees and the Nonconformist clergy on the other. Evangelical fervour, though not typical of the former and widely regarded as a dangerous form of rabble-rousing, was on the other hand by no means rare either. There was a formal allegiance to belief, but any intense profession of sincerity of conviction was regarded with suspicion. Just so the Sadducees 'believed' the first five books of the Old Testament but absolutely nothing else; and, as the New Testament reminds us on several occasions, they regarded the credulity of the Pharisees on such topics as the existence of angels, the resurrection of the just and everlasting life with an amused contempt. The typical life of a Sadducee, surrounded and supported by the wealth, ceremony and relaxed harmony of the temple precinct, needed no compensations drawn from another world to render this one palatable. Ordinary people, on the other hand, were more than grateful to the Pharisees for the hope they offered of a better life hereafter to compensate for all the pain and misery of this one, and seemed determined to overlook – as people in great need have a habit of doing – the possibility that such a hope was quite likely to be illusory.

At the political level also the comparison largely holds. The Sadducees were essentially gentlemen. Formal conduct of ceremonies, formal professions of belief were required, but did not preclude friendly and interested contact with outside influences. Just as in England the parsons traditionally supported the existing political set-up, and were well aware that the comfort of their own existence depended on their doing so, in the same way there had been priestly supporters of (or at least priests anxious to avoid any hostilities with) Antiochus in 167 BC; and the Sadducees adopted much the same attitude towards the Romans in Jesus' day. To the Pharisees on the other hand both these things – the receptiveness to outside cultural influences and the readiness to co-operate with foreign politicians – were matters of the utmost scandal. The Pharisees regarded the Sadducees (with justice) as temporizers; the Sadducees regarded the Pharisees (again with justice) as irresponsible agitators. When disaster came a generation after Jesus' time with the destruction of Jerusalem (yet again) in AD 70, the Sadducees – whose views had they prevailed would have prevented the disaster – were swept away by it for ever; the Pharisees – who, next to the Zealots, were largely responsible for it – survived it, rallied the tattered remnants of the nation on which they had brought destruction, and went on to be the creators of what we know today as Judaism.

The other two contrasting groups can be fairly briefly dealt with, because actual information about both Zealots and Herodians is hard to come by. Very little exists outside the New Testament, and as the reader will discover from looking at a concordance, very little exists within it either. We assume (see note 5 on page 377) that the Zealots must be the same as the Cananeans. We also assume, but a little less confidently, they must be the same as the 'Galilaeans' mentioned by Josephus as one of the major Palestinian sects of his day. Such an equation helps to explain, for instance, who the Galilaeans were 'whose blood Pilate had mingled with their sacrifices' (Luke 13.1): they weren't just north-country men, apparently, but political activists. The same assumption also throws light on 'Judas the Galilaean' in Acts 5.37. We should probably think of them as a kind of political wing of an uncompromising form of Pharisaism. Outright Zealots were probably few in number, but some form of Zealot thinking was held by the overwhelming majority of the population – think of nationalism in the Irish republic for a modern comparison. Hence the ease with which they launched two disastrous uprisings (with outspoken support from the Pharisees) in AD 69 and 135, the second one followed by the permanent expulsion of the Jews from Palestine by the emperor

Hadrian. What we call the Palestinian problem is very much the legacy of these Zealots to the modern world.

With regard to the Herodians we have no worthwhile information at all, and the entire picture has to be based on probabilities. We assume that like the Sadducees they had no real popular following and that their political importance derived solely from the importance of those whose interests they promoted. The Herod in question was presumably Herod Antipas, the tetrarch of Galilee; and the reason why he needed to have his interests promoted was that the Herods were an imposed dynasty who had no real claim on the loyalties of the people they governed. Herod Antipas was son of Herod the Great, who had been made king of the whole of Palestine by the Romans in 37 BC. He died in 4 BC and his kingdom was divided between his three sons, half to Archelaus and the other half between Antipas and Philip (the word 'tetrarch' means 'ruler of a quarter'). Ten years later Archelaus was deposed and his territory thereafter administered by Roman governors, one of whom was Pontius Pilate. When Philip died in AD 34 and Antipas in 39, the whole of the original kingdom was restored to Herod Agrippa, a grandson of Herod the Great by one of his sons who had died before Herod himself. It is this Herod who features in Acts 12. Some years after his death (of which it would be unwise to take Acts 12.20–23 as an altogether reliable account) in AD 50 his son, also Agrippa, was made king over parts of his territory. It is this Agrippa who features in Acts 25.23–26.32. One of the major difficulties in the position of all the Herods was their having to be pagans in presence of pagans and Jews in the presence of Jews. The potential embarassment of this situation is well brought out in this later passage of Acts – see particularly 26.24–28.

The natural pairing that one therefore would expect in Mark's gospel is of Zealots with Pharisees and Herodians with Sadducees. So the fact that on two occasions (Mark 3.6 and 12.13) we find the Pharisees and Herodians acting together, apparently in an attempt to destroy Jesus, is surprising and not easily explained. On the other hand we have no reason to think that Mark is mistaken. If we only knew a bit more about the background of this strange alliance, it would probably also throw light on Luke 13.31–33, a passage which in the present state of knowledge is a total mystery. In the event neither party seems to have had any hand in Jesus' destruction, all four gospels being agreed that for this the Sadducees were almost solely responsible. As the fourth gospel puts it in John 11.49–50 – perhaps not historically, but certainly with a wonderful aptness – for a Sadducee no price is ever too high to pay for political stability. The Herodians would have agreed with that; the Pharisees, on the other hand, most certainly would not have.

4

Jesus and the New Israel

(Mark 3.13–35)

> And he went up on the mountain, and called to him those whom he desired; and they came to him. And he appointed twelve to be with him, and to be sent out to preach and have authority to cast out demons: Simon whom he surnamed Peter; James the son of Zebedee and John the brother of James, whom he surnamed Boanerges, that is, sons of thunder; Andrew and Philip, and Bartholomew and Matthew, and Thomas and James the son of Alphaeus, and Thaddaeus, and Simon the Cananaean, and Judas Iscariot, who betrayed him. (3.13–19a)

Having explored Jesus' evergrowing rupture with the official religious leaders in the previous chapter (which we have reason to believe on the basis of Luke's gospel that Mark exaggerates) Mark now goes on to describe those who make up the new Israel. Of whom does this Israel consist? According to Matthew 21.31, as we have seen, 'the publicans and harlots go into the kingdom of God' before the scribes and Pharisees. According to Luke (who on this point agrees with Matthew 8.11 but directly contradicts Matthew 10.5) 'men will come from east and west, and from north and south, and sit at table in the kingdom of God' (Luke 13.29). Mark has some point of contact with Matthew in his description of the call of Levi in the previous chapter (2.14); he has none at all with Luke. The one point that he does seem to be making is the one that Paul makes in Romans and Galatians: that whereas membership of the old Israel had been chiefly by heredity, membership of the new Israel is by 'adoption' (Rom 8.23; Gal 4.5). Jesus' family appears twice very prominently in this chapter, but the reason for this prominence does not seem to be any concern on Mark's part with Jesus' relations as such (though he does, as we shall see, throw interesting light on that); he is much more concerned to show that the ties of natural relationship are less significant than the *chosen* relationship of belonging to the Christian body.

It was no doubt common enough in Mark's day that when the head of the house was baptized, then all the other members were included probably without having very much say in the matter (Acts 10–11.18; 16.15; 16.33; 18.8). But there must also have been frequent occasions when a single and perhaps rather junior member of a household wanted to be a Christian against the wishes of the other members. (The idea that these other members had no right to interfere on such a question would of course have been unintelligible – even to the defecting member himself.) In such cases, as very many passages in the gospels remind us, he must be prepared to choose between family and calling, and to make a complete break with the former in order to meet the requirements of the latter. That is the real point that the concluding material of this chapter is trying to make.

'And he went up on the mountain ...' To the original readership that phrase will immediately have suggested Mount Sinai which Moses ascends in Exodus 19.3 and doesn't finally leave until Numbers 10.33. Israel was identified above all as the people of the Law – the Law which had been given to Moses by God on Mount Sinai. The twelve tribes also, though rather earlier than the Law, like the Law are a defining characteristic of Israel. The mention of 'the mountain' (which may well have not the slightest reference to any actual locality where Jesus chose his twelve apostles – if indeed he ever chose them all at once or in a particular locality any way) coupled with the selection of twelve apostles establishes for the reader that Jesus is here setting up a new Israel to replace the old.

'And he appointed twelve ... to cast out demons': The dual function of the twelve apostles is teaching and healing. 'Casting out demons' and 'healing' for Mark are, as previously noted, one and the same activity.

Some of the questions raised by the list of twelve names that Mark gives have already been mentioned. We have been told the story of the call of the first four of these names (but why does Andrew stand fourth, instead of next after his brother Peter, as in Matthew 10.2 and Luke 6.14?), but we know nothing whatever about any of the other eight except Judas Iscariot. And Levi, whose call we have been told about, does not appear on the list. Philip, who has a large part to play in the fourth gospel, is a name only in the other three and in

Acts. (All references to Philip in Acts apart from 1.13 seem to be to Philips other than the apostle.) Bartholomew is simply a name, which does not even occur in John's gospel (whose author covers his tracks by never giving us a full list of the twelve apostles as such). The same would be true of Matthew, were it not for the substitution of Matthew's name for Levi's where Matthew's gospel describes Jesus' call of the publican to be a disciple. Thomas, like Philip, is a name only in the synoptic gospels and Acts, but has a real part to play in John's gospel. James the son of Alphaeus again appears in all four lists of the twelve but is never otherwise mentioned. Where Mark and Matthew (presumably following Mark) list the tenth apostle as Thaddaeus and the eleventh as Simon the Cananaean, Luke and Acts give the tenth apostle as Simon the Zealot and the eleventh as Judas the son of James; Simon the Cananaean has already been dealt, and Judas Iscariot, even these days, will need no special introduction to the vast majority of readers.

> Then he went home; and the crowd came together again, so that they could not even eat. And when his family heard it, they went out to seize him, for people were saying, 'He is beside himself'. And the scribes who came down from Jerusalem said, 'He is possessed by Beelzebul, and by the prince of demons he casts out the demons'. And he called them to him, and said to them in parables, 'How can Satan cast out Satan? If a kingdom is divided against itself, that kingdom cannot stand. And if a house is divided against itself, that house will not be able to stand. And if Satan has risen up against himself and is divided, he cannot stand, but is coming to an end. But no one can enter a strong man's house and plunder his goods, unless he first binds the strong man; then indeed he may plunder his house.
>
> 'Truly, I say to you, all sins will be forgiven the sons of men, and whatever blasphemies they utter; but whoever blasphemes against the Holy Spirit never has forgiveness, but is guilty of an eternal sin' – for they had said, 'He has an unclean spirit'. (3.19b–30)

He went home presumably to Capernaum, presumably to the house which is frequently mentioned in connection with the place, whether his or not. The size, persistence and clamorousness of his popular following – which he seems to have made no attempt to discourage or to evade – must have prompted the idea that he had gone mad, so much so that his family get together to try and seize and restrain him. This potentially embarrassing detail has been carefully omitted by both Matthew and Luke; it is clear that there was also a Q version of this incident which already suppressed the detail, and which they both seem to have preferred for that reason. John's gospel on the other hand not merely revives the suggestion but even gives it emphasis (John 7.20; 8.48; 8.52; 10.20); the use of the phrase 'he has a demon' is particularly effective, both because it draws attention to the derivation of the theme from this passage in Mark, but even more because in John's gospel – in the most extreme contrast to what we find in Mark – Jesus is the only person we encounter who is ever thought to have any connection with demons. The omission of the idea in Matthew and Luke badly spoils the idea that Mark (and quite possibly Jesus himself) is making. 'Truly, I say to you, all sins will be forgiven the sons of men, and whatever blasphemies they utter; but whoever blasphemes against the Holy Spirit never has forgiveness, but is guilty of an eternal sin.' Mark clearly means by this that blasphemies such as the suggestion that Jesus is mad are readily forgiven; but blasphemies such as the suggestion that the power by which he works is an evil power cannot be. Both Matthew and Luke include this saying, but since they omit the first of the two incidents to which it relates in Mark, in both these other gospels it largely loses its point.

What should we understand the point to be? The point of the first half is easy enough: mere insults scarcely matter. But what is this blasphemy against the Holy Spirit – this eternal sin which never has forgiveness? If the saying stood by itself we would have no means of knowing, and we have to bear in mind that since the meaning here totally depends on the context, the meaning Mark has given it is not necessarily the meaning that Jesus himself intended, assuming that he ever actually said the words. But the meaning implied by the context is once again not difficult to grasp. The test of virtue – the *only* test of virtue – is the performances of virtuous acts (this partially ties up, perhaps, with 9.38–41 later in the gospel), and similarly virtuous acts must be accepted as the *proof* of virtue. The eternal blasphemy is the suggestion – common enough, I'm afraid, in all enthusiastic sects, including Christianity – that the virtuous acts performed by one's opponents must not be allowed to be virtuous at all, but must be seen as attempts to deceive people into admiring such acts with the sinister intention of entrapping them in doctrinal error. It is this eagerness to denounce virtue as itself a manifestation of evil that is the eternal sin.

A small puzzle still remains for the modern reader. That makes sense of the saying, and of the context in which it occurs, but what connection does it have with the Holy Spirit? As we nowadays use the term, none at all; but I am assuming, as I do throughout the gospel, that the Holy Spirit specifically refers to the power of God that descended on Jesus at his baptism and remains with him thereafter (compare John 1.33), by virtue of which power it is that he performs his works of healing/exorcism. Jesus does not deny he is possessed. The Pharisees have blasphemed the Holy Spirit in Jesus by suggesting that his power is in fact an emanation of Beelzebul.

And that brings us conveniently to the next point of comment. Who is this Beelzebul? The Authorized Version (following the Vulgate) here has 'Beelzebul' to make it agree with the references in II Kings 1.2, 3, 6, 16. And it is in this form that it has passed into the common stock of the language, where William Golding's novel *Lord of the Flies* has probably ensured its enduring place: for Beelzebub in fact means 'Lord of Flies'. Despite this, the New Testament form is undoubtedly Beelzebub, and once again the point of the passage is lost unless this form is preserved. It is fairly certain that in Jesus' time the references in II Kings were still (correctly) to Beelzebul, and it is only since his day that the Hebrew text has been altered. The purpose of the change was part of a systematic process of defacing all references to heathen deities in the Bible, and converting their titles of honour into titles of shame.[1] Thus Beelzebul, which means 'Lord of the House' (i.e. his temple at Ekron), has been changed to Beelzebub which means (as noted above) 'Lord of Flies'. But a glance at the passage before us makes it clear that Jesus fully understands the literal meaning of Beelzebul, and that he bases his refutation of the Pharisee's jibe on an exploitation of that meaning.

And his mother and his brothers came; and standing outside they sent to him and called him. And a crowd was sitting about him; and they said to him, 'Your mother and your brothers are outside asking for you'. And he replied, 'Who are my mother and my brothers?' And looking around on those who sat about him, he said, 'Here are my mother and my brothers! Whoever does the will of God is my brother, and sister, and mother.' (3.31–35)

The meaning of this passage for Mark and his reasons for including it here have already been dealt with above. But it provides a useful opportunity for discussing a topic in which Mark himself seems to have little interest but which the modern reader may well find not merely intriguing but even highly important.

The Christian religion, as its leaders in all denominations tend to insist, places great emphasis on the family; and a remarkable importance has been given to the first two chapters of Luke's gospel in particular to show that this emphasis derives directly from Jesus' own family life. Now any one reading the first two chapters of Luke's gospel will scarcely need convincing that *as history* they have very little value; and the same is true of the first two chapters of Matthew's gospel, which to a lesser extent have been used for the same purpose. I have already set out at length in the second section of the introduction why *for the purposes of history* we can also discount the whole of the fourth gospel. In case anyone suggests I am throwing out the evidence wholesale, this leaves the whole of Matthew 3–28, the whole of Mark, and the whole of Luke 3–24 still available for scrutiny as history; that is, out of a total of eighty-nine chapters in all four gospels, we still have sixty-four under inspection. It is a surprising fact that the overwhelming majority of references to the family throughout this material is at least capable of being understood as hostile. And this is even truer of the (admittedly only two) references by Jesus to his mother. It would be going too far to insist that the evidence actually demands this interpretation, but the point must still be made that the most natural interpretation of it is that Jesus was in fact on bad terms with his family, and may have felt a particular animus towards his mother. If I now simply list the relevant passages below without further comment, for most readers the point will be made. I list the apparently favourable passages first:

> Or what man of you, if his son asks him for bread, will give him a stone? Or if he asks for a fish, will give him a serpent? If you then, who are evil, know how to give good gifts to your children, how much more will your Father who is in heaven give good things to those who ask him! (Matt. 7.9–11–13)

> And why do you transgress the commandment of God for the sake of your tradition? For God commanded, 'Honour your father and your mother', and 'He who speaks evil of father or mother, let him surely die'. But you say, 'If any one tells his father or his mother,

What you would have gained from me is given to God, he need not honour his father'. So, for the sake of your tradition, you have made void the word of God. (Matt. 15.3–6 = Mark 7.9–13)

And Pharisees came up to him and tested him by asking, 'Is it lawful to divorce one's wife for any cause?' He answered, 'Have you not read that he who made them from the beginning made them male and female, and said, "For this reason a man shall leave his father and mother and be joined to his wife, and the two shall become one flesh"? So they are no longer two but one flesh. What therefore God has joined together, let not man put asunder.' They said to him, 'Why then did Moses command one to give a certificate of divorce and to put her away?' He said to them, 'For your hardness of heart Moses allowed you to divorce your wives, but from the beginning it was not so. And I say to you: whoever divorces his wife, except for unchastity, and marries another, commits adultery.' (Matt. 19.3–9 = Mark 10.2–12)

The disciples said to him, 'If such is the case of a man with his wife, it is not expedient to marry'. But he said to them, 'Not all men can receive this saying, but only those to whom it is given'. (Matt. 19.10–11)

I take this second paragraph to mean that the disciples take the view that if from now on you are not allowed to divorce your wife, you are better off doing without sex altogether. I read Jesus' reply as implying that ideally he agrees, but in practice most men can't do without sex. There are huge questions unanswered here, but that is Matthew's fault, not mine; and although the Marcan passage looks genuine, I express no opinions at this stage about the authenticity of this appendage to it in Matthew. Also it only doubtfully belongs with material favourable to the family. But about the hostility of the following there can be little doubt:

Brother will deliver up brother to death, and the father his child, and children will rise against parents and have them put to death; and you will be hated by all for my name's sake. (Matt. 10.21–22a)

For I have come to set a man against his father, and a daughter against her mother, and a daughter-in-law against her mother-in-law; and a man's foes will be those of his own household. He who

loves father or mother more than me is not worthy of me; and he
who loves son or daughter more than me is not worthy of me ...
(Matt. 10.35–37 – verses 35–36 are a paraphrase of Micah
7.5–6)

(Matt. 12.46–50 = Mark 3.31–35 above = Luke 8.19–21)

Then Peter said in reply, 'Lo, we have left everything and followed
you. What then shall we have?' Jesus said to them, 'Truly, I say
to you, in the new world, when the Son of man shall sit on
his glorious throne, you who have followed me will also sit on
twelve thrones, judging the twelve tribes of Israel. And every one
who has left houses or brothers or sisters or father or mother or
children or lands, for my name's sake, will receive a hundredfold,
and inherit eternal life.' (Matt. 19.27–29 = Mark 10.28–30 =
Luke 18.28–30)

And call no man your father on earth, for you have one Father,
who is in heaven. (Matt. 23.9)

As they were going along the road, a man said to him, 'I will
follow you wherever you go'. And Jesus said to him, 'Foxes have
holes, and birds of the air have nests; but the Son of man has
nowhere to lay his head'. To another he said, 'Follow me'. But he
said, 'Lord, let me first go and bury my father' [*that is*, 'Let me
wait until after my father has died']. But he said to him, 'Leave the
dead to bury their own dead; but as for you, go and proclaim the
kingdom of God'. Another said, 'I will follow you, Lord; but let
me first say farewell to those at my home'. Jesus said to him, 'No
one who puts his hand to the plough and looks back is fit for
the kingdom of God'. (Luke 9.57–62 – verses 57–60 = Matt.
8.19–22)

As he said this, a woman in the crowd raised her voice and said to
him, 'Blessed is the womb that bore you, and the breasts that you
sucked!' But he said, 'Blessed rather are those who hear the word
of God and keep it!' (Luke 11.27–28)

Do you think that I have come to give peace on earth? No, I tell
you, but rather division; for henceforth in one house there will be
five divided, three against two and two against three; they will be
divided, father against son and son against father, mother against
daughter and daughter against her mother, mother-in-law against

her daughter-in-law and daughter-in-law against her mother-in-law. (Luke 12.51–53 = Matt. 10.34–36 above)

Now great multitudes accompanied him; and he turned and said to them, 'If any one comes to me and does not hate his own father and mother and wife and children and brothers and sisters, yes and even his own life, he cannot be my disciple'. (Luke 14.25–26)

Two final points needs to be made. First, in the crucifixion scene of John's gospel Jesus' mother at one point makes a prominent appearance (John 19.25–27); but in none of the other gospels is there any certain mention of her even being present (see the discussion of Mark 15.40 on page 343). Second, in Acts 1.14 we find that the band of disciples has now been joined by Jesus' mother and brothers. I see no reason either to doubt the historicity of this, or to suppose that it in any way conflicts with what has been said above. Indeed, the fact that she is specifically mentioned here, along with the other women, in my view gives added significance to the fact that there is no similarly specific mention of her in connection with the crucifixion.

5

The Teaching of the Kingdom

(Mark 4.1–34)

Just as the last two chapters formed a contrasting pair, so do this and the following chapter. We have already noted the sporadic occurrence in the early part of Mark's gospel of a formula pairing the activities of teaching/preaching on the one hand and healing/exorcism on the other as summarizing the dual nature both of Jesus' own ministry and that of his disciples (1.39; 3.14–15; 6.12–13). The present chapter gives us a kind of concentrate of Jesus' preaching activity, the next of his works of healing.

It is in this chapter that we first encounter that tiny word with the enormous meaning – 'parable'. Just what is a parable? None of the gospels ever tells us, and all three synoptics try to give the impression that the idea behind them is in any case impossible for the outsider to grasp (Matt. 13.10–17; Mark 4.10–12; Luke 8.9–10); they cannot quite decide whether – in contrast to outsiders – the true disciple should find them easy (as suggested in the passages just referred to), or whether on the contrary even the elect are often led astray by them (Matt. 15.15–16; Mark 7.17–18). But all of this must surely have been the attitude of the tradition to them rather than that of Jesus himself. Can he *ever* have intended – what all three synoptics claim – that his hearers should be mystified by the parables; that they should feel, not that everything was now clear, but that they were being offered profound riddles whose meaning could only be unravelled after a long and arduous membership of the Christian body? We can easily see why later preachers may have often wanted to suggest that; but it is hard to believe that it comes from Jesus' own mouth.

The suggestion that parables are difficult to grasp does not start with the New Testament however. It is frequent throughout the Old Testament, and this is no doubt what has in part prompted the attitude of the tradition to Jesus' parables, in contrast to that of Jesus himself. For the Old Testament, saving doctrine comes from remote antiquity in riddles (Ps. 78.1–3) which only those with special training can hope to unravel (Prov. 1.2–6). This view is the more extraordinary in that it is in fact quite hard to find a parable/riddle/proverb/illustration in either testament which the modern reader will have much difficulty in unravelling, even where (as is by no means rare) the author of the passage has himself clearly misunderstood it.

Some readers will find this an astonishing claim which needs a great deal of proof; and in a moment I intend to give it. But first let us return to the question of definition: just what *is* a parable? I remember as a very small boy being told that 'a parable is an earthly story with a heavenly meaning'. In fact they don't usually have a particularly heavenly meaning at all, not even in the New Testament; and where the meaning obviously *is* heavenly, it is often a sign that the meaning – or even the story itself – is not an authentic parable of Jesus. It would be nearer the truth to say that a parable is a small story with a large meaning. But in some ways this whole concentration on *meaning* is something of a false scent, though admittedly one that has been started by the gospels themselves – we get few parables that are not accompanied by meanings, even if sometimes the meanings are wildly inappropriate. We tend to assume therefore, as the gospel writers themselves seem to have done, that the purpose of the parables is to *explain*: without them the meaning would be difficult, but the parable makes it easy (at least for the inner circle of the disciples). But in fact the ideas behind most parables would be easy to grasp even without the parable. So what then is the point of them?

Let me take an illustration from the Old Testament. The book of Proverbs seems to have been compiled for the use of the ancient Israelite equivalent of university students. The two pervading temptations of university life, as anyone who has experience of it knows, are idleness and lechery. Elaborate and intriguing warnings against both can be found throughout the book, but I hope the reader will not be too disappointed if I concentrate solely on the theme of idleness. Some of the finest 'parables' in the collection deal with just this topic:

Go to the ant, O sluggard;
   consider her ways, and be wise.

Without having any chief,
     officer or ruler,
she prepares her food in summer,
     and gathers her sustenance in harvest. (6.6–8)

How long will you lie there, O sluggard?
     When will you arise from your sleep?
A little sleep, a little slumber,
     a little folding of the hands to rest,
and poverty will come upon you like a vagabond,
     and want like an armed man. (6.9–11)

Like vinegar to the teeth, and smoke to the eyes,
     so is the sluggard to those who send him. (10.26)

The way of a sluggard is overgrown with thorns,
     but the path of the upright is a level highway. (15.19)

The sluggard says, 'There is a lion outside!
     I shall be slain in the streets!' (22.13)

As a door turns on its hinges,
     so does the sluggard on his bed. (26.14)

The sluggard buries his hand in the dish;
     and it wears him out to bring it back to his mouth. (26.15)

In nearly all these instances the meaning is immediately clear even to the modern reader. (The third and fourth excerpts may need explaining to some. 'Like vinegar to the teeth' etc. means that a lazy man is an infuriating employee. And the next illustration is the ancient equivalent of 'Where there's a will, there's a way': in other words a lazy man is for ever inventing difficulties.) But the real point I want to make is that in none of these instances would the meaning be at all hard to understand anyway. The illustration is being offered, not to make the meaning clear, but to make it *memorable*. Some of these illustrations will now stick in the reader's mind, as they have in mine, for life. And that is the point of them. And that we can also assume is the real point of Jesus' own parables.

So memorable have Jesus' illustrations proved that, as we pointed out above, in the gospels it is often evident that though the illustration itself is authentic, the meaning we are being offered is not. In the chapter before us, as we shall see, the interpretation of the parable of the sower is demonstrably different from what Jesus himself seems to have meant by it. In the parable of the mustard seed, first the meaning of the parable has been changed, and then the parable itself has been changed to make it a better fit to the changed meaning. This also is a process we observe in the Old Testament, and it is no doubt the origin of the otherwise perfectly groundless idea that parables are 'difficult'. As promised above, let us now examine a few illustrations of this process from the Old Testament.

For reasons we can only guess at, the author of the book of Judges, more than any other author in either testament, is all but incapable of relating a verbal illustration without obviously misunderstanding it and misinterpreting it. In Judges 6.36–40 for instance we find described what is quite clearly a rain-making ceremony, of a kind one would have thought the author of Judges would be familiar with and the modern reader can hardly be expected to be. The fleece of wool is a cloud; the priest sprinkles water on the fleece, carefully leaving the ground dry; the assistant then wrings out the fleece on to the dry ground. This is transparent to the modern reader, yet the significance seems to have totally eluded the author himself. In Judges 9.7–15 we have an excellent parable to the effect that only the most useless of human beings is ever made a king: useful people prefer to do whatever it is they are good at; kings, on the contrary, are expert at devouring their subjects and useless at protecting them. Once again this meaning, perfectly obvious to the modern reader, seems to have eluded the author. In the Samson stories in chapters 13 to 16 (which themselves are patently solar mythology – this may not be so obvious to the modern reader, who is unlikely to know Hebrew; the original author, however, had no such excuse) we find the following transparently obvious riddle:

What is sweeter than honey?
What is stronger than a lion? (Judg. 14.18)

There are not many schoolboys who could not answer – quite correctly – 'Love'. But the author of Judges apparently can't. We have the most elaborate paraphernalia of a lion being torn, and bees nesting inside the carcase and so forth to explain something that to the modern reader needs no explanation at all.

In fact, of course, he may not be quite so stupid as he seems. Except in the last instance, which to me remains inexplicable, he could have a very good reason for pretending not to realize the true significance of the rain-making ceremony or the fact that the Samson stories are solar mythology; he may be deliberately 'baptizing' material that he knows has pagan connotations that he wants to conceal. In the case of the anti-monarchy parable, we know from the later chapters of the book that he lived under the monarchy and either was or pretended to be an ardent supporter.[1] We know from I Samuel chapters 8 to 12 that originally there had been almost as much opposition to as enthusiasm for the idea of instituting a monarchy; and we can shrewdly guess that this parable gained the currency it obviously achieved as a plank in the opposition platform. It may well be that, since the opposition was the losing side, the author is here deliberately obscuring the meaning.

There are those who would like to trace the same kind of intentional falsification of the meaning in the gospel accounts of Jesus' parables also. But as I think I can show in what follows, the nature of the process, though producing similar results, seems in the New Testament to be more innocent and accidental.

Again he began to teach beside the sea. And a very large crowd gathered about him, so that he got into a boat and sat in it on the sea; and the whole crowd was beside the sea on the land. And he taught them many things in parables, and in his teaching he said to them: 'Listen! A sower went out to sow. And as he sowed, some seed fell along the path, and the birds came and devoured it. Other seed fell on rocky ground, where it had not much soil, and immediately it sprang up since it had no depth of soil; and when the sun rose it was scorched, and since it had no root it withered away. Other seed fell among thorns and the thorns grew up and choked it, and it yielded no grain. And other seeds fell into good soil and brought forth grain, growing up and increasing and yielding thirtyfold and sixtyfold and a hundredfold'. And he said, 'He who has ears to hear, let him hear'.

And when he was alone, those who were about him with the twelve asked him concerning the parables. And he said to them, 'To you has been given the secret of the kingdom of God, but for those outside everything is in parables; so that they may indeed see but not perceive, and may indeed hear but not understand; lest they should turn again, and be forgiven'. And he said to them, 'Do you not understand this parable? How then will you understand all the parables? The sower sows the word. And these are the ones along the path, where the word is sown; when they hear, Satan immediately comes and takes away the word which is sown in them. And these in like manner are the ones sown upon rocky ground who, when they hear the word, immediately receive it with joy; and they have no root in themselves, but endure for a while; then, when tribulation or persecution arises on account of the word, immediately they fall away. And others are the ones sown among thorns; they are those who hear the word, but the cares of the world, and the delight in riches, and the desire for other things enter in and choke the word, and it proves unfruitful. But those that were sown upon the good soil are the ones who hear the word and accept it and bear fruit, thirtyfold and sixtyfold and a hundredfold'. (4.1–20)

'The sower sows the word', we read in verse 14; and this is the key to understanding, first, what Jesus himself meant by the parable, secondly how very different from that meaning is the one given here. The point has not been lost on either of the other two synoptics. Matthew leaves out the key sentence altogether. Luke makes it if anything more pointed still, and may even be giving us a more authentic version of the saying than Mark's: 'The seed is the word of God' (Luke 8.11). In the 'meaning' which Mark gives us, and the other two writers follow, the seed is not the word of God at all; it has suddenly become the *people* to whom the word of God is preached. So we must try and find an interpretation of the parable in which the seed really is, once again, the word of God: not the people who hear it, but the word that is spoken to them.

What seems to have happened is that between the time that Jesus spoke the parable and Mark recorded it the whole nature of discipleship had completely changed. The change was never planned, and even those involved in it were quite possibly unaware that it was taking place. But it was absolutely fundamental. To Jesus the mark of a true disciple was that he had no worldly ties or responsibilities (because he had simply repudiated them), and that like Jesus himself he no longer had visible means of support. But by Mark's day a disciple was a family man, earning his living (and strongly disapproved of if he did not – Ephes. 4.28; I Thess. 4.11–12; II Thess. 3.10–11; Titus 3.1) and meeting his responsibilities (I Tim. 5.8). In a word, to Jesus a disciple was essentially a vagabond, while to Mark's readers he was essentially a respectable churchgoer. And what has happened to the parable is that an illustration which originally applied to vagabonds has been reinterpreted so that it now applies to churchgoers.

What then was the original meaning? The preacher is like the sower. He doesn't plant seeds carefully and then keep a watchful eye on them like a gardener, but simply scatters them and hopes; and everything then depends on what sort of ground they fall on. It is only to be expected therefore that a high proportion of the seed is simply wasted; and yet in spite of this the harvest amply repays his labour. The biggest difference between the original meaning and the meaning that Mark gives us is in the very end of the parable. By 'thirtyfold and sixtyfold and a hundredfold' Jesus quite certainly meant that the scattering of the word produces *disciples*; but Mark's readers are undoubtedly meant to interpret the words as meaning the *good works* that true disciples characteristically perform. In the original parable therefore details such as the path, the birds, the rocky ground, and so forth had no particular meaning at all: they were simply features that were required by the narrative to make it lifelike. The semi-allegorical treatment that Mark gives them here is very typical of the gospels generally,[2] but is unlikely to have had anything to do with Jesus' original intentions.

The disciple as vagabond is a carefree spirit, and has an open-ended approach both to virtue itself and to his fellow men. The disciple as churchgoer, on the other hand, cannot entirely leave behind the disciplines of the ledger even in his Sunday worship. This is even more strongly emphasized in Mark than it is in Matthew's and Luke's later versions. In these the allegorical details have a general application: 'When *anyone* hears the word ...' (Matt. 13.19) – or in Luke: 'The ones along the path ... The ones on the rock ...' and so on. But in Mark, 'And *these* are the ones along the path ... And *these* in like manner are the ones sown upon rocky ground ...' (Notice first of all *ones*, i.e. people, not the word at all.) One can even see where the actual list of names has fallen out from the version that Mark eventually heard from his local resident parson. 'They heard the word all right. But it did them no good. And why?' And so on.

'And when he was alone ... turn again and be forgiven.' There can be no doubt that Jesus did give instruction to the disciples privately in the absence of the crowd. But particularly in Mark's gospel one tends to feel that, as in the present instance, what follows is not so much the instruction that Jesus himself originally gave as the reinterpretation with which the tradition has subsequently overlaid it. (This is particularly true of the later chapters of the work where there is a much greater emphasis on this aspect of Jesus' teaching.) The 'secret of the kingdom of God' has in part been discussed already. It is quite likely that in Jesus' own thinking there was no secret at all, apart from the one dangerous secret that he was the fulfilment of Messianic prophecy. If the saying is authentic, that is the only secret it can plausibly have referred to. There does not seem much to be said for the idea that the parables were by deliberate intention a hidden teaching which the crowd could not hope to understand, and even the disciples themselves could only grasp with difficulty. Verse 12 ('so that they may indeed see ...' etc.) adapts and paraphrases Isaiah 6.10, where its significance is the same as it will have been when Jesus himself used it: not that it was the preacher's actual intention to mystify the audience but (an experience every preacher will be familiar with) no matter how he tried – with argument, with illustration, with exhortation – to convince them, they remained fixedly and stubbornly uncomprehending.

Mark here leaves some of the evidence lying around which shows us just how he put his gospel together. Most readers will scarcely need convincing that verse 13 ('And he said to them, "Do you not understand this parable?"') originally followed straight on from verse 10 ('And when he was alone, those who were about him with the twelve asked him concerning the parables'). The intervening material does not specifically relate to the parable of the sower at all. Mark has here found a context for what came to him as a loose saying, and done it very cleverly. No doubt he has often done it elsewhere – so cleverly that we are not always aware of it.

> And he said to them, 'Is a lamp brought in to be put under a bushel, or under a bed, and not on a stand? For there is nothing hid, except to be made manifest; nor is anything secret, except to come to light. If any man has ears to hear, let him hear'.
> And he said to them, 'Take heed what you hear; the measure you give will be the measure you get, and still more will be given you. For to him who has will more be given; and from him who has not, even what he has will be taken away.' (4.21–25)

'Is a lamp brought in to be put under a bushel ...?' There are readers who will protest, 'Surely bushel is wrong? Surely it must be an error that has crept in, either by mistranslation or by faulty oral transmission?' There is no question but the imagery is ludicrous, but this trait can be so very closely paralleled in other parts of the gospel tradition that it becomes itself an indication that we are here very close to Jesus' actual words. The most obvious parallels are:

> Why do you see the speck that is in your brother's eye, but do not notice the log that is in your own eye? (Matt. 7.3 = Luke 6.41)

> Again I tell you, it is easier for a camel to go through the eye of a needle than for a rich man to enter the kingdom of God. (Matt. 19.24 = Mark 10.25 = Luke 18.25)

> You blind guides, straining out a gnat and swallowing a camel. (Matt. 23.24)

We have every reason therefore to believe that this kind of absurd and jokey imagery was a characteristic of Jesus' original style.

We think we know what this parable means, but only because when we read it we unconsciously remember Matthew's much fuller version:

> You are the light of the world. A city set on a hill cannot be hid. Nor do men light a lamp and put it under a bushel, but on a stand, and it gives light to all in the house. Let your light so shine before men, that they may see your good works and give glory to your Father who is in heaven. (Matt. 5.14–16)

If we now look at Luke's rather less well-known version, we will find our confidence somewhat shaken:

> No one after lighting a lamp puts it in a cellar or under a bushel, but on a stand, that those who enter may see the light. Your eye is the lamp of your body; when your eye is sound, your whole body is full of light; but when it is not sound, your body is full of darkness. Therefore be careful lest the light in you be darkness. If then your whole body is full of light, having no part dark, it will be wholly bright, as when a lamp with its rays gives you light. (Luke 11.33–36)

One cannot be quite sure just what the meaning is that Luke gives to the parable, but one *can* be sure that it is a very different meaning from the one that Matthew gives. The most obvious difference is that for Matthew the light is the good works of the disciple, but for Luke it seems to be his inner purity and illumination. Both, I suspect, simply derive from guesses that the tradition has made as to what Jesus meant by the parable.

'For there is nothing hid ... will be taken away.' The passage we are at present commenting on (Mark 4.21–25), though presented by Mark as a unit, in fact consists of four, possibly five, entirely separate sayings of which this is the second. We can see this is so by comparing what we have here with what we find in Matthew and Luke. Matthew should have included the passage between 13.23 and 13.24, after the explanation of the parable of the sower and before the next parable – also about a sower. (Matthew, however, substitutes what is traditionally known as the parable of the tares and the wheat in 13.24–30 for what we find in Mark 4.26–29.) In fact, although all these sayings occur in Matthew, they all occur in entirely different contexts: Mark 4.21 (as we have seen) = Matthew 5.15; Mark 4.22 = Matthew 10.26; Mark 4.23 is a recurrent formula in all three synoptic gospels, and presumably therefore one that was characteristic of Jesus himself; Mark 4.24 is not exactly paralleled in Matthew but is close to what we find in Matthew 7.2; and Mark 4.25 = Matthew 13.12, and also 25.29. Luke, in contrast, does have a parallel to this whole passage in Luke 8.16–18. (Note that he here omits the formula, 'He that has ears to hear' etc., though it does occur elsewhere in the gospel – 8.8 and 14.35). But he also, like Matthew, gives all four other sayings in totally different contexts throughout his gospel: Mark 4.21 (as we have seen) = Luke 11.33; Mark 4.22 = Luke 12.2; Mark 4.24 = Luke 6.38 (both here and in 8. 18, however, Luke's version is significantly different from Mark's); and Mark 4.25 = Luke 19.26.

I could, if I thought it would be interesting to the reader, examine these three other sayings in the same way as I examined the first – quote them from Matthew and Luke in their different contexts and show how each of the sayings in each of their contexts acquires a different meaning. But the interested reader is probably now quite capable of doing that. For the moment I will be content with the general point that this can be done, and that the meaning of any saying, now matter how authentic, usually seems to depend on the context in which the gospel writer who records places it; and that this meaning (as here) is often very different in each different context. If any reader is still hostile to the suggestion made in note 1 of the Introduction that nothing in any of the four gospels can be taken as the actual words of Jesus himself, the consideration here raised should have convinced him – assuming he is capable of being convinced. I have been able to demonstrate the process in connection with Mark 4.21–25, but we need not doubt that the same process is often at work even where it can't so easily be demonstrated.

> And he said, 'The kingdom of God is as if a man should scatter seed upon the ground, and should sleep and rise night and day, and the seed should sprout and grow, he knows not how. The earth produces of itself, first the blade, then the ear, then the full grain in the ear. But when the grain is ripe, at once he puts in the sickle, because the harvest has come.'
>
> And he said, 'With what can we compare the kingdom of God, or what parable shall we use for it? It is like a grain of mustard seed which, when sown upon the ground, is the smallest of all the seeds on earth; yet when it is sown it grows up and becomes the greatest of all shrubs, and puts forth large branches, so that the birds of the air can make nests in its shade.'
>
> With many such parables he spoke the word to them, as they were able to hear it; he did not speak to them without a parable, but privately to his own disciples he explained everything. (4.26–34)

'And he said, "The kingdom of God ... because the harvest has come."' One would like to be able to say that this is what an original parable by Jesus actually looked like, and one might even be right in saying it. What strikes readers first of all (with considerable pleasure and relief if, like me, they happen to have been brought up in a sermon culture) is that no explanation of the 'meaning' is offered. (I myself suspect that that was Jesus' actual practice: he simply told a story and left the meaning, as here, to take care of itself.) The difficulty with this view is that the parable of the mustard seed which immediately follows it has exactly the same characteristic, and yet – as we shall see – it is most unlikely that we here have the parable as Jesus told it. Even in the parable of the man scattering seed, I would be much more comfortable if the last verse ('But when the grain is ripe ...') were not there, and I do rather suspect that it has been added. Without it the parable would be a story aimed at the disciples themselves: 'Off you go, and all you have to do is preach; the rest you leave to God and the elements.' The additional verse relates – obviously – to the end of time and the judgment. Now Jesus must have had ideas about the end of time and the judgment, and must have mentioned them in his teaching. But of one thing I am certain: the later church was a lot keener on such ideas, and a lot more explicit about them than Jesus himself had ever been. With Matthew it has become something of a favourite notion (10.22; 13.39–40; 13.49; chapter 24 = chapter 13 of Mark, all three parables in chapter 25, and finally 28.20 which may have had a parallel in the original Marcan ending).

The reason for this is very clear. Jesus, unlike his later followers, did not have a tidy mind. There was a difference between good and bad, certainly, but it wasn't always very easy to tell which was which (see note 2 on page 379). To the later followers, almost from the word go, the whole point of Christianity was that now you *did* know – with *certainly* – the difference between good and bad. And the proof of the accuracy of such knowledge was going to be the judgment at the end of time, when the account would be made up, the books balanced, those in credit properly rewarded, those in debit suitably punished. I cannot claim to have evidence for rejecting verse 29 here; all I can say is that it reminds me of that kind of thinking, which does not seem to have been Jesus' own attitude at all. The final irony is that Matthew at this point has rejected this parable altogether, thinking perhaps – and perhaps with justice – it was too like his own parable of the wheat and the tares to be worth including.

'And he said, "with what can we compare the kingdom of God ... can make nests in its shade."' I have twice suggested that this parable, for which Mark once again has not supplied any explanation, has not only had its meaning changed by the tradition, but has then suffered a change in the actual story to make it fit the new meaning. On what grounds can this be argued? The striking feature of the parable as it stands is that just about everything it tells us about the mustard plant is wrong. The mustard seed is small, but then most seeds are small; it certainly won't do to insist that this particular seed is the smallest. And then at the other end of the process, it does not become a shrub, and certainly never puts forth large branches, nor would any bird ever dream of nesting in it. The one characteristic for which the mustard plant is known is that it grows with extreme rapidity; and we can be certain that this was the point that Jesus made in his original parable. The point we are here being offered is the rather commonplace one that 'great oaks from little acorns grow' – and indeed *any* tree would do to convey this meaning. Such a highly

inept and misleading development of the original parable brings
home to us a point which has already been hinted at in the contrast
above between the disciple as vagabond and the disciple as churchgoer. Jesus' original ministry, as his parables show, was overwhelmingly rural; but second generation Christians, as we can see from
Acts and from Paul's epistles, were predominantly townsmen –
artisans, petty traders, household servants one step above the lowest
class and so forth; and it is this section of the populace that has
provided the main support for Christianity ever since. It is they who
have turned the last judgment into a kind of October audit. It is they
who (as here) have emphasized the permanence, the expansion, the
international significance of the gospel (an idea which quite likely
never once entered Jesus' head), almost as though it were a sound
and successful business house. And it is they who have made a
narrative nonsense of this parable, apparently without in the least
being aware that they were doing so.

The final paragraph, I presume, needs no further comment.

6

The Healing of the Kingdom

(Mark 4.35–6.6)

On that day, when evening had come, he said to them, 'Let us go across to the other side'. And leaving the crowd, they took him with them in the boat, just as he was. And other boats were with him. And a great storm of wind arose, and the waves beat into the boat, so that the boat was already filling. But he was in the stern, asleep on the cushion; and they woke him and said to him, 'Teacher, do you not care if we perish?' And he awoke and rebuked the wind, and said to the sea, 'Peace! Be still!' And the wind ceased, and there was a great calm. He said to them, 'Why are you afraid? Have you no faith?' And they were filled with awe, and said to one another, 'Who then is this, that even wind and sea obey him?' (4.35–41)

Why evening? Even if it was in fact the evening, why should anyone have bothered, after perhaps as much as thirty years, to remember that it was? That other notable sea miracle, the walking on the water, also takes place in the evening (Mark 6.47). There the detail is even odder. The walking on the water (6.45–52) takes place immediately after the feeding of the five thousand (6.34–44). Let us take a look at the setting for this feeding miracle:

As he went ashore he saw a great throng, and he had compassion on them, because they were like sheep without a shepherd; and he began to teach them many things. *And when it grew late*, his disciples came to him and said, 'This is a lonely place, and the hour is now late ...' (6.34–35)

The incident that then follows may be highly improbable, but nothing could be more natural and convincing than the setting in which Mark places it: Jesus talks to the crowd for much of the day, and as it grows late begins to realize that they've been without food all day and now have little hope of finding any out in the desert. Let us take the chronology from here. First of all there are five thousand of them.[1] How long must we allow — even in miraculous circumstances — not merely for feeding but for clearing up afterwards? At the very least, I would have thought, a couple of hours, but probably rather longer. Let us now return to Mark's text:

> Immediately he made his disciples get into the boat and go before him to the other side, to Bethsaida, while he dismissed the crowd. And after he had taken leave of them, he went up on the mountain to pray. *And when evening came*, the boat was out on the sea, and he was alone on the land. (6.45–46)

Clearly, as a modern reviewer might observe, the mechanics of the story are adrift. So although Mark connects the story of the walking on the water with that of the feeding miracle, we have grounds at least for suspecting (a) that the original tradition did not, and (b) that the reason for insisting on a night setting for the walking on the water has nothing to do with chronology. And if it has nothing to do with chronology there, it is likely also that it has nothing to do with chronology here either. So what has it to do with?

First of all let us get out of the way a question perhaps in the forefront of most readers' minds. What are we to suppose actually happened? Obviously any answer we care to give to this question will be conjectural; but on the other hand the question cannot be avoided. I assumed in the introduction that the two sea miracles we are told by Mark are two versions of the same event, and *as regards the tradition*, I think this is true. But as regards original history, they might on the one hand derive from any number of events that the tradition has reduced to two; or on the other (and we shall see there is a lot to be said for this view) they might have no connection with anything that actually happened at all, but on the contrary derive from a purely mythological view of Jesus which the tradition has transformed into a miracle. For me it goes without saying that neither of the stories can be accepted as true. For instance in the first story, the stilling of the storm, supposing the wind had dropped — just like that — as soon as Jesus said the words, 'Peace! Be still!'; it would still be an hour or two before the turbulence of the sea had noticeably subsided; but this was the circumstance that was actually endangering of the boat. In the second story, none except the foolishly pious are going to accept that Jesus actually did walk on the water. The fairly pious might try – they often do! – to offer an explanation of how it was that Jesus wasn't really walking on the water but for these and these reasons the disciples thought he was. But where does that get us? It makes the disciples look fools, but worse than that it makes Jesus himself look like a trickster. He presumably knew what they were thinking. Wouldn't an honest man have gone on to enlighten them? But also on any kind of reading there is an even more insoluble problem: if it was night, how could the disciples have seen Jesus? It may be attractive to the romantic artist to portray him as being luminous in the dark, but to the historian the idea is less appealing.

I suggest then that if there is any history at all behind these stories it must be this: that Jesus occasionally accompanied the disciples when they went out on the lake, and that when he did so the kind of weather that would normally have terrified them seemed much less threatening. But as we shall now see, other kinds of explanation are so close to the details of these stories that it may be there is no historical basis to either of them. On the other hand, it is important to bear in mind that Mark himself clearly believed that there was.

What are these other kinds of explanation? Let us first recall what is perhaps the best known passage in the whole Bible:

> In the beginning God created the heavens and the earth. The earth was without form and void, and *darkness was upon the face of the deep*; and the Spirit of God *was moving over the face of the water*. (Gen. 1.1–2)

There is no doubt in my mind that this is the passage that underlies at any rate the walking on the water. It fits the stilling of the storm rather less well, but I suspect that in these two miracles we have two parts of what were originally one story, which described first the walking on the water (along the lines of the Genesis passage above), and then went on to describe the stilling of the storm along the lines of the verse that follows it: 'And God said, "Let there be light"; and there was light.' The two parts of the story may have been separated, and their order then reversed, perhaps to blur the reference to Genesis and the implied claims being made for Jesus – which would not be to everybody's taste, particularly if they were of Jewish rather than Gentile background. This last point is conjecture; but of the connection between Genesis and the walking on the water, and of the connection of these two stories with each other I have not the slightest doubt.

So much for what seems to lie behind what Mark tells us. But how did Mark himself understand it? For I am equally convinced that Mark himself was not aware of any connection with Genesis – if he had been, he would surely have made it more explicit. Despite our own misgivings, we have no reason to doubt that Mark actually thought that it happened. He seems in fact to be telling the story as if it were an *exorcism*, just like all the other exorcisms Jesus performed – the most stupendous of all the works of healing, no doubt (which is why it now stands at the head of a whole section devoted to that theme), but essentially nevertheless just one of a series of acts that Jesus performed in order to bring wholeness to a disordered world. It is perhaps worth listing the various exorcism commands that Jesus utters in the early chapters of Mark's gospel:

> Be silent, and come out of him! (1.25)
> ... be clean. (1.41)
> ... rise, take up your pallet and go home. (2.11)
> Stretch our your hand. (3.5)
> Come out of the man, you unclean spirit! (5.8)
> ... go in peace, and be healed of your disease. (5.34)
> Little girl, [I say to you,] arise. (5.41)
> Be opened. (7.34)

and comparing them with what we have here:

> Peace! Be still!

The reader I am sure can see that this utterance is one of a series, and that the only distinction that Mark draws between this and the rest is the vast scale of this particular exorcism. When the disciples ask at the end of the story, 'Who then is this, that even wind and sea obey him?', as we have seen in the introduction, for Mark this means that this is one of four miracles that more than any of the others should have persuaded the disciples that Jesus is the Messiah. He got this from the tradition; but he does not seem to appreciate the point the tradition was making. He seems to assume this was because these four miracles were a little bit more miraculous than any of the others; but the tradition behind him seems to have been hinting at very much larger claims, claims that had Mark been aware of he would perhaps not have been enthusiastic about.

They came to the other side of the sea, to the country of the Gerasenes. And when he had come out of the boat, there met him out of the tombs a man with an unclean spirit, who lived among the tombs; and no one could bind him any more, even with a chain; for he had often been bound with fetters and chains, but the chains he wrenched apart, and the fetters he broke in pieces; and no one had the strength to subdue him. Night and day among the tombs and on the mountains he was always crying out, and bruising himself with stones. And when he saw Jesus from afar, he ran and worshipped him; and crying out with a loud voice, he said, 'What have you to do with me, Jesus, Son of the Most High God? I adjure you by God, do not torment me'. For he had said to him, 'Come out of the man, you unclean spirit!' And Jesus asked him, 'What is your name?' He replied, 'My name is Legion; for we are many'. And he begged him eagerly not to send them out of the country. Now a great herd of swine was feeding there on the hillside; and they begged him, 'Send us to the swine, let us enter them'. So he gave them leave. And the unclean spirits came out, and entered the swine; and the herd, numbering about two thousand, rushed down the steep bank into the sea, and were drowned in the sea.

The herdsmen fled, and told it in the city and in the country. And people came to see what it was that had happened. And they came to Jesus, and saw the demoniac sitting there, clothed and in his right mind, the man who had had the legion; and they were afraid. And those who had seen it told what had happened to the demoniac and to the swine. And they began to beg him to depart from their neighbourhood. And as he was getting into the boat, the man who had been possessed with demons begged him that he might be with him. But he refused, and said to him, 'Go home to your friends, and tell them how much the Lord has done for you, and how he has had mercy on you'. And he went away and began to proclaim in the Decapolis how much Jesus had done for him; and all men marvelled. (5.1–20)

If the stilling of the storm could be dismissed as having no connection whatever with history, the present story, however improbable its main feature seems, must in fact be quite close to a historical event. What most persuades us of this is the obviously Gentile setting of the incident, coupled with the fact that Mark makes no explicit reference to such a setting in his telling of it. It is clear indeed that he has only a hazy idea about precisely where the incident took place. But he mentions the Decapolis at the conclusion of the story, and for the commentator this makes sense. The Decapolis (the name in Greek literally means a group of ten cities) was an area to the south-east of the Sea of Galilee, roughly corresponding to the Old Testament Gilead but in Jesus' time, as one could pretty well guess from the name, largely pagan in culture. But the incident must surely have occurred on the actual shore of the lake, whereas Gerasa – which Mark implies was the place – is a considerable distance from it. Matthew, perhaps more familiar with the geography of Galilee than the Jerusalem-born Mark, corrects to Gadara – much closer to the lake than Gerasa is, but still not really close enough. A third suggestion in the manuscript tradition is 'Gergesenes', which some ancient commentators (notably Origen) prefer to either of the other two, but perhaps on no better grounds than that in their view the other two were obviously wrong. All three suggestions are found in all three gospels in the existing manuscripts, but the evidence suggests that Mark actually wrote Gerasenes, and so did Luke, and Matthew actually wrote Gadarenes; where Gergesenes came from is something of a mystery.

'… there met him a man with an unclean spirit …' Matthew, for reasons which are hard to discern, has two demoniacs here, just as he has two blind men in 9.27–31, and – weirdest of all – two asses in the Palm Sunday triumph in 21.1–7 (in that case, though, we know why he has done so). What puzzles the reader here is why, if we are in Gentile territory (as the rest of the story makes clear we are), Jesus reaction to the demoniac should be so very different from his later almost hostile reaction to the much less offensive Syrophoenician woman in chapter 7:

> And from there he arose and went away to the region of Tyre and Sidon. And he entered a house, and would not have any one know it; yet he could not be hid. But immediately a woman, whose little daughter was possessed by an unclean spirit, heard of him, and came and fell down at his feet. Now the woman was a Greek, a Syrophoenician by birth. And she begged him to cast the demon out of her daughter. And he said to her, 'Let the children first be fed, for it is not right to take the children's bread and throw it to the dogs' … (7.24–27)

Here no one is in any doubt, not even the woman herself, about who Jesus is referring to as 'the children' – namely his fellow Jews; nor who he means by 'the dogs' – that is pagans like the woman herself. (When Mark tells us she 'was a Greek', he means by religion; it was by nationality that she was a Syrophoenician.) She shows that she understands all this perfectly well by her reply:

> But she answered him, 'Yes, Lord; yet even the dogs under the table eat the children's crumbs'. (7.28)

When you are asking a favour, humility is the proper attitude; otherwise I don't think she would have been quite so good-humoured in her reply.

Why then is there nothing like this here? If Jesus' instinctive attitude to paganism was one of near contempt, as his reply to the woman seems to imply, why is there no hint of such contempt here? Why indeed – if that's how he felt about paganism – did he ever set foot in what he knew was pagan territory in the first place? Part of the answer may lie in the fact the order of events in Mark's gospel is not a historical order. It may very well be that the incident in chapter 7 is earlier than the present one. Perhaps his experiences in the region of Tyre and Sidon had taught him to be much less dismissive of paganism than his upbringing had encouraged him to be. But if so, on some points, as the story here makes clear, he still had much to learn – the most obvious one being that even pigs have feelings.

'And when he saw Jesus ... "do not torment me".' I don't think we need make too much of the fact that the man already knows he is talking to 'Jesus'. Mark gives us no indication of how he himself would explain it – we are left to toss a coin in deciding whether the man knows it is Jesus because his demons have told him so, or because long before Jesus reached the shore there was already a crowd gathering by the side of the lake excitedly telling each other, 'It's Jesus, it's Jesus!' But how about the epithet 'Son of the Most High God'? Isn't this incompatible with Mark's supposedly adoptionist view of Jesus? There is one other notable instance in Mark's gospel where Jesus is hailed as 'the Son of God', and that is by the centurion guarding the cross in 15.39. In neither instance does Mark make the point that the speaker is a pagan, and yet in both cases this is overwhelmingly likely to be the explanation. Both speakers will therefore have meant something very different by the words both from Mark's adoptionism and from traditional Christian talk about an incarnation. If we want an illustration of what they did mean, a passage in Acts comes near to supplying it:

> Now at Lystra there was a man sitting, who could not use his feet; he was a cripple from birth, who had never walked. He listened to Paul speaking; and Paul, looking intently at him and seeing that he had faith to be made well, said in a loud voice, 'Stand upright on your feet.' And he sprang up and walked. And when the crowds saw what Paul had done, they lifted up their voices, saying in Lycaonian, 'The gods have come down to us in the likeness of men!' Barnabas they called Zeus, and Paul, because he was the chief speaker, they called Hermes. And the priest of Zeus, whose temple was in front of the city, brought oxen and garlands to the gates and wanted to offer sacrifice with the people. (Acts 14.8–13)

I am not suggesting that this story is to be believed as history, but it does give quite a good illustration of the very different way in which pagans viewed the possibility of the gods manifesting themselves among men, in contrast to Mark's Jewish-based adoptionism. The only odd point here in Mark chapter 5 is the one already indicated: that Mark makes no reference to the pagan background, even though to us it seems important to explain what is going on. The same suggestion would also make sense of a detail at the end of the story which is puzzling as it stands:

> And as he was getting into the boat, the man who had been possessed with demons begged him that he might be with him. But he refused, and said to him, 'Go home to your friends, and tell them how much the Lord has done for you, and how he has had mercy on you'.

It's not like Jesus to turn down an offer of discipleship, and neither he nor Mark tells us why he does so. But if we assume that the man was a pagan, that is the point that could explain it.

'And Jesus asked him ... "for we are many".' All the commentaries suggest that the reason why Jesus asks the demon's name is that to know the name is to have power over the demon. There may have been some such belief current in Jesus' time, but it is noticeable that this is the only occasion on which Jesus ever asks the demon's name; and if that was Jesus' reason in asking, one wonders why the demon was so very ready to reply. It makes more sense to me to interpret this bit of dialogue as part of the cure, the first step being to get the patient to realize the nature of his condition. It seems to be the name 'Legion' which suggests to Jesus – and perhaps also to the man himself – the means by which a cure might be effected. Another bit of traditional explanation which also does not ring true is the suggestion of 'coincidence': it just so happened that at the same time as the man was cured there was this totally inexplicable stampede of the herd of swine rushing to their destruction in the lake. It seems much more likely to me that the man 'acted out' his cure by deliberately chasing the swine, and that Jesus himself encouraged him to do so. In Jesus' eyes they were of course unclean animals.

'The herdsmen fled ...' and who is to blame them! What I find puzzling here is how Jesus got away with it so lightly. A herd of two thousand may well be an exaggeration, but even a tenth of that figure would be a very considerable loss which in ordinary circumstances one would not expect the owners to be ready to overlook. Did they feel that someone like Jesus had no money anyway so there was no point in pressing for compensation? A more likely explanation, as the text suggests, is that they were thoroughly frightened, and were ready to put up with the loss provided they could get rid of this dangerous maniac (i.e. Jesus himself rather than the man he cured).

And when Jesus had crossed again in the boat to the other side, a great crowd gathered about him; and he was beside the sea. Then came one of the rulers of the synagogue, Jairus by name; and seeing him, he fell at his feet, and besought him, saying, 'My little daughter is at the point of death. Come and lay your hands on her, so that she may be made well, and live'. And he went with him.

And a great crowd followed him and thronged about him. And there was a woman who had had a flow of blood for twelve years, and who had suffered much under many physicians, and had spent all that she had, and was no better but rather grew worse. She had heard the reports about Jesus, and came up behind him in the crowd and touched his garment. For she said, 'If I touch even his garments, I shall be made well'. And immediately the haemorrhage ceased; and she felt in her body that she was healed of her disease. And Jesus, perceiving in himself that power had gone forth from him, immediately turned about in the crowd, and said, 'Who touched my garments?' And his disciples said to him, 'You see the crowd pressing around you, and yet you say, "Who touched me?"' And he looked around to see who had done it. But the woman, knowing what had been done to her, came in fear and trembling and fell down before him, and told him the whole truth. And he said to her, 'Daughter, your faith has made you well; go in peace, and be healed of your disease'.

While he was still speaking, there came from the ruler's house some who said, 'Your daughter is dead. Why trouble the Teacher any further?' But ignoring what they said, Jesus said to the ruler of the synagogue, 'Do not fear, only believe'. And he allowed no one to follow him except Peter and James and John the brother of James. When they came to the house of the ruler of the synagogue, he saw a tumult, and people weeping and wailing loudly. And when he had entered, he said to them, 'Why do you make a tumult and weep? The child is not dead but sleeping'. And they laughed at him. But he put them all outside, and took the child's father and mother and those who were with him, and went in where the child was. Taking her by the hand he said to her, 'Talitha cumi'; which means, 'Little girl, I say to you, arise'. And immediately the girl got up and walked (she was twelve years of age), and they were immediately overcome with amazement. And he strictly charged them that no one should know this, and told them to give her something to eat. (5.21–43)

Jesus is now back on the Galilaean or Jewish side of the lake, but we get no indication of exactly where. It could be Capernaum, but it doesn't say so. The main miracle of the excerpt – the raising of Jairus' daughter – must have strained the credulity even of the very first readers of the gospel. Second or third generation Christians, once the New Testament as a whole had begun to take shape, will perhaps have noticed the close similarity between the healing formula in verse 41 above ('Talitha cumi') and the formula found in a story in Acts – which apart from the formula itself has little in common with our present story except that both are about someone being raised from the dead – 'Tabitha, rise' (Acts 9.40). If they had pious minds (as Christian readers throughout history have always thought that virtue required them to have), they will have insisted to themselves that both stories are equally and absolutely true, and that the similarity is purely coincidental. A lot of modern readers, however, do not have pious minds, and it is unlikely that they will be satisfied with this explanation of coincidence. They will argue (to my mind correctly) that despite the differences in the two stories, the similarity between the two formulae is not an accident.

And the evidence itself (particularly of Mark's gospel) suggests that they are right. The *very* earliest disciples seem to have been extraordinarily interested in the formulae that Jesus had used in his exorcisms/miracles of healing. If we turn back to page 144 we see there a list of nine of them that occur in the first seven chapters of this gospel. And for two of them (the present example and *Ephphatha*, 'Be opened' in 7.34) we are given the actual Aramaic word that Jesus used. It has been plausibly suggested that this interest was initially due to the belief that the actual word that Jesus had used would be particularly effective in performing the kind of miracles that he had performed.

But the evidence equally suggests that if there was any such belief it quickly declined: these two examples of Aramaic formulae in Mark are the only two that we have; and neither of them survive in Matthew and Luke, while in Acts it is the name 'Tabitha' alone which connects the Greek formula we find there with the Aramaic one that Mark gives us here. Matthew omits any mention of a formula in the raising of the girl in 9.25; Luke gives it in a purely Greek form in 8.54. The story in Mark 7.31–37 ('Ephphatha') is replaced by a general summary of various miracles in Matthew 15.29–31, and is omitted altogether by Luke (who perhaps was still paralysed with rage at the treatment of the Syrophoenician woman in the story that immediately precedes it in Mark, which he also omits). If we want a hypothesis to explain this rapid decline in interest in these Aramaic formulae, the first possibility is that since at a very early stage the gospel began to spread among people who had no connection with Palestine, and in many cases not much with Semitic culture of any kind, these formulae meant little to them and so were dropped from the collective memory. And this may indeed be part of the explanation. But to me an even more plausible hypothesis is that healers found from experience that the effectiveness of their ministry in no way depended on the power of these semi-magical formulae; if one lacked the power in one's self, no formula could provide a substitute for it.

So then 'Talitha, cumi' originally survived because it was known to be the actual formula that Jesus used in performing a notable miracle. The incredulous reader at this point may be tempted to toss the book aside. Am I seriously asking people to believe, as a matter of history, that Jesus really did raise Jairus' daughter from the dead? No, that would, I agree, be going too far. But it seems to me likely that he did raise her, and that he did use this formula in doing so. If we look at the formula alone and forget about its present context, we shall begin to notice that it does not by itself imply that the person being raised is dead; only that he is lying ill in bed. It could appropriately have been used, for instance, in curing Peter's mother-in-law of her fever in 1.30–31. This explanation is admittedly complicated by the fact that we find a near identical formula implied in Acts 9.40. One of the two stories – possibly both of them – must be a fabrication, created on the basis of the formula with a view to 'explaining' its origin. My inclination is to *guess* that the raising of Jairus' daughter is the original, while the raising of Jairus in Acts is the fabrication; but I would also have to admit that I have no actual evidence for this view.

What of the sub-plot, the healing of the woman with the flow of blood? The story has some unusual features. This is one of two surprising instances of narrative 'cutting-in' in Mark: the miracle comes to us sandwiched between the two halves of the raising of Jairus' daughter. (The other is the death of John the Baptist in the next section.) Even if that is how it actually occurred, isn't it strange that after an estimated thirty years of oral tradition this connection should be preserved? Another feature is that Jesus doesn't actually perform this miracle at all: it happens, and he then becomes aware of it. How are we to understand this aspect of the story? We must bear in mind that the only person who could give us a totally reliable answer to our question is Jesus himself. When Mark tells us that *'Jesus, perceiving in himself that power had gone forth from him, immediately turned about in the crowd, and said, "Who touched my garments?"'*, any implied explanation of how Jesus knew what had happened is Mark's rather than Jesus'; and we have no compelling reason to believe that Jesus himself would necessarily have explained it in the same way. A further question is just what kind of disease it was that the woman was suffering from: a twelve year haemorrhage and she is still alive to complain about it does not sound all that likely to modern medicine. And was she cured 'mechanically' just by touching Jesus' garment, as Mark seems to imply, or did the cure also require Jesus to say, 'Be healed of your disease'? If not the latter, why does Jesus nevertheless say it?

So far I have raised a whole series of questions without so far giving answers to any of them. This is not just because such answers would be speculative – that kind of admission, horrifying to the professional scholar, has never inhibited me – but because *illuminating* suggestions do not readily occur. If I had more experience of the phenomenon we know as faith-healing (which so far as I am aware even the sceptical are nowadays prepared to allow actually does occur) I might be of more help to the reader than at present I feel I am being; because this story, more than any other in the gospel, seems to be very much about faith-healing, as Jesus himself implies at the conclusion: 'Daughter, your *faith* has made you well ...' Was it her faith that made her well? If so, why did she need to touch Jesus' garment at all? Does Jesus' ability to work miracles depend on the faith of those who are to be healed? The very next section of the gospel seems to suggest that it does: 'And he could do no might work there, except that he laid his hands upon a few sick people and healed them. And he marvelled because of their unbelief' (6.5–6). (Matthew, evidently shocked at the implications of could not, changes this to 'did not' – 13.58). On the other hand, up to now the evidence on this point has been ambiguous. The text in 1.21–26 and 5.1–13 suggests that the possessed men felt threatened rather than relieved by Jesus' power to cure them. There is no suggestion that the man with the withered hand in 3.1–5 was cured because of his faith. In the stilling of the storm above, what sort of faith could be attributed to the elements in any circumstances? The same ambiguity is manifested in the remainder of the gospel. The Syrophoenician woman shows that she has faith, and it is because of this faith that Jesus changes his mind and is willing to help her. But later in the gospel (9.14–29) the suggestion is clearly made that faith is required not so much in the patient as in the healer. It was the *disciples'* lack of faith which prevented them healing the epileptic boy. I understand that this is the view that faith-healers themselves tend to take: it is they, and not the patients, who need to have faith.

What Jesus' own views were on this subject – and even Mark's views – cannot unambiguously be deduced from the gospel text. The position is if anything vaguer still in Matthew and Luke. We have seen that Matthew, in describing Jesus' apparent lack of success as a miracle worker in his home town, unlike Mark insists that he simply was not willing to work miracles in such an unbelieving environment. It is as if Mark is suggesting that faith in the patient is a prerequisite of the healing miracle, whereas Matthew prefers to think of the miracle as independent of faith except insofar as it is a deserved reward for it. The dog's dinner is in the dish anyway; but he only gets it if he is prepared to beg. But Matthew also is far from consistent about this; elsewhere he implies far more strongly than Mark ever does that the miracle does actually depend on the faith of the recipient. The following passage is found only in Matthew:

> And as Jesus passed on from there, two blind men followed him, crying aloud, 'Have mercy on us, Son of David'. When he entered the house, the blind men came to him; and Jesus said to them, 'Do you believe that I am able to do this?' They said to him, 'Yes, Lord'. Then he touched their eyes, saying, 'According to your faith be it done to you'. And their eyes were opened ... (Matt.9.27–30a)

Luke, more than either of the other two, has no doubt that the miracle does depend on the faith of the recipient. He is so convinced of this that he sometimes forces the interpretation on material which carries no such implication. In Mark's gospel Jesus twice uses the phrase, 'Your faith has made you well' (here in 5.34, and also 10.52), and both times appropriately to the situation. Luke produces it four times, twice in the parallel passages to the above (Luke 8.48 and 18.42), but twice in passages found only in Luke (7.50 and 17.19). In 7.50 (the 'woman of the city' who poured ointment on Jesus' feet) apart from the obvious improbability of the story [2] the phrase is fairly appropriate to the context. But what was the point of Jesus saying the same thing to the Samaritan leper who returned to give thanks to him in 17.19; if out of ten lepers faith had cured this one, what was it that had cured the other nine?

It seems clear that the tradition as a whole is simply not agreed on whether miracles actually depend on the faith of the recipient, or are simply to be thought of as a reward for faith, or (as in the stilling of the storm) can be performed solely on the basis of the miracle-worker's own inner power. And it is not difficult to suggest a reason for the inconsistency of the tradition on this question. As we have seen already, and as will be stressed even more in the later chapters of the gospel, the disciples themselves were expected to be able to perform miracles of the kind that Jesus himself performed. No doubt, particularly in the early years, they often tried, and no doubt the degree of success was varied. And no doubt equally varied were the explanations offered of why some of the disciples could do it and some couldn't, some could do it sometimes but not always, and so forth. It is that kind of perplexed argument, I suggest, which underlies the inconsistency we find on the question of how much the miracle depended on Jesus' power, and how much on the faith of the recipient.

> He went away from there and came to his own country; and his disciples followed him. And on the sabbath he began to teach in the synagogue; and many who heard him were astonished, saying, 'Where did this man get all this? What is the wisdom given to him? What mighty works are wrought by his hands! Is not this the carpenter, the son of Mary and brother of James and Joses and Judas and Simon, and are not his sisters here with us?' And they took offence at him. And Jesus said to them, 'A prophet is not without honour, except in his own country, and among his own kin, and in his own house'. And he could do no mighty work there, except that he laid his hands upon a few sick people and healed them. And he marvelled because of their unbelief.
>
> And he went about among the villages teaching. (6.1–6)

Very little needs to be added to what has already been said about this passage. We have noted that although in 1.9 Mark has told us that 'Jesus came from Nazareth of Galilee' he here makes no mention of Nazareth. The reaction of the crowd in the synagogue is not unlike that of the synagogue in Capernaum in 1.22, except that to this crowd it seems inexplicable that someone they have known since boyhood (and had always thought perhaps was a little bit odd) should now be taken so seriously by so many other people. Jesus, who one would have thought had a good grasp of the way the human mind works, nevertheless seems to have been surprised and perhaps even hurt by their reaction. His summing up of the situation ('A prophet is not without honour ...') has become a proverbial source of consolation for many another young dreamer who cannot persuade his family and friends to react to his ambitions with anything other than laughter.

We might as well, though, take the opportunity to put down as much as we know about Jesus' family, though as we have seen at the end of chapter 4, this is a topic on which it is all but impossible not to give offence. We note first of all that Mark knows nothing whatever about Jesus' father; there is no mention of Joseph anywhere in the gospel. Both Matthew and Luke, in nativity accounts which otherwise have almost nothing in common, are agreed in naming Jesus' father as Joseph, so the tradition is likely to be an early one and may even be historical. Was he a carpenter? All Mark knows is that *Jesus* was a carpenter. The tradition that his father was one derives from Matthew's alteration of Mark's text. Where Mark wrote, 'Is not this the carpenter ...?', Matthew has substituted (13.55) 'Is not this the carpenter's son?' Luke in his own equivalent passage (4.22) makes the crowd ask, 'Is not this Joseph's son?" Thus both of them seem to circumvent – perhaps deliberately – Mark's potentially odd description of Jesus as being the son of his mother instead of his father.

We note that Jesus had four brothers and at least two sisters, the entire family therefore being a minimum of seven. The impression the modern reader gets from the gospels and Acts is that during Jesus' lifetime his family were opposed to him, but that after his death they joined the band of disciples. On the first of these two points John's gospel is explicit (7.3–5), but is probably only drawing the same kind of inference from the synoptic material that the modern reader is inclined to draw. On the second point Acts 1.14 is unambiguous. James seems to have become the first bishop of Jerusalem, and to be mentioned as such in Acts 12.17, 15.13, 21.18, probably I Corinthians 15.7; also Galatians 1.19, probably 2.9, and certainly 2.12. We are also meant to think that the epistle of James is by him, and it just possibly might in fact be so. If it is a forgery, the omission of any mention of 'the Lord's brother' from the superscription is a clever touch.

Of Joses (Matthew 13.55 changes this to Joseph – compare also Mark 15.40 with Matthew 27.56) we know nothing at all. Perhaps he stuck robustly to his original view that his brother was a nutcase, and so grew old as a humble workman in Galilee.

It seems likely that Jesus' brothers Simon and Judas are the original pair of saints whose feast day is celebrated in the Western church on 28 October. The reason why this is obscured in the liturgy of the day (Simon, for instance, being made out to be the apostle of that name) is readily accounted for. Though Mark seems never to have heard of the virgin birth, the fact that both Matthew and Luke give accounts of it indicates that the story is early and had wide appeal. At that stage the tradition seems to have been that although Mary remained a virgin up to the birth of Jesus, beyond that point Joseph and Mary had a normal married life together (Mat. 1.25). However, the later view was that Jesus' mother remained a virgin throughout her life. The idea that Jesus had at least six brothers and sisters is clearly inconsistent with that view, and Jerome explains these brothers and sisters as Joseph's children by a previous marriage; but the church as a whole seems to have been less than confident that everyone would accept this explanation, and to have thought it more expedient that the very existence of these brothers and sisters should be played down. Hence, presumably, the misleading impression given by the liturgy for the feast of Simon and Jude.

Even in that liturgy however Jude is identified with the author of the epistle of Jude. This letter, despite its weirdness, may also just possibly be genuine. It has a close literary connection with II Peter which must (as we saw on page 1) be a very late document, possibly belonging to the early years of the second century. But this by itself tells us nothing about the date of Jude's epistle – only that the author of II Peter was very familiar with it. In the superscription the author describes himself as 'a servant of Jesus Christ and brother of James', and we are undoubtedly meant to understand this as James the Lord's brother and the author of James' epistle. If the claim is false, why doesn't he go the whole hog and describe himself as Jesus' brother? On the other hand we can see a possible reason why. With the example of the epistle of James before him, a forger might have thought it was giving the game away to advance on his own behalf a very much bolder claim than that letter actually makes.

7

The Mission of the Kingdom

(Mark 6.7–56)

And he called to him the twelve, and began to send them out two by two, and gave them authority over the unclean spirits. He charged them to take nothing for their journey except a staff; no bread, no bag, no money in their belts; but to wear sandals, and not put on two tunics. And he said to them, 'Where you enter a house, stay there until you leave the place. And if any place will not receive you and they refuse to hear you, when you leave, shake off the dust that is on your feet for a testimony against them.' So they went out and preached that men should repent. And they cast out many demons, and anointed with oil many that were sick and healed them. (6.7–13)

All three synoptic gospels are agreed that Jesus' purpose in creating a band of apostles was mission. It is in fact something of a tautology to make the observation: as already noted, 'mission' derives from the Latin equivalent of the Greek word from which 'apostle' derives. But what was the mission itself intended to achieve? The traditional answer is the founding of the Christian church, but the evidence in fact suggests that nothing could be further from the truth:

He said to them, 'But who do you say that I am?' Simon Peter replied, 'You are the Christ, the Son of the living God'. And Jesus answered him, 'Blessed are you, Simon Bar-Jona! For flesh and blood has not revealed this to you, but my Father who is in heaven. And I tell you, you are Peter, and on this rock I will build my church, and the powers of death shall not prevail against it. I will give you the keys of the kingdom of heaven, and whatever you bind on earth shall be bound in heaven, and whatever you loose on earth shall be loosed in heaven'. Then he strictly charged the disciples to tell no one that he was the Christ. (Matt. 16.15–20)

But compare this with what the author of Matthew's gospel actually read in Mark:

> And he asked them, 'But who do you say that I am?' Peter answered him, 'You are the Christ'. And he charged them to tell no one about him. (Mark 8.28–30)

We can tell from this that were Matthew alive today he would be a delighted and enthusiastic ultramontane Roman Catholic. But we certainly can't deduce that Jesus would have been. The very use of the word 'church' (Greek *ecclesia*) jars on the critical reader both times it occurs in Matthew's gospel (above and in 18.17). Had Jesus really used the word, what could he have been referring to? And if he did use it, why does it never occur in any of the other three gospels? It seems far more likely that Matthew has incorporated into his gospel ideas which had gained currency since Jesus' time, and which he (Matthew) found particularly inspiring and attractive.

So far as we can tell, the very idea of resident Christian communities never entered Jesus' head. The religious needs of people who wanted houses and families and lands were catered for by the synagogues, and Jesus seems to have had no desire to entice people out of the synagogue and into a separate Christian church. What he did want was to entice them away from this concern with houses and families and lands, and to persuade them to join him in his care-free life on the road. And why? So far as we can tell, not because he thought there was anything evil in itself in a settled, bourgeois existence, but presumably because he honestly did think that by doing so they would become better, happier, kinder, more loving, more generous people. People are sordid and mean, he seems to have thought, because they have sordid and mean concerns; they have dependents to worry about, and a standard of living to maintain. If they would only realize that 'life is more than food, and the body more than clothing' they would be released from a web of unnecessary worries and concerns, and would then have an opportunity of actually discovering *life*.[1]

That may be so, the modern reader objects; but it can only be so for a minority – whose freedom even so depends on (is in fact parasitic on) the readiness of others to shoulder the burden of making provision (as it clearly was even in Jesus' own case – Mark 15.41 = Matt. 27.55, and see Luke 8.3). This is a question nowhere discussed in the gospels. As we have seen (page 133) it gets quite a lot of discussion in the epistles (which, we should remember, are mostly rather earlier even than Mark's gospel), where the verdict tends to be the exact opposite of what Jesus himself would have approved (compare, for instance, Luke 9.57–62 with I Tim. 5.3–8). We have no means of knowing from the gospels, therefore, whether the question had ever occurred to Jesus, and if so, what sort of answer he would have given. Did he tell himself that there was no likelihood of more than a very small proportion of his hearers heeding his call to take to the road, and therefore no danger of the begging-bowl becoming exhausted; or did the problem simply not occur to him? We have no means of knowing.

'And he called to him the twelve ... over the unclean spirits.' The purpose of sending them out two by two is presumably practical: 'For if they fall, one will lift up his fellow; but woe to him who is alone when he falls, and has not another to lift him up' (Eccles. 4.10). If the man travelling from Jerusalem to Jericho (Luke 10.30) had had someone with him, it is quite likely he would have reached his destination unmolested. We note also 'he gave them *authority* over the unclean spirits'. Why, one wonders, was that? If the apostles were capable of casting out unclean spirits, why would they need any one else's authority to do so; if they were not capable (and Mark admits in 9.14–29 they often were not), no amount of authority would remedy the deficiency. That is our view; but as far as Mark is concerned (and it cannot be pointed out too often) Jesus' power over unclean spirits was not something he was born with or had as part of his own nature; he acquired it when the spirit of God descended on him at his baptism. And just as God communicated it to him, so he is capable – or God is capable through him – of communicating it to others (see the discussion of Numbers chapter 11 in the appendix at the end of this chapter). Jesus performs his miracles of healing by virtue of the spirit of God resting on him; and now the apostles, having a portion of the same spirit, will have power to perform the same miracles.[2]

It is odd that Mark at this point makes no mention of the preaching of the apostles. The parallel passage in Matthew is in chapter 10, and is worth quoting at length. It is noticeable that the opening verse of the chapter (not quoted below) like Mark makes no mention of preaching but implies that the sole purpose of the mission is the performances of works of healing; but the much more detailed material that follows says a great deal more about preaching than it does about works of healing:

These twelve Jesus sent out, charging them, 'Go nowhere among the Gentiles, and enter no town of the Samaritans, but go rather to the lost sheep of the house of Israel. And preach as you go, saying, "The kingdom of heaven is at hand". Heal the sick, raise the dead, cleanse lepers, cast out demons. You received without pay, give without pay. Take no gold, nor silver, nor copper in your belts, no bag for your journey, nor two tunics, nor sandals, nor a staff; for the labourer deserves his food. And whatever town or village you enter, find out who is worthy in it, and stay with him until you depart. As you enter the house, salute it. And if the house is worthy, let your peace come upon it; but if it is not worthy, let your peace return to you. And if any one will not receive you or listen to your words, shake off the dust from your feet as you leave that house or town. Truly, I say to you, it shall be more tolerable on the day of judgment for the land of Sodom and Gomorrah than for that town.' (Matt. 10.5–15)

Much of this additional detail looks to be authentic, notably the opening injunction that they should 'go nowhere among the Gentiles', even though – as we have seen in the previous chapter – Jesus himself did not always keep to this rule. The message that the disciples are to preach ('The kingdom of heaven is at hand') is the basic slogan given in all three synoptic gospels to summarize the message both of Jesus and of John the Baptist.

Despite our just having read about the raising of Jairus' daughter, most readers will be startled to read Jesus' injunction to the disciples to 'raise the dead'. Did the early disciples ever actually manage to raise people from the dead? The New Testament insists that they did (Acts 9.36–43; 20.7–12) but for most of us this is not a believable claim. One does not have actual evidence that they did not; one simply knows that they can't have. When studying historical documents, particularly documents as early as the gospels, we do not begin with the assumption that, 'Here we have the evidence'; we begin with the question whether the evidence we have here is likely to be reliable. Prior to believing what a document tells us, we have to evaluate it; and the first thing we look for in evaluating a document is such manifest impossibilities as accounts of people rising from, or being raised from, the dead. Whenever we read that, we *know* that this document has to be read with caution and scepticism. This is a prior assumption, agreed, with which one approaches the evidence, and not a conclusion one derives from it. But without such an assumption it would simply not be possible to make sense of the record. If this particular miracle in this particular document is to be accepted as true no matter how improbable, what means do we have of evaluating the evidence at all? *All* miracles in *all* documents would have to be accepted as at least potentially true; or if not, then criteria would have to be offered by which we can tell which miracles are true and which are not. It may be that such criteria will one day be found, but in the meantime, 'The bishop says so', falls far short of being satisfactory.

It will be noticed that Matthew's list of what the disciples are to do without goes just a little over the top. He seems to clarify one point in Mark, though. Why should Jesus have told his disciples they were not to 'put on two tunics'? What he in fact seems to have told them was that they were not to take a change of clothing with them – they were to possess simply what they stood up in. (It is likely that the early disciples – quite possible even Jesus himself – were close to God in their ideas about simple living, but far from him in their ideas about hygiene.) Apart from that, Mark's allowing the apostles to wear sandals and carry a staff seems much more convincing than Matthew's insistence they should do without either.

'So they went out ... many that were sick and healed them'. Here at the very end of the passage we get an acknowledgement from Mark that preaching, as well as healing, was an important aspect of the mission. But he also manages to spring a further surprise on us right at the last moment: they 'anointed with oil many that were sick' and healed them. Anointing, as we have seen in the introduction (pages 31 and following), was primarily a ceremony of consecration in the Old Testament; we also read occasionally of its being a cosmetic practice to signify cheerfulness and well-being (Ex. 30.22–33; Deut. 28.40; Ruth 3.3; II Sam. 14.2; Ps. 141.5; Dan. 10.3; Amos 6.6; Micah 6.15 – see also Matt. 6.17; Luke 7.46) but we never read there of its being a ceremony of healing. Even in the New Testament there are only two references to the practice – here and James 5.14 (just possibly also John 9.6). If it was well-known, why are there so few references to it? But if it was not, it is exceedingly strange that it should have found its way into Mark's gospel at this point.

King Herod heard of it; for Jesus' name had become known. Some said, 'John the baptizer has been raised from the dead; that is why these powers are at work in him'. But others said, 'It is Elijah'. And others said, 'It is a prophet, like one of the prophets of old'. But when Herod heard of it he said, 'John, whom I beheaded, has been raised'. For Herod had sent and seized John, and bound him in prison for the sake of Herodias, his brother Philip's wife; because he had married her. For John said to Herod, 'It is not lawful for you to have your brother's wife'. And Herodias had a grudge against him, and wanted to kill him. But she could not, for Herod feared John, knowing that he was a righteous and holy man, and kept him safe. When he heard him, he was much perplexed; and yet he heard him gladly. But an opportunity came when Herod on his birthday gave a banquet for his courtiers and officers and the leading men of Galilee. For when Herodias' daughter came in and danced, she pleased Herod and his guests; and the king said to the girl, 'Ask me for whatever you wish, and I will grant it'. And he vowed to her, 'Whatever you ask me, I will give you, even half of my kingdom'. And she went out, and said to her mother, 'What shall I ask?' And she said, 'The head of John the baptizer'. And she came in immediately with haste to the king, and asked, saying, 'I want you to give me at once the head of John the Baptist on a platter'. And the king was exceedingly sorry; but because of his oaths and his guests he did not want to break his word to her. And immediately the king sent a soldier of the guard and gave orders to bring his head. He went and beheaded him in the prison, and brought his head on a platter, and gave it to the girl; and the girl gave it to her mother. When his disciples heard of it, they came and took his body, and laid it in a tomb. (6.14–29)

The first question one asks one's self is why this story is included in the gospel at all. It is obvious for a start that its historical worth is small. Kings who offer dancing girls half their kingdom, or cut off other people's heads simply to oblige them, belong (one would have thought) in the *Thousand and One Nights* rather than in the record of Jesus' earthly ministry. Even more to the point, his 'kingdom' wasn't his to give; he was after all not so much a hereditary monarch as an appointee of the Roman state. As regards John the Baptist, the only really worthwhile information we have in the gospels is what we find in the Q material. The summary of his ministry and preaching in Matthew chapter 3 (= Luke 3.1–22) and the account of the visit of his disciples to Jesus in Matthew 11.2–19 (= Luke 7.18–35) both look reasonably authentic. But the birth stories in Luke chapter 1 and the story of his death here (= Matt. 14.1–12) are clearly fiction.

For some reason Luke does not include this story in his gospel at all. He has already told us in 3.18–20 that the end of John's ministry was his arrest and imprisonment by Herod, and he also tells us why. The Lucan parallel for Mark chapter 6 is Luke chapter 9, where he gives us his own version of Mark 6.14–16 in Luke 9.7–9, but then omits the whole of the rest of the story. There are commentators who would like to make this the basis of a claim that Luke has a finer sense of historical probability than Mark and Matthew, but the truth overall appears to be the opposite of this: of the three synoptic gospels it is Luke's that seems to contain the highest proportion of clear fiction. In this particular instance, though, it may just be that Luke actually did know something about the case. It is noticeable for instance that in 3.19, though he calls Herodias Herod's brother's wife, he omits any mention of Philip (see the Josephus extracts below) – at any rate in our better texts.

Our only source for knowledge about John outside the New Testament is Josephus, and he suggests – much more plausibly than the gospels – that Herod's reasons for executing him were much the same as those attributed in the gospels to the priests for wanting to get rid of Jesus, namely the fear of his growing influence with the crowd, and that the enthusiasm that accompanied it was a threat to political stability. That there was some business about Herod's marriage affairs is also confirmed by Josephus; but he makes no connection between that and John's death, and gives a rather different (and much more convincing) account of who Herodias was:

> In the meantime, a quarrel, whose origin I shall relate, arose between Aretas, King of Petra, and Herod. The tetrarch Herod had taken the daughter of Aretas as his wife and had now been married to her for a long time. When starting out for Rome, he lodged with his half-brother Herod, who was born of a different mother, namely the daughter of Simon the High Priest. Falling in love with Herodias, the wife of this half-brother (she was a daughter of their brother Aristobulus and sister to Agrippa the Great), he brazenly broached to her the subject of marriage. She accepted and pledged herself to make the transfer to him as soon as he returned from Rome. It was stipulated that he must oust the

daughter of Aretas. The agreement made, he set sail for Rome. (*Jewish Antiquities* XVIII, v. 1)

Had Herodias been (as Mark states) the wife of Herod's brother Philip, it is not at all clear that there would have been anything irregular in Herod marrying her. True she was his brother's wife, and we read in Leviticus:

> If a man takes his brother's wife, it is impurity; he has uncovered his brother's nakedness, they shall be childless. (Levi. 20. 21)

On the other hand we also read in Deuteronomy:

> If brothers dwell together, and one of them dies and has no son, the wife of the dead shall not be married outside the family to a stranger; her husband's brother shall go in to her, and take her as his wife, and perform the duty of a husband's brother to her. (Deut. 25. 5)

The apparent contradiction between these two passages is recreated not merely in the New Testament but actually in the text of Mark's gospel. When Mark makes John tell Herod, 'It is not lawful for you to have your brother's wife', he undoubtedly has the passage from Leviticus in mind. But when in 12. 18–23 he makes the Sadducees tease Jesus with a question to show how absurd the idea of resurrection from the dead is, he there has in mind the passage from Deuteronomy.

Under the stipulations of Deuteronomy, Herod's marriage to Philip's wife (had he in fact married her) would have been not merely lawful but actually obligatory, since Philip had died childless in AD 34, and Josephus relates his death prior to the passage above. At first sight this chronology causes difficulty in 'fitting in' Jesus' execution: if he was 'crucified under Pontius Pilate', the latest possible date is AD 36, and we have to allow time for (*a*) Philip's death in 34, (*b*) Herod's marriage to the widow, (*c*) John's denunciation, arrest and eventual execution, (*d*) Jesus' emergence as his successor, (*e*) Jesus' own eventual arrest and execution. But Josephus makes no mention of Jesus at all, and the more likely explanation is that John's death took place before any of Herod's matrimonial entanglements, which does in fact seem to be Josephus' understanding of events. He narrates the death after the passage above, but in a way that implies it had taken place quite some time before. Here is how that passage continues:

> On his return after transacting his business in Rome, his wife, who

had got wind of his compact with Herodias, before any information reached him that she had discovered everything, asked him to send her away to Machaerus, which was on the boundary between the territory of Aretas and that of Herod. She gave no hint, however, of her real purpose. Herod let her go since he had no notion that the poor woman saw what was afoot. Some time earlier she herself had dispatched messengers to Machaerus, which was at that time subject to her father, so that when she arrived all preparations for her journey had been made by the governor. She was thus able to start for Arabia as soon as she arrived, being passed from one governor to the next as they provided transport. [*The most likely explanation of this is that Aretas had a good relationship with the various nomadic sheikh's in the region, who therefore provided his daughter with protection and facilities for her journey.*] So she speedily reached her father and told him what Herod planned to do. Aretas made this the start of a quarrel. There was also a dispute about boundaries in the district of Gamala. Troops were mustered on each side and they were now at war, but they dispatched others as commanders instead of going themselves. In the ensuing battle the whole army of Herod was destroyed when some refugees, who had come from the tetrarchy of Philip and had joined Herod's army, played him false ...

[*The authenticity of what follows has been questioned, but not entirely convincingly. The main argument against its being a Christian interpolation, which is what some scholars suggest, is that it so directly conflicts with the gospel account.*] But to some of the Jews the destruction of Herod's army seemed to be divine vengeance, and certainly a just vengeance, for his treatment of John, surnamed the Baptist. For Herod had put him to death, though he was a good man and had exhorted the Jews to lead righteous lives, to practice justice towards their fellows and piety towards God, and so doing to join in baptism. In his view this [*i.e. virtuous living*] was a necessary preliminary if baptism was to be acceptable to God. They must not employ it [*i.e. baptism*] to gain pardon for whatever sins they committed, but as a consecration of the body, implying that the soul was already thoroughly cleansed by right behaviour. When others too joined the crowds about him, because they were aroused to the highest degree by his sermons, Herod became alarmed. Eloquence that had so great an effect on mankind might lead to some form of sedition, for it looked as if they would be guided by John in everything they did. Herod decided therefore that it would be much better to strike first and be rid of him before his work led to an uprising than to wait for an upheaval, get involved in a difficult situation and see his mistake. Though John, because of Herod's suspicions, was brought in chains to Machaerus, the stronghold that we have previously mentioned, and there put to death, yet the verdict of the Jews was that the destruction visited upon Herod's army was a vindication of John, since God saw fit to inflict such a blow on Herod. (XVIII v. 1b-2)

The reader now knows everything there is to know about John the Baptist, and can also see how little worth is the story of his death that Mark relates. But let us return to the question with which we began this whole discussion: why did Mark include the story in his gospel at all? We shall find the answer to this, I suspect, if we concentrate on just one aspect of it: why did he include it *here*?

The mission of the disciples is briefly summarized in verses 12–13: 'So they went out ... and healed them.' Mark could then have gone straight on to verse 30: 'The apostles returned to Jesus ...' This is very like what Luke actually does in his chapter 10. There we find in verse 16 the closing sentence of Jesus' advice to the seventy, and immediately in the next verse we are told of their return after completing the mission – and the effect is in the utmost degree naive and clumsy. But surely, some readers will object, a man like Mark wasn't worried about that? I'm entirely convinced that he was; indeed, I hope by now I have managed to convince most readers that the underlying framework of Mark's gospel is an extremely sophisticated structure – more so than either Matthew or Luke – more so, perhaps, even than John. *One* of the reasons for putting the John the Baptist story here is undoubtedly to create a sense of the passage of time between verse 13 and verse 30.

But if I am right in my analysis of the gospel as a whole, he must also have had a thematic reason for including it; he must have thought the material appropriate to a chapter devoted to the theme of mission. It would in fact have suited his theme much better, one feels, had his exposition of the reasons for John's death been a little more like those that Josephus offers. That would have made the connection between martyrdom and mission very much more explicit; because that, I am convinced, is the relevance he is claiming for the story. Up to now there has been no suggestion of any connection between these two ideas; once we get to Peter's acknowledgment that Jesus is the Christ in 8. 29 it becomes the dominating theme of the gospel.

> The apostles returned to Jesus, and told him all that they had done and taught. And he said to them, 'Come away by yourselves to a lonely place, and rest awhile'. For many were coming and going, and they had no leisure even to eat. And they went away in the boat to a lonely place by themselves. Now many saw them going, and knew them, and they ran there on foot from all the towns, and got there ahead of them. As he went ashore he saw a great throng, and he had compassion on them, because they were like sheep without a shepherd; and he began to teach them many things. And when it grew late, his disciples came to him and said, 'This is a lonely place, and the hour is now late; send them away, to go into the country and villages round about and buy themselves something to eat'. But he answered them, 'You give them something to eat'. And they said to him, 'Shall we go and buy two hundred pennyworth[3] of bread, and give it to them to eat?' And he said to them, 'How many loaves have you? Go and see'. And when they had found out, they said, 'Five, and two fish'. Then he commanded them all to sit down by companies upon the green grass. So they sat down in groups, by hundreds and by fifties. And taking the five loaves and the two fish he looked up to heaven, and blessed, and broke the loaves, and gave them to the disciples to set before the people; and he divided the two fish among them all. And they all ate and were satisfied. And they took up twelve baskets full of broken pieces and of the fish. And those who ate the loaves were five thousand men. (6.30–44)

We were not told in verse 7 from where it was that Jesus sent the apostles out, but we reasonably presume it was Capernaum, to which therefore the apostles are here returning. The situation now is as we have already had it described to us in 2.1–2 and 3.19b–20 – a constant chaos of outsiders pressing in, either to listen to Jesus preaching or to ask for his help as a healer. But everyone needs a rest sometimes, no matter how much other people need them. And the apostles also need to recover from their journey and to tell Jesus how it all went. Capernaum is on the north west shore of the Sea of Galilee. A feature of the lake is that the western shore is mostly low-lying and therefore fairly well populated, while the eastern shore is mountainous and therefore largely deserted. Jesus gets into a boat (presumably belonging to one of the disciples) and sets sail for the eastern shore. But the crowd see him going and decide to make the same journey on foot, no doubt also explaining to everyone they meet on the way where they are heading for and why. When Jesus puts to shore, therefore, he finds himself surrounded by much the same kind of crowd as he thought he was leaving behind.

Up to now the story has been related as though it were history, and there is no doubt that Mark himself believed that's what it was and expected his readers to do the same. He has plenty of readers to this day who insist on agreeing with him, and whose attitude to a commentator like myself (who takes it for granted that such a story cannot be true) will be a mixture of scorn and outrage. The readership as a whole must be the jury to decide whether it is believers or sceptics that have the better case. But even the believer when coming to verse 34 ('... because they were like sheep without a shepherd') has to admit that this is not so much an insight of history as of what we have come to call typology; that is to say, a reference back to the Old Testament which is treated as being symbolically rather than historically significant. In this case the Old Testament passage is:

> The Lord said to Moses, 'Go up into this mountain of Abarim, and see the land which I have given to the people of Israel. And when you have seen it, you also shall be gathered to your people, as your brother Aaron was gathered, because you rebelled against my word in the wilderness of Zin during the strife of the congregation, to sanctify me at the waters before their eyes'. (These are the waters of Meribah of Kadesh in the wilderness of Zin [*see* Num. 20.2–13].) Moses said to the Lord, 'Let the Lord, the God of the spirits of all flesh, appoint a man over the congregation, who shall go out before them and come in before them, who shall lead them out and bring them in; that the congregation of the Lord may not be as *sheep which have no shepherd*'. And the Lord said to Moses, 'Take Joshua the son of Nun, a man in whom is the spirit, and lay your hand upon him; cause him to stand before Eleazar the priest and all the congregation, and you shall commission him in their sight ...' (Num. 27.12–19)

We can take it for granted that Mark had a significant purpose in echoing the phrase he does. Yet in spite of lengthy cogitation, I find it hard to see just what the significance was he intended. The suggestion that leaps first to mind in the event leads nowhere: it so happens that the successor commissioned by Moses in the above passage has the same name as Jesus himself – Jesus being the Greek form of the Hebrew/Aramaic Joshua or Jeshua. Considering that their earliest contests were almost all against the Jews for possession of the pagan mind (the battles against the pagans themselves came later), one would have expected Christian apologists to have clutched at the possibilities which this coincidence suggests. Jesus, the successor to Moses, achieves what Moses failed to achieve and finally brings the Israelites into the promised land. There is a single passage which alludes to (rather than exploits) this idea in Hebrews 4.8–10; and even there, though Jesus is earlier contrasted with Moses in chapter 3, at that point there is no mention of Joshua; while in chapter 4, where Joshua *is* mentioned, it is only the two Joshuas that are being compared, to the detriment (of course) of the former. Nowhere else in the New Testament do we find even the slightest allusion to this coincidence. It is as if, so far from wanting to exploit the idea, early Christian apologists were actually embarassed by it. And it is easy to see why they may have been: Jews could very easily have countered (and perhaps did so) that although Joshua is Moses' successor, the Old Testament unquestionably portrays him as a very much lesser figure than Moses himself.

But there are also undoubted Old Testament foreshadowings of the impending miracle to which Mark makes no allusion at all. The most obvious is:

> A man came from Baalshalishah, bringing the man of God [i.e. Elisha] bread of the first fruits, twenty loaves of barley, and fresh ears of grain in a sack. And Elisha said, 'Give to the men that they may eat'. But his servant said, 'How am I to set this before a hundred men?' So he repeated, 'Give to the men, that they may eat; for thus says the Lord, "They shall eat and have some left,"'. So he set it before them. And they ate, and had some left, according to the word of the Lord. (II Kings 4.42–44)

Compared with Jesus' miracle this is of course small beer: twenty loaves, as against Jesus' five, and on the other hand a mere hundred men compared with Jesus' five thousand. But one feature they have very much in common (besides the fact of making very little food go round among a lot of people): the sole point of both stories seems to be that a miracle like this proves what an extraordinary man the miracle-worker is – and as we now have them there does not seem to be any profounder implication to either story. This, I suspect, was always so with the Elisha story. Moses and Elijah in the Old Testament are both of them also workers of miracles, but for both of them the working of miracles is an incidental activity. Elisha, alone of all Old Testament heroes, survives in the record almost solely as a miracle-worker (II Kings 3.4–8.6) – so much so that if we did not have a convincing account of his involvement in the political upheaval that swept away the house of Ahab and brought Jehu to the throne (II Kings 8.7–9.3), we would be tempted to doubt whether he ever existed. Most of his miracles we would be inclined to dismiss as exaggerated accounts of mere conjuring tricks. Jesus' miracles in Mark's gospel, on the other hand, even if in many cases no more true, can usually be seen as more profound.

One exception we have already encountered – where a story which may have been profound in the earlier tradition has had much of its significance reduced by Mark's determination to see it as an event which actually happened – is the stilling of the storm. The difficulty of offering a convincing interpretation of the two feeding miracles may well be due to the fact that we are here in much the same kind of situation, but this time it is not easy to see what part of the Old Testament supplied the original imagery. As we shall see in the appendix, Numbers chapter 11 is the likeliest guess, but there are serious difficulties about this – as there seem to be about any – identification.

The author of John's gospel, as is well known, refers his readers back to the manna in the wilderness as a paradigm of the true significance of the feeding miracle (like Luke he gives us only one). Is this likely to be the original significance which Mark has forgotten or suppressed? The most obvious difficulty is the fish: how do these tie up with Old Testament imagery relating to the manna in the wilderness? Then again, bearing in mind the close connection between the feeding miracles in Mark and the sea miracles (a connection which John's gospel also thinks it worth preserving), and given that the sea miracles seem to have derived from Genesis and may even have been a covert claim that Jesus is to be identified with the divine being that created the world, how far does the image of the manna in the wilderness achieve (for want of a better word) com-

plementarity with this idea? It seems to me that the claim implied by
the sea miracles is far grander, weightier, sublimer than anything
that can be squeezed out of the feeding miracles. True, the God who
created the world, and created man to be lord of it (don't blame me
for what Genesis plainly states – 1.28; 9.1–7), can also be seen as the
God who preserves and sustains the beings he has created; and the
giving of the manna in the wilderness is the supreme Old Testament
example of him doing that. I am satisfied that this was part of John's
thinking; I am far less satisfied that this was the original implication
of the story.

One thing that can be said with certainty is that regardless of any
connection the miracle may have had with the Old Testament of the
past, it has an undoubted connection in Mark's mind with the church
of the present and the future; for we need not doubt that he sees this
as the first eucharist of the church, the first participation in a sacred
meal by the assembled body of Jesus' followers. The event belongs in
a chapter on mission because this is the end at which the missionaries' journey was aimed at the outset. The original promise was
that the disciples would become 'fishers of men' (Mark 1.17); it is
here for the first time (the first of many) that that promise is fulfilled.
And it may well be that this is the real significance of the inclusion of
the fish. Matthew repeats the Marcan phrase above (Matt. 4.19) but
his is the only other gospel to do so. Luke gives us his own version of
the saying as the conclusion to a miracle story which is clearly meant
to have the same significance (Luke 5.1–11). John develops the
Lucan idea even further: the disciples become fishers of men, not
when Jesus first calls them in chapter 1, but only after his death and
resurrection when he calls them again in chapter 21, a narration
totally lacking in history but packed with more significance and
charm than any story of comparable length perhaps in the whole of
literature.

Immediately he made his disciples get into the boat and go before
him to the other side, to Bethsaida, while he dismissed the crowd.
And after he had taken leave of them, he went up on the mountain
to pray. And when evening came, the boat was out on the sea, and
he was alone on the land. And he saw that they were making
headway painfully, for the wind was against them. And about the
fourth watch of the night he came to them, walking on the sea. He
meant to pass by them, but when they saw him walking on the sea

they thought it was a ghost, and cried out; for they all saw him, and were terrified. But immediately he spoke to them and said, 'Take heart, it is I; have no fear'. And he got into the boat with them and the wind ceased. And they were utterly astounded, for they did not understand about the loaves, but their hearts were hardened.

And when they had crossed over, they came to land at Gennesaret, and moored to the shore. And when they got out of the boat, immediately the people recognized him, and ran about the whole neighbourhood and began to bring sick people on their pallets to any place where they heard he was. And wherever he came, in villages, cities or country, they laid the sick in the market places, and besought him that they might touch even the fringe of his garment; and as many as touched it were made well. (6.45–56)

Here in Mark after the feeding miracle Jesus sends the disciples away *to* Bethsaida. In the parallel passage in Luke (9.10–17), Bethsaida is the place where the miracle takes place. Presumably Luke, like me, thought that Capernaum (on the west side of the lake) was the likeliest spot for the original return of the disciples, and that the miracle itself must therefore have taken place on the east side – which Bethsaida is, if only just. Matthew also seems to have thought there was something amiss in Mark's topography and gets round it by omitting place names altogether (14.13–22). The healing of the blind man in Mark 8.22–26 (to which – as we have seen in the introduction – Mark attaches very great significance) also takes place in Bethsaida; but apart from that, and the probably fanciful information in John's gospel that the disciple Philip came from there (1.44 and 12.21), our existing accounts make very little of Jesus' connection with the place. But a memorable Q passage leads us to believe that in fact it had considerable importance in his ministry:

> Woe to you, Chorazin! woe to you, Bethsaida! for if the mighty works done in you had been done in Tyre and Sidon, they would have repented long ago [sitting] in sackcloth and ashes. (Matt. 11.21 = [Luke 10.13])

This is also the only reference anywhere in the gospels to Chorazin (a few miles to the north of Capernaum), though it is clear that Jesus must have made several important visits.

Despite the fact that Jesus sends the disciples off to Bethsaida,

Mark is unembarassed to tell us that they in fact landed at Gennesaret, a place name which Matthew at last feels confident enough to include (14.34). Commentators seem to agree, but on remarkably slight evidence, that Gennesaret was the district name for the low-lying country in which Capernaum stood. Luke in 5.1 (his only reference to Gennesaret) implies that the lake of Gennesaret is the same as the sea of Galilee – which commentators again accept, but again only on this very slight evidence.

The conclusion of the section is once again one of those general summaries of Jesus' various works of healing. It is, however, the last of them, which may be why it is also the longest. From now on – though not immediately and never completely – Mark places less and less emphasis on Jesus' public ministry, and more and more on his private instruction of the disciples on the dark and difficult theme of his own impending death, its form, its meaning and its outcome. But before this theme gets properly under way we still have one more chapter to go which can be read as a kind of interlude – in part completing the idea of mission with which this seventh chapter has been concerned, in part anticipating the theme of illumination which will be that of the ninth.

APPENDIX

The following passage from Numbers combines in a very remarkable manner the two main themes of this seventh section of Mark's gospel: which are the giving of authority by taking some of the spirit which dwells in the divine leader and sharing it among a chosen few of his followers, and the feeding of the whole multitude by miraculous means:

> Now the rabble that was among them had a strong craving; and the people of Israel also wept again, and said, 'O that we had meat to eat! We remember the fish we ate in Egypt for nothing, the cucumbers, the melons, the leeks, the onions and the garlic; but now our strength is dried up, and there is nothing at all but this manna to look at'.
>
> Now the manna was like coriander seed, and its appearance like that of bdellium. The people went about and gathered it, and ground it in mills or beat it in mortars, and boiled it in pots, and made cakes of it; and the taste of it was like the taste of cakes

baked with oil. When the dew fell upon the camp in the night, the manna fell with it.

Moses heard the people weeping throughout their families, every man at the door of his tent; and the anger of the Lord blazed hotly, and Moses was displeased. And Moses said to the Lord, 'Why hast thou dealt ill with thy servant? And why have I not found favour in thy sight, that thou dost lay the burden of all this people upon me? Did I conceive all this people? Did I bring them forth, that thou shouldst say to me, "Carry them in your bosom, as a nurse carries the sucking child, to the land which thou didst swear to give their fathers?" Where am I to get meat to give to all this people? For they weep before me and say, "Give us meat, that we may eat". I am not able to carry all this people alone, the burden is too heavy for me. If thou wilt deal thus with me, kill me at once, if I find favour in thy sight, that I may not see my wretchedness.'

And the Lord said to Moses, 'Gather for me seventy men of the elders of Israel, whom you know to be the elders of the people and officers over them; and bring them to the tent of meeting, and let them take their stand there with you. And I will come down and talk with you there; *and I will take some of the spirit which is upon you and put it on them;* and they shall bear the burden of the people with you, that you may not bear it yourself alone. And say to the people, Consecrate yourselves for tomorrow, and you shall eat meat; for you have wept in the hearing of the Lord saying, "Who will give us meat to eat? For it was well with us in Egypt". Therefore the Lord will give you meat, and you shall eat. You shall not eat one day, or two days, or five days, or ten days, or twenty days, but a whole month, until it comes out at your nostrils and becomes loathsome to you, because you have rejected the Lord who is among you, and have wept before him, saying, "Why did we come forth out of Egypt?"' But Moses said, 'The people among whom I am number six hundred thousand on foot; and thou hast said, "I will give them meat, that they may eat a whole month!" Shall flocks and herds be slaughtered for them, to suffice them? Or shall all the fish of the sea be gathered together for them, to suffice them?' And the Lord said to Moses, 'Is the Lord's hand shortened? Now you shall see whether my word will come true for you or not'.

So Moses went out and told the people the words of the Lord;

and he gathered seventy men of the elders of the people, and placed them round about the tent. Then the Lord came down in the cloud and spoke to him, and took some of the spirit that was upon him and put it on the seventy elders; and when the spirit rested upon them, they prophesied. (Num. 11.4–25)

Nevertheless, when we try to trace in detail the influence this passage may have had on Mark's account, considerable difficulties appear. The most obvious and unaccountable is that in the above passage the people to be fed are a rabble, and that at the end of the chapter (not quoted here) the people fed by the miracle are then punished and killed. But the description of the taking of part of Moses' spirit and putting it on the seventy elders is an excellent illustration of the kind of thing Mark will have had in mind when he describes Jesus as giving the disciples authority. And the fact that Mark does also specifically quote the text of Numbers elsewhere in the chapter gives weight to a suspicion that there is deliberate reference back to Numbers throughout the section.

We shall encounter a similar problem when we come to the Jerusalem material in chapter 12, where we find a series of references in the narrative to imagery which can be traced with certainty to the later chapters of Zechariah, and where, although on this occasion we can easily recognize the references, it is once again difficult to see how they are meant to be interpreted. Possible explanations in both cases are: (*a*) that these references go right back to Jesus himself, to whom they were highly significant personally, though he never succeeded in communicating to the disciples why he felt them to be so; or (*b*) the imagery was highly siginificant to the earliest tradition, but had a declining appeal as the years went by, so that by Mark's time, though it was still in use, it was less and less understood, and by Mark himself perhaps not at all. A similar decline has taken place in my own life time of the use of sacrificial imagery as explaining the significance of Jesus' death; we still use the word atonement, but we no longer seem to me an anything at all by it.

8

The Kingdom and the Gentiles

(Mark 7.1–8.10)

Now when the Pharisees gathered together to him, with some of the scribes, who had come from Jerusalem, they saw that some of his disciples ate with hands defiled, that is, unwashed. (For the Pharisees, and all the Jews, do not eat unless they wash their hands, observing the tradition of the elders; and when they come from the market place, they do not eat unless they purify themselves; and there are many other traditions which they observe, the washing of cups and pots and vessels of bronze.) And the Pharisees and the scribes asked him, 'Why do your disciples not live according to the tradition of the elders, but eat with hands defiled?'

And he said to them, 'Well did Isaiah prophesy of you hypocrites, as it is written,

"This people honours me with their lips,
    but their heart is far from me;
    in vain do they worship me,
    teaching as doctrines the precepts of men."

You leave the commandment of God, and hold fast the tradition of men.'

And he said to them, 'You have a fine way of rejecting the commandment of God, in order to keep your tradition! For Moses said, "Honour your father and your mother"; and, "He who speaks evil of father or mother, let him surely die"; but you say, "If a man tells his father or mother, What you would have gained from me is Corban" (that is, "given to God") – then you no longer permit him to do anything for his father or mother, thus making void the word of God through your tradition which you hand on. And many such things you do'.

And he called the people to him again, and said to them, 'Hear me, all of you, and understand: there is nothing outside a man which by going into him can defile him; but the things which come out of a man are what defile him'. And when he had entered the house, and left the people, his disciples asked him about the parable. And he said to them, 'Then are you also without understanding? Do you not see that whatever goes into a man from outside cannot defile him, since it enters not his heart but his stomach, and so passes on?' (Thus he declared all foods clean.) And he said, 'What comes out of a man is what defiles a man. For from within, out of the heart of man, come evil thoughts, fornication, theft, murder, adultery, coveting, wickedness, deceit, licentiousness, envy, slander, pride, foolishness. All these evil things come from within, and they defile a man.' (7.1–23)

I have suggested more than once that Jesus' approach to the Gentiles was at best cautious, and that he may well have in fact (as Matthew 10.5 relates he did) instructed the disciples to avoid contact with them altogether. How then can there be a section of Mark's gospel which deals with the topic of Jesus and the Gentiles – particularly in that when you come to look at the actual material, apart from a short story in the middle (the story of the Syrophoenician woman), the section doesn't seem to say anything about Gentiles at all? Despite this objection, the above passage is certainly, and therefore the concluding material presumably, all about Jesus and the Gentiles. It is admittedly not obvious that this is Mark's theme; and of course this topic must be thought of as Mark's theme rather than Jesus' own, for the reason already given – it is likely that not only Jesus himself had very little to say on the subject of Gentiles, but that for some time after his death his disciples also tended to follow his advice quite closely.

If we look at the early chapters of Acts, the Christian community (or the sect of the Nazoreans as the Jews themselves seem to have insisted on calling it – Acts 24.5; 24.14; 28.22) is a totally Jewish body wholly confined to Jerusalem – if not indeed wholly centred on the temple.[1] This seems to be so until we are told of the martyrdom of Stephen at the end of chapter 7. Even in chapter 6, when we read of an argument between the 'Hellenists' and the 'Hebrews' over which of the two groups is getting the lion's share of charitable donations, we should understand this as an argument between the Greek-speaking and the Aramaic-speaking Nazoreans; and we can take it for granted that at this stage both groups are entirely and exclusively Jewish. Stephen seems to have caused his own death by insisting on the highly provocative idea that this fixation with the Jewish temple and the Jewish law belonged to the past, and that God had a much wider purpose to fulfil by means of the new community. He seems to have had a considerable following, and presumably it was these disciples of his who were the chief target of the persecution that arose 'against the church in Jerusalem' after his martyrdom (Acts 8.1b), whose consequence was perhaps the most important development in the whole of the church's early history. It seems to have been chiefly these disciples who were scattered (at any rate in Acts 8.14 we find the most prominent leaders of the church still at Jerusalem). There are two passages which describe their activities (Acts 8.1b and 11.19–21). The first tells us that 'they were all scattered throughout the region of Judaea and Samaria'; in other words they seem at first not to gone outside the confines of Palestine. It was daring of them to include Samaria (8.5) in their itinerary, particularly in view of Jesus' warning in Matthew 10.5; but these people spoke the same language (so perhaps they argued), and had a semblance of the same religion, so why not try it? The response, though more than likely exaggerated in Acts 8.6, must still have been impressive, the more so for being unexpected. We therefore find the leaders of the Jerusalem sect setting their seal of approval on what seems to have started as a maverick venture (Acts 8.14).

However, the really big trauma for the conservative faction of the emergent church – as we can tell from the length and detail with which the incident is related – was the inclusion of the unmistakably Gentile Cornelius in the Christian community. It takes the forty-eight verses of Acts chapter 10 to relate the incident itself; and then the first eighteen verses of chapter 11 go on to describe the acrimonious debate that followed what obviously seemed to many to be Peter's very precipitate action. On one point also – possibly their major point – their fears were fully and immediately realized: once the barrier was breached there was no holding back the torrent. The second half of Acts 11 (the second of the two passages describing the consequences of Stephen's martyrdom referred to above) continues:

> Now those who were scattered because of the persecution that arose over Stephen travelled as far as Phoenicia and Cyprus and Antioch, speaking the word to none except Jews. But there were

some of them, men of Cyprus and Cyrene [*i.e. the kind of people described as 'Hellenists' in Acts 6.1*] who on coming to Antioch spoke to the Greeks also [*the Greek text calls them 'Hellenists', but it is undoubtedly pagans who are meant*], preaching the Lord Jesus. And the hand of the Lord was with them, and a great number that believed turned to the Lord. (Acts 11.19–21)

Once again the response may well be exaggerated, but we need not doubt that it was both considerable and unexpected. It was a surprise which seems to have changed the whole course of Christian history. We do not know the date of Stephen's martyrdom, but we can be pretty sure that a rapid consequence of it was a split between those Jews who felt (and seem to have had good historical grounds for feeling) that the new development was a betrayal of the intentions of the master[2] and those who welcomed it as offering the possibility – soon to be spectacularly realized – of a worldwide (the Greek term is 'catholic') religious community.

The account of Cornelius' conversion itself is heavily overlaid with embarassed and self-justifying comments. Peter's very first utterance on meeting the man falls far short of what we would nowadays consider a warm and friendly approach: 'You yourselves know how unlawful it is for a Jew to associate with or to visit any one of another nation ...' (Acts 10.28). The tone of the conversation scarcely improves as it procedes: 'Truly I perceive that God shows no partiality, but in very nation any one who fears him and does what is right is acceptable to him ...' (10.34b–35) – pagans of Cornelius' day would have taken all that absolutely for granted. The final decision is taken almost in a spirit of defiance, as though Peter is fully aware he is going to have to do a lot of explaining to others about this: 'Can any one forbid water for baptizing these people who have received the Holy Spirit just as we have?' (10.47). And the reaction back at Jerusalem is exactly what Peter expected: 'Why did you go to uncircumcised men and eat with them?' (11.3). Fortunately Peter has no less than six witnesses who can testify: 'As I began to speak, the Holy Spirit fell on them just as on us at the beginning ...[3] If then God gave the same gift to them as he gave to us when we believed in the Lord Jesus Christ, who was I that I could withstand God?' (11.15, 17) Reluctantly (even though the text states otherwise – 'they glorified God') some of them seem to have been convinced: 'Then to the Gentile also God has granted repentance unto life' (11.18).

I have purposely held back the most obvious exercise of all in this self-justification, because this is the passage that makes it absolutely clear that Mark 7.1–23, despite the lack of any obvious indications, is in fact about Jesus and the Gentiles. Cornelius lived at Caesarea; Peter at the time was staying at Joppa, about a day's journey away in the days when most travellers went on foot. The day after Cornelius sees his vision of the angel telling him to contact Peter, and before his deputation has actually arrived at Joppa, Peter himself sees a vision. The relevance of its subject matter to our passage in Mark will be obvious, as will also be the extreme unlikelihood of this resemblance being in any way coincidental:

> The next day, as they were on their journey and coming near the city, Peter went up on the housetop to pray, about the sixth hour. And he became hungry and desired something to eat; but while they were preparing it, he fell into a trance and saw the heaven opened, and something descending, like a great sheet, let down by four corners upon the earth. In it were all kinds of animals and reptiles and birds of the air. And there came a voice to him, 'Rise, Peter; kill and eat'. But Peter said, 'No, Lord; for I have never eaten anything that is common or unclean'. And the voice came to him again a second time, 'What God has cleansed, you must not call common'. This happened three times, and the thing was taken up at once to heaven. (Acts 10.9–16)

It could be objected that I have exaggerated, or perhaps even invented this coincidence. The two passages are similar in that they are both about forms of ritual cleanliness; but they are no less evidently about very different forms of it. The Marcan passage is about ritual cleanliness insofar as it relates to the washing of hands and utensils before eating; the passage from Acts is about ritual cleanliness insofar as it relates to the kinds of food that may or may not be eaten. But this objection fails when we notice that Mark himself has drawn attention to it and done his best to get round the discrepancy. Notice in particular verses 18 and 19 of the Marcan passage (see below). Above I have quoted them exactly as in the RSV translation, but the translators at the end of verse 19 have somewhat expanded what they read in the Greek. There is no doubt that their version accurately represents what Mark meant to say, but it is worth drawing the reader's attention to what he actually did say, or rather to the way he actually said it. The passage would be more accurately rendered thus:

And he said to them, 'Then are you also without understanding?
Do you not see that whatever goes into a man from outside cannot
defile him, since it enters, not his heart but his stomach, and so
passes on' – cleansing all foods.

In other words the bit in inverted commas is what Mark had in the
traditional sources from which he compiled the gospel; but the last
three words are his own grammatically clumsy addition, to try and
make the passage mean what it obviously does not mean. And it is
Peter's vision in Acts 10.9–16 which makes it clear to us why he
wants to do this, and what (for Mark) is the whole significance of this
lengthy, and at first glance not terribly relevant dispute about ritual
cleanness. Everything in all the gospels is relevant; the gospel-writers
were only interested in what was relevant. Nor were they the first:
the tradition behind them only preserved what it thought was
relevant. Some of the gospel material, as we have seen, is close to
authentic history; some, as we have also seen, is pure invention;
some is a combination of the two, so naturally intertwined that we
have no hope now of discerning just where history ends and invention begins. But the touchstone of *all* the material in *all* the gospels is
its relevance to the message that either the tradition as a whole, or
this particular part of it, wishes to convey. In any given passage, if we
have not yet worked out its relevance to those who preserved or
created it, we have not yet arrived at the meaning.

Acts is later than Mark, but the assumptions underlying the vision
in Acts 10 are probably earlier than the gospel. What follows is
admittedly conjecture, but I think we can nevertheless trace the
course of the argument with which universalists like Paul overcame
or silenced the objections of the primitivists among the early Christians. Whether Peter actually saw the vision in Acts cannot of course
be known, but I doubt it. It makes the point just a little too
opportunely for someone like me at any rate to be convinced. Let us
suppose that after Stephen's death, his more eager disciples take
refuge in the remote countryside. Let us suppose that word begins to
get back to Jerusalem that in the strangest possible way all sorts of
people for whom Jesus' message was never originally intended are in
fact beginning to respond to it with enthusiasm. Peter – and perhaps
some of the others – go on travels to see for themselves. While at
Joppa he receives this enquiry from Cornelius, takes the risk and
responds – once again with unexpected and dramatic success. In
justifying his actions afterwards, he does not need to lay claim to any

vision, which his early opponents in any case would have treated with as much scepticism as the modern reader; the fact that he had six witnesses who could testify that Peter's hearers all spontaneously 'received the gift of the Spirit' (see above) would for the moment justify his action.

My guess is that it was the continuing controversy which gave rise to the story about the vision – but even that wasn't quite enough. Wasn't there anything in what any of the original disciples remembered about Jesus himself which, with a little massaging, could be presented as 'proof' that Jesus himself – 'rightly interpreted' – intended that his followers should make no distinction between Jews and Gentiles? (We see exactly the same kind of forced exegesis practiced repeatedly in our own day as enthusiasts for the latest 'ism' suddenly discover that Jesus was in fact a Marxist, in fact a liberationist, in fact a feminist, and so on.) The material with which this chapter opens is the answer. The actual debate looks to be close to authentic history; but the relevance which Mark evidently wants to find in the debate has no connection at all with the history of Jesus himself, but relates entirely to the history of his followers after his death. We do not know just how long after his death, but certainly I would have thought within a decade, and perhaps well within a decade. Paul's persecution of the church, his eminence in that activity (Acts 9.1–2), his conversion, his periods of retirement (Acts 9.30; 11.25–26; Gal. 1.18; 2.1), his various missionary journeys and the length of time he stayed in some localities (Acts 18.11; 19.8–10; 20.31; 24.27; 28.30), all have to be fitted in between Jesus' death and the writing of Mark's gospel, a period we have reason to believe is no more than about thirty years.

The only other point that needs to be made about this quite lengthy excerpt (the reader will probably be relieved to hear) is the fact that, though Mark presents the whole passage as a single conversation, when we examine it closely we notice that the middle section ('And he said to them, "You have a fine way … And many such things you do"') is an insertion. What has happened is that Jesus' comment, 'You leave the commandment of God, and hold fast the tradition of men', could obviously do with illustration (particularly for the benefit of non-Jewish readers), but the original version of the debate did not contain one. Mark himself seems to have supplied one from another of the many fragments that went up to make his sources, and to have done it with exemplary skill.

And from there he arose and went away to the region of Tyre and Sidon. And he entered a house, and would not have any one know it; yet he could not be hid. But immediately a woman, whose little daughter was possessed by an unclean spirit, heard of him, and came and fell down at his feet. Now the woman was a Greek, a Syrophoenician by birth. And she begged him to cast the demon out of her daughter. And he said to her, 'Let the children first be fed, for it is not right to take the children's bread and throw it to the dogs'. But she answered him, 'Yes, Lord; yet even the dogs under the table eat the children's crumbs'. And he said to her, 'For this saying you may go your way; the demon has left your daughter'. And she went home, and found the child lying in bed, and the demon gone. (7.24–30)

Tyre and Sidon are two ancient Phoenician ports to the north of Palestine, Tyre being about twenty miles south of Sidon. Their frequent pairing in the later Old Testament books (Jer. 25.22; 27.3; 47.4; Joel 3.4; Zech. 9.2) is presumably due to the fact that although both had their own independent rulers, they were by far the most prominent Phoenician cities. I have already drawn attention to the Q passage – which looks to be reasonably authentic – in which Jesus mentions them:

Woe to you, Chorazin! woe to you, Bethsaida! for if the mighty works done in you had been done in Tyre and Sidon, they would have repented long ago in sackcloth and ashes. But I tell you, it shall be more tolerable on the day of judgment for Tyre and Sidon than for you ... (Matt. 11.21–22 = Luke 10.13–14)

The implications here – which are in part confirmed, in part contradicted by the above excerpt from Mark – are that Tyre and Sidon, not being Jewish territory, have not been favoured with mighty works; whereas Chorazin and Bethsaida, which are Jewish, have been abundantly favoured. Mark here portrays Jesus as being instinctively reluctant to perform mighty works for Gentiles, but not so reluctant as to be obdurate. The passage also implies that the reluctance may be due not so much to Jesus' rejection of Tyre and Sidon (if that were the case, what would be the point of visiting them at all, which the Q passage above confirms that he did) as to uncertainty – uncertainty as to whether Gentiles have the kind of faith which makes it possible to perform works of healing. That is certainly the implication of the Marcan excerpt here; the woman only has to persist, and she gets the miracle she asks for.

This is also the only example in Mark's gospel of healing by (as it were) remote control. Jesus does not come with her – as he did with Jairus, enter her house, take hold of her daughter's hand and raise her up. Without moving from where he stands he tells her, 'Yes, I've done that for you', and without any further assurance she has to set off home and hope that everything will be as promised when she gets there. This, once again, raises severe problems of credibility for most of us – so severe that we cannot hope for any kind of 'explanation', but have to be content merely with pointing it out. The theme, though, is one that is taken up by all three of the other gospels (Matt. 8.5–17 = Luke 7.1–10, and see also John 4.46–54). The point that is *heavily* stressed in this Q fragment is that the centurion is a gentile (a variant of the Cornelius theme?), that his faith is very much greater than that of Jesus' fellow Jews, and that it is people like him who go first into the kingdom of heaven. It may well be that the same ideas are at the back of Mark's mind as he writes this story up; if so, it virtually relieves us of the need to accept as fact that the miracle was performed at a distance.

> Then he returned from the region of Tyre, and went through Sidon to the Sea of Galilee, through the region of the Decapolis. And they brought to him a man who was deaf and had an impediment in his speech; and they besought him to lay his hand upon him. And taking him aside from the multitude privately, he put his fingers into his ears, and he spat and touched his tongue; and looking up to heaven, he sighed, and said to him, 'Ephphatha', that is, 'Be opened'. And his ears were opened, his tongue was released, and he spoke plainly. And he charged them to tell no one; but the more he charged them, the more zealously they proclaimed it. And they were astonished beyond measure, saying, 'He has done all things well; he even makes the deaf hear and the dumb speak.' (7.31–37)

To 'return from the region of Tyre ... through Sidon to the Sea of Galilee' is a bit like travelling from London to Brighton via Watford. Nor, as we have seen, is this the only occasion where it is clear that Mark is either careless of topography or (more probably) does not know the area. The Decapolis is that same part of the world where the healing of Legion took place. We decided then that however unlikely the central event of that story sounded in the telling, it was in all probability close to what actually happened. I feel less confident here. I have given reasons (see page 151) for thinking that, like 'Talitha cumi', the formula 'Ephphatha' is one that Jesus actually used, and it has been remembered in the hope that for that very reason it will be additionally effective when used by the disciples in their healing ministry. But, like the story of Tabitha in Acts, it looks to me as if the story here owes more to the remembered formula than it does to history. By that I mean it's quite likely that at an earlier stage in the tradition only the single word 'Ephphatha' was remembered, and this story has been totally invented to create a setting for it.

Even if the story does derive from an actual event, it seems likely to me that its present form has been influenced by the formula in two possible ways. The first and most obvious is that the story we have is more miraculous than any original event can have been; the second is that certainly for Mark, and perhaps also for the tradition behind him, it has a significance which has nothing to do with history at all. Bearing in mind the thematic structure of Mark's gospel – something which I feel has now been sufficiently demonstrated to require no further argument – and the position of this story in it, we are probably justified in interpreting it as a suggestion that Jesus is here opening the ears and loosening the tongue of the Gentile world, so that they too can not only hear the gospel, but can also now go on to preach it to others. Although it could be argued that the concluding two verses of the excerpt (from 'And he charged them to tell no one …') are against this interpretation, on the other hand these two verses are themselves inconsistent with what Mark has told us earlier in verse 33 ('And taking him aside from the multitude privately …') – in verse 33 there are apparently no witnesses, while in verses 36 and 37 there are lots of them. It is possible also (though some readers may find this fanciful) that these last two verses summarize the history of Jesus and the Gentiles: Jesus himself wanted his message kept from them, but in the event this was not possible.

In those days, when again a great crowd had gathered, and they had nothing to eat, he called his disciples to him, and said to them, 'I have compassion on the crowd, because they have been with me now three days, and have nothing to eat; and if I send them away hungry to their homes, they will faint on the way; and some of them have come a long way'. And his disciples answered him, 'How can one feed these men with bread here in the desert?' And he asked them, 'How many loaves have you?' They said, 'Seven'. And he commanded the crowd to sit down on the ground; and he took the seven loaves, and having given thanks he broke them and gave them to his disciples to set before the people; and they set them before the crowd. And they had a few small fish; and having blessed them, he commanded that these also should be set before them. And they ate, and were satisfied; and they took up the broken pieces left over, seven baskets full. And there were about four thousand people. And he sent them away; and immediately he got into the boat with his disciples, and went to the district of Dalmanutha. (8.1–10)

It is not possible that Mark included what appear to be two variants of much the same story so close together in his gospel by inadvertence, and the suggestion is not new that he intended the first feeding miracle to stand for the gathering of the Jews into the kingdom, and the second to stand for the gathering of the Gentiles. I headed the previous chapter 'The Mission of the Kingdom', and this 'The Kingdom and the Gentiles'; but it might have been neater to describe the previous chapter specifically as 'The Mission of the Kingdom to the Jews', and this one as 'The Mission of the Kingdom to the Gentiles'. However remote the idea seemed at first, it became clear on examination that even the lengthy debate in the first half of the present chapter on the subject of the clean and the unclean is in fact a kind of cryptogram for the mission to the Gentiles – historically inaugurated not by Jesus himself but by the conversion of Cornelius. Just as the section dealing with the mission to the Jews ends with the story of their being miraculously fed in communion with Jesus, so here the section dealing with the mission to the Gentiles ends similarly.

There are those who would want to suggest that the different numbers involved in the two stories actually imply such an interpretation. In the first story five thousand are fed by five loaves and two fish, and twelve baskets of fragments remain; in the second story four thousand are fed by seven loaves and 'a few small fish', and seven baskets of fragments remain. There is an obvious congruity between the twelve baskets in the first story and the twelve tribes of Israel, but any alleged correspondence between the seven baskets and the supposed number of Gentile nations is much less obvious;[4]

but as we shall see, the case – though far from strong – is stronger than it seems at first. It is worth comparing Mark in this connection not so much with Matthew as with Luke. Matthew here seems to take Mark pretty much as he finds him; the feeding of the five thousand is given in 14.13–21, that of the four thousand in 15.32–39. All numbers in both versions are the same, with the exception that Matthew both times increases the actual size of the crowd by adding 'besides women and children' (14.21; 15.38). Against his usual practice, Matthew offers not a word of explanation to the puzzled reader why the story should be told twice. Perhaps on this occasion he himself was puzzled; though if that were so, one would have expected him simply to omit one of the two variants.

But the comparison with Luke is very much more interesting. He gives the feeding of the five thousand only, in 9.12–17. Did he leave out the other feeding miracle because he felt the repetition was unnecessary? He may have, of course; but a close scrutiny of his gospel suggests two other possible reasons. First, it is noticeable that after Mark 6.44 (= Luke 9.17) Luke leaves out everything until he gets to Mark 8.27 (= Luke 9.18b); moreover Luke 9.18a as it stands is almost gibberish: 'Now it happened that as he was praying alone, the disciples were with him ...' It is very plausibly suggested that Luke's copy of Mark's gospel had a tear in the roll, and that the first fragment ended with Mark 6.46 ('And after he had taken leave of them, he went up on the mountain to pray') while the second began with Mark 8.27b ('... and on the way he asked his disciples ...'). This would explain both why Luke 9.18b reads as it does, and also why everything in Mark between these two verses is missing. But it is easy also to suggest a second explanation. As far as I am concerned all four gospels – even the Old Testament-minded Matthew – were written mainly for a Gentile readership; but it is particularly obvious that Luke was. Once this is understood, there are obvious reasons why he should have omitted the whole of the debate about ritual purity in Mark 7.1–23 – most readers would not grasp what the real implications were and would be either bored or mystified; those that did grasp them might well be offended. All would be offended by the implications of the healing of the Syrophoenician's daughter. On either side of this material, the walking on the water may have been left out either as coming dangerously close to making Jesus look like a pointless exhibitionist; or Luke may simply have felt, as the modern reader feels, that this reduplicates the stilling of the storm

(Mark 4.35–41 = Luke 8.22–25). The sense of reduplication would overwhelmingly apply also in the case of the second feeding miracle.

So far the argument along these lines is strong; we come now – not so much to the weak points, but to points that are less strong. We are left with four passages: the Ephphatha miracle (Mark 7.31–37), the refusal of a sign (Mark 8.11–13), the discussion of the significance of the feeding miracles (Mark 8.14–21) and the healing of the blind man of Bethsaida (Mark 8.22–26). The Ephphatha miracle may have been left out for the very reason that Mark included it, the use of the Aramaic formula. None of Luke's readers would have any acquaintance with Aramaic, and any idea that such original formulae had unique power in performing healing miracles would have long been out of date. The refusal of a sign may have struck Luke, as it strikes the modern reader, as being inconsistent with Jesus' activity throughout the rest of the gospel. The discussion of the feeding miracles (the arguments, I'm afraid tend to get progressively weaker) loses its force if only one of the miracles has been included. And no one seems yet to have had the ingenuity to offer a convincing reason why the healing of the blind man of Bethsaida has been omitted.

But, to return to the original point, there is a third possible explanation why Luke may have deliberately omitted the second feeding miracle, which has nothing to do with any of the arguments above. Although Matthew and Mark have two feeding miracles, they have only one mission of the apostles (Matt. 10.5–42; Mark 6.7–13); although Luke has only one feeding miracle, he has two missions: the first of the twelve apostles only (Luke 9.1–6), the second of a band of seventy disciples other than the apostles in 10.1–20. Did Luke think of the first as being a mission to the Jews, and the second as being a mission to the Gentiles? The account of the first mission gives no indication; but the inference would be a fair one if we could find a definite clue in the second mission that it is a mission to the Gentiles – and we can. It is in the course of his instruction to the seventy that Luke makes Jesus say (this is the third time I have quoted the passage):

> Woe to you, Chorazin! woe to you, Bethsaida! for if the mighty works done in you had been done in Tyre and Sidon, they would have repented long ago, sitting in sackcloth and ashes. But it shall be more tolerable in the judgment for Tyre and Sidon than for you. And you, Capernaum, will you be exalted to heaven? You shall be brought down to Hades. (Luke 10.13–15)

In other words, Jesus' instruction to the seventy disciples includes a condemnation of the Jewish world in which his ministry has been conducted for having rejected him, and an implication that the Gentile world, given the chance, will be more receptive.

Is the figure of seventy disciples therefore also meant to indicate that this is a mission to the Gentiles? Because if it does, we then have a much stronger case for supposing that the seven baskets of fragments at the end of Mark's second feeding miracle are also an indication that this miracle relates to the Gentiles, while the earlier one relates to the Jews. Unfortunately some early manuscripts of Luke's gospel give the figure as seventy-two, and this – just because of its inconvenience – is likely to be the correct reading. Indeed the alteration to seventy may very well have been made precisely to support the argument I am now putting forward. Some people may feel that seventy-two is close enough, and still accept it. Beyond that point I think it is impossible to go.

9

The Solving of the Riddle

(Mark 8.11–9.1)

The Pharisees came and began to argue with him, seeking from him a sign from heaven, to test him. And he sighed deeply in his spirit, and said, 'Why does this generation seek a sign? Truly, I say to you, no sign shall be given to this generation'.

And he left them, and getting into the boat again he departed to the other side. Now they had forgotten to bring bread; and they had only one loaf with them in the boat. And he cautioned them, saying, 'Take heed, beware of the leaven of the Pharisees and the leaven of Herod'. And they discussed it with one another, saying, 'We have no bread'. And being aware of it, Jesus said to them, 'Why do you discuss the fact that you have no bread? Do you not yet perceive or understand? Are your hearts hardened? Having eyes do you not see, and having ears do you not hear? And do you not remember? When I broke the five loaves for the five thousand, how many baskets full of broken pieces did you take up?' They said to him, 'Twelve'. 'And the seven for the four thousand, how many baskets full of broken pieces did you take up?' And they said to him, 'Seven'. And he said to them, 'Do you not yet understand?' (8.11–21)

The first of these two paragraphs is one of those few occasions (even in the synoptic gospels) when one is fully confident that one is in close encounter with actual history. One is confident of this precisely because the implications of the passage are so entirely contradicted by almost everything else in the record. Out of the eight sections of the gospel examined so far, only three of them (the first, the fourth and the fifth) have contained no miracles at all; the sixth is devoted to nothing else, and the seventh and eighth contain more than one each, including the two stupendous feeding miracles. What sense does it now make to have the Pharisees asking for a sign? It makes so little sense that one is confident they must have actually done so.

As regards what sort of sign they were asking for, I believe I have said enough in the Appendix which starts on page 37. But the position of the material here does raise a further question, which is this: Mark does not himself offer any explanation why the Pharisees ask for a sign. Assuming that the explanation I have offered in the Introduction is the true one, how could Mark's original readers have known that? And in fact we can raise the same question retrospectively about most of the gospel so far. It does indeed seem to be true that the gospel has been constructed on a thematic framework, and the recognition of this framework is often important for understanding the meaning of a particular passage (the debate about the clean and the unclean at the beginning of the previous section is the most obvious example of this); but how could the original readers possibly have known about this framework when they get so little help from the author himself in recognizing it?

The answer is that the original readership was probably a small local body or church, and that the author and the readers were intimately known to each other. When the original community (those that could read) got their copy of the gospel, or borrowed someone else's copy in order to have one made, what they read was all of it already familiar. Had they come across anything new they would very likely have protested, very likely indeed rather angrily. They read – they wanted to read – only what they had already heard in church over and over again. The significance that it takes us years of reflection to rediscover they already took completely for granted; it is *because* they took it for granted that we have such difficulty rediscovering it. How do I know this? It is admittedly not so much a case of having the evidence to hand as of looking round for a hypothesis which will explain puzzling but undeniable facts. But there is also evidence of a sort:

> Then it seemed good to the apostles and the elders, with the whole church, to choose men from among them and send them to Antioch with Paul and Barnabas. They sent Judas called Barsabbas, and Silas, leading men among the brethren, with the following letter: 'The brethren, both the apostles and the elders, to the brethren who are of the Gentiles in Antioch and Syria and Cilicia, greeting. Since we have heard that some persons from us have troubled you with words, unsettling your minds (although we

gave them no instructions), it has seemed good to us, having come to one accord, to choose men and send them to you with our beloved Barnabas and Paul, men who have risked their lives for the sake of our Lord Jesus Christ. We have therefore sent Judas and Silas, *who themselves will tell you the same things by word of mouth* ...' (Acts 15.22–27)

The controversy here is a continuation of the one we discussed in the previous chapter: conservative Jewish Christians were still trying to insist that Gentile converts must first become Jews before they could be Christians; here the leaders of the church come down decisively in favour of the universalist or catholic view. The letter itself was probably not even thought of as the primary means of communication. That was the task of the speakers, and the actual document would be thought of more as the guarantee that what the speakers said was true than as being itself the message. Once we realize this, it also helps explain yet another (to us) astounding feature of early manuscripts. It is likely that the copy that left Mark's hand, or the hand of the scribe to whom he dictated it, contained no punctuation at all, and may even not have used word divisions. To show what this means, let me write that again: andmayevennothaveusedworddivisions. But how could such a document possibly be read? It is very likely that even at the time to an outsider it would have been all but useless; the only people who could 'read' it were those who already knew what it said.

But having solved one problem, haven't we created another? We start from a situation in the early sixties AD with copies of Mark's gospel circulating among the members of a local (probably Roman) congregation in a format which only they could read. Certainly less than twenty years later, and quite possibly less than ten, we find two other writers – one of them (Matthew) right at the other end of the Mediterranean (Antioch) – both of them independently deciding to use Mark's gospel as the narrative framework of their own rather larger accounts. The evidence suggests therefore that within ten years of Mark's gospel being written it had become *the* standard document about Jesus' life throughout the Christian world. How can this be reconciled with what I have suggested about the way it came into being?

One detail which would help resolve the difficulty is to suppose (as scholars commonly do) that the document originated at Rome. The second point is that the amount of punctuation, or other assistance to the eye of the reader, which a manuscript contained depended on the scribe's personal assessment of how much assistance the intended reader would need. The first scribe judged it to be very little, and therefore offered very little.[1] The question of how punctuation came to be added so that the work could then circulate more widely does not arise; the reality is that as the work circulated more widely, the punctuation was added as a matter of course. How then did it happen that the punctuation was agreed on? In the early years it probably wasn't; agreement on this would develop at an even later stage, as the work became widely acknowledged as standard. How do we know that this is the punctuation that the author actually intended? Again we don't, and at some points we may well have got it wrong; just as even now the traditional division of the work into chapters does not correspond to what seem to be the original sections.

All this also helps to explain why it is – as there is no denying that it is – that both Matthew and Luke have missed the significance of a great deal of Mark, principally in that neither of them shows any sign of having understood or appreciated the thematic structure of Mark's gospel. Their view of it seems to have been much the same as the conventional view ever since: that it is a simple, narrative work, with only minimal interest in the actual teaching of Jesus. They took this view for the same reason that traditional scholarship takes it: because they both of them had to hand a great deal of what was primarily teaching material which Mark's gospel does not include. (As to whether this material is authentic, though we would not nowadays feel bound to accept their evaluation of it, on the basis of our own judgment we feel confident that quite a lot of it is.) Thus they both decided, apparently independently, to use Mark's gospel to provide the narrative framework for their own much larger and more complete accounts.

As we noted above, Matthew in particular often sees the need to add explanatory clauses to what he finds in Mark wherever he feels his readers will not understand the plain Marcan version. It is on the basis of these passages that some Christians still insist on the traditional view that Matthew's gospel is earlier than Mark's, and that the undeniable interdependence between them is the reverse of what it really is: that Mark is the abbreviator of Matthew. (One can see, for instance, if one compares the two passages quoted on pages 158–9, why some Christian bodies would prefer to think that

Matthew's version is the original, and that Mark's is an 'abbreviation' of it!) In some passages it does admittedly look like that; but on the other hand, compared with the amount of related material in the two gospels where there can be *no* doubt that Matthew is the abbreviator, these contrasting passages are only very occasional and rather unpersuasive.

It so happens that one of these passages is Matthew's version of the second paragraph of the above excerpt; and a detailed comparison of the two versions will be very instructive, as it illustrates all the points made so far in this chapter. It will first be seen that, although at some points Matthew's version is longer, there is still no doubt that Mark's is the original version and that Matthew is in the main abbreviating it; it will further be seen that Matthew has completely missed the point that Mark was trying to make. I first of all repeat the excerpt from Mark, this time italicizing those words and phrases which Matthew does not include; then I follow with Matthew's version italicized on the same principle. Where one author simply has a different word or phrase from the other without the sense being affected (for instance, 'And being aware of it, Jesus said ...' (Mark), 'But Jesus, aware of this, said ...' (Matthew)) I have ignored the variation. I have also ignored for the moment the very considerable variant where Mark has 'the leaven of the Pharisees and the leaven of Herod' and Matthew has 'the leaven of the Pharisees and Sadducees'.

> And he left them, *and getting into the boat again* he departed to the other side. *Now* they had forgotten to bring bread; *and they had only one loaf with them in the boat. And he cautioned them,* saying, 'Take heed, beware of the leaven of the Pharisees and the leaven of Herod'. And they discussed it with one another, saying, 'We have no bread'. And being aware of it, Jesus said to them, 'Why do you discuss the fact that you have no bread? Do you not yet perceive *or understand? Are your hearts hardened? Having eyes do you not see, and having ears do you not hear? And do you not remember? When I broke* the five loaves for the five thousand, how many baskets full of broken pieces did you take up?' *They said to him, 'Twelve'.* 'And the seven for the four thousand, how many baskets *full of broken pieces did you take up?' And they said to him, 'Seven'. And he said to them, 'Do you not yet understand?'* (Mark 8.13–21)

So he left them and departed. *When the disciples* reached the other

side, they had forgotten to bring *any* bread. *Jesus* said to them,
'Take head and beware of the leaven of the Pharisees and Sadducees'. And they discussed it among themselves, saying, 'We
brought no bread'. But Jesus, aware of this, said, '*O men of little
faith*, why do you discuss *among yourselves* the fact that you have
no bread? Do you not yet perceive? Do you not remember the five
loaves of the five thousand, and how many baskets you gathered?
Or the seven loaves of the four thousand, and how many baskets
you gathered? *How is it that you fail to perceive that he did not
speak about bread? Beware of the leaven of the Pharisees and
Sadducees'. Then they understood that he did not tell them to
beware of the leaven of bread, but of the teaching of the Pharisees
and Sadducees.* (Matt. 16.4b–12)

The difference in the opening is due to the fact that whereas Mark,
having related the feeding of the four thousand, tells us that
'immediately he got into the boat with his disciples, and went to the
district of Dalmanutha' (this is the only occurrence of Dalmanutha in
the entire record of history, which may be why Matthew omits it),
Matthew makes the incident of asking for a sign take place immediately after the feeding miracle, thus dramatizing the unbelief of the
Pharisees in a way that Mark did not intend. The evidence that
Matthew is the abbreviator, though, is clear in such omissions from
Mark as:

… and they had only one loaf with them in the boat.

And he cautioned them …

Are your hearts hardened? Having eyes do you not see, and
having ears do you not hear?

They said to him, 'Twelve'.

And they said to him, 'Seven'. And he said to them, 'Do you not
yet understand?'

In contrast, the only apparently redundant phrases in Matthew are
'O men of little faith', and 'among yourselves'. The major interpolation is his non-Marcan conclusion: 'How is it that you fail to perceive
that I did not speak about bread? Beware of the leaven of the
Pharisees and Sadducees'. But this is clearly not at all redundant, but
rather Matthew's attempt (in the event, as we shall see, a mistaken

attempt) to explain to his mystified readers just what point this strange altercation was trying to make.

First of all, though, let us comment on the major discrepancy noted earlier – the fact that Matthew substitutes 'the Sadducees' for Mark's 'Herod'. And even before that, we should perhaps note that some manuscripts of Mark read 'the Herodians' in place of the accepted reading. It is quite likely (and I will assume) that this alternative reading is intended to explain (which it does correctly) what Mark meant; but it is also obvious that the reading which seems to require explanation is more likely to be original than the one which seems to be offering one. So then Mark makes Jesus warn the disciples against the leaven of the Pharisees and of Herod. The idea of leaven as being not merely something corrupt in itself (I Cor. 5.6b–8), but as something which, even when small in quantity, can work to corrupt an infinitely larger mass than itself (Gal. 5.9), is one we find in the New Testament but not in the Old. On the other hand it is more than likely that Paul's imagery was not invented by himself, but derives from the wider Jewish tradition of his day, in particular from attempts to explain to the laity why it was that for seven days after the Passover festival Jews were forbidden to eat any but unleavened bread. To the above references we must add a Q saying about leaven which looks to be authentic:

> The kingdom of heaven is like leaven which a woman took and hid in three measures of flour, till it was all leavened. (Matt. 13.33 = Luke 13.21)

The significance here is close to that of Galatians 5.9, but adds to it, I think, the important idea that leaven works secretly. The evidence for Jesus' awareness of a secret, malevolent and constantly growing opposition to his message from both these groups has already been discussed.

But to return to Matthew, and to the alteration of Mark's 'Herod' to 'the Sadducees', we noted above that Matthew, achieving a dramatic effect not intended by Mark, joined the asking for a sign on to the conclusion of the second feeding miracle. And he makes the alteration here to continue the same effect; for although in Mark it is the Pharisees alone that ask for a sign (see above), in Matthew it is 'the Pharisees and Sadducees'.[2] In Matthew therefore the leaven of the second paragraph has clearly become the doctrinal unbelief implied by the asking for a sign in the first paragraph. But in Mark

the real connection between the two incidents is that in the first the
Pharisees are asking for a sign to test the claim they suspect Jesus is
making (to be the Messiah); while in the second, the disciples, by
failing to perceive that Jesus was not literally speaking about bread,
make it clear that they have not yet grasped the real significance of
the feeding miracles – that Jesus *is* the Messiah. And this offers an
excellent illustration of the extent to which Matthew, not merely in
this instance but repeatedly in his gospel, fails to grasp the meaning
of what he read in Mark. We note that Mark's story ends: 'And he
said to them, "Do you not yet understand?"', and that Matthew
omits this altogether. Why? The most likely reason is that he just
could not see what Mark was getting at. In Mark the reference to
leaven is secondary; it merely provides the setting for the real point
that he wants to make, that the disciples have not yet grasped the
significance of the feeding miracles. All this seems to be lost on
Matthew. He takes it for granted that the point of the story must be
found to lie in the reference to leaven; and in an attempt to do this he
invents an explanation for the reference which the modern reader
can easily see is mistaken.

And they came to Bethsaida. And some people brought to him a
blind man, and begged him to touch him. And he took the blind
man by the hand, and led him out of the village; and when he had
spit on his eyes and laid his hands upon him, he asked him, 'Do
you see anything?' And he looked up and said, 'I see men; but they
look like trees walking'. Then again he laid his hands upon his
eyes; and he looked intently and was restored, and saw everything
clearly. And he sent him away to his home, saying, 'Do not even
enter the village'.

And Jesus went on with his disciples to the villages of Caesarea
Philippi; and on the way he asked his disciples, 'Who do men say
that I am?' And they told him, 'John the Baptist; and others say
Elijah; and others, one of the prophets'. And he asked them, 'But
who do you say that I am?' Peter answered him, 'You are the
Christ'. And he charged them to tell no one about him.

And he began to teach them that the Son of man must suffer
many things, and be rejected by the elders and the chief priests and
the scribes, and be killed, and after three days rise again. And he
said this plainly. And Peter took him, and began to rebuke him.
But turning and seeing his disciples, he rebuked Peter, and said,

'Get behind me, Satan! For you are not on the side of God, but of men'. (8.22–33)

We can tell from its position in the gospel that Mark intended his readers to find a much greater significance in the story of the blind man than merely as an account of yet another of Jesus' miracles. Even the miracle itself is strange and new; we seem for the first time to be reading about a work of healing that Mark does not obviously regard as an exorcism. There are, for instance, no actual words of healing; there is therefore no command to any indwelling unclean spirit to cease from its unclean activity. The second point to note is that the miracle is gradual: just as there are two sea miracles and two feeding miracles, so Jesus now has two goes before the man can properly claim to be able to see. And immediately there follows, as we see, the sudden recognition by Peter that Jesus is in fact the Messiah. Note also how closely parallel the structure of the miracle story and the recognition story are. In the first Jesus is alone with the blind man, in the second with the disciples; Jesus makes two attempts to heal the blind man, and twice asks the disciples for an opinion about himself; in both stories, once eyes are completely opened, the closest secrecy is asked for. I doubt if any of this is mere coincidence.

What are we to make of the various answers that Jesus gets to his first question, 'Who do men say that I am?' The kind of thinking behind such answers as 'Elijah' or 'one of the prophets' is quite fully discussed in the Appendix to chapter 1 (pages 74–6). The way a modern reader would explain this is that the crowd see Jesus as identifying himself with some figure from the Old Testament – which we know that in fact he did, though not with any of the figures actually suggested here.[3] This does not quite do justice to the way people in those days actually thought; and though it would be hard to suggest a more adequate description that the modern mind could grasp, let us at least try to point the arrow in the right direction. The suggestion above thinks of Jesus as playing a role in a way that is both *voluntary and conscious*, and it is these two ideas that are misleading. Jesus, not only in his own mind but in that of his hearers – both friendly and hostile (see Mark 3.21–22) – has been possessed by a spirit not his own; and what we have here is a short-list of guesses as to the identity of that spirit. The suggestion of 'John the Baptist', as we hinted earlier, seems at first to raise difficulties of chronology, in that to us the implication is surely that John must have been long dead before this suggestion could have been made. But in fact we have no real need to suggest that John must have been dead for years; it makes perfectly good sense if we suppose that the relationship between Jesus and John the Baptist was taken to be the same as that between Elishah and Elijah, as in:

> When they had crossed, Elijah said to Elisha, 'Ask what I shall do for you, before I am taken from you'. And Elisha said, 'I pray you, let me inherit a double share of your spirit'. And he said, 'You have asked a hard thing; yet if you see me as I am being taken from you, it shall be so for you; but if you do not see me, it shall not be so'. And as they still went on and talked, behold, a chariot of fire and horses of fire separated the two of them. And Elijah went up by a whirlwind into heaven. And Elisha saw it and he cried, 'My father, my father! the chariots of Israel and its horsemen!' And he saw him no more.
>
> Then he took hold of his own clothes and rent them in two pieces. And he took up the mantle of Elijah that had fallen from him, and went back and stood on the bank of the Jordan. Then he took the mantle of Elijah that had fallen from him, and struck the water, saying, 'Where is the Lord, the God of Elijah?' And when he had struck the water, the water was parted to the one side and to the other; and Elisha went over.
>
> Now when the sons of the prophets who were at Jericho saw him over against them [*i.e. on the opposite bank of the Jordan*], they said, 'The spirit of Elijah rests on Elisha'. (II Kings 2.9–15a)

That is the kind of thing the crowd may also have meant by suggesting that Jesus 'was' John the Baptist. And though it certainly implies that John was dead, it does not necessarily imply that he had been long dead. Bearing in mind also that the bulk of the Elisha material in the Old Testament portrays him chiefly as a miracle worker (the only Old Testament figure of whom this is true), this popular conception of Jesus may well have had a considerable influence in shaping the development of the whole tradition, and would help to explain the excessive emphasis (I do not think the word is too strong) on miracle stories in the gospels.

Needless to say, the crowd has made no suggestion along the lines that Jesus himself would like hear. The idea that Jesus might be who he would like to think he was has apparently not occurred. There could be contradiction here also, in that the refusal to give the

Pharisees a sign – the incident with which the chapter opens – suggests to me that the Pharisees at any rate had a strong suspicion of who Jesus felt himself to be; and if that is so, and they were also opposed to him, it is hard to think of any reason why they should want to keep their suspicions to themselves. On the other hand, there are good reasons why the crowd should be so unaware. The concept of the Messiah was, in those days and in that part of the world, a very *popular* idea; and the reason why it would never occur to the crowd to think of Jesus as the Messiah is that his idea of what the Messiah was like bore no relation at all to theirs. The popular idea was of a warlike leader, a second King David (probably the literal meaning of any belief they may have had that he would be a 'Son of David'), who would first of all throw out the Romans – as David had thrown out the Philistines – and then, as David had also gone on to do, subjugate most of the known world and incorporate it into a new Israelite world empire. Chapter 7 of Daniel does have some connection with these ideas, and if Jesus in fact (as all four gospels say he did) went round calling himself 'the Son of man', clever hearers (like, perhaps, the Pharisees) might be able to work out why he did so. On the other hand there was one big obstacle to such a realization: both in Hebrew and in Aramaic the phrase 'Son of man' simply means a human being – it simply means that even in Daniel chapter 7 itself; one would have to be malevolent as well as clever (once again, perhaps, like the Pharisees) to work out the new meaning that Jesus was trying to give to the phrase. On the other hand the ideas of Isaiah chapters 40–53, which seem to have defined the Messiah for Jesus himself, not only had no connection with popular notions about the Messiah; they were the exact antithesis of such notions. So from that point of view Jesus' secret was entirely safe.

All this immediately explains the whole of what happens in the last paragraph of the excerpt. When Peter at the end of the previous paragraph blurts out that Jesus is the Messiah, he has in mind not Jesus' own ideas of what the Messiah was like but the popular notions of a warlike leader, and Jesus is aware if this. (In this gospel be it noted, as in Luke 9.18–21, there is no idea that 'flesh and blood has not revealed this to you, but my Father who is in heaven' – Matthew 16.17.) Jesus is also aware that any one else who hears that he is the Messiah will entertain exactly the same notions as Peter does. That is why his first response must be to charge them 'to tell no one about him'. He then first introduces an idea with which the whole of the remainder of the gospel will be largely concerned: the true nature of his Messiahship. Whether he ever hoped to convince the people as a whole as to what the Messiah was 'really' like, we cannot know. His immediate aim is to convince the disciples. Verse 31 (And be began to teach ...', is no doubt a summary of what was originally a lengthy discourse setting out his view of the Messiah in terms in particular of Isaiah 53. The picture is so totally unlike anything that Peter recognizes as being of the Messiah that he is outraged; and Jesus, aware of the worldy (not to mention dangerous) ideas that Peter holds, goes on to issue his sharpest reproof to anyone anywhere in this gospel – the description of Peter as Satan seems particularly harsh. This incident possibly underlies the obviously fictional account of the third temptation that we find in Matthew 4.8–11 (or the second in Luke 4.5–7), where Matthew's 'Begone, Satan' strongly reminds of Jesus' rebuke to Peter here.

> And he called to him the multitude with his disciples, and said to them, 'If any man would come after me, let him deny himself and take up his cross and follow me. For whoever would save his life will lose it; and whoever loses his life for my sake and the gospel's will save it. For what does it profit a man to gain the whole world and forfeit his life? For what can a man give in return for his life? For whoever is ashamed of me and of my words in this adulterous and sinful generation, of him will the Son of man also be ashamed when he comes in the glory of his Father with the holy angels'. And he said to them, 'Truly, I say to you, there are some standing here who will not taste death before they see the kingdom of God come with power'. (8.34–9.1)

Although there has been no lack of material about discipleship in the earlier part of the gospel, in the next two chapters it appears to be Mark's major theme. But whereas up to now the description of discipleship has been chiefly from the point of view of its external features – what they must wear, how they must behave, what they must do to qualify – here the emphasis is on the inner experience of being a disciple, and particularly from the standpoint of how that experience relates to Jesus' own experience as he approaches Jerusalem for the final catastrophe. It is tempting in some ways to view the earlier material as authentic, and this later intensely personal and rather rugged view of discipleship as perhaps owing more to the subsequent experience and reflection of the disciples themselves. But as in all these cases of distinguishing between what is likely to be history and what is likely to be later development, we must remind ourselves (and thus be on our guard) that there are usually personal as well as scholarly reasons for including whatever we include, and rejecting whatever we reject, as history.

In the present instance the injunction that we should 'deny ourselves and take up our cross' and follow Jesus has undeniably inspired a great deal of stark and unyielding heroism; but it also lies at the root of an unpleasant streak of morbidity that seems to run right through the Christian tradition. But other reasons can also be given for wondering whether this apparently new attitude towards discipleship was Jesus' own. In the early part of the all three synoptic gospels (and the structure of Mark's gospel is probably the reason for this unusual agreement), discipleship tends to be portrayed not so much as self-sacrifice but as something much more like plain self-indulgence. Possessions, for instance, are to be discarded not because they are a temptation, but on the contrary because they are a burden: the disciple will be much freer, much happier – in an odd but still perfectly literal sense much richer (Mark 10.29–30) – as a result of becoming a vagabond than he ever was as a family man with possessions and responsibilities. And all this seems rather at odds with the opening sentence of the above excerpt.

On the other hand it cannot be denied that what we have characterized as the morbid streak of Christianity – at any rate as regards voluntary suffering and self-denial[4] – must also go back to Jesus himself. The indication of this is above all the clear connection between Jesus' conception of his Messiahship and the ideas of Isaiah 53 – a connection without any antecedent in Judaic thinking at all, and which Mark reiterates three times very deliberately in this second section of the gospel (8.31; 9.31; 10.32–34). The fuller implications of this aspect of Jesus' thinking are reserved for discussion in the appendix to the chapter.

It is noticeable in the above excerpt, as it usually is when any of the synoptic gospels puts a continuous speech into Jesus' mouth, that the passage is made up of a collection of sayings which at an earlier stage of the tradition may well have existed independently of each other. Every sentence that Mark gives Jesus here could well stand by itself, and most of them probably once did so. It is important to point this out because these sayings can become coloured by their context in a way that, once we have unpicked the material, we can see is misleading. 'For whoever would save his life ...' is a good illustration of this. Christians have always interpreted this as meaning that willingness to offer up one's life for Jesus in this world is the gateway to life in the next, while unwillingness to do so means loss of life in the next. The tradition itself has encouraged this interpretation, and may already have been doing so before Mark put pen to paper. But if we detach the saying from the context and look at it again, it seems to offer a very different – and to my mind much more sensible – meaning. It may even be the case that the words 'for my sake and the gospel's' are not original, but have been added as the saying became reinterpreted in the sense given above. But even if we include them, it is still possible to read the saying – and probably accurate to do so – as a call to discipleship in the earlier, sunny and serene sense of the word. Jesus is telling potential disciples that in his view they are sacrificing their lives to what we would nowadays call their 'standard of living'; they have only to let that go – even, perhaps, 'for my sake and the gospel's' – and they will at last discover what the meaning of life really is. But whatever the original meaning of the saying, I feel certain that it had no connotations whatever (as it always has had in the tradition) of 'life after death'. As the last saying in the excerpt makes clear (and see also Ch. 7, note 1 on page 380) the first generation of Christians had no need of any idea of 'life after death'.

Such an interpretation of verse 35 ('For whoever would save his life ...') is confirmed by the two verses that follow. Verse 36 for instance ('For what does it profit a man ...') is unlikely to mean (though this is how it is usually interpreted) 'What is the point of being miraculously successful in this life if you find yourself eternally damned in the next?'; Jesus almost certainly meant something more like, 'What is the point of sacrificing the whole of life to the pursuit of gain?' And the next verse ('For what can a man give ...') may in this instance actually belong to the previous verse, so that it means something like, 'To spend the whole of your life making money is like spending gold to buy sawdust; what you have spent is infinitely more worthwhile than what you have bought with it'. Nothing, absolutely *nothing*, is more precious than the gift of life; so be very careful you are not throwing it away on something scarcely worth having.

If this interpretation is accurate (as I am certain that it is), the mood abruptly changes once again with verse 38 ('For whoever is ashamed of me and of my words ...'). Mark obviously felt this verse simply continued the ideas of the previous verses, whereas as I have interpreted them they don't. We are therefore up against the same difficulty in interpreting this verse as we were at the beginning of the excerpt. If Jesus basically just wanted to be a hippy, and to preach the virtues of hippiedom to others, no doubt this was not something that the authorities would encourage, but is it likely they would go to any great lengths to suppress it? In what circumstances therefore did Jesus envisage the disciples might ever be ashamed of him and of his words? On the other hand, though we may feel less than confident in accepting the gospel's themselves as a record of history, there is no reason why we should have the same misgivings about Josephus; and we have his confirmation (pages 166–7) that the disciples – if of John, then presumably also of Jesus – had every reason to be aware of the opposition of the authorities, and the serious lengths to which they could go in expressing that opposition. There is a short passage later on in Mark which well illustrates Jesus' warning here:

> But take heed to yourselves; for they will deliver you up to councils; and you will be beaten in synagogues; and you will stand before governors and kings for my sake, to bear testimony before them. (13.9)

In 3.6 we found the Pharisees (the popular religious leaders) and the Herodians (the first century equivalent of the security police) combining to think of ways of putting a stop to Jesus – though apart from this one shared ambition, the two groups appear to have been natural and irreconcileable enemies. The same combination against Jesus was hinted at earlier in this present section of the gospel in 8.15. It is explicitly referred to again in 12.13 where the famous question, 'Is it lawful to pay taxes to Caesar, or not?', is contrived by the two opposed parties in the belief that whichever answer Jesus gives renders him a prey to one or other of them. If he says it is lawful, he forfeits all popular support and becomes powerless as against the Pharisees; if he says it isn't, the Herodians will then have grounds for handing him over to the Romans on a charge of sedition. These are in essence the alternative fates about which the disciples are being warned in the short excerpt above. The Pharisees had power to inflict beatings in the synagogues; the Herodians to charge with most serious offences before governors and kings. Both would certainly happen to any number of them, warns Jesus; and there must be no flinching or turning back, no matter what the dangers of the situation.

As a reason for this he hints at that other great image of his Messiahship, Daniel 7:

> I saw in the night visions, and behold, with the clouds of heaven there came one like a son of man, and he came to the Ancient of Days and was presented before him. And to him was given dominion and glory and kingdom, that all peoples, nations and languages should serve him; his dominion is an everlasting dominion which shall not pass away, and his kingdom one that shall not be destroyed. (7.13–14)

How seriously Daniel meant this as a literal prophecy of what was going to happen we cannot be sure. It was probably the kind of question he himself would prefer not to have to think about. Presumably he made the vision up and was conscious of having done so. To him the vision was a description, not so much of what was going to happen, as of what had *got* to happen; and the greater the emphasis on the word 'got', the more sickening the underlying awareness that in all probability nothing like it would ever happen at all. But there seems little doubt that Jesus read all this not merely as straight prophecy of what would actually be happening, but went a great deal further than this in supposing that the 'Son of man' that Daniel talks about, to whom would be given 'dominion and glory and kingdom, that all peoples, nations and languages should serve him,' was none other than himself: that he, Jesus, after he had undergone the Messiah's fate as described in Isaiah 53, would receive the Messiah's reward as described in Daniel 7. Should he find on his return that in their various earthly trials any of the disciples have concealed or gone back on their acknowledgment of him as the Messiah, they would find that at this final – and heavenly – judgment he too would no longer acknowledge them; and the punishment for this would be infinitely greater than any they had avoided by their previous apostasy.

And when would all this be? 'While some of you, the listeners, are still alive.' We need not doubt not only that Jesus meant this quite literally, but that he was also believed quite literally. In Paul's day it was evidently thought of as a serious problem that members of the Christian community were actually dying (I Cor. 11.30) and still there was no sign of Jesus' return. This is incidentally the best proof we have that first generation Christians had no belief in any kind of life after death – nor even apparently in any resurrection from the dead apart from Jesus' own resurrection, even though the book of Daniel (from which Jesus seems originally to have derived his belief in his own second coming), does have such a belief:

> And there shall be a time of trouble, such as never has been since there was a nation till that time; but at that time your people shall be delivered, every one whose name shall be found written in the book. And many of those who sleep in the dust of the earth shall awake, some to everlasting life, and some to shame and everlasting contempt. (Daniel 12.1b-2)

Had the Christians at Corinth also believed that, the fact that some of their number had died would have caused them no problem at all. But we can tell from Paul's letter that on the contrary it was causing them dreadful heartsearching. It is important to bear in mind that what we have as the two letters to the Corinthians are clearly collections of fragments probably from a much larger number of documents, and that we have no reason to believe that I Corinthians 11 and 15 originally belonged to the same letter. Chapter 15 may well be Paul's second stab at explaining the difficulty once the number and conspicuous virtue of the dead had become so large as to make the suggestion of chapter 11 look unconvincing as well as uncharitable.

APPENDIX

Of the two crucial passages (as it seems to me) in Jesus' thinking about his Messiahship, the above says perhaps as much as can usefully be said on the subject of Daniel 7. Isaiah 53 on the other hand is a much more complex topic, and I think it worthwhile to devote this appendix to an attempt to unravel it. And we will need to begin by a brief consideration of the whole structure of the book of the prophecies of Isaiah as we now have it in the Old Testament.

The superscription, which is of course the descriptive contents of the collection added by a later editor, reads:

> The vision of Isaiah the son of Amoz, which he saw concerning Judah and Jerusalem in the days of Uzziah, Jotham, Ahaz, and Hezekiah, kings of Judah. (Isa. 1.1)

The indications are that whoever added this superscription had no

separate source of information about Isaiah's dates apart from what
he found in the collection of documents themselves. It is true that in
the later portion of the book the poet at one point (44.28–45.1)
refers to Cyrus king of Persia (died 529 BC), which if understood
literally would have extended the prophet's activity to well beyond
the death of Hezekiah (687 BC). Although the ancient editor very
likely did not have as accurate a knowledge of the chronology of
events as we have, he would know enough to know that anyone who
had been a mature young man at the time of Uzziah's death in about
740 BC (see Isa. 6.1) could not still have been alive when Babylon fell
to Cyrus about two hundred years later (538 BC). He probably
explained this reference to Cyrus as an example of Isaiah's ability to
'prophesy', a hypothesis which would be equally useful in explaining
the other references to Babylon which occur in all parts of the book.
If we discount the reference to Cyrus, the latest identifiable historic
events we find in the book are those of the reign of Hezekiah in
chapters 36–39. Thus he concluded, and probably correctly, that
Isaiah was active during the reigns listed above. We know that
Hezekiah's illness described in chapter 38 occurred fifteen years
before his eventual death; so it is reasonable to assume that Isaiah
died some time after 700 BC, and it may have been quite shortly after.
If he was about twenty when Uzziah died, he would have been
perhaps sixty-odd when he himself died.

Those central four chapters 36–39 give us the information we
need for interpreting the book's most obvious peculiarity: which is
(as already noted) that the material stretches in date from the death
of Uzziah in 740 BC till at least two hundred years after that, and
probably even further. Chapters 36–37 describe the siege of
Jerusalem by the King of Assyria; we don't know precisely when –
but suspect it may have been shortly before 700 BC; nor whether
Jerusalem really managed to hold out against Sennacherib as the
biblical account claims, or in fact was subdued by him as Sennacherib's own account (which survives) rather suggests. The
important points for us are that in Hezekiah's time, towards the end
of Isaiah's life, the Assyrian empire was a major threat to the
southern kingdom of Judah's independence (the northern kingdom
of Israel had already been overthrown some twenty years earlier);
and that, whether Jerusalem was taken or not, the kingdom managed
to preserve its integrity and survive the threat. Chapter 39 describes a
visit from Babylonian envoys – ostensibly to congratulate Hezekiah

on his recovery from the illness described in 38, but in reality (as the conclusion of the account makes obvious) to discuss the possibility of an alliance between Judah and the rising power of Babylon against the waning power of Assyria. Isaiah warns that Babylon will before too long be a far more dangerous threat than Assyria ever was, and will succeed where Assyria has failed. We have no reason to doubt that he actually did make such a prophecy (which he did, of course, on the basis of common sense rather than divine inspiration), nor that a major factor in the successful resistance of Hezekiah to Assyria had been Isaiah's assurance that Israel's tenacity would be vindicated.

On what basis then do we decide which portions of Isaiah are the prophet's own words, and which portions are (as a great deal of it must be) those of later poets? We have no reason to doubt that the description of his call in chapter 6 is genuine; but then what of chapters 1–5, or alternatively, why isn't chapter 6 the actual opening of the book? The opening of chapter 2 is particularly suspect in that exactly the same poem is attributed to a contemporary of Isaiah's in the opening verses of chapter 4 of Micah; which brings home to us the fact that just about the only technique we have for assessing the genuineness of prophetic material is what appears to be the date of the material and whether this agrees with our estimated dates for the prophet. So the only real answer we can give about the genuineness of chapters 1–5 is that they seem to be about right as regards date. Whether it was Isaiah, or Micah, or even someone totally different from either of these (whether known to us or unknown) who wrote the opening poem of chapter 2 we have absolutely no means of knowing.

Much the same must be said about most of the material following chapter 6 as well – right up to chapter 35, which also presents us with problems. It is unmistakably about the return of exiles to Zion (the mountain on which Jerusalem is partly built) and is normally read as a 'prophecy' of the return of the exiles after the fall of Babylon. If that interpretation is correct, then this poem also must be later than Isaiah; but it should be noted that, though consistent with such a reading, the poem does not in fact demand it. There must have been many who fled the country at the approach of Sennacherib's invasion, and the poem could equally well be (and my guess is that in fact it is) a prophecy about the return of these fugitives; in which case it is genuine. Provisional and tentative conclusions of this kind are on most occasions all that is possible in interpreting the prophetic books, and this is true also of the rest of the material we shall be considering.

By and large most of these early chapters (6–39) look as if they could be genuine. A certain difficulty is presented by a group of poems (chapters 13–19 and 21–23) which seem to be prophecies of the downfall of Israel's neighbours and rivals. In feel these poems remind us of Jeremiah 46–51 or Ezekiel 25–32, which enables us to say two things about them: first it is likely they were originally intended to stand at the end of a collection, as the Jeremiah poems do; second, that whoever wrote them was attempting thereby to console his hearers for some national disaster that Israel itself had suffered. Collections of prophecy tend to be arranged on the principle of first the brimstone, then the treacle: first the poems prophesying doom and destruction to Israel, then those prophesying consolation. It is an unfortunate but undeniable feature of Old Testament thinking that death and destruction to Israel's neighbours are a source of joy and consolation to Israel itself.

Are we to think of these poems also as genuine? If they are, the presumption would be that they were the closing poems of the original Isaiah collection, which would make Isaiah a rather short book (chapters 6–23) as against the very long one we have today. Against this it could be argued that if the poems earlier than chapter 6 could be genuine (as there is no denying that they could) then the poems after chapter 23 could also be genuine – as they also seem to be (but note that to anyone whose ears are attuned, Isaiah 24.1 reads very distinctly like the beginning of an entirely new book: compare Isaiah 1.2, Amos 1.2, Micah 1.2, Zephaniah 1.2). But there are much stronger reasons than this for doubting whether these chapters really belong where we find them. The first two of them (chapters 13 and 14) predict the downfall of Babylon in a way that makes it clear that this downfall will be a matter of great satisfaction to the poet and his likely audience. Isaiah, as we saw, predicted the rise of Babylon, but it is hard to see why he should have predicted its downfall quite so vindictively. The presumption is overwhelming that they were written at much the same time and in much the same spirit as the Jeremiah collection referred to above, once again quite possibly by someone of whom we have never heard. Note also that in 23.13a we seem to have an editorial comment that has crept into the text, which seems to bear witness to the fact that scholars were aware of the chronological difficulty presented by these chapter at an early date.

The reader now knows all that it is necessary to know (perhaps even slightly more) about Isaiah 1–39, who Isaiah was and how much of the material is likely to be his. It has always been recognized that the remaining twenty seven chapters are to some extent a separate book. Even in those unsophisticated days when it was taken for granted that the whole collection must be from the single pen of Isaiah, it was acknowledged that in chapters 1–39 he was speaking largely of his own time, in chapters 40–66 he was 'prophesying' about events that would be taking place long after his death. It was in the course of the last century that the feeling gathered strength that this kind of explanation of the material was not convincing. If the material gave indications that the author was familiar with the events of Cyrus' reign, then this was the *proof* that that was when the material was in fact written. The conclusion began to be accepted that these later chapters must have been written by an entirely separate author, whom scholars agreed to call Deutero-Isaiah, or the Second Isaiah. They did not stop there. It also began to be felt that chapters 40–53 could convincingly be detached from the whole of the rest of the book and treated as a unity, so that it would be helpful to attribute these poems alone to Deutero-Isaiah, and to suggest yet another author – to be known as Trito-Isaiah – as the author of the remainder of the book.[5]

It is with these fourteen chapters 40–53 that we are concerned in connection with Jesus' view of his Messiahship. We need to ask two questions: firstly what the original author seems to have meant; secondly how Jesus himself seems to have understood them? But first of all I need to show that they really are a literary unity. There are four clearly identifiable themes running through these chapters, which are largely peculiar to them, or if they are echoed elsewhere, it is never so forcefully and repeatedly as here. These themes are: (*a*) the universality of God as proved by his sole creation of the world; (*b*) his sole direction, therefore, of the course of all human history; (*c*) the utter worthlessness and delusion of the worship of idols; (*d*) Israel's unique mission, for which the troubles of the recent past must be seen as a preparation, to proclaim the true nature of God to the whole world. I shall be arguing on the assumption (which is by no means generally agreed) that the 'servant' in these chapters never refers to anyone else but Israel. The basic proclamation, made in 40.12–26, is the universality of Israel's national God, whose name was traditionally Yahweh or Jahveh, and who in earlier times, even by Israel itself, was thought of as only one God among many. But even as early as Elijah (ninth century BC) we find this idea being questioned (I Kings 18.21), while the classical prophets such as Isaiah (Proto-Isaiah) and Jeremiah clearly think of Israel's God as very much more than that – as being real in a way that no other god ever has been. However, in these chapters of Deutero-Isaiah the idea is made much more explicit than ever before (or, in the event, subsequently either) that this national God is the only God that exists, and is thus the God of all nations; and that it is Israel's task and destiny to reveal him to those nations, and to cure them of the blindness that has afflicted them up to now. *All* the material from 40.12 to the end of chapter 53 can effortlessly be classified under one of the above four heads – a degree of thematic unity all but unparalleled in the Old Testament in any passage of similar length.

The figure we are primarily concerned with in these chapters, as already observed, is that of the 'servant' mentioned no less than twenty times. Of these the following are certainly references to Israel: 41.8, 41.9, 44.1, 44.2, 44.21, (note that 44.26, though not certainly referring to Israel, makes it clear that though 'servant' is singular, it refers to a plural body – 'messengers' in the next line), 45.4, 48.20 and 49.3; out of twenty references therefore, eight are certainly to Israel. On the other hand 49.5 and 49.6 seem on the surface to imply that the servant is quite definitely *other* than Israel (and 49.7 could easily be interpreted the same way), and that the servant's mission is as much to restore Israel as it is to be a light to the nations? And how many of the remaining nine references are more consistent with this second sense than the alternative? At once we have to admit that the most crucial chapter of all for our purposes (chapter 53, or as some would plausibly start the poem, 52.13) comes into this second category. And having admitted that, without going into the remaining references one by one, we have drawn up the battle lines – across which controversy still rages – as to just how these poems are to be interpreted. There are basically two questions: (*a*) is the servant to be understood as Israel itself, or on the contrary as an individual Israelite, charged by God with the task of making his true nature known, first to Israel and then to the nations; and (*b*) is the suffering servant of chapter 53 an individual to whom these terrible things actually happened, or on the contrary are they a kind of fictionalized portrayal of the sufferings of Israel as a whole?

There is no doubt in my mind that Jesus took the servant to be an individual, and many scholars to this day agree with that interpretation, though few would still maintain (as Jesus himself obviously believed) that from the first they were written with no other intention than to prophesy the sufferings that he (Jesus) would have to undergo; they would prefer to suggest that the poem describes the historic martyrdom of an individual who was contemporary with the poet, of whom we know nothing but what the poet tells us. The other view is that, despite the awkward instances of chapter 49, the servant always refers to Israel, and that the sufferings described in chapter 53 are a description of the sufferings of the nation, and the purpose God has in mind in inflicting them. Nor are the chapter 49 references an insurmountable difficulty: after all, Christian writers throughout history have drawn a distinction between the 'true' church – those whose membership is validated by God's acceptance of them – and the larger body of professing Christians whose membership makes no difference to their lives and whose professions are dismissed by God as worthless; that essentially is the distinction being made in chapter 49 between Israel and the servant. My own vote is for this second view.

We discussed in an earlier appendix (page 74) whether it would not be sensible simply to conclude that Jesus was mad; and at the time we decided that in the context of the culture of which he was a product he probably wasn't. Many even of those who accepted the argument there will feel that here it is a lot harder to maintain. Three times in Mark's gospel, as Jesus journeys towards Jerusalem he tells his disciples that when he gets there he will be arrested, tortured and executed horribly. If any one of us were talking to a friend who confided to us that kind of anticipation, wouldn't we immediately point out, 'In that case, my dear chap, if I were you I wouldn't go'; and wouldn't we also start wondering to ourselves how we could get this fellow to a hospital before the delusions became any more dangerously crazy? And I don't think we can *totally* set aside these misgivings. The suggestion that the culture was different from ours may be some help, but to most of us not quite enough.

On the other hand, within the context of Christianity itself this is the absolute core of the message. Anyone who spends much time (utterly unlike, let me add, the present author) offering the hope and consolation of religion to despairing poverty will tell you that the one image that brings relief more than any other is this one; compared with it promises of increased benefits or improved housing often sound (as indeed they often are) totally unreal. It will be pointed out, what I would not dream of denying, that this is a cynical point of view: potentially an immoral cynicism in the mouth of an individual like myself, and a malevolent cynicism if openly professed by society as a whole. And yet if it is true, it must surely also be said. And it is true, and can be observed, that there are people in the grip of circumstances that on any rational analysis really are hopeless who, without any outward change in those circumstances, will contemplate this image and find hope; and not just hope, but what feels like a God-given, quite literally supernatural redemption – as if a ship had appeared out of the night, and some one had thrown them a life-belt and hauled them out of the sea.

10

The Road to Jerusalem I

(Mark 9.2–50)

We saw that up to the end of chapter 6 Mark gives us clear indications of where his various sections end. The end of chapter 6 is the end of the seventh section. The end of the eighth section is less clearly marked, but assuming we are right that its theme is 'Jesus and the Gentiles' we can be confident that it ends with the conclusion of the second feeding miracle in 8.10. Do we have any indication of the various sections beyond this point? I think we do. The ninth section begins with the Pharisees asking Jesus for a sign, clearly (to those in the know) to test (a) whether in fact he claims to be the Messiah, (b) whether in fact he is. It might at first be thought to end with Peter's acknowledging that claim; but then we seem bound to tack on to that, first Jesus' explanation of what the true Messiah is like (8.31), and following that the brief sermon on the implications of this true Messiahship for true discipleship (8.34–9.1). We have already noted that the explanation of true Messiahship is given three times in all (the above, 9.31 and 10.33–34); and if we look closely, we see that on all three occasions it is followed by a brief sermon on the nature of true discipleship. I shall assume therefore that these little sermons (the second one – 9.33–50 – perhaps not so little) also indicate the conclusion of a section. This takes us up to 10.45, and beyond that point there is once again no ambiguity. There follows an inordinately long section (for reasons to be explained at the proper place) on Jesus and Jerusalem (10.46–12.44), chapter 13 concludes the teaching ministry with a section devoted to Jesus' prophecy about the end of the world, (connected in his mind with what he foresaw as the imminent fall of Jerusalem), and chapters 14–16 are equally obviously a self-contained account of the passion, death and resurrection of Jesus.

When Mark originally wrote the gospel there was of course no problem of a lost ending. Now that there is, in order to discuss it we have to detach the resurrection from the rest of the passion narrative, in a way which I doubt if Mark would have approved. So we have one more section at the end than Mark intended. But the reader should from now on begin to feel that the end is in sight – just as Mark's account of the transfiguration which now follows seems itself intended to point us forward to the resurrection appearance with which the gospel almost certainly originally ended.

> And after six days Jesus took with him Peter and James and John, and led them up a high mountain apart by themselves; and he was transfigured before them, and his garments became glistening, intensely white, as no fuller on earth could bleach them. And there appeared to them Elijah with Moses; and they were talking to Jesus. And Peter said to Jesus, 'Master, it is well that we are here; let us make three booths, one for you and one for Moses and one for Elijah'. For he did not know what to say, for they were exceedingly afraid. And a cloud overshadowed them, and a voice came out of the cloud, 'This is my beloved Son; listen to him'. And suddenly looking around they no longer saw any one with them but Jesus only.
>
> And as they were coming down the mountain, he charged them to tell no one what they had seen until the Son of man should have risen from the dead. So they kept the matter to themselves, questioning what the rising from the dead meant. And they asked him, 'Why do the scribes say that first Elijah must come?' And he said to them, 'Elijah does come first to restore all things; and how is it written of the Son of man that he should suffer many things and be treated with contempt? But I tell you that Elijah has come, and they did to him whatever they pleased, as it is written of him'. (9.2–13)

There are only two instances of apparent temporal connection in the whole of Mark's gospel: 'And after six days' above, and 'It was now two days before the Passover' in 14.1. These two instances alone would not in any case undermine the notion that the work is constructed round a thematic rather than a narrative framework; but it is interesting to note that on examination it turns out that neither of them are in fact temporal connections at all. The opening of 14.1 means, not that the events about to be related took place two days after those at the end of chapter 13, but only that what the author is about to tell us took place 'two days before' – that is by our reckoning 'the day before' – the Passover. The present instance is a great deal more intriguing: in the event, it doesn't look as though it is meant to be read as any kind of temporal reference. Its real function is to trigger off an association of ideas, specifically the following idea:

> Then Moses went up on the mountain, and the cloud covered the mountain. The glory of the Lord settled on Mount Sinai, and the cloud covered it six days; and on the seventh day he called to Moses out of the midst of the cloud. (Ex.24.15–16)

We are at the exact mid-point of the gospel, and the transfiguration (as it is traditionally known) is the marker that the author has carefully placed to indicate the fact. It simultaneously looks back to the very beginning and forward to the very end. A direct reminder of the beginning are the words 'This is my beloved Son ...', echoing the voice that was heard at Jesus' baptism; a direct pre-echo of the end (assuming as I do that the ending of Matthew's gospel was also the original ending of Mark's) is the mountain-top setting common to both visions – and also Jesus' words to the disciples as they come down from the mountain: he orders them to tell no one what they have seen 'until the Son of man should have risen from the dead'. But it has two other references also: first it is a retelling in vision form of the incident that has just been related, in which Peter has acknowledged that Jesus is the Christ; and second, as we have seen, it compares God's vindication of Jesus' claims (which is what the resurrection essentially is) with God's original descent on Mount Sinai to hand over a copy of his own law, supposedly written by his own hand.

This is the one occasion in the gospel where I feel it is quite pointless even to consider the question, 'What originally happened?'. Plausible answers to such a question can be suggested (it is not certain that they ought to be, but undoubtedly they can be) for the two sea miracles and the two feeding miracles; but the transfiguration story seems to have been solely created by the corporate imagination without reference to any idea of an original event. It was actually created as a vision, and the point of that vision only ever was its 'meaning'. It follows that travel books and commentaries which ruminate the question on which particular mountain the transfiguration took place have entirely missed the point.

The traditional suggestion of Mount Tabor, for instance, can be shown to be all but impossible. We have occasionally noted in the first part of the gospel how careless Mark can be about geography. But in the second part quite suddenly all that changes. Mark seems to have written it with pen in one hand and a map in the other. Caesarea Philippi, where Mark places Peter's confession, is just about the most northerly location in the gospel narrative (we pointed out at the time how geographically peculiar the reference to Sidon is in 7.31, and the reason for this may well be that Mark had only a vague idea where Sidon was); it was in all probability also the most northerly point of Jesus' personal world. It is from this most northerly point that Jesus begins his long journey to Jerusalem which occupies us over the next two chapters. Mark makes no mistakes about this. We find Jesus in Galilee in 9.30, in Capernaum (for the last time) in 9.33, and in the 'region of Juda and beyond the Jordan' in 10.1. They are 'on the road going up to Jerusalem' (but still presumably on the other side of Jordan) in 10.32, they recross the Jordan to arrive at Jericho in 10.46, and they finally approach Jerusalem in 11.1. There can be no question but that this consistency is intentional. If I point out therefore that Tabor is well to the south of Capernaum, we can conclude with certainty that, even supposing Mark had a particular mountain in mind, it cannot have been that one. For this reason scholars who wish to insist that the transfiguration was an actual event have tended to plump for Hermon – which is possible in that it is not far to the north of Caesarea Philippi; but the inherent improbability as history of what is alleged, and the heavy symbolism with which the account is loaded, both seem to indicate it would be more sensible not to enquire about any actual mountain.

Since a major (perhaps *the* major) reference of the imagery is to Mount Sinai, can one see the subsequent journey to Jerusalem as a parallel to Israel's journey in the wilderness and arrival in the promised land? (Remember also that in Hebrew and Aramaic Joshua, who led them into the promised land, has the same name as Jesus.) It looks as though Luke may have wanted to bring out this idea. Where Mark and Matthew simply tell us that Moses and Elijah were talking to Jesus, Luke makes a guess at what they were talking about. For some reason the transfiguration seems to have gripped Luke's fancy, and his account of it is far more brightly coloured than either of the other two:

Now about eight days after these sayings he took with him Peter and John and James, and went up on the mountain to pray. And as he was praying, the appearance of his countenance was altered, and his raiment became dazzling white. And behold, two men talked with him, Moses and Elijah, who appeared in glory and spoke of his departure, which he was to accomplish at Jerusalem. Now Peter and those who were with him were heavy with sleep, and when they wakened they saw his glory and the two men who stood with him. And as the men were parting from him, Peter said to Jesus, 'Master, it is well that we are here; let us make three booths, one for you and one for Moses and one for Elijah' – not knowing what he said. As he said this, a cloud came and over-shadowed them; and they were afraid as they entered the cloud. And a voice came out of the cloud, saying, 'This is my Son, my Chosen; listen to him!' And when the voice had spoken, Jesus was found alone. And they kept silence and told no one in those days anything of what they had seen. (Luke 9.28–36)

There are several notable differences here – perhaps due to Luke's knowing another version of the story besides Mark's, or perhaps simply due to his own invention. Though he clearly recognizes the Sinaitic implications of the imagery, he has apparently failed to spot that Mark's 'After six days' is an indication of this, treats it (as many commentators since his time have done) as a temporal link and therefore 'corrects' it to the equivalent of 'After about a week'. Mark, unlike Luke, makes no mention of praying; Luke totally omits Mark's discussion about Elijah as they come down from the mountain. But the big difference is the description of Moses and Elijah themselves. In Mark they just appear and talk; in Luke they make a solemn entrance, and he tells us what they talked about: they 'spoke of his departure which he was to accomplish at Jerusalem'. The Greek behind that word 'departure' is *exodus*, and the implication seems to be that Luke does think of the journey to Jerusalem as the equivalent of the journey through the wilderness.

In contrast, any such influence in Mark seems hard to spot, perhaps because he had a better idea than Luke of how imagery works, and wanted to keep the Jerusalem stories clear for quite other associations. This impression is confirmed when we notice that although in Matthew and Luke Jesus is addressed as 'Son of David' throughout both gospels, particularly by people wanting to be healed, in Mark we have to wait till 10.47 for the first instance of this, when Jesus is at Jericho, the very last staging post before he finally reaches Jerusalem. He is indirectly hailed as that again on his entry into the city in 11.10 (actually the crowd implies that all of them are sons of David, but that Jesus is their leader), and there is a discussion of the Messiah as son of David (in which Jesus in fact seems to reject this traditional Messianic claim for himself) in 12.35–37. All mention of the son of David in Mark therefore is associated with Jerusalem, and there is little doubt that this is deliberate. He clearly thinks of the triumphal entry as a reenactment of David's original conquest of the city.

There is not much in the story itself which needs comment apart from one puzzling feature: '... let us make three booths, one for you, and one for Moses and one for Elijah'. First of all just what here these booths; secondly, and even harder to explain, what here is supposed to be the purpose of them? The likeliest explanation of what they were is provided by the following:

> On the fifteenth day of the seventh month [*approximately our October*], when you have gathered in the produce of the land, you shall keep the feast of the Lord seven days; on the first day shall be a solemn rest, and on the eighth day shall be a solemn rest. And you shall take on the first day the fruit of goodly trees, branches of palm trees, and boughs of leafy trees, and willows of the brook; and you shall rejoice before the Lord your God seven days. You shall keep it as a feast to the Lord seven days in the year; it is a statute for ever throughout your generations; you shall keep it in the seventh month. You shall dwell in booths for seven days; all that are native in Israel shall dwell in booths, that your generations may know that I made the people of Israel dwell in booths when I brought them out of the land of Egypt: I am the Lord your God. (Lev. 23.39–43)

Despite the last sentence of this excerpt, scholars are agreed that in origin this festival is purely a harvest festival, probably inherited from the original non-Israelite inhabitants of Canaan, and that this final sentence is no more than a clumsy Israelite attempt (somewhat like our Christmas) to 'baptize' a ceremony whose pagan origins were well understood, but whose overwhelming popularity made it impossible to suppress. Long before Jesus' day, however, (once again like Christmas) this superimposed orthodox interpretation had become the universally accepted one, so that the harvest festival aspect had become secondary, and for many (particularly town-dwellers) perhaps even irrelevant. It is somewhat odd in the above excerpt that 'the fruit of goodly trees' should be part of a list which goes on to mention various kinds of branches, since we think we know what the purpose of both the fruits and the branches were, and they were in fact very different. The fruits we assume to have been both the main object of the festival and also the means of celebrating it – the 'wine and summer fruits and oil' of Jeremiah 40.10 (see also 40.12 and 48.32); the original purpose of the branches seems to have been for the making of the booths themselves, which were presumably makeshift lean-to shelters. (It is suggested by the very irreverent that the original purpose of these booths was to provide a minimal privacy for the kind of thing that Ruth and Boaz get up to on just this kind of occasion in Ruth chapter 3.) We are by no means sure whether in Jesus' time the booths were still being made at all, and we seem to gather from Mark 11.1–10 (the Palm Sunday entry) that the chief function of the branches had become as something to wave in procession. It is because this theme of the Feast of Booths or Tabernacles is relevant to Palm Sunday as well as to the Transfiguration that it seems worthwhile to go into this kind of detail into its background.

We have some idea now what these booths were that Peter was suggesting he should make, but still very little about what purpose they were intended to serve. The irreverent suggestion in the previous paragraph in this kind of context is of course out of the question. But there is another suggestion, possibly quite attractive to a number of modern readers, which many of Mark's original audience would have found equally shocking: the last thing Peter is likely to have intended to make is three little shrines at which the three notables could be worshipped. Certainly in the case of Moses and Elijah, and probably also at this early date in the case of Jesus himself, a fair proportion of the audience would have denounced any such suggestion as flat idolatry. But having pointed out what the booths cannot have been for, it is very much harder to make a convincing suggestion what they must have been for. Luke as we have seen, perhaps taking his cue from the closing sentence of the Leviticus excerpt, seems to connect them with the original Exodus journey to the promised land; and (assuming that Mark did not himself compose the story but is relating part of a received tradition) this may also have been the intention of the original creators of the episode. But if so, the idea seems to have passed Mark by, so that he simply leaves us dangling.

The significance of Moses and Elijah here as a visual representation of the law and the prophets will be obvious to most readers. It is clear to us (though it may not have been so clear to Matthew and Luke, since both their accounts omit the Marcan phrases that bring this meaning out) that what Mark thought they were doing was bearing witness to the fact that Jesus was the Messiah, and the incident is therefore a retelling in visionary form of the incident of Peter's confession. The actual phrase 'the law and the prophets', though not rare in Matthew and Luke, strangely enough never occurs at all in Mark, and this is his only hint of any equivalent. In what sense the law (specifically the first five books of the Old Testament) contains any Messianic prophecies at all will not be clear even to many pious readers – though all three gospels apart from Mark appear to insist on the claim, and John's gospel with great emphasis. The answer to the riddle is probably that we should understand the phrase 'the law and the prophets' simply to mean 'the Bible' (by that of course meaning the Old Testament only). John's gospel has one reference that is in substance to 'the law and the prophets' (1.45), one to 'the prophets' alone (6.45), but a considerable number to 'the law' alone; and in all these instances also we should understand 'the law' to mean simply the Bible.

If any one doubts that the meaning of the story is that Jesus is the Messiah and that this is what Moses and Elijah were testifying to, the sequel makes this clear. Luke as we have seen omits this part of the episode, presumably as being of little relevance to his exclusively Gentile readers. Matthew seems to have felt that Mark's description of the descent from the mountain was so cryptic that his readers would have difficulty understanding it, and this is another of those passages that he expands in order to explain it – principally by adding a final sentence: 'Then the disciples understood that he was speaking to them of John the Baptist' (Matt. 17.13). It seems astounding to me that Matthew's readers would not have worked this last point out without his help. Similarly a high proportion of popular biblical commentary throughout the ages seems to make a point of telling the reader what he could perfectly well gather from the text, while ignoring all the points about which he is actually likely to be puzzled. Matthew's explanation well illustrates both these failings. What the reader wouldn't grasp in Mark is the reasoning behind the question: 'Why do the scribes say that first Elijah must come?', and Matthew gives them no help with it. What has in fact gone through the disciples' heads is something like this: *So it seems that Jesus really is the Messiah, because that's what we heard Moses and Elijah saying. But the scribes say that before the Messiah comes Elijah must reappear.* Then follows the question of the text.

The scribes say that first Elijah must come because they have in mind the 'prophecy' of Malachi:

> Behold, I will send you Elijah the prophet before the great and terrible day of the Lord comes. And he will turn the hearts of fathers to their children, and the hearts of children to their fathers [*i.e. he will come to a divided community and restore it to being a united one*], lest I come and smite the land with a curse.' (Mal. 3.23–24 in the Hebrew, 4.5–6 in the Greek)

And Jesus has exactly the same quotation in mind when he replies as he does. But his actual words are so eliptic that rather than explain them Matthew has thought it better just to cut them out – and for once he has my sympathy. The full version would be something like as follows:

'Yes, it is true that "Elijah does come first to restore all things". You're puzzled because as yet there has been no sign of Elijah, and already the Messiah – that is, myself – has appeared. You ask how this can be. Two points, my friends. First, don't always assume the scribes are accurate when they interpret scripture. There are some things they have patently got wrong. For instance, their description of the Messiah is totally different from the true biblical description, which is that the Son of man "should suffer many things and be treated with contempt". The second point is that "Elijah has come, and they did to him whatever they pleased, as it is written of him".' This last sentence seems to imply that as far as Jesus is concerned the martyrdom of Elijah/John the Baptist is foretold by scripture, but it is impossible to think of any passage that he might have had in mind.

And when they came to the disciples, they saw a great crowd about them, and scribes arguing with them. And immediately all the crowd, when they saw him, were greatly amazed, and ran up to him and greeted him. And he asked them, 'What are you discussing with them?' And one of the crowd answered him, 'Teacher, I brought my son to you, for he has a dumb spirit; and wherever it seizes him, it dashes him down; and he foams and grinds his teeth and becomes rigid; and I asked your disciples to cast it out, and they were not able'. And he answered them, 'O faithless generation, how long am I to be with you? How long am I

to bear with you? Bring him to me'. And they brought the boy to
him; and when the spirit saw him, immediately it convulsed the
boy, and he fell on the ground and rolled about, foaming at the
mouth. And Jesus asked his father, 'How long has he had this?'
And he said, 'From childhood. And it has often cast him into the
fire and into the water, to destroy him; but if you can do anything,
have pity on us and help us'. And Jesus said to him, 'If you can! All
things are possible to him who believes'. Immediately the father of
the child cried out and said, 'I believe; help my unbelief!' And
when Jesus saw that a crowd came running together, he rebuked
the unclean spirit, saying to it, 'You dumb and deaf spirit, I
command you, come out of him, and never enter him again'. And
after crying out and convulsing him terribly, it came out, and the
boy was like a corpse; so that most of them said, 'He is dead'. But
Jesus took him by the hand and lifted him up, and he arose. And
when he had entered the house, his disciples asked him privately,
'Why could we not cast it out?' And he said to them, 'This kind
cannot be driven out by anything but prayer'. (9.14–29)

Since there is no doubt that the transfiguration derives its imagery
from Moses on Mount Sinai in Exodus 24.15–18, it is tempting to
try and see this incident as a reenactment of the scene which
confronts Moses when he comes down from the mountain again in
chapter 32 – the worship of the golden calf; but, apart from the
general contrast between the glory of the mountain vision and the
terrestrial clumsiness of the disciple's failure, Mark gives little
indication that he has any such idea in mind. What we can say with
certainty is that for the first time he is not here primarily interested in
the miracle. The material in this and in the following sections is
concerned with the disciples: the disappointments and perplexities
they face (as in the above), the attitudes of mind they must cultivate
(9.33–37), who they are to regard as their friends (9.38–41), and so
on. During these two chapters the concerns of the crowd – to whom
up to now Jesus' mission has been principally directed, as will be that
of the disciples after he has gone – are put to one side. The crowd
themselves are still on stage, and their presence is in fact necessary to
those incidents which provide Jesus with the basis for his teaching.
But for the moment they function as extras, whereas up to now they
have tended to be principals of the drama.

The first detail to catch one's eye is that when Jesus gets back to the
disciples, not only are they surrounded by a crowd but, we are told,

there were also 'scribes arguing with them', a detail which Mark never explains, nor do the scribes themselves make any further appearance. Back in 3.22–30 we found scribes arguing with Jesus, on that occasion in at attempt to discredit his success as a miracle-worker. One presumes that here they have a complementary ambition to exploit the disciples' lack of it. It is interesting here to compare Matthew's version with what we have every reason to believe was his sole original:

> And when they came to the crowd, a man came up to him and kneeling before him said, 'Lord. have mercy on my son, for he is an epileptic and he suffers terribly; for often he falls into the fire, and often into the water. And I brought him to your disciples, and they could not heal him'. And Jesus answered, 'O faithless and perverse generation, how long am I to be with you? How long am I to bear with you? Bring him here to me.' And Jesus rebuked him, and the demon came out of him, and the boy was cured instantly. Then the disciples came to Jesus privately and said, 'Why could we not cast it out?' He said to them, 'Because of your little faith. For truly I say to you, if you have faith as a grain of mustard seed, you will say to this mountain, "Move from here to there" and it will move; and nothing will be impossible to you.' (Matt. 17.14–20)

The first thing to catch the eye (apart from the fact that this is a drastically shortened version – except at the end, where Matthew's radically altered version is longer than the original), is that Mark's 'demon' has been cut very much down to size. He is still there ('Jesus rebuked him, and the demon came out of him'), but now reduced from a star role to a bit part. Instead of Mark's elaborate description of how the demon normally carries on, Matthew briskly substitutes the single word 'epileptic', a word to which initially he seems reluctant to attach any ideas of demon possession at all. (Mark: 'wherever it [the demon] seizes him ...' Matthew: 'often he [the boy] falls ...') If he gives in later, it looks as though it is because the structure of Mark's tale forces him to do so. Should we accept Matthew's suggestion that the boy was epileptic? The tradition has tended to do so, labelling this miracle 'the healing of the epileptic boy'; and the symptoms are approximately right. The difficulty is in accepting that epilepsy could ever be 'cured' in this way – if indeed it could ever be really cured at all.

The other notable difference, as already hinted, is the conclusion. In both versions the disciples ask Jesus, 'Why could we not cast it out?'; but the answers they get bear no relation to each other. Prayer (and in some texts fasting also) will do the trick as far as Mark is concerned; but Matthew in our best texts makes no mention of either. He substitutes a short Q passage which occurs in Luke as:

> The apostles said to the Lord, 'Increase our faith!' And the Lord said, 'If you had faith as a grain of mustard seed, you could say to this sycamine tree, "Be rooted up, and be planted in the sea", and it would obey you.' (Luke 17.5–6)

I call this a Q passage because the 'grain of mustard seed' that both Matthew and Luke refer to appears nowhere in Mark in this kind of context. The reader will have noted though that Luke's 'sycamine tree' is a 'mountain' in Matthew, and this 'mountain' can make a good claim to belong to P:

> As they passed by in the morning, they saw the fig tree withered away to its roots. And Peter remembered and said to him, 'Master, look! The fig tree which you cursed has withered'. And Jesus answered them, 'Have faith in God, Truly I say to you, whoever says to this mountain, "Be taken up and cast into the sea", and does not doubt in his heart, but believes that what he says will come to pass, it will be done for him ...' (Mark 11.20–23)

Note that Mark agrees with Luke against Matthew in mentioning the sea, and with Matthew against Luke in talking about a mountain rather than a tree; though the context in which Mark places the miracle could well explain Luke's otherwise curious substitution. But the real point to make is that Matthew also gives the P version of the saying in its proper place in 21.21–22. So why then does he here balk at Mark's reply that, 'This kind cannot be driven out by anything but prayer [and fasting?].' In part I suggest this is yet another example of his habitual embarrassment about demons. But a further possibility is not hard to come by: repeated failure by the disciples, after the most intensive prayer and the most heroic fasting, to achieve the same convincing results that Jesus had by Matthew's time had persuaded many Christians that a more lenient excuse for failure needed to be found.

> They went on from there and passed through Galilee. And he would not have any one know it; for he was teaching his disciples, saying to them, 'The Son of man will be delivered into the hands of men, and they will kill him; and when he is killed, after three days

he will rise'. But they did not understand the saying, and they were afraid to ask him.

And they came to Capernaum; and when he was in the house he asked them, 'What were you discussing on the way?' But they were silent; for on the way they had discussed with one another who was the greatest. And he sat down and called the twelve; and he said to them, 'If any one would be first, he must be last of all and servant of all'. And he took a child, and put him in the midst of them; and taking him in his arms, he said to them, 'Whoever receives one such child in my name receives me; and whoever receives me, receives not me but him who sent me'.

John said to him, 'Teacher, we saw a man casting out demons in your name, and we forbade him, because he was not following us'. But Jesus said, 'Do not forbid him; for no one who does a mighty work in my name will be able soon after to speak evil of me. For he that is not against us is for us. For truly, I say to you, whoever gives you a cup of water to drink because you bear the name of Christ, will by no means lose his reward.

'Whoever causes one of these little ones who believe in me to sin, it would be better for him if a great millstone were hung round his neck and he were thrown into the sea. And if your hand causes you to sin, cut it off; it is better for you to enter life maimed than with two hands to go to hell, to the unquenchable fire. And if your foot causes you to sin, cut it off; it is better for you to enter life lame than with two feet to be thrown into hell. And if your eye causes you to sin, pluck it out; it is better for you to enter the kingdom of God with one eye than with two eyes to be thrown into hell, where their worm does not die, and the fire is not quenched. For every one will be salted with fire. Salt is good; but if the salt has lost its saltness, how will you season it? Have salt in yourselves, and be at peace with on another'. (9.30–50)

The excerpt starts with the second of the three warnings to the disciples of Jesus' approaching end. It is interesting here to compare both the other versions of this passage:

As they were gathering in Galilee, Jesus said to them, 'The Son of man is to be delivered into the hands of men, and they will kill him, and he will be raised on the third day.' And they were greatly distressed. (Matt. 17.22–23)

But while they were all marvelling at everything he did, he said to his disciples, 'Let these words sink into your ears; for the Son of man is to be delivered into the hands of men.' But they did not understand this saying, and it was concealed from them that they should not perceive it; and they were afraid to ask him about this saying. (Luke 9.43b–45)

Matthew has dispensed with Mark's idea (perhaps because he hasn't noticed it) of a final continuous sweep of a journey, starting from Caesarea Philippi on the occasion of Peter's confession, and ending with the triumphal entry into Jerusalem. He clearly intends us to think that the journey starts at this later point, and that this announcement of Jesus' approaching passion is the beginning of it. In Mark the disciples do not understand the saying; in Matthew they are greatly distressed by it. The likeliest reason for the change is that Matthew had misgivings about what he saw as the excessive emphasis in Mark on the disciples' not understanding Jesus. In contrast Luke puts greater stress on just this aspect of the story than even Mark's does.

As before noted, each time Mark puts this forewarning into Jesus' mouth of the ordeal that awaits him, he follows it with a little sermon on the nature of discipleship; and in this second instance the sermon is noticeably longer than the other two. But it also seems to have (what I hope I have now convinced the reader is very rare in Mark) an odd fault in construction. In verses 33–37 ('And they came to Capernaum ... "not me but him that sent me"') we have a discussion about who is the most important of the disciples, a question which Jesus refuses to answer immediately, but instead uses a child as an illustration of the way it might be answered one day. Verse 42 ('Whoever causes one of these little ones ...') takes up the theme of the child again as if it had never been interrupted, and Mark clearly intends the reader to suppose that as Jesus says 'one of these little ones', he indicates the same child that he put among them in verse 36. So verses 38–41, which deal with those who do mighty works in Jesus' name without being actual followers, appear to disrupt this flow of imagery. I have thought long and hard about how the sequence might be interpreted in a way that made the fault disappear, but confess myself up to now to be defeated.

But there are two observations that may turn out to be relevant. First is that the third and final prophecy by Jesus of his passion, which occurs in the next chapter in verses 32–34, is followed by private conversation which, as here, is between James and John on the one hand and Jesus on the other. If that conversation were transposed to this position, it would then be appropriate to the context. Second is the concluding sentence of the intrusive episode: 'For truly, I say to you, whoever gives you a cup of water to drink because you bear the name of Christ, will by no means lose his reward.' Matthew has a very similar saying in a very different context: 'And whoever gives to one of these little ones even a cup of cold water because he is a disciple, truly, I say to you, he shall not lose his reward' (10.42) Curiously, if the Marcan version appeared in the Matthean context and *vice versa*, the flow both passages would be improved. In Matthew there has been no previous mention of 'one of these little ones', and if we didn't also have the Marcan passage to explain it, it is quite likely we wouldn't have a clue what he is talking about.

A more contentious point is the general implication of the dispute about which of the disciples was the greatest. I know nothing of the traditions of the Eastern church, but in the West it seems to be accepted – even by Protestants – that Peter was the greatest disciple, the one that Jesus clearly intended should be the leader after he had gone. Yet if we take Mark's gospel in isolation, there seems to be no confirmation whatever of this view, which derives chiefly from Matthew 16.17–19 reinforced by the late and historically doubtful John 21.15–19. Within Mark's gospel there are three disciples – Peter, James and John – who are more prominent than any of the others. Of these three we know that James and John were ambitious to be joint leaders, and even tried to come to a private arrangement with Jesus to that effect (Mark 10.35–45). Although we have no reason to question that it was Peter who first acclaimed Jesus as the Messiah (Mark 8.29), there is no record in Mark of Jesus offering any special commendation to Peter because of this realization, and when it emerges that Peter's idea of what the Messiah is like is diametrically opposed to Jesus' own idea, he earns himself, as we have seen, the most savage rebuke that Jesus delivers anywhere in the gospel. When Jesus is directly asked which of them is the greatest (see the excerpt above), he refuses to give a straight answer. And that is the whole of the evidence on the question *within the pages of Mark's gospel*. It is clear, however, both from Acts and from Paul's epistles, that in the event Peter did become the leader after Jesus' death; and if his leadership was ever contested, we certainly have no trace of evidence of such a contest.

The *pericope* of the man casting out demons has already been alluded to earlier in connection with the nature of the body that Jesus brought into existence, where the point was made (and cannot be repeated too often) that if Christians had given due emphasis to the saying, He that is not against us is for us, European history would be a different and a kindlier story. The mischief may be said to have started with Matthew who finds no place for the Marcan version of the saying at all – his Q version is the exact opposite of Mark's:

> He who is not with me is against me, and he who does not gather with me scatters. (Matt. 12.30 = Luke 11.23)

(Luke, with slightly unintelligent evenhandedness, gives both versions – the above, and also the P version in 9.50.) The apparent contradiction is obvious, but so also is the difficulty of dismissing the Q version of the saying as inauthentic. The fact that (*a*) the Q saying is in parallel form and in no way ambiguous, and (*b*) the actual wording is identical in both Matthew and Luke makes this difficult. Matthew presumably cut out the Marcan passage just because of the contradiction; but interestingly it is possible that Mark deliberately omitted the Q saying for the same reason. Both Matthew and Luke agree, after all, that the saying is part of the 'casting out demons by Beelzebul' controversy, and we noticed earlier (pages 83–4 that Mark seems to have doctored his source in relating this incident.

Coming to the last section of the excerpt, we hardly need to draw attention to its extraordinarily miscellaneous content. Most readers, I am sure, will detect no connection whatever between the following five sections:

> Whoever causes one of these little ones who believe in me to sin, it would be better for him if a great millstone were hung round his neck and he were thrown into the sea.

> And if your hand causes you to sin, cut it off; it is better for you to enter life maimed, than with two hands to go to hell, to the unquenchable fire. And if your foot causes you to sin, cut it off; it is better for you to enter life lame, than with two feet to be thrown into hell. And if your eye causes you to sin, pluck it out; it is better for you to enter the kingdom of God with one eye, than with two

eyes to be thrown into hell; where their worm does not die, and the fire is not quenched.

For every one will be salted with fire.

Salt is good; but if the salt has lost its saltness, how will you season it?

Have salt in yourselves, and be at peace with one another.

Some, though, will have noted the verbal connections. The first two, for instance, have in common the phrase 'cause ... to sin'; the end of the second has in common with the third the word 'fire'; the third, fourth and fifth the word 'salt'. 'But', they may well say to themselves, 'so what? These catchwords hardly amount to connecting ideas, do they!' To us – no, but to the first generation of disciples these catchwords were of more practical use than any real ideas. They were in the position of having to learn off by heart long strings of disconnected sayings which no one had ever yet committed to paper – and in the very early days there may well have been a kind of ritual objection to anybody trying to do so. The use of catchwords such as we see in the above seems to have provided the technique which enabled them to do this. The end of chapter 9 of Mark's gospel is an untidy and haphazard jumble, but we are extraordinarily lucky to have it. Nothing like it survives elsewhere in this or in any other gospel; but it is likely that the bulk not only of Mark's gospel but also of the Q material came to the evangelists in this form, and that all three of them were faced with the task, first of unpicking the separate sayings, and then of rearranging them in a more literary and acceptable form. Why didn't Mark, then, unpick this passage with all the rest? I suggest because as the gospel now stands he has no section where any of this material would be specially appropriate, so he leaves it as he finds it. The use of catchwords would also explain another curious feature of the gospel material: the fact that different versions of what appear to have been originally the same saying, by means of only tiny variants, sometimes offer widely different meanings. As with all learning by rote, the significance of a saying, particularly for the less intelligent (of whom we may presume there was no lack among the early disciples), would tend to attach to the actual form of the words rather than to what we should consider to be their meaning.

And now, finally, what should we consider their meaning to be?

The question is difficult because one suspects (particularly in the case of the third and fifth sayings) not only that Mark himself had little idea of what they meant, but that whoever it was he got the sayings from was equally in the dark. With the first, second and fourth sayings, though, the problem is less severe. The first will perhaps have a certain piquancy for some of my more hostile readers, who will be in no doubt about *exactly* what the saying means: people who write books like this are upsetting the simple faith of simple believers, and it would be better – if not for them, then certainly for everyone else – if a great millstone ... and so forth. I have to confess that my obduracy is such that it would not greatly distress me if that really *were* the meaning, and in any case I accept that one can't altogether avoid an interpretation along those lines; but I think one could also fairly insist that the above is an oversimplification.

In this interpretation, for instance, 'one of these little ones who believe in me' is taken to mean not just children (although they are a paradigm of the simple believer), but any person of whatever age who just 'believes' in a trusting and uncomplicated way, and is so little interested in – and incapable of – considering the supposed 'intellectual difficulties' of belief that it causes a pointless bewilderment and distress even to try and make them aware of them. The hostile reader then interprets thus: 'In upsetting such a person's faith, you also shatter their moral framework (probably true), and that is why Jesus utters such a harsh condemnation of people like you.' On the other hand Jesus may have actually meant just 'children' (and it is clear from the context that Mark so interprets); the words 'who believe in me' are not necessarily original (it is hard to imagine, for instance, what Jesus himself could have meant by them), and even if they are, they certainly have no reference to anything remotely resembling a traditional catechism, or even a traditional creed. And one's defence also has to be that the truth really does matter, and that often it cannot be told without such believers getting hurt. It can also be said that much of the pain they feel is the fault, not of those who try to undeceive them, but of those who in many cases wilfully and knowingly deceived them in the first place. Could it not just as well be argued that it is *they* who have caused the little ones to stumble?

The rather savage tone of the second saying seems to have deterred Luke from including it in his gospel at all – and to have attracted Matthew sufficiently to relay it in two separate versions (Matt. 5.29–30; 18.–9). Its most useful function for me is as a check on the enthusiasm Christians have always had for equating virtue with whatever is forbidding or burdensome. 'Jesus prohibited divorce; therefore divorce is always wrong.' Or even worse: 'Jesus had no sex; therefore sex is always wrong.' (Perhaps I could, and perhaps I should be able to, think of other examples, but sex has always been the number one favourite for this kind of pointless condemnation. It is notable, for instance, that the first of the two Matthew passages referred to above follows immediately after Jesus' condemnation – somewhat unreal to most of us – not merely of adultery, but even of just fancying the notion. It is almost as if Matthew is hinting as strongly as he dare just which part of the anatomy in his view is prime candidate for abscission.) In this one instance, if in no other, we can be *absolutely* sure that Jesus had no intention of being taken literally, and Christians have never seriously suggested that he should be. But if we are allowed to use our common sense here, why should we not equally be allowed to use it elsewhere? Thus it is true that Jesus 'condemns' divorce (10.2–9). To interpret the passage as meaning that Jesus disapproved of divorce is fine; but to deduce from that that he therefore prohibited it is to be in love with agony for its own sake. I have not the slightest doubt that Jesus would have been as deeply repelled by the traditional 'Christian attitude to sex'[1] as he seems to have been by the pointless severity and inconvenience of the Sabbath laws of his own time.

So much for what he didn't mean – but what *did* he mean? Despite first impressions, this is a fine, perceptive and even witty observation. There are two words in it which will automatically mean something very different to most readers than Jesus intended: the first is 'life', and the second is 'hell'. Most readers traditionally assume that by 'life' Jesus here means 'life after death'; but he doesn't. And most readers assume that by 'hell' Jesus means a place of everlasting fire and torment where wicked people will be condemned to spend the eternity of life after death; and once again he doesn't – although the traditional Christian view of hell very much derives from passages like this. On the first point it is clear, as we have noted before, that by 'life' Jesus means not 'life after death' but what we should call 'the quality of life'. And the true explanation of 'hell' is even more intriguing. The Greek word here is *geenna*, a corruption of a Hebrew phrase meaning 'the valley of Hinnom', or (as it is more usually rendered in the Old Testament) 'the valley of the son[s] of Hinnom'. All is explained with marvellous brevity by the following:

> And he defiled Topheth, which is in the valley of the sons of
> Hinnom, that no one might burn his son or his daughter as an
> offering to Molech. (II Kings 23.10)

The 'he' is King Josiah, and the date is about 623 BC when the
monarchy, urged on by the Jerusalem priests, instituted a drastic
reform of the whole of the traditional religion of the southern
kingdom. Topheth was the name of the temple, while the valley of
the sons of Hinnom was the area outside Jerusalem in which it was
situated. It needs no further explanation why it was that in Jesus'
time this area had long been the rubbish dump for the city – a scene of
perpetual fires and perpetual decay – and was thus a powerful
symbol of the destruction that was due to everything that was
unclean or evil. Although in Mark's gospel Jesus is nowhere near
Jerusalem when he says this, we should almost certainly think of him
as being outside the city as he spoke, and able to point to the ever-
burning fires of *geenna* as he said it. So what he really means is
something like this: 'Which is more important – life itself, or the
mere accessories of life? You may think that the last thing you would
ever want to lose is a hand, or a foot, or an eye. But not quite the last.
The last thing you would ever really want to lose is life itself. No
matter how reluctant you would be to lose a limb, if you could save
your life by doing so, you would do it.' The point he was getting at is
easily illustrated from contemporary experience. I know all sorts of
people, for instance living 'life in the fast lane' who openly admit they
would do anything – *anything* – to be able to get out of it and live at a
more reasonable pace; but while in the 'acceleration lane' they took
on all sorts of financial commitments which they feel now make this
impossible. Jesus is here talking to just such people – and perhaps
just such people should now be talking to Jesus!

It remains to deal with verse 48: '... where their worm does not
die, and the fire is not quenched.' Some readers will have a text before
them that contains no verse 44 nor 46, and some of these will have a
marginal note explaining that these verses, which simply repeat verse
48, are not found in our better manuscripts. Whoever it was that
interpolated the additional verses was professionally at fault, no
doubt, but I can't help agreeing with him that the interpolation is an
improvement on what Mark actually wrote, and stylistic considerations seem to demand it. The verse in question is a quotation of the
last verse of Isaiah, where it has much the same meaning as Jesus

gives it here, and may well indeed have the very same source for its inspiration: the incessant burning and decay of the rubbish dump outside Jerusalem. Although Isaiah himself lived rather earlier than Josiah, the later portions of the book – as we saw in the appendix to the previous section – are much later.

Finally we have the three sayings about salt. Let us take the middle one first, since at least we can be sure that one does have an actual meaning. It is of course intended as a joke, though the joke is usually lost when the passage is read aloud in church. One gets the impression that some readers seriously believe it is possible for salt to lose its saltness – and certainly Luke seems to have thought that. His version runs:

> Salt is good; but if salt has lost its taste, how shall its saltness be restored? *It is fit neither for the land nor for the dunghill; men throw it away.* (Luke 14.34–35)

It is certain that the words I have italicized do not belong to any saying about salt, and likely that they originally referred to a saying about compost which we no longer have. However Matthew also does very little better:

> You are the salt of the earth; but if salt has lost its taste, how shall its saltness be restored? It is no longer good for anything except to be thrown out and trodden under foot by men. (Matt. 5.3)

This also makes the same crazy assumption that salt actually can lose its savour. The Marcan version, on the other hand, may be fairly close to what Jesus actually said. When read aloud we usually hear: '... if the salt has lost its saltness, how will you *season* it?' But the sense that Jesus had in mind was more like: '... if the *salt* has lost its saltness, how will you season *it*?' Perhaps in English one ought to take the liberty of translating: 'If the salt itself *were ever* to lose its savour ...' and so on. Christians normally apply the saying to the church; and though we have no reason to believe that Jesus ever foresaw anything like what finally emerged as the Christian church, the basic idea is not far from what he does seem to have meant. I take it that he is telling the disciples that they are different from the rest of the world, and meant to be different, and that is the point of them. They season the world by being something that the world lacks, and something that the world needs; and that if they ever become totally like the world, they will no longer be serving any useful purpose. I have to confess I very much like this interpretation, because it carries an implication that Christians do not intend, but which is just as true, as useful and as perceptive as any of the implications that they do intend. One of the most significant characteristics of salt, after all, is that it is perilously easy to use too much of it!

The other two sayings are absurdly cryptic, probably because they have been handed down, not just by one, but by a series of disciples who hadn't a clue what they meant and were obviously afraid to ask. It is still possible, nevertheless, to make a reasonable shot at interpreting them. First, 'Everyone will be salted with fire'. 'Fire' is above all a purifier, and is therefore used throughout the Bible as a frequent symbol of the kind of adverse fortune which tests what a man is made of and thus renders him nobler and wiser (Ps. 12.6; Prov. 17.3; 27.21; Eccl. 2.5; I Cor. 3.10–15; I Peter 4.12). If the saying were, 'Everyone will be *tested* with fire', there would be no problem, and one suspects in any case that that is really what it means. So where does 'salt' come in? The only thing I can think of by way of *partial* explanation is the following:

> You shall season all your cereal offerings with salt; you shall not let the salt of the covenant with your God be lacking from your cereal offering; with all your offerings you shall offer salt ... And the priest shall burn as its memorial portion part of the crushed grain ... it is an offering by fire to the Lord. (Lev. 2.13, 16)

By itself not even this gets us very far. But just as we suspected in the passage quoted from Luke above that the second half of the saying originally belonged to a completely different context which has not survived, so I suspect here not that we actually *do* have a reference to the above passage from Leviticus, but that there once was such a reference, only a faint trace of which now survives.

Finally, 'Have salt in yourselves, and be at peace with one another'. Part of this is already explained by the Leviticus quotation above, where reference is made to the fact that salt symbolizes a covenant or agreement. The reason for this is that the ratification of an agreement in ancient times was effected by the sharing of a meal by the parties agreeing, and salt was an essential ingredient in such a meal (Gen. 31.51–54; Num. 18.19; Josh. 9.14–15; Ezra 4.14). The first part of the saying unquestionably means, 'Be in agreement among yourselves ...', and one's perplexity is due only to the fact that this seems a very odd way of saying it.

11

The Road to Jerusalem II

(Mark 10.1–45)

And he left there and went to the region of Judaea and beyond the Jordan, and crowds gathered to him again; and again, as his custom was, he taught them.

And Pharisees came up and in order to test him asked, 'Is it lawful for a man to divorce his wife?' He answered them, 'What did Moses command you?' They said, 'Moses allowed a man to write a certificate of divorce, and to put her away.' But Jesus said to them, 'For your hardness of heart he wrote you this commandment. But from the beginning of creation "God made them male and female." "For this reason a man shall leave his father and mother and be joined to his wife, and the two shall become one flesh." So they are no longer two but one flesh. What therefore God has joined together, let not man put asunder.'

And in the house the disciples asked him again about this matter. And he said to them, 'Whoever divorces his wife and marries another, commits adultery against her; and if she divorces her husband and marries another, she commits adultery.' (10.1–12)

I don't mind admitting that the opening sentence of this excerpt is inconvenient for the theory on the basis of which I expounded the previous section of the gospel, in that in the middle of a section which is no longer supposed to be interested in the crowd as such, but to be concentrated on the disciples, Mark specifically states that the following material was directed at the crowds. When we look at the actual material though, it is by no means clear that we should believe him. The controversy with the Pharisees over divorce, for instance, may have been conducted in public. But what Jesus says out loud to all is general in tone; and when he becomes specific in the next paragraph, it is to the disciples alone that he is talking. The episode about the children which follows it does not relate to the crowd at all, except insofar as it is they who have brought the children along to be the topic of the dispute; the controversy itself solely concerns the disciples. When we look at the rest of the chapter up to verse 45, I think there is no doubt but that all this material relates to the instruction of the disciples. I wonder therefore whether Mark didn't put this sentence in solely in order to be able to contrast the discussion with the Pharisees in verses 2–10 with that with the disciples in verses 10–12.

What was the point of the controversy in any case? What is it the Pharisees are trying to prove (for who could be so naive as to imagine they ask the question in all innocence simply for the sake of information)? And how does Jesus' answer circumvent their hostile intention – something else we take for granted in expounding the controversy? The text itself gives us no clue on either of these points, and though the reader may be puzzled, the modern scholar can make a very good guess why. An earlier form of the story would probably have shown how Jesus yet again outsmarted the Pharisees in public debate and left them looking foolish – very much along the lines of a whole series of such stories we now have in 11.27–12.37. The difference here is that at some stage in the tradition interest seems to have switched to what Jesus actually says about marriage, so that the original depiction of a sparring match has become secondary. The story in this earlier form probably ended with verse 9: 'What therefore God has joined …'; and the next paragraph, containing the 'explanation' to the disciples, has been added later.

What justification can I offer for such a view? In particular there will be those to accuse me, with some show of probability, that all this is an exercise not in explaining the text but in explaining it away. I dislike the implications of verses 10–12 ('And in the house … "she commits adultery"'), and so I invent this elaborate hypothesis as an excuse for ignoring it. I do not for a moment deny that a strong motive for my interest in the hypothesis is my dislike of the implications of the concluding verses; but I think I can also honestly claim to be able to defend it on grounds of probability. Let us first of all make a comparison between this and some of the other equally striking sayings in the gospel:

> Those who are well have no need of a physician, but those who are sick; I came not to call the righteous, but sinners. (Mark 2.17)

The sabbath was made for man, not man for the sabbath; [so the Son of man is lord even of the sabbath]. (Mark 2.27–28)

Here are my mother and my brothers! Whoever does the will of God is my brother, and sister, and mother. (Mark 3.34b–35)

Render to Caesar the things that are Caesar's, and to God the things that are God's. (Mark 12.17)

I don't believe I am being fanciful in suggesting to the reader that 'What therefore God has joined together, let not man put asunder' fits very well into the style of the above sayings, and the verses which follow it do not. The authentic style of Jesus seems to have consciously rejected the formation of precise rules – an attitude which the disciple-as-vagabond naturally found congenial, and which the disciple-as-churchgoer just as naturally found deeply unsatisfying. It comes as no surprise to the historian that in the tradition as a whole it is the disciple-as-churchgoer who has triumphed, and who has imposed his preferences first on all his fellow Christians, and then (and often with deplorable consequences) on all his fellow human beings. Mark 10.10–12 can be taken as the opening verses of that distressing chapter in human history. A saying which Jesus seems to have intended – as he usually did – to be deliberately imprecise and merely hortatory has been reinterpreted as the basis of a horribly precise and legalistic discipline.

Comparison with Matthew's version (Luke suppresses the entire episode) will again be instructive from several points of view:

And Pharisees came up to him and tested him by asking. 'Is it lawful to divorce one's wife for any cause?' He answered, 'Have you not read that he who made them from the beginning made them male and female, and said, "For this reason a man shall leave his father and mother and be joined to his wife, and the two shall become one flesh"? So they are no longer two but one flesh. What therefore God has joined together, let no man put asunder.' They said to him, 'Why then did Moses command one to give a certificate of divorce, and to put her away?' He said to them, 'For your hardness of heart Moses allowed you to divorce your wives, but from the beginning it was not so. And I say to you: whoever divorces his wife, except for unchastity [makes her commit adultery] and [he who] marries another, commits adultery; [and he who marries a divorced woman commits adultery]'.

The disciples said to him, 'If such is the case of a man with his wife, it is not expedient to marry.' But he said to them, 'Not all men can receive this precept, but only those to whom it is given. For there are eunuchs who have been so from birth, and there are eunuchs who have been made eunuchs by men, and there are eunuchs who have made themselves eunuchs for the sake of the kingdom of heaven. He who is able to receive this, let him receive it'. (Matt. 19.3–12)

I have included this second paragraph because we then have the *whole* of Jesus' views, whether authentic or merely attributed, on the subject of marriage. (I am assuming that Mark 12.18–27 = Matt. 22.23–32 = Luke 20.27–38 is about marriage only incidentally, and is really concerned with resurrection.) As for the material in square brackets at the end of the first paragraph, it is nowadays generally agreed that it is not part of Matthew's authentic text, and any one with a modern translation will find these additions given only in a footnote – if at all. But it is in fact quite important to show them since for well over fifteen hundred years they were part of the received text of the gospel (as anyone can check by referring to the Vulgate and the Authorized Version) and have had a determining influence on the *whole* of Christian teaching relating to marriage until quite recent times.

Despite their appalling rigour, the first thing to notice is that they are in fact intended to be a *softening* of the potentially greater rigour of the Marcan text, which allows for no divorce at all under any circumstances. Whereas in Mark the Pharisees simply ask Jesus 'Is it lawful for a man to divorce his wife?', in Matthew they add the words 'for any cause', which is clearly intended to prepare the way for a much more important addition later. In Mark Jesus states peremptorily, 'whoever divorces his wife and marries another, commits adultery against her'; between 'another' and 'commits' Matthew inserts 'except for unchastity'. Presumably rank-and-file Christians in the locality for which Matthew was writing were insisting on this proviso. The later additions to Matthew's text mentioned above have the effect – probably intentional – of restoring some of Mark's original rigour to Matthew's laxer version.

Nor should we necessarily see the second Matthew paragraph as being (in intention) as rigorous as the tradition has tended to make it. Despite the fact that it is peculiar to Matthew it may well closely derive from something Jesus actually said, though probably not in any connection with its present context. When Jesus says, 'Not all men can receive this precept ...', as the text itself makes clear, Matthew intends this precept to refer to '... it is not expedient to marry' (which is not in fact a precept) rather than to the condemnation of divorce (which is). The join between the two passages is therefore rather tenuous and unconvincing. The meaning of Jesus' remarks can be paraphrased as follows: 'You suggest that perhaps it's better not to get married at all. That's all right for some, but not everyone is capable of living up to that idea. But there are some who can. Some people naturally have a very low sex-drive. Some people have had the misfortune to be castrated. Some, who otherwise would very much like to marry, deliberately refrain from doing so in order to be free to take to the road and spread the gospel. Only those who are capable of it should contemplate this kind of sacrifice.' As is fairly well-known, the Christian scholar Origen interpreted 'there are eunuchs who have made themselves eunuchs' in a startlingly different sense, which the church at large has rightly condemned, not only on grounds of what is fitting, but quite simply on grounds of accuracy; neither Jesus (if he said it) nor Matthew meant anything like that.

More controversial is the question whether Jesus is recommending *caelibatus* in its original sense or in its ecclesiastical one – to a Roman the word had no connotations of chastity at all, though it always has had for churchmen. Is he simply recommending that one refrain from marriage in order to be free (he is without question doing at least that), or does he also mean – as the church has always insisted – that refraining from marriage means refraining from sexual activity altogether? The evidence on the question is slender, but inclines to the harsher view. In the wider world of Jesus' day sex and marriage were by no means the same thing, nor was fornication considered particularly immoral by ancient paganism. But the specifically Jewish outlook on this question was very much gloomier than that, and there is moreover the likelihood that Jesus knew of no other attitude than the Jewish one. It is noticeable that in Acts (15.29; 21.25) we are twice given lists of the kind of behaviour to which paganism attached no moral significance but which converts from paganism must now avoid, and both lists conclude with a prohibition of unchastity. On the other hand – unlike a large majority of his followers – Jesus seems to have had an essentially practical mind as far as morality was concerned; and if he insistently condemned Sabbatarianism, apparently on the ground that its restrictions were purely ritualistic, served no genuinely moral purpose, and in practice often resulted in quite unnecessary hardship, it is hard to see why he should have insisted on any kind of total chastity, to which much the same objections could be made. Either way I see no reason to doubt that the passage closely resembles actual words of Jesus. As we have already seen on pages 125–7, despite Christianity's wish to present itself very much as the religion of the family, Jesus himself seems to have taken a rather caustic view of married and family life, and we should probably add this passage to the list of sayings we there gave to illustrate the point.

Let us at last return to Mark and look at an obvious question that remains. If we are right in suggesting that verses 10–12 should be regarded as an attempt by the tradition to turn Jesus' saying in verse 9 into something it was never intended to be, namely an absolute ban on divorce, we then have to ask ourselves just what *did* Jesus mean? There is no doubt that here he disapproves of divorce, and is suggesting that in a perfect world there would not be any such thing. But those words 'in a perfect world' are here crucial. We do not in fact live in a perfect world, and Jesus seems to have been perfectly aware that we do not. What he is saying is that *ideally* there should be no divorce. Had he survived to witness the agony and contortions brought about by treating his words as some kind of legal ban, none of us need doubt that he would have been the first to condemn them.

> And they were bringing children to him that he might touch them; and the disciples rebuked them. But when Jesus saw it he was indignant, and said to them, 'Let the children come to me, do not hinder them; for to such belongs the kingdom of God. Truly, I say to you, whoever does not receive the kingdom of God like a child shall not enter it.' And he took them in his arms and blessed them, laying his hands upon them. (10.13–16)

We need not doubt that this is historical, but we are still quite right to be amazed by it. Assuming that it happened, why did the tradition think it important to preserve such an unessential detail? What point was it supposed to be making? What relevance to the tradition as a whole was it supposed to have? One could connect it, I suppose, with the incident in the previous chapter of a child being used to illustrate the unassuming simplicity which should be the mark of true greatness. The same idea is obviously recalled here: 'Truly, I say to you, whoever does not receive the kingdom of God like a child shall not enter it.' But the truly remarkable feature of the passage is that children are not primarily being used as an illustration of anything at all. The only point that Jesus seems to be making – and the tradition which preserved the incident does not seem to have made any alteration to it – is that children are lovable just for themselves.

This is a view which to some extent we take for granted nowadays, but the very remarkable fact is that it is hard to think of anyone else in antiquity, whether Christian or pagan, who is on record as having thought the same way. Our own view is no older than the eighteenth century, and seems to have been developed by the prosperous and domestic-minded middle classes. Even at the time it was still incompatible with the dynastic thinking of the aristocracy, or the desperate-struggle-for-survival outlook of the poor. If it now seems all but universal (in utterance if not necessarily in reality), this is because for the present age the image of middle-class prosperity is held up as *the* ideal at which all should be aiming. It is also true that in prosperous countries this is by far the largest and most influential section of the population. Should growth capitalism one day come to an end (as presumably it will when the exhausted planet can no longer supply the resources needed to keep it going), it is likely that the economic basis of this class will also disintegrate, and our present attitude to children will perhaps seem as improbable to those that come after us as I dare say Jesus' view has often done to subsequent generations of Christians.

> And as he was setting out on his journey, a man ran up and knelt before him, and asked him, 'Good Teacher, what must I do to inherit eternal life?' And Jesus said to him, 'Why do you call me good? No one is good but God alone. You know the commandments: "Do not kill, Do not commit adultery, Do not steal, Do not bear false witness, Do not defraud, Honour your father and mother".' And he said to him, 'Teacher, all these I have observed from my youth.' And Jesus looking upon him loved him, and said to him, 'You lack one thing; go, sell what you have and give to the poor, and you will have treasure in heaven; and come, follow me.' At that saying his countenance fell, and he went away sorrowful; for he had great possessions.
>
> And Jesus looked around and said to his disciples, 'How hard it

will be for those who have riches to enter the kingdom of God!'
And the disciples were amazed at his words. But Jesus said to them
again, 'Children, how hard it is to enter the kingdom of God! It is
easier for a camel to go through the eye of a needle than for a rich
man to enter the kingdom of God.' And they were exceedingly
astonished, and said to him, 'Then who can be saved?' Jesus
looked at them and said, 'With men it is impossible, but not with
God; for all things are possible with God.' Peter began to say to
him, 'Lo, we have left everything and followed you.' Jesus said,
'Truly, I say to you, there is no one who has left house or brothers
or sisters or mother or father or children or lands, for my sake and
for the gospel, who will not receive a hundredfold now in this
time, houses and brothers and sisters and mothers and children
and lands, with persecutions, and in the age to come eternal life.
But many that are first will be last, and the last first.' (10.17–31)

We shall leave aside here the obvious implications of Jesus' initial
reply to the young man ('Why do you call me good?'), since these
have already been dealt with, and consider a point which comes very
much to the fore in these later chapters of the gospel. I suggested
earlier that Jesus' original intention in telling his disciples, 'Go, sell
what you have and give to the poor, and you will have treasure in
heaven', was more like one of self-indulgence rather than of self-
denial, in that he sincerely believed they would be happier as
vagabonds than they ever had been as householders and providers.
Yet the story here seems to imply that there was a moral obligation
for a disciple to do this whether he thought it would make him
happier or not. One could in fact make the dichotomy more stark
even than this. Is there not a contradiction between my suggested
portrait of a band of blissful, carefree vagabonds and the implications – whose authenticity I do not question – of Jesus' thrice
repeated prophecy of his own horrifying death and his determination
to go forward to meet it (Mark 8.31; 9.31; 10.33–4)? I admit there is
such an apparent contradiction, and my only answer must be to
draw attention to the passage which above all makes it clear that the
picture of the carefree vagabond is also undeniably authentic:

Therefore I tell you, do not be anxious about your life, what you
shall eat or what you shall drink, nor about your body, what you
shall put on. Is not life more than food, and the body more than
clothing? Look at the birds of the air: they neither sow nor reap

nor gather into barns, and yet your heavenly Father feeds them. Are you not of more value than they? And which of you by being anxious can add one cubit to his span of life? And why are you anxious about clothing? Consider the lilies of the field, how they grow; they neither toil nor spin; yet I tell you, even Solomon in all his glory was not arrayed like one of these. But if God so clothes the grass of the field, which today is alive and tomorrow is thrown into the oven, will he not much more clothe you, O men of little faith? Therefore do not be anxious, saying, 'What shall we eat?' or 'What shall we drink?' or 'What shall we wear?' For the Gentiles seek all these things; and your heavenly Father knows that you need them all. But seek first his kingdom and his righteousness, and all these things shall be yours as well. (Matt. 6.25–33 = Luke 12.22–31)

The conflict therefore once again seems to be in the actual evidence, and not just in my interpretation of it. The reader may perhaps still complain of a one-sided emphasis, in that I lay stress on the theme of self-indulgence, but seem to want to avoid that of self-denial. I think I'd admit that. I do it because I find traditional Christianity to be onesided in the other direction: to the onlooker it is very much the religion of useless and self-inflicted agony. And although for the moment the theme does here seem to be that of self-denial rather than of self-indulgence, as we shall see, Jesus still seems to be giving this unwelcome advice in the sincere belief that it will actually make the young man happier, in that it will both disencumber him, and also resolve that inner feeling of dissatisfaction which he clearly feels.

One feature of the story has often been commented on: when given the basic recipe for inheriting eternal life, the young man reacts with disappointment: 'I know all that – that's what I've been doing since boyhood.' Commentators have often wanted to see this as an indication of the morally unsatisfactory condition the young man is in; but there is no indication in the text that Mark thought that, or that he thought of Jesus as thinking so. Jesus' rules are for an every day, unheroic sort of virtue, and the young man's reply simply protests – in a way that he intends, and Jesus accepts, to be reasonable – that in that sense he always has been virtuous. But he still feels dissatisfied. Jesus believes he knows why – and my even be right. But no *sensible* person is going to be all that critical of the young man if his immediate reaction is that such a vast and irreversible change in his mode of life at the very least needs thinking about.

The text implies that Jesus was disappointed with his response; but it does not suggest that he necessarily condemned him for it.

The words, 'And Jesus looking upon him loved him …', in contrast have usually been passed over in silence – and in recent years an increasingly awkward silence. The former bishop of Birmingham, Dr Hugh Montefiore, once suggested that Jesus was probably homosexual, and these words were part of the evidence he put forward for that view. On the general point it can be stated flatly that nothing in any of the four gospels gives us any information about Jesus' sexuality whether psychic or sarcic. All later suggestions on the subject can therefore be at once classified as speculation. But equally we should reject the insistence of the tradition-minded enthusiast that Jesus could not possibly have experienced any kind of sexuality – either because it is unthinkable that the holy Son of God could have 'defiled' mind or body in that way, or simply because the idea is too embarrassing to think about. I would have to take professional advice to know whether it is possible for a human being to experience no kind of sexual impulse at all. But the one thing I could be sure of before I raised the question is that whatever answer I got would have absolutely no *moral* significance. Christianity, as I have noted before, seems to have a kind of fixation with sexuality – chiefly, I suspect, because of the peculiar thinking of Paul on the subject; and this is one area where its influence has been uniformly malign.

On what grounds can we insist that the words have no connotations of sexuality? Just what kind of response *was* Jesus making to the young man? A moment's reflection will show that this is the wrong question to be asking. As I think I have by now illustrated to most people's satisfaction, between the events of the gospel and the account we have of them in Mark's gospel there is a probable gap of about thirty years, and unquestionable evidence of constant retelling, rearranging and reinterpreting of the material. The real question therefore is, Did the tradition, or did Mark himself, intend the words to convey any suggestion of Jesus' sexuality? And to this I think we can give a definite answer, No. But then what *did* Mark think the words meant? He does not seem to be offering them as some kind of superfluous detail (of the kind, for instance, that we find in 6.39, where he thinks it worthwhile to point out that the grass was green); they are clearly meant to provide the motive firstly for Jesus making the suggestion that he does, and then for his obvious disappointment when the young man turns down the idea. The words are surely meant to imply that this was one of those situations where two up-to-now perfect strangers, within a very few minutes of starting to talk to each other, had come to realize the enormous rewards they could give each other in the way of companionship and like-mindedness. Even these days I think most people would agree that it's absurd to suggest this kind of response necessarily has anything at all to do with sex.

A final point that strikes the reader is contained in the words, '... go, sell what you have, and give to the poor, and you will have treasure *in heaven* ...' What does Jesus mean by 'heaven'? Or, if you prefer, what does the tradition, or Mark himself, mean by it? Up to now we have consistently argued that both Jesus and his followers had little use for any idea of a life after death of the kind that throughout its history the church has insisted on. For first generation Christians the reward held out to them was that they would still be alive at the time of Jesus' return to set up his perfect and eternal kingdom on earth; or if not that, then they would be raised from death and restored to a new earthly life to reign with Christ eternally. All the evidence suggests, for instance, that Paul intended the following to be understood absolutely literally:

> But we would not have you ignorant, brethren, concerning those who are asleep [*i.e. dead*], that you may not grieve as others do who have no hope. For since we believe that Jesus died and rose again, even so through Jesus God will bring with him those who have fallen asleep. For this we declare to you by the word of the Lord, that we who are alive, who are left until the coming of the Lord, shall not precede those who have fallen asleep. For the Lord himself will descend from heaven with a cry of command, with the archangel's call, and with the sound of the trumpet of God. And the dead in Christ will rise first; then we who are alive, who are left, shall be caught up together with them in the clouds to meet the Lord in the air; and so we shall always be with the Lord. (I Thess. 4.13–18)

It could be argued that the words 'in the air' above are a contradiction of my thesis; on the other hand they could equally well be simply Paul's attempt to adjust his imagery to match that of Daniel 7.13–14 where, despite the heavenly setting for the ceremony of actual investiture, there is not the slightest doubt that it is an *earthly*

kingdom that is being inaugurated. The points I would stress in the
above are the unquestionable *physicality* of the entire episode, plus
the fact that Jesus has to 'descend from heaven' in order for it to take
place.

In contrast to all this, talk of 'treasure in heaven' has an undeniable
ring of a purely spiritual treasure in a purely spiritual world,
something much more like the traditional and familiar imagery of
heaven. And the possibility cannot be ruled out that the tradition
behind Mark actually was thinking along such lines – we must
remember that, comparatively early though it is, Mark's gospel is
significantly later than Paul's genuine epistles, and may even be later
than some of the spurious ones. But assuming (as I do) that the
conversation is reasonably authentic, and however the later tradition
may have reinterpreted it, we have an *excellent* summary of what
will have been Jesus' original meaning towards the end of the above
excerpt:

> Truly, I say to you, there is no one who has left house or brothers
> or sisters or mother or father or children or lands, for my sake and
> for the gospel, who will not receive a hundredfold now in this
> time, houses and brothers and sisters and mothers and children
> and lands, with persecutions, and in the age to come eternal life.

There is an *immediate* hundredfold reward for people who walk out
on their commitments and dependents and join Jesus on the road;
there will be an even greater reward 'in the age to come', which here
has clearly no connection at all with our traditional ideas of heaven.
That age to come will be a new age of the terrestrial world.

Jesus is clearly disappointed by the young man's turning the
proposal down, and it is probable that Mark intends us to sense a
bitter flavour in his utterance about rich men and the kingdom of
God. So overwhelming has been the victory of the pale Galilaean
over European thought and history that we tend to take the truth of
what he here observes for granted. It is refreshing and salutary
therefore to note that the disciples to whom he first said it simply
could not believe their ears. If rich men will have difficulty entering
the kingdom of God, how can it even be *possible* for poor men to do
so! Jesus' first attempt to convince them takes the form of explaining
what he meant: 'It is easier for a camel to go through the eye of a
needle than for a rich man to enter the kingdom of God.' There have
been all sorts of attempts in popular interpretations of the gospel to

make this saying just a little less absurd than it seems to be. The two most frequent seem to be that 'camel' does not really mean camel but is in fact a thick rope; alternately that 'the eye of a needle' really means a small wicket gate beside the main gate of a city. But in fact we have no grounds whatever for questioning the perfectly ordinary meaning of both these terms, and in any case the whole *point* of the imagery is its absurdity. In Jesus' part of the world from earliest times up to our own day the camel was first and foremost a kind of heavy goods vehicle, first of all as richly caparisoned as its owner could afford as a means of advertising his own standing as a successful merchant, secondly heavily burdened with the merchandise itself. All this has to go, Jesus points out, for this bulkiest of creatures to get through this tiniest of apertures. Our everyday lives are overburdened by the trappings of supporting them. To enter the kingdom you must get rid of all these trappings and take with you only the life itself. And the life itself, by itself, is no more than the merest whisper, which can easily pass through even the tiniest of apertures.

Even this explanation initially fails, however. The hearers are still incredulous: 'And they were exceedingly astonished and said to him, "Then who can be saved?"' – not 'Who can be *saved*?', but 'Who *can* be saved?' Jesus' rather lame reply sounds to modern ears like a pious version of, 'Well, I give up', and that may be part of Mark's intention. On the other hand it looks to my eyes as if the tradition here has conflated two separate incidents, or else two separate versions of the same incident, and that is why verse 26 ('And they were exceedingly astonished ...') is virtually a repetition of verse 24 ('And the disciples were amazed at his words ...') In that case Jesus' two replies would also originally have belonged to entirely separate stories.

With verse 28 ('Peter began to say to him, "Lo, we have left everything ..."') we come to a new stage in the discussion. The point has been made, though not perhaps understood, that rich men find difficulty in entering the kingdom because they find difficulty in detaching themselves from the supposed comforts – but in reality encumbrances – of their possessions. Peter's next remark as it stands seems in rather bad taste, but I suspect this is only because the passage we are now dealing with came to Mark as an independent story and it was his decision to fit it into its present context. The most obvious reason for thinking this is that the preceding material suggests that the disciples still could not grasp how it could be that rich men could hardly get into the kingdom at all, and yet the kingdom would still be very populous. But Peter's present comment shows that he understands this perfectly. The context also (and I am convinced it is the context that is to blame for this) presents him in a rather undignified light, almost as though he were a dog wagging his tail in the hope of being thrown a biscuit – an impression which Matthew makes very considerably worse by adding, apparently off his own bat, 'What then shall we have?' (19.27). The implications of Jesus' reply have already been dealt with, but I would like to draw attention to the concluding verse of the passage: 'But many that are first will be last, and the last first.' Matthew uses these words to introduce the parable (found only in his gospel) of the workers of the vineyard, and repeats them again at the end to drive the point home (Matt. 19.30–20.16). The saying and the parable match each other so well that if we did not have Mark's gospel we would be convinced that they actually belonged to each other and had done so from the very first. Yet the full evidence suggests that it is Matthew himself that has made the connection. In just the same way we can be sure that there are many joins of just the same kind in Mark which we now have no hope of being able to detect.

And they were on the road, going up to Jerusalem, and Jesus was walking ahead of them; and they were amazed, and those who followed were afraid. And taking the twelve again, he began to tell them what was to happen to him, saying, 'Behold, we are going up to Jerusalem; and the Son of man will be delivered to the chief priests and the scribes, and they will condemn him to death, and deliver him to the Gentiles; and they will mock him, and spit upon him, and scourge him, and kill him; and after three days he will rise.'

And James and John, the sons of Zebedee, came forward to him, and said to him, 'Teacher, we want you to do for us whatever we ask of you.' And he said to them, 'What do you want me to do for you?' And they said to him, 'Grant us to sit, one at your right hand and one at your left, in your glory.' But Jesus said to them, 'You do not know what you are asking. Are you able to drink the cup that I drink, or to be baptized with the baptism with which I am baptized?' And they said to him, 'We are able.' And Jesus said to them, 'The cup that I drink you will drink; and with the baptism with which I am baptized you will be baptized; but to sit at my right hand or at my left is not mine to grant, but it is for those for whom it has been prepared.' And when the ten heard it, they began to be indignant at James and John. And Jesus called them to him and said to them, 'You know that those who are supposed to rule over the Gentiles lord it over them, and their great men exercise authority over them. But it shall not be so among you; but whoever would be great among you must be your servant, and whoever would be first among you must be slave of all. For the Son of man also came not to be served but to serve, and to give his life as a ransom for many.' (10.32–45)

The second of these paragraphs is the one that concerns us, the substance of the first of them having been encountered twice before. It cannot be a coincidence that last time Jesus informed his disciples of his approaching ordeal, the warning was immediately followed by the disciples squabbling about which of them should be the leader. And here again the same kind of warning is followed by the same kind of dispute. A new interest begins with Jesus' words: 'You do not know what you are asking. Are you able to drink the cup that I drink, or to be baptized with the baptism with which I am baptized?' Here I could open up a vast dissertation on what is symbolized in the Bible by the 'cup' and by 'baptism'. What follows is necessarily a little meagre, but for what it is worth here goes.

Even in modern English we are still fairly familiar with two quasi-proverbial expressions about a 'cup', both of them directly borrowed from the Bible. 'My cup runs over' quotes Psalm 23.5b and indicates that we are being overwhelmed by a tide of good fortune. A cup of sorrow or of affliction in most people's minds is connected with Jesus' words in the garden of Gethsemane immediately before his arrest: 'Abba, Father, all things are possible to thee; remove this cup from me; yet not what I will, but what thou wilt' (Mark 14.36, see Matt. 26.39 and Luke 22.42). But neither of these uses of the term are all that rare in the Bible, the Old Testament particularly: for the cup of joy see Psalm 16.5, 116.13, while instances of the cup of horror or affliction are too numerous to list. The central image seems to be provided by the following:

I say to the boastful, 'Do not boast',
    and to the wicked, 'Do not life up your horn [*i.e. do not
                behave arrogantly*];

do not lift up your horn on high,
   or speak with insolent neck.'
For not from the east or from the west
   and not from the wilderness comes lifting up;
but it is God who executes judgment,
   putting down one and lifting up another.
For in the hand of the Lord there is a cup
   with foaming wine well mixed;
and he will pour a draught from it,
   and all the wicked of the earth shall drain it down to the
                            dregs. (Ps. 75.4–8)

The speaker is the king, and the implication of what he says is that his is a divine office. As he abases the proud among those about him, so God punishes the iniquity of the world at large. The cup can be taken almost as an image of destiny; it contains what God has in store for human beings. This *can* be a cup of joy, but it is usually thought of as a cup of sorrow and disaster. These are the images that underly both what Jesus says in the garden of Gethsemane, and also what he says to James and John here. In both these passages the cup has become specifically an image of martyrdom. Jesus prays in Gethsemane that he may not have to die; and he is asking James and John here whether or not they are prepared to die.

   The baptism symbolism is harder to grasp. Up to now whenever we have spoken of baptism it has been a baptism of repentance, and references generally to baptism in the New Testament are to this kind of baptism – apart from two: Mark 10.38–9 above, and Luke 12.50. This second reference is worth quoting in full:

I came to cast fire upon the earth; and would that it were already kindled! I have a baptism to be baptized with; and how I am constrained until it is accomplished! Do you think I have come to give peace on earth? No, I tell you, but rather division ... (Luke 12.49–51)

We still have a proverbial expression in English, 'a baptism of fire', and the above passage is where it derives from. But the conjunction of the two images of baptism and fire, instead of the more usual (and more obvious) baptism and water, is not confined to this one passage. The Q material relating to John the baptist contains the following:

I baptize you with water for repentance, but he who is coming after me is mightier than I, whose sandals I am not worthy to carry; he will baptize you with the Holy Spirit and with fire. (Matt. 3.11 = Luke 3.16)

There is an important difference, though, between the Lucan passage above and this from Q, in that the implications of the former are that the baptism Jesus is talking about is an *ordeal*, and I don't think the same is true – or necessarily true – of the Q passage. The true contrast there is not so much between water and fire as between water and the Holy Spirit. The intrusion of fire may well be influenced by the ordeal imagery; but that is the most one can say.

In these two references therefore – Mark 10.38–9 and Luke 12.49–51) – Jesus uses baptism as a symbol of an ordeal; and his use of the symbol of the cup is, as we have seen, not dissimilar. In effect he is telling James and John that to qualify for the positions they are asking for they must be willing to undergo an ordeal. Since all the evidence suggests that right up to the time of the final catastrophe the disciples continued to assume that the fact that Jesus was the Messiah indicated that his ministry would end with a military campaign against the Romans, culminating in the restoration – in a literal, political and territorial form – of the historic empire of King David, we are bound to suppose that they understood him to mean that they must be willing to risk their lives in the field, and so achieve for themselves the position of eminence. And no doubt all that had been part of their calculations, and all of it completely taken for granted, even before they raised the question. It is not surprising therefore that they so readily agree to the conditions. The point that Mark seems to have in mind is that no matter how often Jesus reminds the disciples of what his role as Messiah is really like, they simply won't – or rather simply can't – believe him. The other ten, when they come to hear of this private conversation, have no better understanding of the situation. Jesus yet again – and presumably yet again vainly – tries to convince them of the very different nature of his kingdom compared with the one they have in mind. Just as his victory will be one of submission rather than of conquest, so his rule will be one of service rather than of domination.

The final verse of the excerpt, 'For the Son of man also came not to be served but to serve, and to give his life as a ransom for many', is one of those vast images of the New Testament which, when we stand close to them and ask ourselves exactly what they mean, do not seem to have any precise meaning at all; yet viewed from a distance, and vaguely absorbed rather than closely examined, they create an indelible impression. The specific reference is to Isaiah 53, but the tradition is probably right in also seeing a general reference to the sacrificial theory of the Old Testament, particularly to the idea that the offering of sacrifice cleanses the worshipper from sin. Some modern reader will want to object that in reality it has no such effect. But on the other hand, does anything in reality have that effect? And if not, are we going to be content with the idea that nothing can cleanse us from sin? Better to argue, I would have thought, that if the imagery is effective, there is no way in which it can be, much less needs to be, confuted.

12

Jesus and Jerusalem

(Mark 10.46–12.44)

The inordinate length of this section is in all likelihood due to the fact that Jesus made several visits to Jerusalem in the course of his ministry, all the recollections of which Mark has condensed into a single episode at its close. If only one visit is going to be described, it is obviously going to have to be put at the end, since it is an important feature of the story as a whole that Jesus died in the course of such a visit. Later tradition has condensed the narrative even further than Mark intended. For centuries the church has celebrated Palm Sunday five days before the crucifixion, and the preacher usually makes great play of the contrast between the two events in the belief that this close juxtaposition was the actual history. But it is in fact clear from Mark's gospel that the triumphal entry he describes in the opening verses of chapter 11 took place at the feast of Tabernacles in the autumn (see pages 220–1), while the crucifixion occurred at the spring festival of the Passover. We have no reason to suppose that Mark himself was unaware of this. He may even have intended us to assume that Jesus was in Jerusalem for the whole of that last six months, and that is why the discussion material he records for the visit is so extensive. The traditional Christian Holy Week, profoundly impressive as a ceremony in its stark contrast between the triumph of Palm Sunday, the catastrophe of Good Friday, and the concluding triumph of Easter, is nevertheless implausible as history, while this original Marcan scheme is very much less so.

But even the Marcan scheme, faithfully imitated by Matthew and Luke, is probably not the truth of the matter. In John's gospel, by way of contrast, Jesus goes up to Jerusalem in 2.13 for the Passover, again in 5.1 for an unspecified feast of the Jews, again in 7.10 for the feast of Tabernacles, is still there for the winter feast of the Dedication in 10.22, and returns for the last time six days before the

Passover in chapter 12 where the triumphal entry is also described –
clearly it was John's narrative which originally laid the basis of the
Christian Holy Week. It can easily be demonstrated that John's
reasons for suggesting these repeated visits to Jerusalem are far from
being historical; nevertheless in this particular respect he is likely to
be closer to history than the synoptic gospels. On which particular
visit the triumphal entry took place obviously cannot be known; but
it is important to bear in mind the possibility that it may originally
have had no connection at all with the events leading up to Jesus'
arrest and execution. On two points Mark is almost certain to be
right: the triumphal entry took place in the autumn and the execution in the spring; but the distance between the two events may well
have been far more even than the six months that Mark implies. It
could even be several years. Once again the testimony of John's
gospel, though not historical, could be making a historical point. The
Christian tradition suggests that the incident that more than any
other sealed Jesus' fate was his cleansing of the temple. Yet in John's
gospel this event takes place at the very outset of the ministry in
2.13–17.

> And they came to Jericho; and as he was leaving Jericho with his
> disciples and a great multitude, Bartimaeus, a blind beggar, the
> son of Timaeus, was sitting by the roadside. And when he heard
> that it was Jesus of Nazareth, he began to cry out and say, 'Jesus,
> Son of David, have mercy on me!' And many rebuked him, telling
> him to be silent; and he cried out all the more, 'Son of David, have
> mercy on me!' And Jesus stopped and said, 'Call him.' And they
> called the blind man, saying to him, 'Take heart; rise, he is calling
> you.' And throwing off his mantle he sprang up and came to Jesus.
> And Jesus said to him, 'What do you want me to do for you?' And
> the blind man said to him, 'Master, let me receive my sight.' And
> Jesus said to him, 'Go your way; your faith has made you well.'
> And immediately he received his sight and followed him on the
> way. (10.46–52)

'And they came to Jericho ...' This apparently simple statement
reveals one of the big puzzles relating to the history behind the gospel
accounts, and one that has scarcely been touched on so far: Jesus'
attitude to the Samaritans. If you look at a map of Palestine in the
time of Jesus you will see that the country is divided into three
sections: Galilee on the north, Samaria in the middle, and Judaea in

the south. It hardly needs to be stated that for the country as a whole the supremely important centre was Jerusalem in Judaea; and as we have seen from John's gospel, there was a kind of urge for as many people as possible to celebrate all the major festivals there. But this applied to the Galilaeans and Judaeans only. For historical reasons which we need not go into here, the Samaritans were excluded from orthodox Jewish worship. As John's gospel pithily puts it (4.9b) 'Jews have no dealings with Samaritans' It was for this reason that Galilaeans going to Jerusalem for a festival, instead of passing through Samaria, would cross over to the east side of the Jordan at the bottom of the sea of Galilee and cross back again to the west side at Jericho. This is why the apparently simple statement of 10.46 raises an enormous question. As far as Mark is concerned Jesus adopted the usual – and therefore hostile – attitude of the orthodoxy of his day towards the Samaritans.

How close is he to history on this point? His is our earliest gospel, and if other gospels (notably Luke and John) take a different view, it could easily be because once the split had occurred between Judaism and the Christian church it began to seem not merely unnecessary but actually embarassing to portray Jesus as having shared these prejudices. But there is one particular passage in Luke – which we alluded to on page 1 of the introduction – which is very hard to dismiss as inauthentic:

> When the days drew near for him to be received up, he set his face to go to Jerusalem. And he sent messengers ahead of him, who went and entered a village of the Samaritans to make ready for him; but the people would not receive him, because his face was set toward Jerusalem. And when his disciples James and John saw it, they said, 'Lord, do you want us to bid fire come down from heaven and consume them?' But he turned and rebuked them. And they went on to another village. (Luke 9.51–56)

The story makes no obvious moral point. Some manuscripts add after 'he turned and rebuked them' the words, 'and he said, "You do not know what manner of spirit you are of; for the Son of man came not to destroy men's lives but to save them"'; but this is transparently an attempt to make up the deficiency – to insert a moral point where there should be one but at present doesn't seem to be. No one comes out of the incident all that well, neither the Samaritans nor the two disciples. Jesus' answer is on the side of virtue, but the modern reader can't help feeling that an honest man might have laughed, and said something like, 'Yes, do by all means call down fire from heaven, and let's see what happens.' Even in Luke's own day there would have been a good proportion of his readership to whom that idea would also have occurred. On the one hand we can easily see why other traditions would have suppressed the story, and on the other it is hard to see why the Lucan tradition should have made it up; the conclusion must be therefore that the story is authentic.

And we do also have evidence of actual suppression in Mark's gospel on the whole subject of Samaritans. He never once mentions them, or anything to do with them. Matthew's gospel has a single mention in 10.5, where he makes Jesus instruct his disciples to have nothing to do either with them or with the Gentiles; and we have seen that, however much it contradicts our usual suppositions about Jesus, this instruction may well be authentic. The distinctly pro-Samaritan gospel is Luke's, but it also cannot be denied (see Ch. 3, note 2 on page 375) that much of the material about them seems to have a considerable element of fiction in it. The parable of the good Samaritan, for instance, is a fine and improving tale, but I do not for a moment believe it has any connection with the original teaching of Jesus; and the story of the Samaritan leper in 17.11–19 cannot possibly be true. But the above story must be, and is enough by itself to cast the strongest doubt on Mark's total silence about Samaritans in his gospel. Did Jesus' in fact cross and recross the Jordan when on his way to Jerusalem? It's quite possible, of course, that sometimes he did and sometimes he didn't. A very likely explanation is that, having occasionally tried to show goodwill towards the Samaritans and been rebuffed, in later years he decided that orthodoxy, if not necessarily best, was certainly more practical.

'... Bartimaeus, a blind beggar, the son of Timaeus, was sitting by the roadside.' This may well be true, but do we need to know, for instance, even the beggar's name, let alone why he was called that? Why not simply, 'A blind beggar was sitting by the roadside', as we pretty well find it in Luke (18.35)? We nowhere else find Mark giving the actual names of casual beneficiaries of the healing ministry, so why here? It is just possible that Mark actually knew either the man himself or a close relative. We find in the passion narrative, for instance, that all three synoptic gospels mention Simon of Cyrene (Matt. 27.32; Mark 15.21; Luke 23.26), the man who was press-ganged into carrying Jesus' cross for him; but Mark alone adds that he was 'the father of Alexander and Rufus', and expositors have plausibly suggested the implication is that these two men were members of the congregation for which Mark was writing. A similar factor may be present here. The name Bartimaeus is itself something of a puzzle. Mark, though he tells us that his father was called Timaeus, does not tell us that this is in fact what 'Bartimaeus' means. (Indeed, and rather alarmingly, if we didn't have behind us a tradition of confident identification of the author of this gospel with the John Mark that is mentioned in Acts 12.12, 12.25, 15.39, and who must certainly have been Aramaic-speaking, on the basis of this passage we would tend to assume that the author simply didn't know what 'Bartimaeus' means.) The other oddity here is that while Timaeus is an idiomatically Greek name, Bar is an equally idiomatic Aramaic prefix. The effect is rather like that of an Italian being called MacVerdi.

'Jesus, Son of David ...' This is the first of only three instances throughout the gospel where reference is made to any possible claim Jesus might have to this transparently Messianic title. It is no accident either that all three of them are embedded in the Jerusalem material. It may also be intentional that the three references are 'shaped'. Here on the first occasion the title is offered quite casually, without even any hint that it has a particular significance. In the next section of the gospel (11.1–10), though the actual title is saved up for the conclusion, the whole of the incident is a deliberate and quite unmistakable enactment of Jesus' claim to such a title, and is a major point of climax in the gospel as a whole. The third instance therefore (12.35–37) is something of a puzzle. The immediate implication of the passage is that Jesus makes no claim to be the Son of David. The wider implication is that despite the fact that he is not the Son of David, he is nevertheless the Messiah. The point he is making is that the tradition is mistaken in supposing that the Messiah will be Son of David, and he uses the quotation from Psalm 110 to 'prove' this. The implications of the triumphal entry therefore are in direct conflict with this later passage – a problem we will be exploring later in the chapter.

And when they drew near to Jerusalem, to Bethphage and Bethany, at the Mount of Olives, he sent two of his disciples, and said to them, 'Go into the village opposite you, and immediately as you enter it you will find a colt tied, on which no one has ever sat; untie it and bring it. If any one says to you, "Why are you doing this?", say, "The Lord has need of it and will send it back here immediately".' And they went away, and found a colt tied at the door out in the open street; and they untied it. And those who stood there said to them, 'What are you doing untying the colt?' And they told them what Jesus had said; and they let them go. And they brought the colt to Jesus, and threw their garments on it; and he sat upon it. And many spread their garments on the road, and others spread leafy branches which they had cut from the fields. And those who went before and those followed cried out, 'Hosanna! Blessed is he who comes in the name of the Lord! Blessed is the kingdom of our father David that is coming! Hosanna in the highest!'

And he entered Jerusalem, and went into the temple; and when he had looked round at everything, as it was already late, he went out to Bethany with the twelve. (11.1–11)

At this point, for reasons which are not immediately clear but will become so as we proceed, we find ourselves having to take a look at one of the most puzzling books in the Old Testament – the prophecies collected under the name of Zechariah. As the book stands it consists of fourteen chapters, but even at first reading most will be able to see that it separates into two sections, chapters 1–8 and 9–14, and that these two sections have nothing whatever to do with each other. The first section contains its own share of problems – but which book of the Old Testament does not! – but the basic situation is clear. The book opens with the words: 'In the eighth month, in the second year of Darius [i.e. 520 BC], the word of the Lord came to Zechariah ...', and we have no reason to doubt the accuracy of this dating or the substantial authenticity of the following eight chapters. Chapters 9–14 on the other hand must be treated as a totally anonymous and undated fragment: we literally have no idea who wrote it, and have to guess from the actual contents when it was written and what kind of political situation it relates to.

The one direct clue the material contains looks to my eye to be wholly misleading. 9.13b reads: 'I will brandish your sons, O Zion, over your sons, O Greece, and wield you like a warrior's sword.' I would agree with those who argue that these words date at the earliest from the time of Alexander the Great, and that it is his empire or some successor to it that is referred to. But for me this one short passage is not enough to date the entire fragment to that period. It could easily be, and it looks to me as though it is, an interjection by the hand of a later scribe who was probably carried away by some imagined relevance of the text he was working on to his own view of his own time. Without that one passage such indications as there are point to a pre-exilic date for the writing. If we take the first eight verses of chapter 9, we notice a great many references to place names: the land of Hadrach, Damascus, the cities of Aram, Hamath, Tyre and Sidon, Ashkelon, Gaza, Ekron, Ashdod, Philistia. All of these are places which before the exile could have constituted some kind of threat to Israel; but with the exception of Tyre and Sidon, none of them was of any real significance after it. The indications of chapter 10, if accepted as genuine, would point to a date roughly mid-eighth century BC. There are, for instance, two independent Israelite kingdoms – of Ephraim [i.e. Israel] and Judah (10.6–7), while the dominant world powers appear to be Assyria and Egypt (10.10–11). And the material certainly originates from the southern rather than the northern kingdom. But even if we accept that date and that provenance, it gives us no real clue as to what a great deal of the actual imagery is about.

Why then is it so important to Mark 11.1–10? A frivolous answer would be that I wish I knew; but more seriously, though we cannot see *why* it is, we are forced to acknowledge *that* it is. One need look no further than 9.9 to see this:

> Rejoice greatly, O daughter of Zion!
>   Shout aloud, O daughter of Jerusalem!
> Lo, your king comes to you:
>   triumphant and victorious is he,
> humble and riding on an ass,
>   on a colt the foal of an ass.[1]

There is no question but that the incident of the triumphal entry is based upon the imagery of this passage, not merely in Mark's mind or that of the tradition but in the mind of Jesus himself. But why? The passage itself is not obviously Messianic at all. What seems to have caught Jesus' imagination is the apparent contrast between the second couplet and the third. In the second couplet the king is triumphant and victorious, in the third he is humble and riding on an ass. He seems to have thought of this as a way of communicating to the crowd that, yes, he was the Messiah but, no, not the Messiah of their dreams. There is a strong tradition of exegesis which insists that the crowd would have automatically called the passage to mind, and so grasped the point Jesus was trying to make. Personally I am sceptical about that; but I do not doubt either that that was in Jesus' mind, or that the triumphal entry took place very much as Mark describes it.

While we are on the subject, we may as well draw attention to the several other instances where the imagery of – let us call it Deutero-Zechariah – has influenced the gospel narrative leading up to and including the passion. From 11.4 of Zechariah to the end of the chapter is a mystifying section starting: 'Become the shepherd of the flock doomed to slaughter.' Apart from the fact that the 'sheep' must be the ordinary Israelites of both kingdoms, nothing in this section is clear. Verses 12–13 read:

> Then I said to them, 'If it seems right to you, give me my wages; but if not, keep them.' And they weighed out as my wages thirty shekels of silver. Then the Lord said to me, 'Cast it into the treasury [*the Hebrew actually says* potter]' – the lordly price at which I was paid off by them. So I took the thirty shekels of silver and cast them into the treasury [*same word*] in the house of the Lord.

Most readers will already have been reminded without my help of the following from Matthew's gospel:

> Then one of the twelve, who was called Judas Iscariot, went to the chief priests and said, 'What will you give me if I deliver him to you?' And they paid him thirty pieces of silver. And from that moment he sought an opportunity to betray him. (Matt. 26.14–16)

and even more of:

> When Judas, his betrayer, saw that he was condemned, he repented and brought back the thirty pieces of silver to the chief priests and the elders, saying, 'I have sinned in betraying innocent blood.' They said, 'What is that to us? See to it yourself.' And throwing down the pieces of silver in the temple, he departed; and he went and hanged himself. But the chief priests, taking the pieces of silver, said, 'It is not lawful to put them into the treasury, since they are blood money.' So they took counsel, and bought with them the potter's field to bury strangers in. Therefore that field has been called the Field of Blood to this day. Then was fulfilled what had been spoken by the prophet Jeremiah, saying, 'And they took

the thirty pieces of silver, the price of him on whom a price had been set by some of the sons of Israel, and they gave them for the potter's field, as the Lord directed me.' (Matt. 27.3–10)

So far as we can tell, the whole of this (which is found only in Matthew) is a fabrication derived – and as the reader can see, somewhat loosely and confusedly derived – from the passage in Zechariah, which Matthew here wrongly attributes to Jeremiah, which he wildly misquotes anyway, and which even in the original is itself not a little confused.

We have no reason therefore to connect these particular ideas with any thinking of Jesus. But Mark has a passage which does seem to have such a connection:

And Jesus said to them, 'You will all fall away; for it is written, "I will strike the shepherd, and the sheep will be scattered."' (Mark 14.27)

The quotation is fairly close to a line from Zechariah 13.7; but that is pretty well all that can be offered by way of explanation.

The final passage which has reference to the gospel narrative brings us back conveniently to the very topic which is supposed to be our concern – the triumphal entry. It would be well worthwhile for the reader to look at the whole of chapter 14 of Zechariah; there's not much he will actually understand, but it may cheer him up to know that that is the case with all of us. If he already knows chapters 11–13 of Mark well, he will be continually reminded of them even while remaining mystified. There is the mention of the Mount of Olives in verse 4. Verse 9 ('And the Lord will become king over all the earth') was probably understood by Jesus as a prophecy of his own coming kingdom. Verses 16–19 are a declaration that not merely Israel but 'all nations' must go up every year to Jerusalem for the feast of booths or Tabernacles. And finally there is the closing sentence of the book: 'And there shall no longer be a trader in the house of the Lord of hosts on that day.' When Jesus cleanses the temple in Mark 11.17, he says, 'Is it not written, "My house shall be called a house of prayer for all the nations"? But you have made it a den of robbers', the translators rightly direct our attention to Isaiah 56.7b ('... for my house shall be called a house of prayer for all peoples'), and Jeremiah 7.11 ('Has this house, which is called by my name, become a den of robbers in your eyes?'). But John just as rightly draws our attention to the relevance of Zechariah to this incident when he makes Jesus say: 'Take these things away; you shall not make my Father's house a house of trade.'

After all this it comes as something of a relief to return to the comparatively lucid text of Mark's gospel. When Jesus tells the disciples: 'Go into the village opposite you, and immediately as you enter it you will find a colt tied, on which no one has ever sat; untie it and bring it', the modern reader tends to assume he is implementing a procedure previously arranged. And if we suppose (as I do) that the triumphal entry is a historical event, this has to be the real situation underlying the text. But I don't think I am being fanciful in suggesting that the text itself is trying to resist that idea and to edge the reader towards a semi-miraculous explanation. We find the same kind of ambiguity in an incident in the early verses of the passion narrative (14.12–16) where Jesus instructs his disciples how to find the upper room where he intends to celebrate the Passover with them.

'And many spread their garments on the road, and others spread leafy branches which they had cut from the fields.' I have previously explained the significance of the leafy branches cut from the fields, and their connection with the feast of Tabernacles. For the significance of the garments we have to go further afield:

> And he [Jehu] said, 'Thus and so he spoke to me saying, "Thus says the Lord, I anoint you king over Israel."' Then in haste every man of them took his garment and put it under him on the bare steps, and they blew the trumpet and proclaimed, 'Jehu is king.' (II Kings 9.12b–13)

In other words the disciples – and also, if the text is to be believed, the crowd – are openly greeting Jesus as king, that is (in this particular historic situation) as the Messiah. Since Jesus appears to have been executed on a charge of claiming to be just that, the traditional Christian Holy Week can claim a certain plausibility in arguing that it was the events of Palm Sunday which provided the grounds of accusation on Good Friday, and this argument may already have come to be accepted by the time John's gospel was written, and thus underlie the order of events there related. But assuming the triumphal entry is historical, and that it in fact took place in the autumn as Mark implies, there is a minimum gap of six months (and as we have seen, it could easily be longer) between the triumphal entry and the events of Passover.

'Hosanna! Blessed is he who comes in the name of the Lord!' The quotation is from Psalm 118.25–26, where the *New Jerusalem Bible* translates, if with characteristic inelegance, nevertheless very close to the original:

> We beg you, Yahweh [*Lord*], save us,
>   we beg you, Yahweh, give us victory!
> Blessed in the name of Yahweh is he who is coming!

(The footnote *g* which is there attached to this last line should really be attached to 'save us' two lines earlier. It is this cry which translates the Hebrew, 'Hoshiah na,' of which the traditional 'Hosanna' is a corruption.) The translators of this version state quite correctly that this psalm is the conclusion of the Hallel (Psalms 113–118) which the Jews recite at the great feasts, including the Passover supper. But it would also be relevant to point out, as G. W. Anderson does in *Peake's Commentary on the Bible*, that 'according to the Talmud it was used at the Feast of Tabernacles.' Verse 10 ('Blessed is the kingdom of our father ...' is not so much a quotation from the psalm as a loose statement of what it actually meant to the crowd at the time. Note that at the second occurrence the cry of 'Hosanna' has been transformed into a cry of jubilation with no precise meaning at all, a function which it has continued to have in the Christian tradition, which actually quotes these words as part of the *Sanctus* hymn at one of the climactic points in the Mass.

'And he entered Jerusalem ...' In both Matthew (21.12–13) and Luke (19.45–46) Jesus' cleansing of the temple is made the concluding act of his triumphal entry. But in Mark, 'as it was already late,' Jesus merely makes a note of what is going on and saves his strength and his anger for another day. Mark seems to think of Jesus as having lodgings in Bethany about two miles outside the city, and we are entitled to assume on the basis of 14.3 that these were 'in the house of Simon the leper'. John's gospel (11.1) suggests that Jesus had a family of friends there – Lazarus, and his two sisters Martha and Mary. But these three figures, if not fictional in themselves, are fictional as John's gospel presents them. The story of the raising of Lazarus, for instance, clearly originates in the ostensibly fictional story of the rich man and Lazarus in Luke 16.19–31; while his 'sisters' Martha and Mary, though borrowed from the possibly authentic story in Luke 10.38–42, seem to have no connection with history as they are presented in John's gospel. Although he does not say so, it is likely that the author of this gospel wanted the reader to assume that Lazarus and Simon the leper were one and the same person, perhaps hoping it would be remembered that the original Lazarus of Luke's gospel was himself a fairly leprous creature. The vexed question of the identity of the woman who anoints Jesus' feet in Mark 14.3 will be gone into when we get to that part of the text.

> On the following day, when they came from Bethany, he was hungry. And seeing in the distance a fig tree in leaf, he went to see if he could find anything on it. When he came to it, he found nothing but leaves, for it was not the season for figs. And he said to it, 'May no one ever eat fruit from you again.' And his disciples heard it.
>
> And they came to Jerusalem. And he entered the temple and began to drive out those who sold and those who bought in the temple, and he overturned the tables of the moneychangers and the seats of those who sold pigeons; and he would not allow any one to carry anything through the temple. And he taught, and said to them, 'Is it not written, "My house shall be called a house of prayer for all the nations"? But you have made it a den of robbers.' And the chief priests and scribes heard it and sought a way to destroy him; for they feared him, because all the multitude was astonished at his teaching. And when evening came, they went out of the city. (11.12–19)

There are those who argue on the basis of Luke 21.37 ('And every day he was teaching in the temple, but at night he went out and lodged on the mount called Olivet') that Jesus was in fact sleeping rough on the Mount of Olives, and that is why he was so hungry in the morning. Against the idea is the fact that Bethany is on the southern slopes of the mountain, and as we have just noted, in Mark 14.3 we find Jesus dining at a house in Bethany; but in favour of it is firstly the fact that the Greek verb *aulizein*, which lies behind the word 'lodged' in Luke, can very easily carry such a meaning. It literally means 'to lodge in the courtyard', but one of its commonest uses is in military language – 'to bivouac'. One also notices that the disciples appear to have no idea where the Passover is going to be celebrated until the very day it happens (that is by our reckoning; by Jewish reckoning, since the day begins at sunset, it is the day before). And perhaps even weightier than that, when Judas wishes to betray Jesus to the temple authorities, he leads them to a 'garden' on the

Mount of Olives where he knows Jesus will be – and seems to know he will be there all night.

The fig tree having leaves but no fruit is yet another indication that the time is late summer or autumn rather than spring, since one of the peculiarities of the fig tree is that the fruit is already well-formed (though not of course ripe) before the leaves begin to appear. The only time of the year when a fig tree has leaves but no fruit is *after* the fruit has ripened and fallen or been harvested. Should we, as some suggest, interpret what is presented here as a miracle (of the cursing of the fig tree) as having originally been a parable that has been reworked? There is a lot to be said for the idea. In Matthew (21.18–19) the fig tree withers away at once, but in Mark's original version, as we see, the story is split into two instalments – and thus resembles the cleansing of the temple, which is also told as a single incident in Matthew but split in two in Mark. And the two halves of the two stories in Mark are interleaved with each other. On day one Mark takes a look at the temple, clearly disapproves of what he sees, but does nothing. On day two he passes by the fig tree, registers his disappointment with what he finds there, and passes on. He then enters the temple and purges it. Next day he passes by the fig tree and finds it has withered. It is clear to me at any rate that the condition of the fig tree – a fine show of leaves, but no actual fruit – is being used as a symbol of the condition of temple religion as Jesus sees it. And thus the fate of the fig tree is being used as a symbol of the fate of the temple – probably not just of its cleansing by Jesus, but also as a prophecy of its eventual destruction by the Romans (see Mark 13.1–2). But what are we to suppose actually *happened*? My own instinct is to settle for the initial disappointment with the fig tree as real; but in the withering away, I suspect that what was originally a sermon using the fig tree as its text has now been transformed into a quasi-event.

The tradition suggests that it was the cleansing of the temple above all that lead to Jesus' death; and the plausibility of this is that all four gospels are agreed that the prime movers in Jesus' execution were the temple authorities, and in this we have no reason to doubt them. That it was connected with the temple in some way therefore cannot be doubted, the strongest indication of this being the to us mystifying testimony which seems to have finally persuaded the council they now had the necessary grounds to proceed:

Now the chief priests and the whole council sought testimony

against Jesus to put him to death; but they found none. For many
bore false witness against him, and their witness did not agree.
And some stood up and bore false witness against him, saying,
'We heard him say, "I will destroy this temple that is made with
hands, and in three days I will build another, not made with
hands."' (Mark 14.55–58)

The impression I get from this is that, rather as Mark in any case
implies, Jesus having spent a great deal of time in the weeks leading
up to his death in the temple teaching the crowd and disputing with
any that offered to debate with him, the priests are hoping to be able
to convict him on the basis of something he might have said which
can be construed as blasphemy – this part for their own satisfaction.
They will then hand him over to Pilate for sentence and execution on
the grounds that he claims to be Messiah, and is thereby proved to be
a political agitator against Roman rule. Even if we assume that the
above testimony does approximate to something that Jesus actually
said, we would still need to ask just how closely, and just what he can
have meant by it. Unfortunately the solution that John's gospel
proposes in 2.19 seems more likely to be his own made-up suggestion
for the very problem we are considering rather than information
obtained from an independent historical source. What I think we can
say with confidence is that Jesus' death was due to the alarm and
irritation felt by the temple authorities over Jesus' attitude towards it
– just as Stephen's later death and Paul's even later arrest were due to
similar causes. But the precise grounds of that alarm and irritation
we shall never know. The cleansing of the temple, assuming it
actually happened, may have been part of the cause. On the other
hand the accounts we have of the trial in all four gospels are fairly
extensive, and none of them brings up this incident as any part of the
accusation; all of them concentrate on what Jesus had *said* as being
the reason for his conviction.

We also need to ask why there was any need for a cleansing of the
temple in the first place. What were buyers and sellers doing there at
all, or what need was there of money changers? One detail in the
Marcan account goes pretty well to the heart of the matter: 'and he
overturned the tables of the moneychangers and the seats of those
who sold pigeons.' Let's take pigeons first. The first five chapters of
Leviticus give a handy summary of the kind of creatures that might
be offered in sacrifice, and the usual reasons for which they might be
offered. Chapters 4 and 5 deal with the sin offering, starting with the

sin offering of 'an anointed priest' in 4.1–12, the sin offering of 'the whole congregation' in 4.13–21, and the sin offering of 'the ruler' in 4.22–26. It then goes into the details of the sin offering of 'one of the common people'. The preferred victim is a female goat or lamb (4.27–35); but it does also take account of the fact that only the comparatively well-off will be able to afford that. For the less well-off therefore it suggests 'two turtle-doves or two young pigeons' (5.7); and for those absolutely on their beam-ends it is even possible to get away with 'a tenth of an ephah of fine flour' (5.11). In those days as in ours the bulk of the population felt no embarassment about not wanting to spend a penny more than they need, but scorned the suggestion that they were absolutely destitute. In all likelihood therefore the temple bazaar (it was actually called that officially) stocked all the kinds of creatures that might be wanted by worshippers intending to offer sacrifice, and the overwhelming demand was for pigeons. Hence the specific mention of them in the Marcan account.

The point about the money-changers was that the coinage in ordinary use in Jerusalem was a Roman coinage, which (as we know from 12.13–17 of Mark's gospel) was stamped with the emperor's portrait. In the eyes of the very orthodox this meant it infringed the second commandment (Ex. 20.4 – 'You shall not make for yourself a graven image, or any likeness of anything that is in heaven above, or that is in the earth beneath, or that is in the water under the earth …'), and so could not be accepted as the means of purchase of temple offerings. The money-changers were there to exchange Roman coinage for temple coinage. It might be thought that ordinary people would have been impatient of a cumbersome and inconvenient piece of ritual like this, but in practice it seems to have been popular as yet another means of expressing hostility to Roman domination. Also we have no good grounds for supposing the whole business had developed into a racket, or that the peoples were being swindled. So far as we can tell, the trade was honestly conducted and met a practical and popular need. Why then did Jesus' object? The two Old Testament passages which Mark makes Jesus cite probably do give us his actual reasons. The Isaiah passage is:

And the foreigners who join themselves to the Lord
to minister to him, to love the name of the Lord and to be his servants,
every one who keeps the sabbath and does not profane it,

> and holds fast my covenant –
> these I will bring to my holy mountain,
>   and make them joyful in my house of prayer;
> their burnt offerings and their sacrifices
>   will be accepted on my altar;
>   for my house shall be called a house of prayer for all peoples.
>
>   (Isa. 56.6–7)

But the situation that actually confronted Jesus in the temple was that Gentiles were admitted only to the court of the Gentiles, and it was precisely in that court that the bazaar was run; not the least possibility therefore of any Gentile being 'joyful in my house of prayer'. The Jeremiah passage (7.11), with its reference to 'a den of robbers', provides the supposed evidence for those who argue that the whole thing had become a dishonest racket. But a simpler and more plausible explanation is that Jesus, like a great many non-commercial people, was automatically offended by the implications of commerce, particularly in a holy place. The very fact that buying and selling were going on at all in the temple was *proof* that it had become a den of robbers. The gift shops that are such a prominent feature of our modern cathedrals strike a great many visitors just the same way. They either do not know or do not want to know that the alternative is that they would be visiting a ruin.

'And the chief priests and the scribes heard it and sought a way to destroy him ...' At first sight this strengthens the case of those who argue that it was the cleansing of the temple that was the chief cause of Jesus' execution. But notice that the passage goes on: '... for they feared him because all the multitude *was astonished at his teaching*'.

> As they passed by in the morning, they saw the fig tree withered away to its roots. And Peter remembered and said to him, 'Master, look! The fig tree which you cursed has withered.' And Jesus answered them, 'Have faith in God. Truly, I say to you, whoever says to this mountain, "Be taken up and cast into the sea", and does not doubt in his heart, but believes that what he says will come to pass, it will be done for him. Therefore I tell you, whatever you ask in prayer, believe that you receive it, and you will. And whenever you stand praying, forgive, if you have anything against any one; so that your Father also who is in heaven may forgive you your trespasses'. (11.20–26)

The withering of the fig tree is made a text on the basis of which Jesus offers his comments about prayer – the only section of the gospel which deals with the subject. If we turn to the parallel passage in Matthew (21.18–22), we find that the last two verses of this passage ('Therefore I tell you, whatever you ask in prayer …') have been omitted. Something very like the last verse of all occurs in Matthew 6.14–15 as an attachment to what the tradition calls 'the Lord's prayer', and that is presumably why Matthew sees no need to repeat the saying here. (This brings to our notice the fact that Mark nowhere includes the Lord's prayer, and the implication of that can only be that he knew nothing of it. This is a topic that is discussed more fully in the appendix to this chapter.) When we consider the other omitted verse, Matthew doesn't include this or anything like it anywhere in his gospel, and it is quite likely that he baulked at the highly subjective view it seems to imply of the way prayers works. Obviously it isn't true that whatever you ask in prayer you receive. So what does it mean to say, 'Believe that you receive it and you will'? Doesn't it seem to suggest that prayer doesn't really work, but that if you use your imagination you can easily persuade yourself that it does? Even if that is not Mark's meaning, it could still be that Matthew omits the verse because that is the meaning that most readily suggests itself. Luke on the other hand, though he doesn't include this actual saying, includes a whole series of sayings which seem to me to point in the same direction as this one – and these also are attached to his version of the Lord's prayer. This is found in 11.2–4, and the series of sayings, runs from 11.5–13. Note in particular that final saying: 'If you then who are evil know how to give good gifts to your children, how much more will the heavenly Father *give the Holy Spirit to those who ask him*'. That is surely the kind of point the Marcan saying is making – prayer is always answered provided you pray for the right things. There will be cynics even tougher than myself to point out that the practical implications of this and what I have suggested is the Matthaean interpretation are much the same. To the observing eye perhaps they are; but to the experiencing heart it is certain that they are not.

And they came again to Jerusalem. And as he was walking in the temple, the chief priests and the scribes and the elders came to him, and they said to him, 'By what authority are you doing these things, or who gave you this authority to do them?' Jesus said to them, 'I will ask you a question; answer me, and I will tell you by

what authority I do these things. Was the baptism of John from
heaven or from men? Answer me.' And they argued with one
another, 'If we say, "From heaven", he will say, "Why then did
you not believe him?" But shall we say, "From men"?' – they were
afraid of the people; for all held that John was a real prophet. So
they answered Jesus, 'We do not know.' And Jesus said to them,
'Neither will I tell you by what authority I do these things.'
(11.27–33)

I find this one of the most interesting debates not merely in the Bible
but in literature. There are three religions (there may well be more,
but there are at least three) which place heavy emphasis on our
ability to *know* with certainty what God wills and what God is
saying to us: and these are Judaism, Christianity and Islam. All three
of them place heavy emphasis on a collection of writings as a means
of knowing this, and claim that these writings are not – as an outsider
would automatically suppose they must be – records of human
experience set down by human writers, but that on the contrary they
give real information about the activity and intentions of God in the
world, which cannot be known by any other means than by these
writings. The writings themselves therefore (so runs the 'argument')
are not simply the production of human authorship, but must be at
the very least a collaboration between the human hand that held the
pen and the divine mind which dictated what it should write.

This claim – common to all three religions, though made on behalf
of three different collections of writings – I believe to be false. But the
longing for certainty of this kind is undoubtedly deeply rooted in the
human heart. History shows both that it cannot be eradicated, but
equally that the conviction that certainty has finally been achieved is
always disastrous. That is how we have long viewed the mediaeval
idea of Christendom, that is how we have recently come to view
Eastern European communism, and my guess is that in the next
generation that is how we will view many of our modern assumptions about capitalism and democracy. For me the task of civilization
is not to eradicate the mischief, which cannot be done. And it is
certainly not to encourage it. It simply tries to contain and question
it.

If we really had the certainty for which we long, this debate
between Jesus and the chief priests would have been unnecessary.
Both of them would already have known the answer to the central
question: 'Was the baptism of John from heaven or from men?'

Because we do not have this certainty, the chief priests can decline to answer the question at all. Because they will not answer the question, Jesus has no basis on which to answer the question they originally asked him: 'By what authority are you doing these things, or who gave you this authority to do them?' The unspoken question underlying the whole debate is: On what kind of grounds do we *ever* decide who is speaking or acting for God? Most of us are convinced that we do not have an answer to that question. Some mistakenly believe that if you work on the assumption that there is no God anyway, the question itself will disappear; but that is not so. You are still left with the debate about what kinds of speech and activity are to be considered virtuous and to be encouraged, and what kinds are to be reproved, or even punished, as wicked. We have no certain answers to this question either. Indeed it is the same question, but translated out of religious and into secular language. And yet the fact that it cannot be answered in no way relieves us of the necessity of trying to answer it somehow or other; for without an answer of some kind, social living cannot begin. We see now why the promise of certainty offered by some religions answers such a deep-seated need. And I think we also see why it is that in practice so many societies give such entirely different and mutually contradictory answers.

And he began to speak to them in parables. 'A man planted a vineyard, and set a hedge around, it, and dug a pit for the wine press, and built a tower, and let it out to tenants, and went into another country. When the time came, he sent a servant to the tenants to get from them some of the fruit of the vineyard. And they took him and beat him, and sent him away empty-handed. Again he sent to them another servant, and they wounded him in the head and treated him shamefully. And he sent another, and him they killed; and so with many others, some they beat and some they killed. He had still one other, a beloved son; finally he sent him to them, saying, "They will respect my son." But those tenants said to one another, "This is the heir; come, let us kill him, and the inheritance will be ours." And they took him and killed him, and cast him out of the vineyard. What will the owner of the vineyard do? He will come and destroy the tenants, and give the vineyard to others. Have you not read this scripture:

"The very stone which the builders rejected
    has become the head of the corner;

> this was the Lord's doing,
>   and it is marvellous in our eyes"?'

And they tried to arrest him, but feared the multitude; for they perceived that he had told the parable against them; so they left him and went away. (12.1–12)

'And he began to speak to them in parables.' It sounds like the beginning of a new section, and this is undoubtedly why the traditional division of the gospel starts a new chapter here; but in the event Jesus tells just one parable, the rest of the chapter continuing with debate. The meaning of the parable is transparent, but one wonders how much of it goes back to what Jesus originally said. It is one of those parables where the particular items in the story seem to 'stand for' something – in other words it is more of an allegory than a parable as such. And as we saw in Chapter 5, and as we have an appallingly crude example in Matthew 13.24–30 and 36–43, that is usually a sign that the tradition has been heavily at work on the interpretation. With this parable the process has continued even beyond Mark's gospel. Whereas Mark above writes: 'And they took him and killed him, and cast him out of the vineyard', [Matthew (21.39)] and Luke (20.15) have: 'And they [took him and] cast him out of the vineyard, and killed him.' The tradition seems at one stage to have made play with the fact that Jesus suffered 'outside the city', notably as in the following:

> For the bodies of those animals whose blood is brought into the sanctuary by the high priest as a sacrifice for sin are burned outside the camp. So Jesus also suffered outside the gate in order to sanctify the people through his own blood. Therefore let us go forth to him outside the camp, bearing abuse for him. For here we have no lasting city, but we seek the city which is to come. (Heb.13.11–14)

It is undoubtedly some consideration of this kind that underlies the reversed order of the last two events of Mark's parable in Matthew and Luke. As I mentioned, the allegory is fairly clear. The vineyard is Israel, whose emblem is frequently a vine in the Old Testament, notably in Psalm 80. 8–16 and Isaiah 5.1–7. The planter of the vineyard is therefore God, the tenants are the religious leaders of the nation, the various servants are the prophets and the son is of course Jesus himself. Despite the fact that the style of this allegory seems very different from what we think of as Jesus' normal style in telling a parable, I am inclined to accept that the story so far may be pretty well as he told it. Note that he here compares himself to the prophets of old, as both he and John the Baptist seem to have done, and he foretells his own death at the hands of the authorities, which we know he had already done in his instruction of the disciples. In what sense Jesus thought of himself as God's son was extensively discussed in the early chapters of this work; bearing in mind what he seems to have meant by this claim, we have no reason to doubt its authenticity here.

It is when we come to the conclusion of the story that we have to start going carefully. 'What will the owner of the vineyard do? He will come and destroy the tenants, and give the vineyard to others.' We are clearly meant to interpret it, and the church always *has* interpreted it, as meaning that God will set up the New Israel, namely the Christian Church, in place of the Old Israel which throughout the ages has always rejected his servants the prophets and now finally has rejected even his own son. Such an interpretation might well have been popular even as early as Mark's gospel; it would have become so as a result of the open split between those who wanted to insist that the new movement must always remain part of traditional Judaism, and those who wanted to insist on the free admittance of Gentiles without there being any need for them to become Jews as well. And this split, as we saw in Chapter 8, may well have occurred within about ten years of Jesus' death; but the same chapter makes it clear why I don't think we an attribute that meaning to Jesus himself. But if we take these final verses, not as a manifesto that the new Christian church will take the place of traditional Judaism, and that God has now set up the former in place of the latter as the means of his grace and redemption, but instead as a prophecy of Jesus' second coming to earth after his death to destroy the unrighteous kingdoms of the world and to inaugurate a righteous kingdom of his own, then with very little alteration the parable as it stands becomes credibly authentic.

And they sent to him some of the Parisees and some of the Herodians, to entrap him in his talk. And they came and said to him, 'Teacher, we know that you are true, and care for no man; for you do not regard the position of men, but truly teach the way of God. Is it lawful to pay taxes to Caesar, or not? Should we pay them, or should we not?' But knowing their hypocrisy, he said to them, 'Why put me to the test? Bring me a coin, and let me look at it.' And they brought one. And he said to them, 'Whose likeness and inscription is this?' They said to him, 'Caesar's.' Jesus said to them, 'Render to Caesar the things that are Caesar's, and to God the things that are God's' And they were amazed at him. (12.13–17)

The point of the question here is that there appear to be only two possible answers, neither of which could Jesus safely utter in public. If Jesus answers that paying Roman taxes is lawful, he is looked on by the crowd as a collaborator and immediately loses all his following; if he answers that it is not lawful, his opponents then have the evidence they are looking for in order to denounce him to the Roman authorities as a threat to public order. Hence the flattering appeal to Jesus' 'fearless honesty': '... we know that you are true, and care for no man; for you do not regard the position of men, but truly teach the way of God.' In other words, 'Throw aside the obvious prudential considerations, and let us have your real opinion.'

The answer Jesus gives has a peculiarly modern feel to it, seeming almost to suggest that there is (and that there should be) a separation between church and state – a doctrine which has only widely become accepted with the rise of capitalism, and may well not long survive its passing. In Jesus' own day it was only the circumstance of Roman domination that made this distinction available to him; it was unknown to the pagan world at large, to whom it was totally obvious that the maintenance and supervision of institutional religion was a function of the state just like any other. For about a hundred years before the Roman annexation of the province of Syria in 64 BC, the Jews had been governed by the descendants of a priestly dynasty – the Maccabees. Their rule, like that of all other rulers of the time, made no distinction whatever between what was due to Caesar and what was due to God. Power was one and indivisible, and it was taken for granted that institutional religion was one of the three great functions that from time immemorial the ruler had always exercised – the other two being the those of justice and of military affairs. The idea that religion was a matter of individual conviction rather than of social obligation was one that has arisen with the spread of Christianity itself; and as we can tell from the Roman attitude to Christianity, originally it was not at all popular.

For that matter, for quite a lot of us it still isn't. Had it never been encouraged it is hard to see how the religious wars and persecutions of modern Europe could have started; they were all but unknown to antiquity. And even now, when we tend to assume that these things belong completely to the past, instead of being born into membership of a state church, where one believes as much or as little of the tradition as one cares to, one has the inconvenience of having to make a choice between a selection of confessional churches, admission to which is made to depend upon accepting a set of 'beliefs'. The nuisance here is not so much that the beliefs themselves nonsense – it is a necessary characteristic of religious 'belief' that it is unreal, and that it obviously belongs to another kind of world than the everyday one we inhabit; it is that the antics that believers feel obliged to get up to in order to win adherents to these beliefs are noisy and potentially dangerous. In history also the principle that Jesus here enunciates has not worked all that well in practice. In the incessant rivalry between religion and the state that has dominated European history, it has usually been possible to see which of them has the real power over the other by asking which of them can better enforce its claim to the right to draw the line of demarcation. In the mediaeval world it was the church, with consequences that very few of us nowadays find attractive. In the modern world it is usually the state; but only because it is the state, and not religion, which holds out hope to the multitude of that ever-increasing prosperity, which is what the multitude has been taught to set its heart on. In years to come, when it seems likely that a sharp decline in prosperity will be forced upon all of us, the wisdom of our separation between church and state may again come into question.

And Sadducees came to him, who say that there is no resurrection; and they asked him a question, saying, 'Teacher, Moses wrote for us that if a man's brother dies and leaves a wife, but leaves no child, the man must take the wife, and raise up children for his brother. There were seven brothers; the first took a wife, and when he died left no children; and the second took her, and died having no children; and the third likewise; and the seven left no children. Last of all the woman also died. In the resurrection whose wife will she be? For the seven had her as wife.'

Jesus said to them, 'Is not this why you are wrong, that you know neither the scriptures nor the power of God? For when they rise from the dead, they neither marry nor are given in marriage,

but are like angels in heaven. And as for the dead being raised,
have you not read in the book of Moses, in the passage about the
bush, how God said to him, "I am the God of Abraham, and the
God of Isaac, and the God of Jacob"? He is not God of the dead,
but of the living; you are quite wrong.' (12.18–27)

As I hinted earlier, in the appendix to Chapter 3, I've always had a
soft spot for the Sadducees. Taking the Old Testament books of
Ecclesiastes and Ecclesiasticus as the best clues we have to their
thinking, they delightfully remind me of the kind of clergyman I was
often familiar with in my own youth – a style that is now supposed
(and more's the pity) to be discredited. They tended on the one hand
to be hidebound by tradition, but on the other to be pretty well
devoid of superstition. Typically they had a deep knowledge of and
affection for antiquity, but unlike their popular rivals the Pharisees
they made a clear distinction between the ancient and the modern
world, and maintained an unclouded – if also unadmiring – view of
the latter. Belief one suspects was something they professed rather
than actually entertained. Their real outlook seems to have been that
of men of culture whose professional life happened to be in religion.
Not all will agree with me, but to my eyes even here they present
themselves in an attractive light. Though they cannot be said to win
the argument, they certainly do not lose it. Rather it goes by default,
for which the Sadducees themselves are chiefly to blame for
approaching the topic frivolously in the first place.

It is typical of such people that they should regard the deeply-held
but in their view groundless beliefs of their rivals with indulgent
amusement. And the joking riddle they here put to Jesus seems to
have been an accepted symbol of that amusement. The classical Old
Testament view of life after death was that there was no such thing:
virtue was rewarded and wickedness punished in *this* life. And this
was the doctrine which, so far as we can tell, the Sadducees still
officially put forward. It is likely, though, that among themselves
they held a more realistic view which it was not convenient to make
too widely known: that though perhaps there ought to be a life after
death, and we'd be living in a much better world if there were, in fact
there isn't; and this may be very regrettable, but that does nothing to
make it untrue.

The Pharisees on the other hand had abandoned the classical view
outlined above in favour of ideas that had their origin in Persian
religion, to which Israel had been exposed during its long inclusion

as part of the Persian empire, from Cyrus' overthrow of the power of Babylon in 536 BC to Alexander the Great's overthrow of the power of Persia in 331. Although Israel had quite likely always been familiar with ideas among its neighbours of a personal immortality that was offered to each individual, up to the time of the exile they had always resisted such ideas and insisted on those outlined above. It was the experience of overwhelming and prolonged national disaster which seems to have gradually made them dubious about rewards for virtue in this life only, and to have convinced them of the desirability of such rewards being offered in another. The idea was popular also with ordinary Israelites (we see that Jesus himself shared it) among whom the Pharisees moved. One feels that the Sadducees in their temple enclosure (and they may even have been aware of this feeling) already experienced in reality a heaven that their rivals had to be content to enjoy only in prospect.

The riddle therefore is a joke, and apparently one of long standing. If it were seven sisters and one husband, there would be no problem. Although by Jesus' time Judaism had universally become a monogamous culture, the numerous and illustrious instances of polygamy in the Old Testament made it impossible for the tradition to condemn polygamy as such. But polygamy worked one way only: it was perfectly all right for a man to have several wives, but utterly unthinkable that a woman should be allowed to have several husbands – unless, of course, she had them one at a time. And a notorious passage from Deuteronomy layed down the rule whereby a woman might not merely be allowed but actually compelled to take her next husband:

> If brothers dwell together, and one of them dies and has no son, the wife of the dead shall not be married outside the family to a stranger; her husband's brother shall go in to her and take her as his wife, and perform the duty of a husband's brother to her. And the first son whom she bears shall succeed to the name of his brother who is dead, that his name may not be blotted out of Israel. (Deut. 25.5–6)

The reasoning behind this procedure seems unconvincing to us, but was clearly felt to have an overwhelming urgency at the time the passage was written. If we look at the the book of Ruth, for instance, the story turns on Ruth's duty and need to give birth to an heir to carry the name of her dead husband in a situation where there is no obvious male candidate who can be obliged to perform the necessary act. The lengths to which she is prepared to go to get round the difficulty, reprehensible in themselves in normal circumstances (Ruth 3.14),[2] are for that very reason an immortal heroism when undertaken for this particular purpose. The same is true of Judah's daughter-in-law Tamar in Genesis chapter 38. It was probably also true originally of the daughters of Lot whose escapades are described Genesis 19.30–38. As this story now stand, it seems meant to be read as a reproach against two frequently hostile neighbours of Israel, the Moabites and the Ammonites; but it is overwhelmingly likely that the author of Genesis got the stories from the Moabites and Ammonites themselves, among whom they were handed down as grounds for heroic pride in their ancestry – as it is clear from the Old Testament that the stories of Ruth and Tamar were both of them heroic ancestral tales of the Davidic house (see Ruth 4.11–12, 18–22).

Despite all this it is likely that by Jesus' time the law of levirate marriage (the technical term given to the provision of Deuteronomy, deriving from the Latin word *levir*, meaning 'a husband's brother') was largely disregarded. I have already pointed out that it in any case contradicts the provisions of Leviticus 18.16 and 20.21, and that this latter view seems to have carried more religious weight in Jesus' day – as it has done also in the Christian tradition until well into the present century. Belief in resurrection may itself have played a part in this development, in that belief in personal immortality may have made the supposed need for physical descendants seem less urgent than it had done in the past. I myself, like the Sadducees, do not believe in any form of personal immortality. But their joke, amusing enough if read simply as a joke – perhaps even moderately effective as an *argumentum ad hominem* – is not in any way a convincing proof of their point, and this is what I meant when I said earlier that they have let the argument go by default. But Jesus' reply of course is equally unconvincing. It tells us that he believed in resurrection, but not that he had any good grounds for doing so. The 'proof' he offers, that God is the God of Abraham, Isaac and Jacob, and that he is not God of the dead but of the living, carries little conviction, not even as an interpretation of what the Old Testament passage he refers to (Ex. 3.6) actually means. And we can in any case be sure that the author of Exodus also had no belief in any kind of personal immortality – all he meant was that the God who was speaking to Moses was the same

God as had spoken to Abraham, Isaac and Jacob, that is to say, the ancestral God of Israel.

> And one of the scribes came up and heard them disputing with one another, and seeing that he answered them well, asked him, 'Which commandment is the first of all?' Jesus answered, 'The first is, "Hear O Israel: The Lord our God, the Lord is one; and you shall love the Lord your God with all your heart, and with all your soul, and with all your mind, and with all your strength." The second is this, "You shall love your neighbour as yourself." There is no other commandment greater than these.' And the scribe said to him, 'You are right, Teacher; you have truly said that he is one, and there is no other but he; and to love him with all the heart, and with all the understanding, and with all the strength, and to love one's neighbour as oneself, is much more than all whole burnt offerings and sacrifices.' And when Jesus saw that he answered wisely, he said to him, 'You are not far from the kingdom of God.' And after that no one dared to ask him any question. (12.28–34)

As noted earlier, this is the only passage in the whole of Mark's gospel where there is any expression of friendliness or admiration between Jesus and what one presumes is one of the official religious leaders. Even this one instance is more than the author of Matthew's gospel has been able to digest, and a comparison of the above with Matthew 22.34–40 will, for readers of any human or moral worth, be a rather distasteful experience. In Mark there is no doubt from the first that the attitude of the scribe is admiring ('... seeing that he answered them well ...'); in Matthew, on the other hand, we are clearly meant to infer that the motive is hostile – the crucial and damning alteration is the gratuitous insertion of the phrase, 'to test him':

> But when the Pharisees heard that he had silenced the Sadducees, they came together. And one of them, a lawyer, asked him a question to test him. (Matt. 22.34–35)

Even more distressing is the deliberate suppression of the whole of Mark 12.32–34, beginning with the words, 'And the scribe said to him, "You are right, Teacher ..."'

We can presume therefore that in Mark, when the scribe asks the question 'Which commandment is the first of all?', he already has his own ideas of what the answer should be, and is distinctly pleased when it turns out that Jesus' answer is much the same as his own would have been – a reference to Deuteronomy 6.4. The scribe had originally asked for just one commandment which could be looked on as the greatest, but Jesus clearly thinks that one alone is not enough; a second must be added, without which the first by itself is meaningless, and Jesus goes on to quote Leviticus 19.18.[3] I take the implication to be that these are not two separate commandments, but merely two different aspects of one and the same commandment: the first by itself is meaningless unless it issues in obedience to the second. Among the later documents of the New Testament the whole of I John can be read as an extended commentary on this one idea; but in particular one should note:

> If any one says, 'I love God', and hates his brother, he is a liar; for he who does not love his brother whom he has seen, cannot love God whom he has not seen. And this commandment we have from him, that he who loves God should love his brother also. (I John 4.20–21)

It has been customary for centuries at this point to insert a comment making a supposed contrast between the religion of Law (i.e. Judaism) and the religion of Love (i.e. Christianity). Even apart from the fact that Jesus is here actually quoting the Law, my own conviction is that the whole business of comparing religions favourably or unfavourably with each other is bogus; a sensible and well-disposed practitioner can make a fine thing out of any religious tradition; an enthusiast or downright believer will make even the best of them into something horrible. It is certainly true that to the outside observer Judaism is a religion which places a wholly disproportionate emphasis on the performance of ceremonies which have a purely ritual significance. And even in the sphere of actual morality, there is a disproportionate emphasis on morality as unquestioning obedience to the known commands of God, rather than (as seems more appropriate to most of us) a personal decision which tries to be a moral one, even though against a background of great uncertainty. But in both respects, if Christianity is anything of an improvement it is so only in degree. The more ritualistic traditions of Christianity manifest to a considerable degree the first 'fault'; and practically all of them display the second, many of them to a degree that even a lot of Jews can find quite shocking. Both religions therefore – and I would even go on to say both of them equally – are religions both of Law and of Love.

The important contrast that I would want to make is that between the religion of Love and the religion of what I would call Candour or Enlightenment; and as regards the latter, while individual Christians may have had a good record, that of the tradition as a whole has been appalling – perhaps distinctly worse than that of Judaism. For myself it is enlightenment, and not love, which is the highest of the virtues. And I think I can defend this preference on the basis of history. The age of Christendom (from about the fifth to the seventeenth centuries) was wholly dominated by the supposed religion of Love, and though the claim looks pretty sour to us, there is no reason to doubt that at the time it was made in all sincerity. None of us, I suspect, would care to go back to the ambience of those times. Towards the end – roughly from the rise of protestantism in the early sixteenth century to the rise of rationalism at the end of the seventeenth – the death throes of Christendom were convulsed by an orgy of torture and murder. It was the rediscovery of enlightenment, a virtue almost totally suppressed in antiquity with the suppression of paganism, which eventually restored Europe to sanity, tolerance and co-operation. Love is certainly a virtue; but we also know that Love is blind, and that unless guided by reason it does a lot of silly things. Above all – as most of us also know from experience – it easily turns into hatred.

> And as Jesus taught in the temple, he said, 'How can the scribes say that the Christ is the son of David? David himself, inspired by the Holy Spirit, declared,
>
> > 'The Lord said to my Lord,
> >   Sit at my right hand,
> > till I put thy enemies under thy feet.'
>
> David himself calls him Lord; so how is he his son?' And the great throng heard him gladly. (12.35–37)

This is the third of the three references in Mark – and by far the most interesting of the three – to the idea that Jesus is the 'son of David'. In the first of them (10.47) Jesus is addressed by someone else by the title and makes no comment of his own, so that we have no indication whether he accepts it or rejects it. But the clear implication of 11.1–10 is that he not only accepts the title himself, but is trying to convey his claim to it to the crowd, whose response in verse 10 should be seen as having been deliberately elicited by Jesus, and not simply volunteered by themselves. But here in contrast he seems to be rejecting it. Which of the two alternatives should we prefer as authentic? The relevant questions are: (*a*) Was he really descended from King David? (*b*) If not, did he nevertheless sincerely believe that he was? (*c*) If not, did he still claim the title – with no intention of deceiving anyone – as an indication of his destiny (that is, Messiahship) rather than of his genealogical descent? (*d*) Or did he reject a title which other people were trying to foist on him, feeling that although it was a familiar and traditional Messianic name, its implications were the opposite of the kind of Messiah he felt himself to be. If we relate these questions to Mark's gospel, the third suggestion gives the most plausible explanation of the situation at the Palm Sunday procession, while the fourth best suits the one we are dealing with here. And if we think about it, there is no necessary contradiction between the two. It could easily be that at one period in his ministry Jesus encouraged the title as conveying his Messianic claims, but that he later took fright and did his best to disclaim it.

But this assumes that the first two options listed above can simply be dismissed, and some readers may feel that this needs at least to be argued. Let us take the first of the four options. There is an interval of just about a thousand years between Jesus and King David. The number of his physical descendent by Jesus' time therefore must have run into hundreds of thousands. But the claim of physical descent, particularly as set out in Matthew chapter 1 and as it has been insisted on by the Christian tradition, means very much more than that. It is trying to claim that had King David's throne and inheritance survived to Jesus' time, it is Jesus who would have had the direct claim to it. We cannot of course prove that the claim is worthless, but there is a fair presumption that it is. And we *can* demonstrate that the genealogy at the opening of Matthew's gospel is fabricated. It falls into three sections: Abraham to David (fourteen generations), David to the exile (fourteen generations), and the exile to Jesus' time (fourteen generations). The first group of fourteen corresponds exactly to what we find in the Old Testament in Genesis 38 and Ruth 4.18–22. In biblical thinking fourteen is very much a round number – twice seven, the sacred number of days in which the world was made; and it seems to have been this happy coincidence that decided the author of the gospel (or his source) to squeeze the other two groups into fourteen generations as well. For in fact when we turn back to the Old Testament, we find there were many more than fourteen generations between David and the exile. Someone – perhaps over-hastily, or perhaps even quite deliberately – has conflated Ahaziah, son of Joram who reigned briefly in 841 BC, both with Azariah (or Uzziah) who reigned from 767 to 740, and with Ahaz, the real father of Hezekiah, who reigned from 732 to 716 BC, and thus clumsily rendered down the number to the desired fourteen. If this happens where we can check the author's tally, it gives us no confidence in accepting his word in those areas where we can't. In that case we have good grounds for supposing that the third section of the genealogy is also worthless, and probably fabricated.

What of Jesus' 'argument' here in Mark's gospel? How successful is it in 'proving' (as seems to be its intention) that the Messiah is not in fact the son of David after all? An honest evaluation would have to be that as an argument it is worthless, but that as a specimen of 'proof' on the basis of scriptural quotation it is no worse than many another example that could be given from Jesus' day – or indeed many centuries afterwards. The quotation Jesus puts forward is the opening verse of Psalm 110; and though it would be a hard matter to offer a literal interpretation of the Psalm as a whole, what one can say with certainty about its opening verse knocks the bottom out of the interpretation that Jesus tries to put on it. In the original Psalm, where it says 'The Lord said (or says) to my lord', it is absolutely clear that the speaker is a court poet or prophet who is addressing himself to the king, poetically feigning that he has heard an oracle from God to the effect that the king ('my lord' – that is, any one of the kings of Judah, not necessarily King David) is about to be victorious over all his enemies. Jesus' own interpretation depends on the erroneous belief (probably shared, though, by all his contemporaries) that the author of the psalm is himself King David, and that he is therefore addressing some other figure greater than himself in the opening verse of the psalm; and this greater figure can only be the Messiah, whose triumph over all his foes was many centuries still to come at the time King David wrote, but which the prophet-king nevertheless confidently predicts and celebrates in the psalm. Jesus' 'argument' is that if King David heralds the Messiah as greater than himself (and on this interpretation, which all Jesus' contemporaries would have accepted, he does) then it follows (!) that the Messiah cannot be the descendent of King David.

To the modern reader, therefore, the proof is doubly worthless: first it rests on what is plainly an erroneous interpretation of the psalm; but second, even if that interpretation were correct, the conclusion Jesus wants to derive from it still doesn't follow. But why is it that 'the great throng heard him gladly'? Presumably the source of their satisfaction was not that the Messiah was not after all the son of David, but the perception that Jesus' purpose in putting this argument forward was in *support* of his claim to be Messiah, even while rejecting any claim to be 'son of David'. And this is why it not only finds a place in Mark's gospel, but never seems to have caused the slightest difficulty to a tradition which from earliest times (see chapter 1 of Matthew discussed above) has always insisted in the most literal way that Jesus was the direct heir to the ancient throne of David.

> And in his teaching he said, 'Beware of the scribes, who like to go about in long robes, and to have salutations in the market places, and the best seats in the synagogues, and the places of honour at feasts; who devour widows' houses, and for a pretence make long prayers. They will receive the greater condemnation.'
>
> And he sat down opposite the treasury, and watched the multitude putting money into the treasury. Many rich people put in large sums. And a poor widow came, and put in two copper coins, which make a penny. And he called his disciples to him, and said to them, 'Truly, I say to you, this poor widow has put in more than all those who are contributing to the treasury. For they all contributed out of their abundance; but she out of her poverty has put in everything she had, her whole living.' (12.38–44)

I find both of these rather sad little anecdotes, if for rather different reasons. I cannot help feeling that this denunciation of the scribes, though moderate enough compared with the extended vituperation of Matthew chapter 23, is almost certainly unfair – in the same way that any kind of insistent anti-clericalism is almost always unfair. That Jesus had his anti-clerical moments I do not doubt, nor that the clergy of his day, like the clergy of any society in any age, tended to manifest vices such as Jesus here denounces. But two points need to be made. First, however justified the criticisms, they are not the whole story. As Luke reminds us, they are not the whole story even as far as Jesus' own attitude to the scribes was concerned; he seems to have been friendly with some of them, and even on occasion (see the previous section of this very chapter from Mark) to have admired their outlook. We all have our failings, and failings such as he denounces here are no doubt typical of the clergy as a whole. It is perfectly all right to denounce such failings, but the attitude should be the same as that of the satirist denouncing politicians. The faults he draws attention to are there, and are inseparable from the profession of politics. But the satirist does not seriously hope (if he has any sense) that his satire is going to remove such faults. His true aim is, by drawing attention to them to minimize the amount of damage they can do. So here, the idea that because the clergy are to some extent like this, the whole of the order which they represent must be swept away, and a new and purer world created, purged of all dissembling, hypocrisy and self-righteousness – visionary notions of this kind are simply the mischievous ravings of enthusiasm. One can be confident, for instance, that even where the experiment is tried, (as perhaps in the attempt to replace religion by communism in Eastern Europe) a new order immediately springs up in the new situation, with much the same vices – and perhaps even much the same virtues – as the former priestly caste.

The second anecdote is sad for a different reason. Had I been Jesus, my own instinct would have been to rush forward and try to forestall the widow's rashness; to point out to her that two copper coins meant a very great deal to her who was giving, and nothing at all to the people to whom she was giving it, and that she would be more than justified, both in morality and good sense, to spend the money on herself rather than on the temple. This is an unfashionable view, but I must confess I feel it deeply. My chief consolation is that such an obviously edifying anecdote is quite likely to be an invention of the tradition in any case, as so many of the more extravagantly romantic passages in Luke's gospel, for instance, so obviously are.

APPENDIX

Although there is no mention of the traditional Lord's prayer as such in Mark's gospel, some consideration of it is not out of place in a work such as this, whose primary interest is in what can confidently be asserted about the historical figure of Jesus. And the obvious echo of that prayer in Mark 11.25 makes this a suitable place in which to reflect upon it. I suspect the question uppermost in the reader's mind is, 'Is it genuine?' The answer to this is more reassuring that one might have expected. Although on the one hand one cannot ignore the likelihood that had Mark ever heard of the prayer he would almost certainly have included it, as we have seen throughout this work it is equally likely that quite a lot of other Q material is genuine, despite the presumption that Mark has never heard of that either. And of one thing we can be sure about the Lord's prayer – it is a translation into Greek of something that was originally created (rather than necessarily written down) in another language.

Here are the two versions as we have them in Matthew and Luke:

> Our Father who art in heaven,
> Hallowed be thy name.
> Thy kingdom come, Thy will be done,
> On earth as it is in heaven.
> Give us this day our [daily] bread;
> And forgive us our debts,
> As we also have forgiven our debtors;
> And lead us not into temptation,
> But deliver us from evil. (Matt. 6.9–13)

> Father, hallowed be thy name.
> Thy kingdom come.
> Give us each day our [daily] bread;
> and forgive us our sins,
> for we ourselves forgive everyone who is indebted to us;
> and lead us not into temptation. (Luke 11.2–4)

As you can see, the Lucan version is considerably shorter and simpler than Matthew's, and the presumption is that it is therefore likely (but no more than that) to be closer to the original. We can be sure that the two evangelists got their versions from different sources, but we can be equally sure that underlying those different sources there was a common original. The clearest indication of this, as also that that original was a translation into Greek from some other language, is the Greek word underlying the traditional English word 'daily', which you will see I have included in square brackets in both versions above. Despite the considerable differences between the two versions, the Greek word here is the same in both; it is also a word which does not occur elsewhere in Greek, and for that reason is not literally translatable at all. The word is *epiousion*.

Jerome's heroic attempt to translate it for the Vulgate is worth analysing. As most readers will not need to be told, it is Matthew's version which has prevailed as the 'received' version of the prayer.[4] In the old days Catholics used to pray, *Panem nostrum cotidianum da nobis hodie*, where *cotidianum* is the word underlying the traditional English 'daily'; but this is not what actually appears in the Vulgate, which at this point talks about *panem nostrum supersubstantialem*. How did Jerome arrive at this strange word *supersubstantialem*, which is quite as foreign to Latin as *epiousion* is to Greek? In fact the thinking behind this extraordinary coinage (and thank goodness the early church thought better of trying to foist it on their congregations) is fairly transparent, and it turns out that it isn't really a translation at all: *epi* is the Greek for the Latin *super* (meaning 'above' or 'upon'). There is no Greek word *ousios* (of which *ousion* would be the accusative), but if there were such a word it would presumably be the adjective derived from *ousia*, for which the Latin is *substantia* (meaning 'substance'), and from which Christian writers (though not pagans) had already derived an adjective *substantialis*. *Supersubstantialem* therefore is in no sense a witness to any kind of 'original' meaning of the puzzling Greek *epiousion*; it simply repeats the same puzzle in Latin.

In Luke's Gospel Jerome seems to have left undisturbed what was probably an already traditional *cotidianum*, and some readers will be wondering how this was arrived at, and how close it is likely to be to Jesus' original meaning. The answer to the first question is that it was probably a guess made on the basis of choosing something (anything) that would reasonably fit. The answer to the second question is more intriguing: we have no means of knowing what was the actual word that Jesus used, but we can make a very good guess at deciding what sort of ideas it was intended to convey. Towards the end of the book of Proverbs we read:

> Two things I ask of thee;
>> deny them not to me before I die;
> Remove from me falsehood and lying;
>> give me neither poverty nor riches;
>> feed me with the food that is needful for me,
> lest I be full, and deny thee, and say, 'Who is the Lord?',
>> or lest I be poor, and steal, and profane the name of my God.
> (Prov. 30.7–9)

Whatever word underlies the Greek *epiousion*, it was almost certainly a reference to this passage. It is suggested therefore that it actually meant something like 'needful', which is as good a guess as any – though I am not of course recommending that after two thousand years (nearly) we should now go ahead and make the substitution.

13

The Last Things

(Mark 13.1–37)

The apparently self-contained discourse of chapter 13 has long been known to scholars as 'the Marcan apocalypse', *apocalypsis* being the Greek word for 'revelation'. The last book in the New Testament, known to English readers as 'The Revelation to John', is in the Greek *Apocalypsis Ioannou*. In both instances, and in scholarly writing about the Bible generally, it is assumed that an apocalypse is about what is going to happen 'at the end of the world'. Scholars have also wanted to suggest that unlike the rest of the gospel – the material for which it is agreed circulated in oral form before Mark collected and arranged it in writing – this particular section was already a written document before it reached Mark. I think this an unnecessary hypothesis which derives solely from the circumstance that commentators have failed to detect the manner in which Mark's gospel has been constructed throughout. It is obvious that this section is a collection of scattered fragments on a unified theme; it is less obvious that the entire gospel is built up out of a series of such sections, as I think by now I can claim to have shown that it is. Previous commentators, not having noticed that, have felt they had to account for the difference between this section and the rest of the gospel. I am arguing that there is no such difference, that the manner in which this section has been constructed is the same as that of all the other sections, and the presumption is therefore that Mark himself constructed it – just as he constructed the others – out of what came to him as independent fragments of oral tradition. There is of course a noticeable difference in the feel of the material, but that arises from the striking difference in the subject matter: all the other sections relate to the world around Jesus, this one relates entirely to the future.

I said above that scholars take the word apocalypse to be a vision of the end of the world, and that this section of Mark's gospel is classified as an apocalypse. But some readers may already have noticed that though the material by and large does seem to be about the end of the world, it is not in fact a vision at all. It is a vision only in the sense that all prophecy is vision – the prophet or 'seer' tells us of things that will be happening in the future that he can see, but as yet the rest of us can't. But this is not how the word 'apocalypse' should really be used: the two great biblical apocalypses – Daniel in the Old Testament, and the Revelation in the New – are both of them 'visions' in a much narrower and more 'miraculous' sense than this. But further, even more perceptive readers may have noticed that the first half of the chapter isn't even about the end of the world. It is prophecy in the non-apocalyptic sense of the word, and down to verse 20 ('And if the Lord had not shortened the days ...') it relates to an entirely non-miraculous foretelling of the destruction of Jerusalem. It is only beyond that point that apocalyptic themes can really be said to begin.

How close is the connection between the two sections? And was the connection made by Jesus himself, or has the tradition – or indeed Mark himself – confounded two ideas that in Jesus' mind were entirely separate? One asks this first because it takes little reflection to realize there is no obvious connection between the two ideas at all. Secondly, although as a matter of historic fact the destruction of Jerusalem took place in AD 70 (about thirty-five years after Jesus' death), the end of the world and Jesus' return to sit in judgment upon it has not yet happened. (In the belief of most of my readers I have no doubt the very possibility of such an event ever taking place in the real world is dismissed altogether; nevertheless it is a real event – and one shortly to be expected – that Mark clearly has in mind in the second half of this chapter.) Thirdly one must also point out that chapter 13 is the only instance in Mark of Jesus being concerned to foretell the destruction of Jerusalem; but he foretells his own return to earth – not in such detail as here, but still every bit as graphically – in two other passages (8.38–9.1 and 14.62), in neither of which does he give any hint that the event is connected with the fall of Jerusalem.

Leaving aside a decision on this point for the moment, the conjunction of the two ideas in this section of Mark is significant evidence on one point: that the gospel was written earlier than the fall of Jerusalem. Had it been written afterwards, we would expect the two ideas to be separated for the reason given above. This may seem not wholly convincing at first, since the same conjunction of these two ideas occurs both in Matthew (chapter 24) and Luke (chapter 21). My argument is that it only occurs there because both authors found it in Mark here. But this still undermines the argument in some degree; for both these authors all but certainly wrote after the fall of Jerusalem, and neither of them saw the need to make the separation which I argue Mark would have made had he also been writing then. The argument therefore depends on whether the reader accepts that Mark is not here incorporating a written document as scholars have argued, but put this chapter together himself, in the same way he seems to have done the rest of the gospel. But if we accepted the scholars' theory, the conclusion would be only that the document Mark used was likely to be earlier than the fall of Jerusalem, and we would have no indication of when he sub- sequently made use of it – a conclusion that those same scholars would find highly inconvenient.

But let us return now to the original question. Who was respon- sible for the conjunction of the two ideas, and what was the 'reasoning' behind it? Why should anyone – whether Jesus himself, or Mark on his behalf, or some unknown early teacher that links the two of them – ever have wanted to connect a prophecy of the destruction of Jerusalem with a prophecy of the end of the world and its final judgment before God? The Old Testament provides us with an obvious pre-echo of the same conjunction, and in doing so points us to the likelihood that the connection that Mark here offers us goes right back to Jesus himself. If we divide the chapter into its two halves, the first dealing with the fall of Jerusalem, the second with Jesus' return to earth to sit in judgment on it, then the crucial image in the first half is contained in verse 14:

> But when you see the desolating sacrilege set up where it ought not to be (let the reader understand) ...

while the crucial image of the second half is contained in verse 26:

> And then they will see the Son of man coming in clouds with power and great glory.

Both images are lifted straight from the book of Daniel, the first from 9.27 (see also 11.31 and 12.11), the second (as we have already noted several times) from 7.13. Since Jesus, on the three occasions on which he foretells his return to earth, makes use of this second image from Daniel, we can reasonably assume that he was in some way strongly fixated upon the book, and that this fixation underlies his foretelling of the destruction of Jerusalem as well.

But this itself raises two further problems for the modern reader, the first to do with the whole idea of prophecy, the second to do with the interpretation of the book of Daniel in particular. On the first point, is it really credible that Jesus should have prophesied an event (the destruction of Jerusalem) which was not to take place until thirty-five years after his death? Wouldn't it be simpler and more convincing to suppose that we are mistaken about the date of Mark's gospel, and that chapter 13 is the *evidence* that the work was written after the fall of Jerusalem, and that the 'prophecy' is in fact a record of something that at the time of writing had already taken place? Certainly we can't dismiss the suggestion altogether. But it is in fact quite credible that Jesus should have foretold the destruction of Jerusalem in this way.

First he had an obvious Old Testament forerunner in Jeremiah – not merely in announcing the destruction of Jerusalem, but in announcing it well before anyone was prepared to believe the real possibility of such an event taking place. We learn in Jeremiah 1.2 that 'the word of the Lord' first came to the prophet 'in the days of Josiah the son of Amon, king of Judah, in the thirteenth year of his reign'. That, by our reckoning, would be 627 BC. The first capture of the city by Babylon was exactly thirty years later in 597 BC, and the second, followed by the city's destruction, eleven years after that in 586 BC. When Jeremiah first began his ministry, his hearers had every reason to believe that a long period of peace and stability was before them. Assyria, the power that a hundred years earlier had destroyed the neighbouring kingdom of Israel and had come within an ace of destroying Judah as well was clearly in decline; and while the potentiality of Babylon had long been noted (we have no reason to doubt, for instance, the substantial truth of the prophecy recorded in Isaiah 39.5–8, nor of Hezekiah's response to it) no one could as yet foresee just how rapid Babylon's rise would suddenly be. But even had they done so, since Judah (with God's help) had survived the onslaught of Assyria, why should it not equally survive the onslaught of whatever power succeeded that of Assyria? It was this misplaced self-confidence which Jeremiah spent so much of his energy vainly denouncing, and which ensured that the eventual fall of Jerusalem was a far greater catastrophe than it need otherwise have been. As it was, Jeremiah seems to have spent the first twenty years of his ministry warning against a disaster that most people could not believe was ever going to occur. We have no reason to doubt the authenticity of this picture, which clearly emerges from the records that we have of him. In comparison (as I believe I have repeatedly shown) Jesus would have had a much easier task foretelling the destruction of Jerusalem, and there was a much greater likelihood of his being readily believed.

The second problem, I suggested above, is to do with the book of Daniel itself. How did Jesus understand the book, and how did this differ from the way the author himself intended to be understoood? And this problem is compounded by the possibility that the author of Daniel intended to deceive his readers anyway. The claim of the book itself is that it was written by one of the exiles after the destruction of Jerusalem in 586, who became a high official at the Babylonian court and was enabled by a series of detailed visions to foretell the nation's history at least down to the time of the desecration of the Jerusalem temple by Antiochus IV in 168 BC. We know that the book was in fact written between this date and the Maccabean uprising in 165 BC (whose early stages are perhaps described in Daniel 11.33–35), and that these 'visions' therefore really *are* in this case summaries of what had already happened, and not predictions of the future at all.

We presume, however, that Jesus himself will have taken the author's claims pretty well at face value as regards his dates being in the sixth rather than the second century BC. He will therefore have thought of the visions as genuine predictions of the future. But here we come up against another uncertainty. People who read the book when it first appeared will have realized that chapter 11 was largely a summary of the events of their own time – indeed, so readily will they have realized this that even if the author had intended to deceive them, most of them will have easily seen through the deceit.[1] But how did Jesus understand it? It seems likely, and chapter 13 of Mark is quite good evidence for this, that he understood *all* the predictions of Daniel as still awaiting fulfilment in the future, and as being literally intended to refer to his own time. When the author of Daniel refers to 'the abomination that makes desolate' he is referring to the image that had already been erected above the altar in Jerusalem; but on the basis of the gospel evidence it looks as though Jesus was convinced that this was a prophecy – made six hundred years before his time – of something that was now shortly going to happen. An important corollary of this conclusion is that whereas (say) in 150 BC most readers of the book will have been conscious of the huge gap between the 'prophecies' that had been fulfilled (down to Daniel 11.39) and those where history had turned out to be very different from what was predicted (11.40–45), or those which were hardly capable of fulfilment anyway (chapter 12), by Jesus' time this awareness had faded. All the prophecies could once again be taken seriously as predictions of an awaited future, and it makes best sense of the Marcan material to suppose that this is how Jesus in fact regarded them.

> And as he came out of the temple, one of his disciples said to him, 'Look, Teacher, what wonderful stones and what wonderful buildings!' And Jesus said to him, 'Do you see these great buildings? There will not be left here one stone upon another that will not be thrown down.'
> And as he sat on the Mount of Olives opposite the temple, Peter and James and John and Andrew asked him privately, 'Tell us when will this be, and what will be the sign when these things are all to be accomplished?' And Jesus began to say to them, 'Take heed that no one leads you astray. Many will come in my name, saying, "I am he!", and they will lead many astray. And when you hear of wars and rumours of wars, do not be alarmed; this must take place, but the end is not yet. For nation will rise against nation, and kingdom against kingdom; there will be earthquakes in various places, there will be famines; this is but the beginning of the sufferings'. (13.1–8)

The prophecy is triggered off by Jesus' rather sour put-down of the innocent expressions of admiration by the disciples in response to the architectural wonders of the Jerusalem temple. Just as in Jeremiah's time the undeniable beauty and holiness of the temple had lead people into a dangerously unreal belief that God would never allow such wonders to be destroyed (Jer. 7.1–15), so Jesus here seems to sense a similar infatuation, which is why he rebukes them so harshly. 'No matter how wonderful the building may be', he seems to be telling them, 'if the worshippers allow themselves to be deluded into foolish opinions about it (as they undoubtedly have done), then the whole magnificent edifice will once again come crashing down.' The scene then shifts to the Mount of Olives for a distant view of the temple, which provides the backcloth for a longer and more detailed prophecy of the imminent course of events. The four disciples ask Jesus for a sign, something that will forewarn them when the disaster is about to occur. For the moment they get no very definite answer to this question, though there is an answer of sorts at the end of the chapter – and probably the only answer that Jesus would have thought appropriate: If you're worried about being taken by surprise, you must be *constantly* prepared for the disaster to happen at any moment. But for the moment Jesus' advice seems almost the opposite of that: Don't be too ready to jump up at every false alarm.

And there are two kinds of false alarm that they must particularly expect. The first is the appearance of a whole series of false Messiahs.[2] The second is an over-readiness to interpret any kind of military conflict as the final stage before the appearance of the Messiah. I am inclined to treat this second warning with a fair amount of caution. What troubles me is that if we assume that Jesus had the book of Daniel at the back of his mind on all occasions when he spoke about the coming disaster, then his own idea must surely have been that 'wars and rumours of wars' were precisely the kind of thing that indicated that 'the end was nigh' – for two reasons. First this is exactly what we would be expect on the basis of an overliteral reading of Daniel 11; but secondly, of course, if these wars and rumours of wars were *not* the indication that 'the end was nigh', why mention them at all? My own inclination is to suppose that on the contrary, Jesus' original advice was unambiguously that wars and rumours of wars *were* the indication of the approaching end. So why has the change been made?

The most obvious possibility is once again inconvenient for the suggestion that Mark's gospel was written earlier than the fall of Jerusalem; an alteration of this kind would most obviously be *required* if Jerusalem had been reduced to rubble some years ago, and still there was no sign of Jesus' promised return. But that is not the only possibility, and there is an important feature of the material that counts against it. The crucial point is, how are we to interpret the phrase, 'the end is not yet'? Which particular end is Jesus here talking about: the end of Jerusalem at the hand of the Romans, or the end of the world at his appearing to the judge it? The suggestion above depends on our reading it in this latter sense; but the actual text of Mark's gospel implies that we should read it in the former. My own favoured position would be that the advice Jesus originally gave had led to many false alarms, even in the short space of time between his own death and the catastrophe he was predicting: and it was the irritation that some leaders felt at repeatedly being made to look fools in this way that led to the modification. Most of my readers will not need to be told that the enthusiastic strain of Christianity – starting I suppose with Jesus himself – has throughout history been eager to predict the end of the world within months rather than years; and repeated and unvarying disappointment has not even modified, let alone cured, this apparently deluded longing.

> But take heed to yourselves; for they will deliver you up to councils; and you will be beaten in synagogues; and you will stand before governors and kings for my sake, to bear testimony before them. And the gospel must first be preached to all nations. And when they bring you to trial and deliver you up, do not be anxious beforehand what you are to say; but say whatever is given you in that hour, for it is not you who speak, but the Holy Spirit. And brother will deliver up brother to death, and the father his child, and children will rise against parents and have them put to death; and you will be hated by all for my name's sake. But he who endures to the end will be saved. (13.9–13)

Here we have an insertion by Mark of material that does not appear to have belonged originally in this kind of context at all. If we turn to Matthew chapter 24, we find that although the first eight verses of that chapter follow very closely what Matthew found here in Mark, when he comes to this paragraph he discards it altogether and substitutes something that may very well be the creation of his own pen. The reason for his doing so is not that he objected to anything in the above excerpt, but that he had already included it very much earlier in his gospel, in 10.17–22. This suggests to me firstly that Matthew encountered the material of Mark 13 in more than one source, and secondly that he judged (and I think I agree with him) that this passage properly belonged to Jesus' instruction to the disciples about their mission rather than to his foretelling of the end of the world. Mark should really have placed the material somewhere in chapter 6; it was presumably the concluding advice, 'But he who endures to the end will be saved' that persuaded him to put it here.

But when you see the desolating sacrilege set up where it ought not to be (let the reader understand), then let those who are in Judaea flee to the mountains; let him who is on the housetop not go down, nor enter his house to take anything away; and let him who is in the field not turn back to take his mantle. And alas for those who are with child and for those who give suck in those days! Pray that it may not happen in winter. For in those days there will be such tribulation as has not been from the beginning of the creation which God created until now, and never will be. And if the Lord had not shortened the days, no human being would be saved; but for the sake of the elect, whom he chose, he shortened the days. And then if any one says to you, 'Look, here is the Christ!', or 'Look, there he is!', do not believe it. False Christs and false prophets will arise and show signs and wonders, to lead astray, if possible, the elect. But take heed; I have told you all things beforehand (13.14–23)

If we look back at Matthew 24, we find that he here follows Mark once again. But he has some interesting additions at the end which are worth drawing attention to. He discards the final sentence of the above excerpt, and continues:

So if they say to you, 'Lo, he is in the wilderness', do not go out; if they say, 'Lo, he is in the inner rooms', do not believe it. For as the lightning comes from the east and shines as far as the west, so will be the coming of the Son of man. Wherever the body is, there the eagles will be gathered together. (Matt. 24.26–28)

All of this can be considered Q material. The first sentence is clearly an alternative version of Luke 17.23; and the next sentence is a much closer version of Luke 17.24. The third sentence is a pretty well exact equivalent of Luke 17.37b. This seems to confirm what I have just suggested, that much of the material in Mark 13 came to Matthew in more than one source.

'For in those days there will be such tribulation ... he shortened the days.' I think it worth reminding the reader of what I said about the 'faithful remnant' on pages 63–4, and in particular of the discussion of I Kings 19.15–18, with its (to us abhorrent) suggestion that a wholesale and prolonged disaster will separate the righteous from the wicked – the former being those who survive the disaster, the latter being those who are destroyed by it. A very similar idea seems to underlie Jesus' words here – that, after all, is the only possible interpretation of: 'And if the Lord had not shortened the days, no human being would be saved ...' Let me remind the reader that up to now I have interpreted the chapter on the assumption that it offers a description of two separate events: first the fall of Jerusalem, then the return of Jesus to judge the world and to set up his own perfect kingdom. But I suspect that the original readership did not necessarily – nor was it meant to – think of separate events at all. Jesus' real meaning was probably that the disaster *is* the judgment: the wicked are destroyed and the righteous preserved by a single event which looks to earthly eyes like the destruction of Jerusalem, but (for those that have eyes to see) is really the return of Jesus to judge the world.

> But in those days, after that tribulation, the sun will be darkened, and the moon will not give its light, and the stars will be falling from heaven, and the powers in the heavens will be shaken. And then they will see the Son of man coming in clouds with great power and glory. And then he will send out the angels, and gather his elect from the four winds, from the ends of the earth to the ends of heaven. (13.24–27)

I wish to draw attention particularly to the words 'after that tribulation' because they seem at first sight to be an outright refutation of the idea I have just put forward that the earthly disaster and the heavenly judgment are not two separate events but two different ways of viewing the one event. These words, on the contrary, seem to insist that *first* comes the earthly disaster, *then* comes the heavenly judgment. My task is not so much one of refuting this view, as of refining it. In a culture like the one we are dealing with, which differs from our own above all in what we see as an extreme inability to express ideas in abstract terms, it also looks as though they get round the 'problem' by the metaphorical use of *concrete* temporal, spatial and dynamic imagery. (The frequent absurdities of Christian fundamentalism are uniquely caused by a refusal to allow that there is any use of methaphor in this way.)

   Let's consider first what function the proclamation of impending judgment is meant to perform. First and foremost it is meant to *frighten* people. That's an unfashionable thing to say, and many Christians (but not fundamentalists) would at first instinctively reject it. But it is easy to show on the basis of the New Testament that the first generation of Christians would have agreed with me. The best illustration I know is, if authentic, very early indeed, part of that sudden burst of revivalist enthusiasm which occurred a few weeks after Jesus' death, and which seems to underly the account in the second chapter of Acts of what the tradition calls the descent of the Holy Ghost. The following is an extract from the first sermon following on from that event:

> 'Being therefore exalted at the right hand of God, and having received from the Father the promise of the Holy Spirit, he has poured out this which you see and hear [*i.e. speaking in tongues*]. For David did not ascend into the heavens; but he himself says,
>
> "The Lord said to my Lord, Sit at my right hand,
>
> till I make thy enemies a stool for thy feet."
>
> Let all the house of Israel therefore know assuredly that God has made him both Lord and Christ, this Jesus whom you crucified.'
>
> Now when they heard this they were cut to the heart, and said to Peter and to the rest of the apostles. 'Brethren, what shall we do?' And Peter said to them, 'Repent, and be baptized every one of you in the name of Jesus Christ for the forgiveness of your sins; and you shall receive the gift of the Holy Spirit. For the promise is to you and to your children, and to all that are far off, every one whom the Lord our God calls to him.' And he testified with many other words and exhorted them, saying, 'Save yourselves from this crooked generation.' (Acts 2.3–40)

It is clear from this extract that the hearers are terrified by the preaching of the disciples ('Brethren, what shall we do?' – i.e. 'How can we escape the destruction with which you threaten us?'). It is not so clear *why* they are terrified, and if we did not have a passage like Mark 13 to explain it, the point would probably evade us altogether. We begin to see now, perhaps, how this dual imagery of judgment – both that of an *imminent* earthly disaster, and that of an *eventual* return of Jesus to earth – work as an inseparable pair. The second image without the first, though terrifying in the long run, is too remote to be so in the immediate situation; the first image on the other hand is terrifying for the moment, but (as with the original destruction of Jerusalem) once the crisis has passed, does that mean that the need for repentance has passed with it? The way the combination has actually worked (and with quite spectacular success) is that the *historic* crisis of impending destruction begets the *mythic* crisis of Jesus' return to earth; and the *mythic* crisis, once established in the thinking of the community, then automatically reattaches itself to whatever historic crisis appears to be on the horizon. This process can (and probably will) go on for ever; and it also explains why it is that, no matter how often prophecies of 'the end of the world' are confidently made and then disappointed, believers in the idea can still remain convinced.

From the fig tree learn its lesson: as soon as its branch becomes tender and puts forth its leaves, you know that summer is near. So also, when you see these things taking place, you know that he is near, at the very gates. Truly, I say to you, this generation will not pass away before all these things take place. Heaven and earth will pass away, but my words will not pass away.

But of that day or that hour no one knows, not even the angels in heaven, nor the Son, but only the Father. Take heed, watch; for you do not know when the time will come. It is like a man going on a journey, when he leaves home and puts his servants in charge, each with his work, and commands the doorkeeper to be on the watch. Watch therefore – for you do not know when the master of the house will come, in the evening, or at midnight, or at cock-crow, or in the morning – lest he come suddenly and find you asleep. And what I say to you, I say to all: Watch. (13.28–37)

These two paragraphs are a perfect conclusion to the see-saw motion of the section as a whole. I have no difficulty in accepting both of them as authentic; but if I am right about that, it follows that both were originally independent of each other. (And – on a more detailed point – it is also clear that the last sentence of the first paragraph did not originally belong to its present context.) They both appear to be offering answers to the question the disciples originally asked in verse 4: 'Tell us, when will this be, and what will be the sign when these things are all to be accomplished?' The first paragraph implies that there will be clear indications of the approaching catastrophe, while the second implies there won't be. If that is so, some may protest, they can't both be genuine. But it would be truer to say they can't both have been uttered at the same time. There is no implausibility in suggesting that Jesus' various pronouncements at various times on the same question were not necessarily always consistent with each other.

But the discrepancy can equally well be explained another way which is well worth considering, and may very well be the explanation that Mark himself (though probably not Jesus) had in mind when he wrote the passage. The first paragraph, which suggests that the accomplishment of all these things will be preceded by definite signs, is intended to relate to the destruction of Jerusalem; the second paragraph, which suggests that the final visitation will be totally without warning, is intended to relate to the more mythical notion of Jesus' reappearance to judge the world. It will be argued that this scheme is incompatible with my own suggestion that the destruction of Jerusalem and Jesus' reappearance are two ways of looking at the one event – and to *some* extent that is true. But there are additional possibilities to be considered. The first is that this dichotomy belongs to Mark's own thinking, or that of the tradition, rather than to that of Jesus himself. The second is that even in Mark's own thinking the distinction between the two 'events' is made concrete only because he lacked the ability to think in abstract terms, as suggested above. The third is that Mark himself, or the tradition, or Jesus, or even all three of them, were by no means entirely clear in their own minds about the nature of the distinction – and this suggestion, I suspect, will seem highly plausible to quite a number of readers.

14

The Passion Narrative

(Mark 14.1–15.47)

As the reader will not need to be reminded, the passion narrative has clearly been constructed on principles very different from those that have prevailed throughout the work so far. Up to now the writing has been in sections, each with its discernible unifying theme, and containing an assortment of smaller units which appear to have had no connection with each other before Mark himself drew them together in constructing the section. But from now on the gospel is a continuous, extended and unified narrative, and we are probably right to suppose that it was already all these things before it reached Mark's hands. Up to this point Mark has himself constructed the gospel; but from this point on one suspects he simply records it.

Why the difference? The most usual explanation, which I find plausible, is that by the time Mark wrote, the custom had already established itself of holding an annual recitation – or perhaps even reenactment – by the Christian communities of the events of Jesus' passion, death and resurrection,[1] and Mark here gives us his own local version of those events transcribed out of liturgical and into narrative form. The length and detail of the story is likely to be due to the fact that, early though Mark's probable date may be, these liturgical enactments already went back a good number of years by the time he wrote. A particular thought that suggests itself therefore is this: If Mark's date is early, and if by his time these liturgies already had some years of tradition behind them, the likelihood is that the material dates from the very earliest days of the Christian community, and is therefore likely also to be an accurate record. At first sight that looks plausible; and it is also noticeable that the last three chapters of Mark's gospel, in the strongest possible contrast to the first thirteen, contain no miraculous or supernatural events whatever, nor anything that even the most sceptical reader would be inclined to dismiss as historically or scientifically impossible. If we bear in mind that the authentic text of Mark's gospel ends with 16.8, this is as true of his account of the resurrection as it is of the crucifixion; and I shall be arguing that it would still have been true even if we had (as most scholars seem to agree we have not) the complete text.

So are we in the passion narrative at last dealing with actual *history*? One cannot absolutely say yes, but the verdict does turn out to be somewhat closer to yes than it is to no. But when one first considers the question, enormous grounds for misgiving present themselves. Consider for instance: we are told a great deal about Jesus' last moments that one would have thought only he could have known; so what has been the source of the tradition's information? The point is most obvious with Jesus' famous prayer in the garden of Gethsemane: 'Abba, Father, all things are possible to thee; remove this cup from me; yet not what I will, but what thou wilt' (Mark 14.36). The sentiments are appropriate and well expressed, and whoever invented them is certainly to be commended; but it is certain also that only invention can account for them. Even earlier than this, though the disciples could well have known subsequently that Jesus' arrest was engineered by Judas' betrayal of him, it is far more likely than not that details of the agreement between Judas and the priests (14.10–11) is an invention of the tradition. Personally I am extremely sceptical of the idea that Judas' motives were mercenary, and am inclined to suspect that this suggestion, in Mark's gospel as much as in Matthew's, derives from Zechariah 11.12–13 (see page 262). Also we get quite a lengthy and detailed account of Jesus' trial before the priests (14.55–65); but who was present at it – apart from Jesus himself, who died without making further contact with any of the disciples – who would have passed on an account of it to them? The same applies also to the trial before Pilate (15.1–5), to the explicit account of the mockery by the soldiers (15.16–20), and above all to the closing scene and Jesus' dying words on the cross – this last for two reasons. The first is that we are assured by medical opinion that after three hours on the cross it is unlikely that the victim would be able to make any utterance at all, let alone one 'with a loud voice' (15.34, 37). The second is that Mark himself tells us that everyone who actually knew Jesus or might have been interested in what he had to say was 'looking on from afar' (15.40).

Someone who seems to have noticed these weaknesses in antiquity, and to have gone to great lengths to rectify them is the author
of John's gospel. There is a very prominent character in the second
half of that gospel whom the author describes as 'the disciple whom
Jesus loved' (John 13.23; 18.15–16; 19.26–27; 20.2–4; 21.7;
21.20–24). The last of these references identifies this disciple with
the actual author of the gospel. But if we look at the other references,
all of them seem intended to explain how the tradition comes to
know what happened in situations where it otherwise had no
obvious source of information. Jesus' prayer in the garden of Gethsemane is suppressed altogether (see John 18.1–2), and admittedly
the major reason for this is the anxiety of the author to avoid any
suggestion that Jesus was capable of either fear or suffering (see
pages 30–1 of the Introduction); but we can equally be confident that
had the author of John's gospel felt the need to record an agony in the
garden, the beloved disciple would have been at Jesus' side to witness
it. The assertion in 18.15 that 'this disciple was known to the high
priest' is intended to explain how the tradition comes to know what
went on at Jesus' trial before Caiaphas – and in doing so it involves
the narrative in an absurdity. How is it, for instance, that the maid at
the gate challenges Peter as being one of the disciples, but not the
beloved disciple? Is it remotely likely that he should have been an
acquaintance of the high priest, but that his status as Jesus' favourite
disciple should not equally be known? Similarly he stands at the foot
of the cross as Jesus dies, accompanied by Jesus' mother (who plays a
very minor role in Mark's account of the crucifixion, if indeed she is
present at all), and thus can answer the question, which Mark can
not, of how he came to know what happened at this point (John
19.35). Even the first appearance of all in 13.23 (which comes
without a word of explanation) can be seen as fulfilling the same kind
of purpose: if we look at Mark's account of this incident (Mark
14.18–21) the identity of the traitor is not disclosed. But even if we
disregard this as too close a reading of the evidence, it cannot be a
coincidence that the beloved disciple first appears at the last supper,
and then goes on to appear at all these otherwise unwitnessed events.
The evidence strongly suggests to me that the character was
originally invented for just this purpose, and that the additional
claim that he is also the author of the gospel may well have been a
happy afterthought.

And yet, despite this obvious and at first sight well-grounded nervousness on the part of the fourth gospel, we shall find as the exposition proceeds that at any rate as regards the two trials (where the problem seems to be most acute) he had no real cause for alarm. Close scrutiny of the trials as Mark records them seems to vindicate the at-first-sight implausible suggestion that the earliest tradition did in fact have good information about what went on at them. (Perhaps then the figure of Joseph of Arimathaea is historical after all!) This is not to deny that considerable distortions seem to have crept in between the earliest versions and the one Mark actually gives us. Showing where these distortions are most likely to have occurred will be the business of the actual exposition.

> It was now two days before the Passover and the feast of Un-leavened Bread. And the chief priests and the scribes were seeking how to arrest him by stealth, and kill him; for they said, 'Not during the feast, lest there be a tumult of the people.' (14.1–2)

Up to now the parties mentioned by Mark as being interested in having Jesus put out of the way are the Pharisees and the Herodians – in 3.6, probably also in 8.15, and finally in 12.13. As regards the Herodians, to the historian the first two of these references, set in a Galilaean context, are plausible, while the Jerusalem context of the third is less so. The Herod in question is the tetrarch of Galilee, and it was in this capacity that he had had John the Baptist put to death, believing (not altogether without reason) that the popular interest which his mission had awakened was a likely threat to good order in general and to his own position in particular. We have grounds therefore for supposing that he would have viewed Jesus' mission with the same kind of suspicion, and there is an indirect confirmation of this in Luke's passion narrative, where we read:

> And Pilate asked him, 'Are you the King of the Jews?' And he answered him, 'You have said so.' And Pilate said to the chief priests and the multitudes, 'I find no crime in this man.' But they were urgent, saying, 'He stirs up the people, teaching throughout all Judaea, from Galilee even to this place.'
> When Pilate heard this, he asked whether the man was a Galilaean. And when he learned that he belonged to Herod's jurisdiction, he sent him over to Herod, who was himself in Jerusalem at that time. When Herod saw Jesus, he was very glad, for he had long desired to see him, because he had heard about

him, and he was hoping to see some sign done by him. (Luke
23.3–8)

I think we can dismiss out of hand the suggestion that a hardboiled
politician of the Roman Empire like Herod was the least bit interested in Jesus' supposed miracle-working capacities, and we can
probably even dismiss the entire suggestion (which is not made by
any of the other gospels) that he took any part in the events leading
up to Jesus' death. In any case it is unlikely that the tetrarch of Galilee
would have concerned himself with Jesus' antics once he had left
Galilee for Judaea. We get confirmation of this idea from an otherwise mystifying passage, also found only in Luke:

> At that very hour some Pharisees came, and said to him, 'Get away
> from here, for Herod wants to kill you.' And he said to them, 'Go
> and tell that fox, "Behold, I cast out demons and perform cures
> today and tomorrow, and the third day I finish my course.
> Nevertheless I must go on my way today and tomorrow and the
> day following; for it cannot be that a prophet should perish away
> from Jerusalem."' (Luke 13.31–33)

This is one of those rare passages – found particularly in Luke – that
are otherwise apparently so pointless that the only plausible
explanation of them is that they are authentic. The fact that the
Pharisees here seem to be *opposed* to the Herodians and actively on
Jesus' side is inconsistent with what Mark tells us, but quite likely to
be historical just the same; and if we take the passage purely on its
own terms, the picture is convincing. The incident takes place in
Galilee, and the Pharisees are urging Jesus to leave and presumably
head south for Jerusalem where he will be out of Herod's power. The
gist of Jesus' rather obscure reply seems to be that, yes, he is going to
head south – not because he is the least bit intimidated by Herod's
threats, but only because he is going to die anyway, and it has to
happen in Jerusalem.

In contrast to all this, the main agents against Jesus throughout the
passion narrative are the Jerusalem priests. Their likely motives for
hostility have already been discussed. Their dilemma is that to do
anything effective they have to be able to persuade Pontius Pilate, the
Roman governor, that Jesus is a *political* threat; i.e. that he is a
fanatical agitator of the kind described in the previous chapter,
whose aim is to stir up a violent revolution aimed at the overthrow of

Roman domination. This is the situation as it is described by all four gospels, and is in any case a plausible explanation of the events described. All four of them are also agreed that Pilate was reluctant to accept this view of Jesus' intentions, preferring to believe the priests had their own ulterior motives for wanting Jesus out of the way, and that the formal accusation was no more than a pretext.

When Mark tells us, 'It was now two days before the Passover ...', as noted earlier this is not a temporal conjunction with the previous material, but simply his way of telling us that the following story begins the day before the Passover. The 'feast of Unleavened Bread' refers to the traditional eating unleavened bread for seven days, the first of which was the Passover itself (see Ex. 12.1–28). Despite the close connection between the two rituals throughout Israel's history, it is likely that in origin they were separate, the Passover deriving from a *nomadic* annual festival connected with the lambing season, the unleavened bread deriving from an *agricultural* festival connected with the spring sowing of grain.

> And while he was at Bethany in the house of Simon the leper, as he sat at table, a woman came with an alabaster jar of ointment of pure nard, very costly, and she broke the jar and poured it over his head. But there were some who said to themselves indignantly, 'Why was the ointment thus wasted? For this ointment might have been sold for more than three hundred pence,[2] and given to the poor.' And they reproached her. But Jesus said, 'Let her alone; why do you trouble her? She has done a beautiful thing to me. For you always have the poor with you, and whenever you will, you can do good to them; but you will not always have me. She has done what she could; she has anointed my body beforehand for burying. And truly, I say to you, wherever the gospel is preached in the whole world, what she has done will be told in memory of her.' (14.3–9)

What is recognizably another version of this story occurs in Luke 7.36–49, even down to the point that in both cases the host is called Simon (Luke 7.40). Insofar as either of them can be considered authentic, this seems more likely to be the original version, and it is important to clear the mind of all echos of the Lucan version in interpreting it. There is for instance no point in suggesting, as popular tradition does, that the woman in question is Mary Magdalene.[3] She is an otherwise unknown figure who appears at this point only in, the gospel, and whose memory depends (as Jesus' own words – or those put into his mouth by the tradition – imply) on this one action. As the two versions of the story testify, the imagery suggested by that action is rivetting. The disciples themselves point out (and not just Judas, as in John 12.4) that it was a grotesque extravagance.[4] A very considerable sum of money (getting on for five hundred pounds if we can believe Mark's valuation – one suspects, though, that Matthew is incredulous and for this reason leaves it out) has been frittered away in an action that, at its highest estimate, amounts to no more than a gesture. Modern church administrators – modern Christians generally – with their deeply serious views on the subject of stewardship, would undoubtedly have sided with the disciples. It is worth noting also that Mark uses the same word here (*enebrimōnto*) to describe the reaction of the disciples to the woman as he had used back in 1.43 (*embrimēsamenos*) in describing Jesus' very odd reaction to the leper he had just cleansed, and that the translation is in both cases misleading in exactly the same way. The disciples here don't just 'reproach' the women; they barrack her.

> Then Judas Iscariot, who was one of the twelve, went to the chief priests in order to betray him to them. And when they heard it they were glad, and promised to give him money. And he sought an opportunity to betray him. (14.10–11)

This refers us back to the beginning of the chapter, where we are told that the chief priests, though anxious to put a stop to Jesus, were reluctant to do so during the festival for fear of causing a disturbance. The narrator wishes us to conclude that it is Judas' spontaneous approach to them that changes their mind on the point. We have only to read the account of Paul's arrest in Acts 21.27–36 (on this occasion with the collusion of the crowd) to appreciate just how noisy a public arrest could be in Jerusalem. Judas' offer of an opportunity for a clandestine arrest seems to remove the difficulty.

I have pointed out above that the mercenary motive that all four gospels put forward as explaining Judas' treachery is probably derived from Zechariah 11.12–13 and is unlikely to be authentic. So what is the real motive likely to be? We have to guess the answer, but a plausible guess readily presents itself. The disciples – *all* the disciples – were attached to Jesus in the belief that he was the Messiah, not in the fanciful sense that Jesus himself gave the term, but in the good old-fashioned sense of a Davidic warrior who would lead the nation to victory over the Romans. Luke's writings uniquely imply that this erroneous expectation survived even the catastrophe of Calvary, and hè portrays the disciples as still confidently awaiting its fulfilment at the very moment of Jesus' final taking leave of them (Acts 1.6). But even if this strains belief, we can still be confident that right up to the last (the last being Jesus' actual death), all the disciples apart from Judas were still under this delusion. Scholars have suggested, to me entirely plausibly, that the motive for Judas' betrayal was the realization that this *was* a delusion. He alone of the disciples had worked out the kind of thing Jesus really meant when he called himself the Messiah; and it was his rage and disappointment at the let-down which prompted him to act as he did. I should be very surprised if he expected or received any money for what to him probably looked like an act of revenge.

> And on the first day of Unleavened Bread, when they sacrificed the passover lamb, his disciples said to him, 'Where will you have us go and prepare for you to eat the passover?' And he sent two of his disciples, and said to them, 'Go into the city, and a man carrying a jar of water will meet you; follow him, and wherever he enters, say to the householder, "The Teacher says, Where is my guest room, where I am to eat the passover with my disciples?" And he will show you a large upper room furnished and ready; there prepare for us.' And the disciples set out and went to the city, and found it as he had told them; and they prepared the passover. (14.12–16)

The first day of Unleavened Bread began, like all Hebrew days, not at sunrise, nor even at midnight, but at the sunset which concluded the previous day (as in: 'And there was evening and there was morning, one – or a second – or a third – day'; see Gen. 1.5,8,13 and so on). It was at this first sunset of the feast that the Passover lambs were eaten, and Mark's description of the above conversation as having taken place 'on the first day of Unleavened Bread' cannot be strictly accurate. He seems to mean that it took place on the morning of what we would call the first day, but which he – to be consistent with his own terminology – should have still been calling 'the day before'. There is no doubt in Mark and Matthew that we are meant to think of the 'Last Supper' as the actual Passover meal. The independent account of Luke seems to agree with Matthew and Mark in the preliminaries (Luke 22.7–13); but during the actual meal (Luke 22.15–20) his words seem to imply that it is still the day before the

Passover. It may have been this that prompts the author of John's gospel to insist on this chronology for the whole of his account:

> Now before the feast of the Passover, when Jesus knew that his hour had come to depart out of this world to the Father, having loved his own who were in the world, he loved them to the end. And during supper ... (John 13.1–2a)

– his reasons for the difference (as so often throughout the work) being better explained on symbolic than on historic grounds. If Jesus died mid-afternoon before the Passover, he died just about the time the Passover lambs were being slaughtered for the evening feast. The experienced reader needs no further explanation for the preference.

'And he sent two of his disciples ...' Most readers will be reminded of the preliminaries to the triumphal entry in 11.1–6. Jesus sends two disciples, to whom he gives detailed instructions which imply to the reader that there has been a previous arrangement; although since in neither case is this actually stated, the author gives the impression he would like us to think of the outcome as at least in part 'miraculous'. In this case there is also the element of timing: 'a man carrying a jar of water', though a rare sight (in those days this would have been women's work) is unlikely to have been a protracted one; it is unlikely, for instance, that he had instructions from his master to take a jar of water and carry it round the city until accosted by ..., and so forth. The arrangements relating to the upper room must certainly have been by prior arrangement, and if this is the case it seems odd that the disciples did not know something of the place already and could not simply have been directed to an address. Tradition suggests, with some plausibility, that this house was the family home of John Mark, the supposed author of the gospel.

> And when it was evening he came with the twelve. And as they were at table eating, Jesus said, 'Truly, I say to you, one of you will betray me, one who is eating with me.' They began to be sorrowful, and to say to him one after another, 'Is it I?' He said to them, 'It is one of the twelve, one who is dipping bread in the same dish with me. For the Son of man goes as it is written of him, but woe to that man by whom the Son of man is betrayed! It would have been better for that man if he had not been born.' (14.17–21)

One of the reasons why one is hesitant about accepting the gospel portrait of Judas is the transparent reference back to Old Testament 'prophecy' in almost everything he does. We have already noted that the payment of thirty pieces of silver for his treachery is more likely to be derived from Zechariah 11.12–13 than it is from history; and here again we are immediately reminded of Psalm 41.9 (which John's gospel actually quotes at this point – John 13.18):

> Even my bosom friend in whom I trusted,
> who ate of my bread, has lifted his heel against me.

To which one could add Psalm 55.12–15, particularly in connection with Judas' alleged subsequent suicide (an incident whose historicity I also suspect, in view of the fact that the two accounts we have of it – Matthew 27.3–10 and Acts 1.18–19 – bear so little relation to each other):

> It is not an enemy who taunts me –
> then I could bear it;
> it is not an adversary who deals insolently with me –
> then I could hide from him.
> But it is you, my equal,
> my companion, my familiar friend.
> We used to hold sweet converse together;
> within God's house we walked in fellowship.
> Let death come upon them; let them go down to hell alive;
> evils are in their habitation, in their midst.

It is at this point in his narrative that the author of the fourth gospel suddenly introduces the character of the disciple whom Jesus' loved (John 13.23). If I am right in supposing that the original function of this character was to be able to vouch for all those incidents which in the synoptic accounts seem to happen without the presence of witnesses, it is not immediately obvious why he should be needed here. There is a presumption in all four accounts that at the time of the actual supper none of the other disciples was aware of the identity of the betrayer, though John's gospel is the only one that is explicit on the point (John 13.28). But surely this by itself raises no difficulties about evidence: if they didn't know it then, they found out at the actual betrayal in the Garden of Gethsemane? This is true as far as the synoptic accounts go; but it is significant that in John's gospel, although it is Judas who leads the band of soldiers to where Jesus is, there is no kiss of betrayal, nor even the suggestion that Judas made himself in any way prominent at the time of the arrest. A further point worth noting is that in all three synoptic accounts Jesus, though aware of Judas' treachery, admits him to the final ceremony which forms the basis of the Christian eucharist. In Luke's gospel there is even specific comment on the point (Luke 22.19–23). The horror which such imagery inspires in the Christian mind is rendered with notable artistry in the fourth gospel:

> So when he had dipped the morsel, he gave it to Judas, the son of Simon Iscariot. Then after the morsel, Satan entered into him ... So, after receiving the morsel, he immediately went out; and it was night. (John 13.26b–27a, 30)

> And as they were eating, he took bread, and blessed, and broke it, and gave it to them, and said, 'Take; this is my body.' And he took a cup, and when he had given thanks he gave it to them, and they all drank of it. And he said to them, 'This is my blood of the covenant, which is poured out for many. Truly, I say to you, I shall not drink again of the fruit of the vine until that day when I drink it new in the kingdom of God.' And when they had sung a hymn, they went out to the Mount of Olives. (14.22–26)

One could almost write a book – indeed a considerable number of books have in fact been written – on this passage alone. Matthew at this point gives a slightly amplified version of Jesus' words which to this day are used as part of the climax of the Christian eucharist. Luke's account is strikingly different, particularly in the reversed order of the distribution of the wine and the bread. In the following I have italicized the material which, though part of the received traditional text, is not found in most early manuscripts and is probably an interpolation. It will be noted that in this traditional text of Luke there are *two* distributions of the cup, one before and one after the distribution of the bread:

> And he said to them, 'I have earnestly desired to eat this passover with you before I suffer; for I tell you, I shall not eat it until it is fulfilled in the kingdom of God.' And he took a cup, and when he had given thanks he said, 'Take this, and divide it among yourselves; for I tell you that from now on I shall not drink of the fruit of the vine until the kingdom of God comes.'[5] And he took bread, and when he had given thanks, he broke it and gave it to them, saying, 'This is my body *which is given for you. Do this in remembrance of me.' And likewise the cup after supper, saying,*

> 'This cup which is poured out for you is the new convenant in my blood.' (Luke 22.15–20)

As for John's gospel, it is well-known that the author omits this episode altogether. It looks as though he preferred to derive the eucharist, not from the last supper with the disciples, but from the miraculous feeding of the multitude which he relates in 6.1–14. The lengthy meditation which runs from 6.25–65 contains everything that the author wants to say about the eucharist; he makes the last supper the occasion for a very much longer meditation (chapters 14–17) on the nature of the church, which he evidently regards (in a manner that is both subtle and profound) as itself the greatest sacrament of all, and the continued 'incarnation' of Jesus after he himself has left the earth.

Inevitably the question arises for most readers, what do Jesus' words actually mean? – and in this connection we must also consider John 6.53–58. Protestant Christianity has always maintained that Jesus was providing the disciples with a *symbol* to be the focus of their unity with him and with each other after his death. Catholics on the contrary insist that the force of the words is not merely symbolic but is actually miraculous; that this unity is not merely enacted by the shared bread and wine, but is actually created and sustained by the miraculous transformation of the bread and wine into the real body and blood of Jesus, as the words of John's gospel at any rate seem to insist. In support of this view they correctly quote the ancient opinion of practically the whole church. Yet for me, and I suspect for most of my readers, however much this proves that the Catholic position is ancient, it still fails to show that it is credible, much less that it is true. Let us also take a closer look at the Johannine passage:

> The Jews then disputed among themselves, saying, 'How can this man give us his flesh to eat?' So Jesus said to them, 'Truly, truly, I say to you, unless you eat the flesh of the Son of man and drink his blood, you have no life in you; he who eats my flesh and drinks my blood has eternal life, and I will raise him up at the last day. For my flesh is food indeed, and my blood is drink indeed. He who eats my flesh and drinks my blood abides in me, and I in him. As the living Father sent me, and I live because of the Father, so he who eats me will live because of me. This is the bread which came down from heaven, not such as the fathers ate and died;[6] he who eats this bread will live for ever.'

> Many of his disciples, when they heard it, said, 'This is a hard saying; who can listen to it?' But Jesus, knowing in himself that his disciples murmured at it, said to them, 'Do you take offence at this? Then what if you were to see the Son of man ascending where he was before? It is the spirit that gives life, the flesh is of no avail; the words that I have spoken to you are spirit and life. But there are some of you that do not believe.' (John 6.53–64a)

The liberal tradition of Christianity – whose ancestry is almost entirely Protestant, though much of Protestantism now rejects what it sees as the compromising tendencies of liberalism – fastens eagerly on the mention of 'the Jews' at the opening of this extract. Throughout John's gospel, it argues, 'the Jews' are portrayed, not so much as rejecting Jesus, as of being incapable of understanding him. What John is emphasizing here is that 'the Jews' reject Jesus' claim because they try to understand it in literal terms: and the author seems to admit that taken literally, the claim is indeed absurd. The whole point, particularly of the second paragraph, is to insist that the 'real' meaning is something very different from the literal meaning.

Conservative Christians of both the Catholic and Protestant variety reject this interpretation as being oversubtle. My own inclination is to reject it as being not nearly subtle enough. It is true that throughout John's gospel 'the Jews' seem to fulfil the function of indicating that Jesus' words at this point do not simply mean what they say. But to my eyes the liberal tradition gives us only half of what the author of John's gospel actually meant to achieve by this device. Take the second paragraph above: 'It is the spirit that gives life, the flesh is of no avail; the words that I have spoken to you are spirit and life.' To the liberal these words indicate that the literal meaning of sayings such as, 'unless you eat the flesh of the Son of man and drink his blood, you have no life in you' is not the meaning Jesus actually intends; his *real* meaning is a spiritual, not a literal, meaning of these words. But the conservative Christian interprets the second paragraph above as meaning that if 'the Jews' were spiritual people (as, for instance, Christians are) they would have no difficulty in accepting the *literal* meaning of Jesus words as the true meaning; they cannot do this because they are *not* spiritual.

To me it seems pointless to ask which of these two undoubtedly contradictory positions the author actually held. My conviction is that he actually intended this dual response. 'The Jews', if you like, are a kind of literary device (practically the whole gospel is an endless series of highly ingenious literary devices) which simultaneously allows the simple believer to insist that the literal meaning *is* the spiritual meaning, and the sophisticated believer to insist on a wide distinction between them. If you read straight through the fourth gospel, you will very likely be infuriated by the repeated failure of the Jews and Jesus to be intelligible to each other. The Jews come across as being quite extraordinarily obtuse, Jesus as being quite extraordinarily evasive. My own guess is that this is not an effect that the author actually intended, but an unwanted by-product of his attempt to achieve the dual response I have outlined, and which he maintains with quite amazing virtuosity.

The catholic or universal teaching of the church up to the time of the Reformation, with its insistence that Jesus' words at the last supper must be interpreted in a miraculous sense, cannot therefore be dismissed out of hand as a mis-interpretation of John's gospel; but then, of course, neither can the post-Reformation insistence that they are to be understood symbolically. The author seems actually to have intended that both interpretations should be possible. It is worth pointing out though that the author's *personal* stance must have been (in our terms) liberal rather than conservative; if this were not the case, he would have had no need of the device in the first place. It is also important to draw attention to the disastrous long-term consequences of the church's ever-increasing insistence that only the 'conservative' interpretation was allowable. The history of Christianity would have been a very much happier affair if the two traditions could both have enjoyed the same equal if mutually contradictory status that the fourth gospel seems to argue for. But that is perhaps an unreal hope. For if the literary device we are considering shows that the author's personal stance was liberal rather than conservative, it also shows that even in his day the 'liberals' felt in some degree threatened by the conservatives. Traditional scholarship suggests that John's gospel deliberately deepened the understanding of his day on the subject of 'what happens' at the eucharist. Myself I doubt that. It seems much more likely to me that he is commenting on a development that has already begun to gather momentum, and is indeed trying to offer some kind of refuge for those reluctant to go along with it.

But after all this, we are still faced with the question how are we to understand Jesus' words as reported in Mark's gospel. There are two contrasting points to be made. The first is that neither Mark himself

nor the other two synoptics give the slightest hint that they understand the words in a miraculous rather than a symbolic sense. I have
no wish to dispute that the miraculous interpretation must be
exceedingly early; but this still doesn't persuade me that it is even the
'original' one, much less the 'true' one. (After all, Mark's gospel itself
– a product of first generation Christianity – contains no lack of
miracles, hardly any of which most of us would be prepared to
believe happened just as Mark relates them.) As far as I am concerned *all* the miracles in *all* the gospels require a symbolic interpretation anyway; and this seems also to have been the view of the
author of John's gospel, though he clearly felt it prudent to be more
chary of saying so than I am. To me the symbolic interpretation of
the words of the eucharist (and indeed of the whole ceremony) is to
be preferred to the miraculous interpretation, if only because the
symbolic interpretation is possible and the miraculous interpretation
is not. And when we have arrived at this conclusion, what I said
about the ceremony of baptism on pages 55–6 equally applies here.
When it comes to interpreting symbolism, interpretations are things
that any one of us has a right to offer, and none of us has a right to
insist on.

> And Jesus said to them, 'You will all fall away; for it is written, "I
> will strike the shepherd, and the sheep will be scattered." But after
> I am raised up, I will go before you to Galilee.' Peter said to him,
> 'Even though they all fall away, I will not.' And Jesus said to him,
> 'Truly, I say to you, this very night, before the cock crows twice,
> you will deny me three times.' But he said vehemently, 'If I must
> die with you, I will not deny you.' And they all said the same.
> (14.27–31)

The quotation, 'I will strike the shepherd …', as we have seen, is from
Zechariah 13.7; and as an equally mystifying quotation from the
same book also lies behind the Palm Sunday event, one is inclined to
accept that the allusion in both cases comes authentically from Jesus.
The same can probably be said of the prophecy of his reappearance
in Galilee after his resurrection, if only because to a sceptical mind it
seems unlikely that the disciples would ever have come to believe in
the resurrection at all unless Jesus himself had encouraged them to
expect it. Equally convincing is the account, first of Peter's protest
that no matter what happens to Jesus there need never be the slightest
doubt of Peter's unshakable loyalty to him, followed by the sub-

sequent ignominious denial (the occasion for which would never have arisen had not Peter been determined to keep his word). There can surely have been only one source for the story, and that is Peter himself. And when we consider the eminent position that (according to the united and impressive testimony of Acts 1–12 and Galatians 1–2) Peter came to hold in the early church, and that this story must have been in circulation throughout the time of that eminence, one has to acknowledge that it reflects the highest credit on the man who gave it currency.

> And they went to a place which was called Gethsemane; and he said to his disciples, 'Sit here, while I pray.' And he took with him Peter and James and John, and began to be greatly distressed and troubled. And he said to them, 'My soul is very sorrowful, even unto death; remain here, and watch.' And going a little farther, he fell on the ground and prayed that, if it were possible, the hour might pass from him. And he said, 'Abba, Father, all things are possible to thee; remove this cup from me; yet not what I will, but what thou wilt.' And he came and found them sleeping, and he said to Peter, 'Simon, are you asleep? Could you not watch one hour? Watch and pray that you may not enter into temptation; the spirit indeed is willing, but the flesh is weak.' And again he went away and prayed, saying the same words. And again he came and found them sleeping, for their eyes were very heavy; and they did not know what to answer him. And he came the third time, and said to them, 'Are you still sleeping and taking your rest? It is enough; the hour has come; the Son of man is betrayed into the hands of sinners. Rise, let us be going; see, my betrayer is at hand.' (14.32–42)

Jesus' separation from the disciples takes place in two stages. The bulk of them he leaves sitting at the edge of Gethsemane,[7] apparently without any further instructions even though he has no expectation of ever rejoining them. He then goes forward with his select inner group of three disciples, whom he asks to keep watch while he goes further off to pray. The second part of this description rings true, but to my mind the first does not. We have noted on several occasions that the tradition insists on the precise number of twelve apostles, but seems surprisingly unclear about just who they were; and on the other hand that the word 'disciple' is in any case of much wider significance than apostle. The tradition envisages the 'last supper' as being a meal shared by Jesus and all twelve apostles, but attended by no one else. It presumes that after the meal Judas went off by himself to complete his business transaction with the priests, and the other eleven apostles followed Jesus to Gethsemane. The party left by Jesus on the edge of the garden will have comprised eight people, while Jesus and the remaining three went on into the garden to enact the scene described above.

I have considerable misgivings whether at any time during Jesus' life-time the twelve apostles were as rigidly fixed a band as the tradition supposes. I do not doubt that Jesus *intended* there to be such a band, but the evidence suggests to me that the reality was rather more fluid than his plan envisaged. First there is the figure of Andrew. In Mark 3.18 he is listed as one of the twelve, but as number four after Peter, James and John. Yet he was Peter's brother, and would surely have resented the fact that his brother was one of the chosen three and he was not; particularly when the other pair of brothers (James and John) were both of them in the first three. Also his position seems to fluctuate: chapter 1 describes the call of both pairs of brothers, without ever hinting that Andrew was 'less important' than the other three. Subsequently there is no mention of Andrew as an active character until the very end of the gospel, where for the moment (13.3) we find Jesus once again accompanied by a select band of four instead of three disciples, the fourth man being Andrew. In the passion narrative we are back to three as the number of Jesus' closest followers. I suspect the true explanation of this is that Andrew was inclined to blow hot and cold as a member of the mission – sometimes in and sometimes out. I also suspect that he was not the only one, and that although there was an *intention* that there should be a band of twelve apostles, it seems much less likely to me that there ever was in fact a fixed *body* of twelve – at least not until after Jesus' death, when the list might have been finally fixed by the election of Matthias to take Judas' place (Acts 1.15–26). Just as the larger body of disciples was almost certainly in flux during Jesus' life-time, with new disciples constantly joining and existing ones constantly leaving, so I suspect even the list of the twelve would have been periodically revised as close associates occasionally lost enthusiasm and distant aspirants showed promise.

Accordingly when we come to the last supper, I would argue we simply do not know how many people were there. It is quite likely that not even those sitting there bothered to work out how many were attending. It is not impossible that some of the diners left early, while others arrived late, and that it was never a very formal occasion anyway. And my own conviction is that when Jesus set off for Gethsemane, he had with him *only* the three disciples listed above. The band of eight left sitting on the edge of Gethsemane I suspect is a fiction made necessary to preserve the idea of a hard-and-fast band of twelve apostles.

Some commentators have seen the 'agony in the garden' as a kind of deliberate counterpoint to the transfiguration scene which Mark describes back in 9.2–8. The indications that such an idea has occurred to Mark are slight, in that the only real feature in common is the presence on both occasions of Peter, James and John. It is more prominent in Luke where in both scenes the sleepiness of the witnesses is drawn attention to (compare Luke 9.32 with 22.45 – but note also that in Luke *all* the disciples seem to be present at the arrest); and it may have been made more so by the insertion of 22.43: 'And there appeared to him an angel from heaven, strengthening him,' which is not found in all texts; (though see note 17 to the Introduction (p. 370), where I argue that this variant is just as likely to be due to excision of what Luke originally wrote as to later insertion). In Mark the scene is well-drawn and convincing (and moving), despite the fact already observed that the substance of it must be fictional. Jesus' closing words ('Rise, let us be going; see, my betrayer is at hand') are something of a puzzle. Are we meant to infer that at the last minute Jesus suddenly decides to make a run for it and is only prevented by circumstances? The question does not admit of a firm answer, but raising it helps to explain a no less puzzling detail at the end of John chapter 14: 'Rise, let us go hence.' My guess is that the Marcan verse had raised the very same query I have drawn attention to in the minds of the congregation for which John's gospel was written, and that the Johannine verse is the author's providing the 'evidence' that refutes such an interpretation.

And immediately, while he was still speaking, Judas came, one of the twelve, and with him a crowd with swords and clubs, from the chief priests and the scribes and the elders. Now the betrayer had given them a sign, saying, 'The one I shall kiss is the man; seize him and lead him away safely.' And when he came, he went up to him at once, and said, 'Master!' And he kissed him. And they laid hands on him and seized him. (14.43–47)

The Jerusalem temple had its own garrison of soldiers under the direction of the high priest. Part of the reason for this was historical, deriving from the struggles under the Maccabees when the chief magistrate, chief general and chief priest of the nation were all of them united in one person, whose inspiration and abilities were responsible for the recovery – for about a century, until the arrival of the Romans – of independence for the nation. And the Romans, following their usual practice, so far from replacing the existing political structure with their own, simply incorporated it. They appointed a governor, answerable at first to the senate – later to the emperor – for the success of all aspects of the local administration. But his day-to-day task was seen more in terms of co-operation with the local politicians than in displacement of them. The duties of this temple guard, however, were far from being merely ceremonial. As Acts 21.27–36 reminds us, the temple could often be the scene of extremely threatening disorders, so much so that (as in Acts) the Roman garrison would have to come to the aid of the temple authorities in restoring order. But however threatening the situation, inside the temple itself only the temple guard could act – a tradition that the Romans scrupulously respected until faced with the need of taking it by assault in AD 70.

The purpose of Judas' kiss of betrayal has from time to time excited a great deal of unilluminating comment. The kiss used to be (as it is beginning to be again) a perfectly normal form of greeting between friends, or those who wished to make a display of friendship before onlookers. The motive behind the sign that Judas agreed with the soldiers was from his (and their) point of view a practical one, rather than anything deliberately or egregiously sinister. It was dark. Quite probably Judas was the only one who knew which of the four men before them was Jesus. And in the dark even he would have to get close before he could be sure; close enough also to be able to hold him in case he realized what was afoot and tried to run away. The gospels insist of course that he realized perfectly. But they may be exaggerating the extent to which he realized; as they may also be exaggerating the extent to which he was prepared for, and ready to face, the appalling fate that was before him. The concluding verse of the previous extract, commented on above, could be taken as a vestigial hint of the truth of that kind of supposition. But also, no matter how prepared Jesus was to meet his fate, Judas – and even more the guard of soldiers – would have been foolish to take any such belief for granted. So the sign that Judas agreed on enabled him to get close to Jesus without arousing suspicion, and then if need be to hold him until the soldiers could secure him.

> But one of those who stood by drew his sword, and struck the slave of the high priest and cut off his ear. And Jesus said to them, 'Have you come out as against a robber, with swords and clubs, to capture me? Day after day I was with you in the temple teaching, and you did not seize me. But let the scriptures be fulfilled.' And they all forsook him, and fled.
>
> And a young man followed him, with nothing but a linen cloth about his body; and they seized him, but he left the linen cloth and ran away naked. (14.47–52)

I am inclined to accept both these events as historical, if only because as they stand they seem so very pointless. The first incident has clearly captured the Christian imagination, and we get considerable embellishment of it in all three other gospels. But the tradition apparently could make nothing of the second event, and it has already disappeared even from Matthew's account.

In commenting on the first incident, I cannot make a better start than by giving the other three accounts and inviting the reader to note the differences (italicized in the case of Matthew's version):

> And behold, one of those who were with Jesus stretched out his hand and drew his sword, and struck the slave of the high priest, and cut off his ear. *Then Jesus said to him, 'Put your sword back into its place; for all who take the sword will perish by the sword. Do you think that I cannot appeal to my Father, and he will at once send me more than twelve legions of angels? But how then should the scriptures be fulfilled, that it must be so?'* At that hour Jesus said to the crowds, 'Have you come out as against a robber …?' (Matt. 26.51–55a)

> And when those who were about him saw what would follow, they said, 'Lord, shall we strike with the sword?' And one of them struck the slave of the high priest and cut off his right ear. But Jesus said, 'No more of this!' And he touched his ear and healed him. (Luke 22.49–51)

> Then Simon Peter, having a sword, drew it and struck the high priest's slave and cut off his right ear. The slave's name was Malchus. Jesus said to Peter, 'Put your sword into its sheath; shall

I not drink the cup which the Father has given me?' (John 18.10–11)

Rather surprisingly it is Matthew who refrains from miraculous embellishment and Luke who introduces it. Matthew's additions are all directed towards offering moral comment – in three areas: first, that violent reactions are liable to elicit an equally violent reply, to the gain of nobody and the fatal loss of many;[8] second, (both less convincing and less elevating than the first) that Jesus could effortlessly be delivered anyway by miraculous intervention; third, that it would be pointless and impious for him, or anyone else on his behalf, to struggle against his prophesied destiny.

If one were to question the ordinary churchgoer about this event, there is none of them to whom it would not be completely familiar; and every one of them would 'know' that the person who drew the sword was Peter, that the person whose, ear was cut off was Malchus, and that Jesus immediately – and miraculously – healed the injury. Yet the first two details are derived only from John's gospel, and the third only from Luke's. Our earliest and presumably best account, Mark's gospel, is silent on all three of them.

With regard to the second incident, it used to be assumed as a matter of course that the young man with the linen cloth can only have been Mark himself. More recent scholarship has tended to dismiss the identification as naive and fanciful. But I have to confess that to me it still looks completely sound. What other possible explanation can there be for its inclusion? Later in the story we are told (once again only by Mark) that Simon of Cyrene, who was compelled by the soldiers to carry Jesus' cross to the place of execution (presumably because Jesus himself was no longer strong enough to do so) was 'the father of Alexander and Rufus' (Mark 15.21). No one has ever doubted, nor is it easy to see how they could doubt, that the explanation of this comment is that Alexander and Rufus were members of the congregation for which Mark was writing. The present hypothesis about Mark is no more fanciful and naive than that about Alexander and Rufus. One could I suppose, if one were desperate to be thought sophisticated, argue that the incident may perhaps relate to someone whom Mark knew personally, but still someone other than himself. But in the case of Alexander and Rufus Mark has no hesitation in giving names; here he leaves the name out. The fact that the incident relates to himself is surely the most plausible explanation of this.

> And they led Jesus to the high priest; and all the chief priests and
> the elders and the scribes were assembled. And Peter had followed
> him at a distance, right into the courtyard of the high priest; and
> he was sitting with the guards, and warming himself at the fire.
> (14.53–54)

This short paragraph sets the scene for the two separate incidents
which follow. The intention behind this narrative dovetailing does
not seem – as it undoubtedly is in the fourth gospel – to be any kind
of attempt to explain how the gospel writers could have known what
went on at Jesus' trial before the priestly council. My own reading is
that Mark implies no more that that both incidents took place at the
same time.

> Now the chief priests and the whole council sought testimony
> against Jesus to put him to death; but they found none. For many
> bore false witness against him, and their witness did not agree.
> And some stood up and bore false witness against him, saying,
> 'We heard him say, "I will destroy this temple that is made with
> hands, and in three days I will build another, not made with
> hands."' Yet not even so did their testimony agree. And the high
> priest stood up in the midst, and asked Jesus, 'Have you no answer
> to make? What is it that these men testify against you?' But he was
> silent and made no answer. Again the high priest asked him, 'Are
> you the Christ, the Son of the Blessed?' And Jesus said, 'I am; and
> you will see the Son of man sitting at the right hand of Power, and
> coming with the clouds of heaven.' And the high priest tore his
> mantle, and said, 'Why do we still need witnesses? You have heard
> his blasphemy. What is your decision?' And they all condemned
> him as deserving death. And some began to spit on him, and to
> cover his face, and to strike him, saying to him, 'Prophesy!' And
> the guards received him with blows.' (14.55–65)

At this point we begin to redeem the promise made earlier that close
scrutiny seems to show that, however improbable the claim may
appear on the surface, the tradition underlying Mark's account of
the trials, particularly that of the first trial before the high priest,
seems originally to have been based on some kind of eyewitness
testimony. Let us begin by reading the narrative backwards: Mark
15.26 reads: 'And the inscription of the charge against him read,
"The King of the Jews".' Matthew fears the reader may find that

slightly cryptic and expands it (27.37) to: 'And over his head they put the charge against him, which read, "This is Jesus the King of the Jews".' In other words, nailed to the cross above his head was a plaque[9] which briefly stated the charge on which Jesus had been executed – namely that of having claimed to be Messiah or King, and therefore of having intended the overthrow of Roman rule. This detail is very likely to be authentic. So the trial before Pilate must have focussed almost entirely on this issue. All the gospels suggest, however, that Pilate was reluctant to believe (*a*) that Jesus was in fact guilty of this charge, or (*b*) that this was the real reason why he had been brought before him. So what was the *real* reason why Jesus had been arrested and condemned by the priests?

Mark's account of the trial before the priests falls into two apparently unconnected halves. Down to verse 59 ('Yet not even so did their testimony agree') no one seems at all interested in who Jesus claims to be, and everything seems to turn on his attitude to the temple. The account suggests that all attempts to convict Jesus on a charge connected with the temple failed, and that it was only after that that the high priest turned his attention to the possibility of convicting him on the alternative grounds of his claims. As it stands this isn't all that plausible; verse 59 just quoted, for instance, is not convincing. If these witnesses also failed to agree, why go into such detail over their testimony, when all the other testimony has simply been passed over? But with little alteration the account becomes very plausible indeed. It seems likely to me that the original version was that although the rest of the testimony failed to stand, this particular accusation did; and that it was when the priests had established his guilt on a charge of blasphemy for their own satisfaction that they turned their attention to one which they hoped would carry more weight with the Roman governor. The Romans after all had the reputation of being impatient with the nuances of the Jewish religion, particularly as regards religious offences (Acts 18.12–16; 23.28–29; 25.18–20, 24–27).

I see no reason therefore to believe the suggestion that the priests could not find testimony against Jesus. The real question is, What was the significance of the strange evidence that Mark records: 'We heard him say, "I will destroy this temple made with hands, and in three days I will build another not made with hands"'? It would be unwise to take John 2.19 as offering the true explanation of what *Jesus* meant. What the author of John's gospel seems to be doing there is offering his own explanation of a feature of Mark's gospel which his congregation evidently found as puzzling as we do. He tells us, in other words, not the answer to our question, but that we are not alone in our perplexity. If we read him as offering his own interpretation of what *Mark* meant, my own guess is that on that point he is close to the truth. Note, though, he has 'improved' what he found in Mark in order to bring out his own double meaning: 'Destroy this temple, and in three days I will raise it up.' To Jesus' hearers ('the Jews') the words 'this temple' mean – and Jesus gives them no indication that he means anything else – the building in which they are standing. But the reader of the gospel knows (in this instance because the author uncharacteristically tells him so in the next verse) that Jesus in fact meant something quite different by 'this temple'; he meant his own body. (It is likely that the author also consciously echoes Paul's description of the believer's body as the true temple of God in I Cor. 3.16–17; 6.19–20, and II Cor. 6.16.)

Although I am confident that John has made a good guess as to what the utterance meant to Mark, I am equally confident that either Mark himself or the tradition behind him has heavily distorted whatever it was that Jesus was originally supposed to have said. Three of the four gospels give us his direct prophecy of the temple's destruction (Mark 13.2 = Matt. 24.2 and Luke 21.5–6), and we need not doubt that in the earliest accounts of the trial the testimony the priests were looking for related to this aspect of Jesus' teaching, and that they were eventually satisfied that they had found such testimony. It seems to me improbable therefore that the testimony originally made any reference to 'made with hands', or that it then went on to say 'and in three days I will build another, not made with hands'. It is much more likely that it referred solely and unambiguously to the actual building, and related to the fact that Jesus had denounced it and foretold its destruction. We need not look as far back as Jeremiah chapter 26 to realize that in the normal way this was looked on by the priests as itself a capital offence. In Jesus' own day or shortly afterwards we have the examples of Stephen in Acts chapter 7 and of Paul in chapter 23, the first of whom lost his life apparently for denouncing the temple, and the second very nearly lost it because it was believed he had desecrated it.[10]

Having satisfied themselves in the first part of the trial that Jesus deserved to die on the grounds that he had spoken against the temple, the priests are now faced with the problem that they have to persuade

Pilate to execute him, and that he is unlikely to do so on the basis of this particular charge. They must therefore find an alternative accusation to bring against him when they hand him over. And that is what the second part of the trial is concerned with. But before we go on to that, we are faced with the strange detail that Jesus is given an opportunity to put forward a defence against this testimony 'And the high priest stood up in the midst, and asked Jesus, "Have you no answer to make? What is it that these men testify against you?"' and, if the account is to be believed, that he declines to do so. The first explanation to suggest itself is that it was prophesied in Isaiah that this was how the Messiah would act:

> He was oppressed, and he was afflicted,
>   yet he opened not his mouth;
> like a lamb that is led to the slaughter,
>   and like a sheep that before its shearers is dumb,
>   so he opened not his mouth.
> By oppression and judgment he was taken away ...
> (Isa 1.53.7–8a)

Was it Jesus himself that had the prophecy in mind when he was questioned by the priests, and was that why – despite his extremely perilous circumstances – he decided to make no reply? Or is it the tradition which, on the basis of this prophecy, has simply assumed that this must have been Jesus' response. Both these solutions are possible, but a third seems to me much more likely than either, if only because Jesus shows not the slightest reluctance to answer the high priest's very next question. That question, I suggest, is historical, and so far from being the exasperated conclusion to the first part of the trial, it is the opening of its second half. Having condemned Jesus in their own minds on the grounds of his blasphemy, they are now looking for grounds on which the Roman governor might be persuaded to condemn him as one who admits to claiming to be Messiah.

The hard question to answer therefore is not why Jesus' was reluctant to make any reply to the first question, but why he was so ready to cut his own throat in answering the second. Both Matthew and Luke are apparently somewhat shattered by Jesus' foolhardiness. Where in Mark's gospel Jesus replies quite emphatically, 'I am', in both the other gospels this is changed to 'You have said so' (i.e. 'Those are your words, not mine' – see Matt. 26.64 and Luke 22.70).

As in the first part of the trial, so here in the second it looks as though an originally plausible narration has been overlaid by distortions that are rather less plausible. The question Jesus is asked is, 'Are you the Christ, the Son of the Blessed?' The affirmative answer that Jesus gives is certainly enough to hang him; but the question is, on what grounds? According to Mark the priests interpret his answer as blasphemy; but why should they? Was it blasphemous to claim to be the Messiah? After all it was officially believed by all present that some day somebody would legitimately make the claim; so how was it necessarily blasphemous for Jesus to make it now? Or was the blasphemy that Jesus, besides claiming to be Messiah, also claimed (or did not deny when the high priest put the claim to him) to be 'Son of the Blessed?' It may be that by the time Mark was writing Christians (and Jews also) were beginning to think in those terms; but they are entirely foreign to the original situation that Mark is describing. If the high priest used any such phrase (and in view of the wording of Psalm 2 he may well have done) we can be sure that he meant no more by it than everyone at the time thought the psalm really meant; i.e. it was an idea that was inseparable from that of Messiahship, and was no more obviously blasphemous than the title of Messiah itself.

Did the blasphemy reside, then, in the fact that Jesus *falsely* claimed to be Messiah? But that would surely have involved the council in some kind of investigation whether the claim *were* false. And Mark's account makes no mention of any such investigation. Admission of what the high priest suggests is immediately accepted as proof of guilt. My own view is that the charge on which the priests convicted was indeed that of blasphemy, but that the blasphemy related to Jesus' attitude to the temple, and that the admission of the claim to be Messiah was elicited with a view to satisfying the Romans.

Why does Jesus make the admission so readily? In considering this point I discount any difficulties raised by the supposed contrast between Jesus' refusal to answer the high priest's first question and his readiness to answer the second. The contrast that does cause difficulty is that between his alleged readiness to affirm before the high priest that he was the Messiah and his refusal to do so before the Roman governor. Is this to be thought of as history, and how do we account for it? It looks to my eye that it very well could be. In answering the first question, Jesus has every reason to believe (as we saw above) that he is standing before a court every member of which believes that the Messiah is shortly to come. They may not believe his own claim to be the Messiah, but what danger can there be in making such a claim before such a court? Presumably he does not realize that they are now no longer trying him themselves but are preparing their case for the Roman governor. Thus Jesus convicts himself in his reply without realizing for the moment he has done so.

The account of the trial ends with a description of the rough taunting of Jesus which, we are told, was initiated by the priests themselves and afterwards carried on by the soldiers. It is by no means clear to me that we should necessarily believe this. When Jesus eventually emerged from Pilate's praetorium to be led to execution, it would be evident to all that he (like all other prisoners in the same situation) had been considerably knocked about. But I doubt if anyone knew any more of the details than that, or if anyone at the time would have cared enough to ask. One item in Mark's account has already puzzled Matthew's readers, and he therefore explains it to them. Mark tells us, 'And some began to spit on him, and to cover his face, and to strike him, saying to him, "Prophesy!"' It is that last word that mystifies, and Matthew plausibly interprets Mark's meaning as, 'Prophesy to us, you Christ! Who is it that struck you?'

And as Peter was below in the courtyard, one of the maids of the high priest came; and seeing Peter warming himself, she looked at him, and said, 'You also were with the Nazarene, Jesus.' But he denied it, saying, 'I neither know nor understand what you mean.' And he went out into the gateway. And the maid saw him, and began to say to the bystanders, 'This man is one of them.' But again he denied it. And after a little while again the bystanders said to Peter, 'Certainly you are one of them; for you are a Galilaean.' But he began to invoke a curse on himself and to swear, 'I do not know this man of whom you speak.' And immediately the cock crowed a second time. And Peter remembered how Jesus had said to him, 'Before the cock crows twice, you will deny me three times.' And he broke down and wept. (14.66–72)

As noted earlier, this story is likely to be substantially true, if only because it must have established itself in the passion narrative at a time when Peter was not only still alive but perhaps *the* most prominent member of the Christian church. The only detail that needs comment is the (to modern ears) over-precise nature of the prophecy, 'Before the cock crows twice, you will deny me three times.' The words themselves would cause no difficulty were it not for the way in which the fulfilment of them is related. If we did not have the fulfilment story, we would interpret Jesus words (probably correctly) as meaning no more than, 'Before it is full daylight tomorrow you will have denied me repeatedly.' It is the tradition which, with or without Peter's help, has taken the words 'twice' and 'thrice' quite literally, and thus given the story a slightly miraculous element which at an earlier stage it probably did not have.

> And as soon as it was morning the chief priests, with the elders and scribes, and the whole council held a consultation; and they bound Jesus and led him away and delivered him to Pilate. And Pilate asked him, 'Are you the King of the Jews?' And he answered him, 'You have said so.' And the chief priests accused him of many things. And Pilate again asked him, 'Have you no answer to make? See how many charges they bring against you.' But Jesus made no further answer, so that Pilate wondered.
>   Now at the feast he used to release for them one prisoner whom they asked. And among the rebels in prison, who had committed murder in the insurrection, there was a man called Barabbas. And the crowd came up and began to ask Pilate to do as he was wont to do for them. And he answered them, 'Do you want me to release for you the King of the Jews?' For he perceived that it was out of envy that the chief priests had delivered him up. But the chief priests stirred up the crowd to have him release for them Barabbas instead. And Pilate again said to them, 'Then what shall I do with the man whom you call the King of the Jews?' And they cried out again, 'Crucify him.' And Pilate said to them, 'Why, what evil has he done?' But they shouted all the more, 'Crucify him.' So Pilate, wishing to satisfy the crowd, released for them Barabbas; and having scourged Jesus, he delivered him to be crucified. (15.1–15)

As pointed out above, two features of the underlying structure of this episode are particularly plausible. Pilate does not believe that Jesus is guilty of what he is accused of, ('why, what evil has he done?'); and even more presuasively he does not believe that what Jesus is accused of is the real reason why he has been brought before him, ('For he perceived that it was out of envy that the chief priests had delivered

him up'). The feature that is hard to accept with confidence is the
Barabbas incident in the second of these two paragraphs. Given the
political situation in this locality at this time, is it conceivable that a
Roman governor would be prepared to act as irresponsibly as this,
not merely on a single occasion but even habitually once a year? All
four gospels insist that it was so – and remember that in the passion
narrative (as distinct from the gospel as a whole) we have three
different accounts, Mark/Matthew, Luke and John, which show
considerable independence of each other; but without confirmation
from a more official source (which we do not have), we are probably
justified in dismissing the incident as a fictional embellishment. Some
commentators have been confirmed in this view by the fact that
Barabbas is the Aramaic for 'Son of the Father'; and the significance
of the name is further enhanced by the fact that some early copies of
Matthew's gospel call the man Jesus Barabbas. As we have seen,
although Matthew's gospel follows Mark's account closely, there
are occasional signs that he was familiar with other versions of the
passion, and it is probably from these that at least some of his
amplifications are derived. My own suspicion is that 'Jesus Barabbas' is the original reading at this point in Matthew, and that later
Christians disliked the implications of the detail and encouraged its
suppression.

The function the story performs in the actual narrative though is a
necessary one. Pilate is un convinced of Jesus' guilt, but condemns
him just the same. Why? Assuming the situation is accurately
portrayed (and we have seen that it is plausible), his real reason will
have been along the lines that he did not think a weirdo like Jesus was
worth sticking his neck out for. Did it matter whether he was guilty
or not? Would there be any comeback if, against his better judgment,
he pacified these fanatics and did what they were asking for?
Probably not. And would there be any comeback if he resisted them?
Probably. One authentic factor that the Barabbas story does bring
out also is that an important part of Pilate's calculation will have
been the extreme volatility of Jerusalem during the festival. The only
other point that needs to be dealt with is the obvious desire of all four
gospels[11] as much as possible to blame the Jews for Jesus' execution,
and as much as possible to exonerate Pilate. For the reasons given
above I doubt if such a view is historically worth-while; the motive
behind this eagerness is likely to be the extreme mutual hostility
which sprang up between Jews and Christians apparently within a

generation of Jesus' death and which has continued pretty well up to
our own time.

> And the soldiers led him away inside the palace (that is, the
> praetorium); and they called together the whole battalion. And
> they clothed him in a purple cloak, and plaiting a crown of thorns
> they put it on him. And they began to salute him, 'Hail, King of the
> Jews!' And they struck his head with a reed, and spat upon him,
> and they knelt down in homage to him. And when they had
> mocked him, they stripped him of the purple cloak, and put his
> own clothes on him. And they led him out to crucify him.
> (15.6–20)

One of the indications that Mark wrote his gospel for a western
rather than an eastern congregation is the fact that here he feels the
need to explain the Greek word *aule*, which can be any large house or
superior residence, with the Latin word *praetorium*, which (in terms
of the provinces of the Roman empire) can only be the official
residence of the governor. And when we add to this the rapid
dissemination of the work and its initially high prestige (as evidenced
by the fact that both Matthew and Luke have used it as their primary
source for the narrative), it makes it credible that that congregation
was at Rome.

What was said about the earlier mocking scene after the trial
before the priests one would have thought applies here also. But two
points are prominent. The description of the mocking is very detailed
and very specific to the charge against Jesus that he claimed to be the
'King of the Jews' or the Messiah. The purple cloak, the crown made
of thorns, and probably even the reed with which Mark tells us they
struck his head,[12] are all clearly intended as parodies of the emblems
of royalty. It is presumably this accumulation of specific detail which
has again raised for the author of John's gospel the question of how
the tradition could know all this; and the incident, found only in
John 19.1–5, in which Pilate brings Jesus out to the crowd wearing
the crown of thorns and the purple cloak seems to be his own attempt
to solve the problem. In Matthew and Mark (Luke does not include
the incident) the entire episode takes place behind closed doors, and
when Jesus emerges he is wearing his own clothes again.

> And they compelled a passer-by, Simon of Cyrene, who was
> coming in from the country, the father of Alexander and Rufus, to

carry his cross. And they brought him to the place called Golgotha (which means the place of a skull). And they offered him wine mingled with myrrh; but he did not take it. And they crucified him, and divided his garments among them, casting lots for them, to decide what each should take. And it was the third hour when they crucified him. And the inscription of the charge against him read, 'The King of the Jews'. (15.21–26)

On the subject of Alexander and Rufus see above. For readers who are looking for — and disappointed that they do not find — some mention of Calvary here, let me quote the Vulgate version of the second sentence above: *Et perducunt illum in Golgotha locum: quod est interpretatum Calvariae locus*. The 'wine mingled with myrrh'[13] seems to have been the ancient world's version of the slug of brandy, which from the sixteenth century (when the process of distilling was discovered) till the nineteenth century (when chloroform — the first really effective anaesthetic — began to be administered) was the only 'painkiller' known to scientific medicine. The wine and myrrh was like the later brandy also in this, that it apparently undermined one's fortitude to pain just as much as one's sensitivity to it, and Jesus' refusal to take it may well have been a perfectly rational one. One thing that is not clear from the account that the reader would probably like to know is who was responsible for offering the drugged wine. Was it charitably-minded citizens who were allowed access by the Romans to condemned men for this purpose? Or was it the Romans themselves?

I point out in note 13 the influence that Psalm 69 seems to have had on Matthew's account of the drugged wine. In 15.24 above ('And they crucified him ...') we seem to have an example of the same thing in Mark, whose account here seems far too closely modelled on Psalm 22.18 for it to be coincidence. Both these Psalms seem to have caught the early Christian imagination as prophecies of the crucifixion (in the case of Psalm 22 perhaps even that of Jesus himself — see below). We find Psalm 69 quoted in the various gospels as follows:

verse 4 = John 15.25
verse 9 = John 2.17 (not part of the passion narrative itself, but nevertheless applied to the cleansing of the temple as part of the explanation of Jesus' death)

verse 21 = Matthew 27.34; Luke 23.36; John 19.29

verse 25 = Acts 1.20 (quoted in connection with Judas's suicide)

Psalm 22, the opening verse of which is quoted by Mark and Matthew as the very last words that Jesus uttered, seems additionally to be referred to in the following passages:

verses 7–8 = Mark 15.29 = Matthew 27.39; and see also Luke 23.35

verses 16–18 = Matthew 27.35; Mark 15.24 (above); Luke 23.34; John 19.24

And with him they crucified two robbers, one on his right and one on his left. [And the scripture was fulfilled which says, 'He was reckoned with the transgressors'] And those who passed by derided him, wagging their heads, and saying, 'Aha! You who would destroy the temple and build it in three days, save yourself and come down from the cross!' So also the chief priests mocked him to one another with the scribes, saying, 'He saved others; he cannot save himself. Let the Christ, the King of Israel, come down now from the cross, that we may see and believe.' Those who were crucified with him also reviled him. (15.27–32)

The robbers also may just possibly be an invention of tradition, one of whose aims throughout has been to match history with prophecy. This is well illustrated by the sentence in square brackets, which does not appear to be integral to the text of Mark's gospel, but was nevertheless until recent times always included in it. On the other hand, this business of questioning the authenticity of all details which seem to be matched by prophecy can easily be taken too far. A certain element of real coincidence is not implausible, and it could even be argued that it is required in order to explain the character of the accounts we have. If there were no coincidences between supposed prophecy and the actual events, how do we account for the origin of the conviction that the events were prophesied in the first place? But when we have given that consideration all the weight it deserves, it still remains overwhelmingly probable that all of the gospel accounts of the crucifixion have also been embellished with a view to heightening the element of prophetic fulfilment.

I would much prefer to think also – though I don't hesitate to admit that this is as much what I want to believe as what I have reason to believe – that the mocking of the crowd, and particularly that of the chief priests, is just such an element of the fulfilment of prophecy. The prophecy in question is not hard to find:

> All who see me mock at me,
>   they make mouths at me, they wag their heads;
> 'He committed his cause to the Lord; let him deliver him,
>   let him rescue him, for he delights in him!' (Ps. 22.7–8)

The words ascribed to the crowd ('Aha! You who would destroy the temple ...') are of course quoted from the adverse testimony given at Jesus' trial before the priests. It is doubtful, though, that we can realistically interpret this as confirmation of that testimony and not rather as a convenient and effective solution to what seems to have been an authorial problem, namely, 'What do I here make the crowd say?' It seems impossible to give any Old Testament provenance for the words ascribed to the priests ('He saved others; he cannot save himself ...'), and I don't mind admitting that I find it worrying that one can't. They seem also to be exquisitely well-chosen to satirize the contrast between Jesus' claims and his predicament, and it may be they have simply been invented by the tradition with that in mind. If so, I can't help feeling that it indicates a sadistic streak in the tradition itself, which Matthew intensifies by adding a paraphrase of Psalm 22.8 (quoted above). Note also that in the Matthew/Mark account there is no suggestion of a penitent thief – an idea found only in Luke 23.39–43, and a good example of his liking for ideas that most of us would find perhaps more attractive than plausible.

> And when the sixth hour had come, there was darkness over the whole land until the ninth hour. And at the ninth hour Jesus cried with a loud voice, 'Eloi, Eloi, lama sabachthani?', which means, 'My God, my God, why hast thou forsaken me?' And some of the bystanders hearing it said, 'Behold, he is calling Elijah.' And one ran and, filling a sponge full of vinegar, put it on a reed and gave it to him to drink, saying, 'Wait, let us see whether Elijah will come to take him down.' (15.33–36)

If you were to ask a churchgoer, you would find he was convinced that Jesus hung on the cross from mid-day (the sixth hour) till three o'clock in the afternoon (the ninth hour). But Mark's chronology is wider than this: according to him Jesus was actually crucified at nine in the morning (the third hour – see 15.25), but that at noon a strange darkness came over the land and lasted until Jesus died three hours later. The popular idea derives from the fact that both Matthew and Luke give us this second bit of information but not the first. What is the explanation of this darkness? Luke sticks his neck out and seems to suppose it was an eclipse of the sun ('while the sun's light failed' – Luke 23.45), presumably overlooking the fact that the crucifixion took place on the day of the passover, which occurs at the full moon, at which time an eclipse of the sun cannot occur. Mark and Matthew wisely offer no explanation, and seem to be assuming that it is some kind of miraculous darkness such as might fittingly shroud the stupendous death of God's Messiah. If such was indeed their meaning, it raises the likelihood that from a historical point of view we should doubt the occurrence of this darkness altogether. It is worth pointing out also that at the very beginning of the Bible God's first act of creation is to say, 'Let there be light'. The tradition that Mark is here recording may very well have been trying to suggest (without plausibility, but nevertheless with considerable artistry) that Jesus' death was a temporary reversal of that act of creation, a moment when primaeval chaos once again almost triumphs over the ordered world.

Jesus' famous last cry quotes the opening of Psalm 22. In what form did he quote it? Mark gives the words more or less in Aramaic, but this makes the narrative as a whole look odd; for the crowd then misunderstand the words and presume that Jesus is calling on Elijah. Had he cried out in Aramaic (*a*) they would presumably have understood him, (*b*) they would have easily told the difference between the sound of 'Eloi' and that of Elijah. It is no doubt for this reason that Matthew feels compelled to Hebraize and to change 'Eloi' into 'Eli' (Matt. 27.46); he overlooks the point though that the Hebrew text has *azabthani* for the Aramaic *sabachthani*.

Did Jesus utter the cry? Or rather, could he have uttered such a cry in a way that bystanders might have heard him? Medical opinion seems to be that if (as Mark implies) he was now close to death, he could not have done. But he might of course have uttered such a cry earlier, perhaps shortly before, or during, or shortly after being fastened to the cross. And if he uttered it, what did he mean by it? Or if he did not, what ideas did the tradition want to convey by attributing the words to him? That he really did die in despair, the onset of death at last persuading him that all his beliefs about himself were illusory, and that he had never been anything other than an ordinary human being with unusually powerful convictions and an unusually vivid imagination? If he did utter the words, historically such an interpretation is of course plausible. On the other hand, it cannot possibly be the way the tradition intended them to be understood, and in interpreting Mark's narrative this second consideration is in many ways more important than the first. So how did the tradition understand them?

I can see no indications in the text that would answer the question, and the following therefore is largely a guess. I suspect that originally the single quotation was intended to stand for the whole psalm, and that its quotation at this point was intended, at least in part, to draw attention to the uncanny degree of coincidence between many of the images of the poem and many of the events of the crucifixion. (As I pointed out above, there can be no doubt both that the tradition has considerably improved this degree of coincidence, but also that there must have been a degree of real coincidence in the first place.) The other intention I suspect was to describe to the worshipper the state of mind with which Jesus met his death, and to offer him the experience of actually sharing in that mental state. It is perhaps worthwhile here to quote the psalm in full, and to suggest that the reader bears both these intentions in mind while reading it:

> My God, my God, why hast thou forsaken me?
>   Why art thou so far from helping me,
>   from the words of my groaning?
> O my God, I cry by day, but thou dost not answer;
>   and by night, but find no rest.
> Yet thou art holy,
>   enthroned on the praises of Israel.
> In thee our fathers trusted;
>   they trusted, and thou didst deliver them.
> To thee they cried, and were saved;
>   in thee they trusted, and were not disappointed.
>
> But I am a worm, and no man;
>   scorned by men, and despised by the people.
> All who see me mock at me,
>   they make mouths at me, they wag their heads;
> 'He committed his cause to the Lord; let him deliver him,
>   let him rescue him, for he delights in him!'
> Yet thou art he who took me from the womb;

thou didst keep me safe upon my mother's breasts.
Upon thee was I cast from my birth,
  and since my mother bore me thou hast been my God.
Be not far from me, for trouble is near
  and there is none to help.
Many bulls encompass me,
  strong bulls of Bashan surround me;
they open wide their mouths at me,
  like a ravening and roaring lion.

I am poured out like water,
  and all my bones are out of joint;
my heart is like wax,
  it is melted within my breast;
my strength is dried up like a potsherd,
  and my tongue cleaves to my jaws;
  thou dost lay me in the dust of death.
Yea, dogs are round about me;
  a company of evildoers encircle me;
they have pierced my hands and feet –
  I can count all my bones –
  they stare and gloat over me;
they divide my garments among them,
  and for my raiment they cast lots.

But thou, O Lord, be not far off!
  O thou my help, hasten to my aid!
Deliver my soul from the sword,
  my life from the power of the dog!
Save me from the mouth of the lion,
  my afflicted soul from the horns of the wild oxen!
. . . .

I will tell of thy name to my brethren;
  in the midst of the congregation I will praise thee:
You who fear the Lord, praise him!
  All you sons of Jacob, glorify him,
  and stand in awe of him, all you sons of Israel!
For he has not despised nor abhorred the affliction of the afflicted;
  and he has not hid his face from him,
  but has heard, when he cried to him.

From thee comes my praise in the great congregation;
  my vows I will pay before those who fear him.
The afflicted shall eat and be satisfied;
  those who seek him shall praise the Lord!
May your hearts live for ever!

All the ends of the earth shall remember and turn to the Lord;
  and all the families of the nations shall worship before him.
For dominion belongs to the Lord,
  and he rules over the nations.
Yea, to him shall all the proud of the earth bow down;
  before him shall bow all who go down to the dust,
  and he who cannot keep himself alive.
Posterity shall serve him;
  men shall tell of the Lord to the coming generation,
and proclaim his deliverance to a people yet unborn
  that he has wrought it.

What the psalm originally meant to whoever wrote it is a question
for another book. What it meant to the early Christians who quoted
it here will by and large be clear. There are two points, though, which
need comment. I have drawn a line two thirds of the way through the
psalm to indicate a sudden and total change of mood, though this
change would probably be obvious even without it. Quite a number
of the psalms have this kind of structure, as though the deliverance
the poet pleads for in the first part of the psalm has actually taken
place at this juncture, and the rest of the poem is a thanksgiving for it.
There is also that curious line: 'they have pierced my hands and feet'.
Can that really be simply a coincidence? As with the passion
narrative as a whole, the answer seems to be yes *and* no. The
traditional Hebrew text at this point literally translates as: *they like a
lion my hands and feet*, and is therefore obviously wrong. The
English version translates the Septuagint, or Greek Old Testament,
and although it is true that this was the Christian version of the Old
Testament and the Jews themselves repudiated it after the rise of
Christianity, it is in fact a Jewish translation and earlier than the
crucifixion — so in that sense the coincidence is a real and natural one.
It is even quite likely that the Septuagint accurately translates the
original Hebrew, and that the present Hebrew reading is a deliberate
distortion made to spoil a coincidence which Jews themselves may
have thought to be so astounding as almost to convince and to

convert. We must remember that the fixing of the received Hebrew text is significantly *later* than the rise and flourishing of Christianity.

Though I have declined to offer an interpretation of the psalm as a whole, I think that some suggestion is needed as to what this particular verse originally meant. Let us begin by taking the next line to the one in question: 'I can count all my bones.' If this stood by itself we would be inclined to interpret that the speaker is so wasted with famine that his bones stick out, and it is in something like that sense that the church has generally understood it. But I doubt if that is the true one. I would look for the explanation of both the pierced limbs and the revealed bones in the imagery of the first line of the verse: 'Yea, dogs are round about me'. It is true that these are purely metaphorical dogs, and that in reality they are 'a company of evildoers'; but it seems to me to make best sense to explain both the lines under inspection by means of this metaphor: the dogs have pierced (i.e. bitten through) his hands and feet, while his flesh is so badly torn that his bones can be seen.

The bystanders, we are told, assume that Jesus is calling on Elijah and mockingly wait for Elijah to come and save him. As we have seen, it was probably this feature that persuaded Matthew to 'Hebraize' the cry he originally found in Mark. The next incident, in the mind of the narrator is clearly linked with the mocking reaction of the crowd: he wants us to think that the offering of 'vinegar' is a derisive taunting of Jesus' distressed condition. If the incident happened at all (as we have seen, it is just as likely to be a fulfilment of the 'prophecy' of Psalm 69.21) it was probably a sincere and compassionate gesture. The Romans had a summer drink which they called *posca*, which basically consisted of vinegar heavily diluted with water; and it is this if anything that Jesus would have been offered. The very trouble involved in getting the drink to his lips surely makes it clear that if the incident happened it was an act of pity rather than scorn.

And Jesus uttered a loud cry, and breathed his last. And the curtain of the temple was torn in two, from top to bottom. And when the centurion who stood facing him saw that he thus breathed his last, he said, 'Truly this man was the Son of God!'

There were also women looking on from afar, among whom were Mary Magdalene, and Mary the mother of James the younger and of Joses, and Salome who, when he was in Galilee, followed him and ministered to him; and also many other women who came up with him to Jerusalem. (15.37–41)

As noted above, the loud cry with which Jesus expires, though dramatically effective, is implausible from a medical point of view. And from the historical point of view the same may be said of the rending of the temple curtain. The significance of this imagery is expounded at length by the author of the Epistle to the Hebrews, but (strangely, in view of what one would have thought was its primary importance for most early Christian communities) nowhere else in the New Testament. For those insterested in exploring the theme, the crucial passage (which, alas, is too long to be quoted) is chapter 9; but the whole of the epistle will repay study.

A similar comment (that it is effective but not entirely plausible) might be made of the centurion's utterance on the death of Jesus. The first point that raises a question mark is the very first word of the utterance – *alēthōs*. There is such a word in Greek, but only as a cognate adverb of the adjective 'true'. But here it is quite plainly an interjection – and equally plainly translates the common Hebrew/ Aramaic interjection *amen*. Then there is also the puzzle of the words 'the Son of God'. The English translation is misleading in that Mark's Greek contains no definite article; 'Son of God' could therefore mean either 'a Son of God', or else its force could be adjectival. Even supposing the incident is historical, I am disinclined to speculate what the centurion may have meant by the words, but there is still the important question of what Mark intended we should understand by them. And here I think we have to go for the adjectival sense, which is fully compatible with the adoptionist theology repeatedly expounded in the early part of this work.

In describing the 'women looking on from afar' Mark gives the careful reader quite a jolt. This is the first hint *anywhere in the gospel* that there were any women at all among Jesus' disciples (and the wording of the second half of the passage makes it clear that that is what essentially they were). On the other hand, the reader who is already familiar with the gospels probably does not react at all to the sudden mention of Mary Magdalene; he has the feeling he already knows all about her. But if we had only Mark's gospel we would be mystified, for this is the first time he has ever mentioned her, and neither here nor in the two references to come (15.47 and 16.1) does he tell us anything about her. Most readers also are already familiar with the account of the crucifixion in John's gospel, so that it escapes their notice that Mark seems to make no mention of Jesus' mother among these women. Orthodoxy insists (not without evidence though – compare Mark 6.3 with Matthew 13.55, and Mark 15.40 with Matthew 27.56, and note that both times Matthew changes Mark's 'Joses' to 'Joseph') that 'Mary the mother of James the younger and of Joses' must be Jesus' own mother; but if so, it is odd first that she is not here actually described as Jesus' mother, second that she should come second after Mary Magdalene, third that she should apparently be included on a list of women 'who, when he was in Galilee, followed him and ministered to him' And how should we interpret this last phrase? If we just had Mark, we should assume their role had been to do the cooking and the washing up, but Luke 8.3 suggests rather that they were comparatively well-off women whose 'ministering' was chiefly financial.

Finally a note about the third of the three women listed. Mark calls her Salome; Matthew drops the name and calls her simply 'the mother of the sons of Zebedee', i.e. the mother of the disciples James and John (Matt. 27.56). Unlike Mark he has previously introduced her into his account. Where in Mark 10.35–40 it is James and John themselves who ask Jesus if they can be Number One and Number Two in his approaching kingdom, in Matthew 20.20–23 (presumably to shift the blame for such worldliness away from two important disciples) it is (once again) 'the mother of the sons of Zebedee'. How far we should accept Matthew's identification, and whether he had any more information about her than Mark had, are points that cannot be settled with any confidence.

And when evening had come, since it was the day of Preparation, that is, the day before the sabbath, Joseph of Arimathaea, a respected member of the council, who was also himself looking for the kingdom of God, took courage and went to Pilate, and asked for the body of Jesus. And Pilate wondered if he were already dead; and summoning the centurion, he asked him whether he was already dead. And when he learned from the centurion that he was dead, he granted the body to Joseph. And he bought a linen shroud, and taking him down, wrapped him in the linen shroud, and laid him in a tomb which had been hewn out of the rock; and he rolled a stone against the door of the tomb. Mary Magdalene and Mary the mother of Joses saw where he was laid. (15.42–47)

It comes as a surprise to the experienced scholar that Mark, apparently within thirty years of Jesus' death, already feels it necessary to explain to a Christian congregation what 'the day of Preparation' is. I mentioned above that the traditional view is that Mark wrote for the congregation at Rome, and the relevant features of the gospel itself are mostly consistent with that. However, we do also happen to have a long letter written to that same congregation, somewhat earlier than Mark's gospel though we don't know how much earlier. The best guess is no more than a decade, since this allows only twenty years from the death of Jesus to the formation of a congregation at Rome (by whom is unknown, but we know it was not by Paul) and time for it to grow to the size and renown it had evidently achieved by the time Paul wrote. If we take a look at that letter, it is inconceivable that the congregation to whom it was written would need to be told what the day of Preparation was. Non-Jewish Christians are admitted, but it is evident that up to now they have been made to feel very much second class citizens, and the whole argument of the letter is an attempt to destroy the ideological basis of this two-tier Christianity. What happened between the date of Paul's letter and Mark's gospel? We can only guess, but it looks as though Paul's efforts have proved only too effective, and many – perhaps most – of the Jewish Christians, no longer permitted the joy of looking down on their Gentile 'brethren', have returned to the synagogue and to the pleasures of superiority.

As we have seen, despite the superficial improbability of the claim, it looks as if the earliest Christian community really did have some sort of eyewitness account, probably of the trial before the priests, and perhaps even of the trial before Pilate also. The real existence of someone in the background not unlike what we are told about Joseph of Arimathaea, a member of the council (that is presumably the council of priests and scribes before whom Jesus had been tried) who is also a clandestine disciple (John 19.38 – but perhaps his own explanation of what he felt were the implications of Mark) is therefore not merely plausible but actually required.

According to Mark Jesus died six hours after being hoisted on the cross. As a method of execution, crucifixion was meant to be a lingering experience of extreme torture – just how lingering is conveyed by Pilate's wondering, after six hours, if he were already dead. In all probability considerably more than six hours: the text tells us it was already evening when Joseph of Arimathaea made his request, and it is significant that when Pilate makes enquiries, the centurion who supervised the execution is apparently on hand to confirm the death. The implication for the reader is that this must have been at least a couple of hours after death occurred. It is only John's gospel which makes any mention of the Jews' requesting Pilate that the legs of the criminals might be broken in order to hasten their deaths so that the bodies could be removed before sundown; and the author may well be reacting to contemporary Jewish criticism of the other three accounts for not containing it. Such criticism would have had in mind the stipulation of Deuteronomy:

> And if a man has committed a crime punishable by death and he is put to death, and you hang him on a tree, his body shall not remain all night upon the tree, but you shall bury him the same day, for a hanged man is accursed by God; you shall not defile your land which the Lord your God gives you for an inheritance. (Deut. 21.22–23)

Roman practice appears to have been to leave the dead body at least for several days as a warning to others. How far they complied with Jewish susceptibilities in Palestine is not known, but it is certainly possible that at least at passover they could have stretched a point to keep the local enthusiasts calm. On the other hand it is equally possible that John's gospel is reacting to a difficulty of its own making. When he tells us that the day after the crucifixion was 'a high day' (19.31), this is because in his chronology the next day is the passover. But Matthew and Mark certainly, and in Luke possibly, the crucifixion takes place on the actual day of the passover, so that the day following, although the sabbath, is *less* sacred.

The hills outside Jerusalem were a honeycomb of tombs, and (as the present text reminds us) in Jesus' time more of them were being excavated year by year. These cave-tombs were not so much individual graves as family vaults. The bodies would be laid on ledges until after decomposition and dehydration, and the bones would then be gathered and placed in an urn, leaving the ledge free for its next occupant. It seems odd at first that Mark should be so precise in stating that 'Mary Magdalene and Mary the mother of Joses saw where he was laid'; but a reason readily suggests itself. Matthew's account of the resurrection for instance (27.62–28.15) is transparently an elaborate fabrication designed to refute the suggestion which he admits is being made by contemporary Jews that the 'disciples came by night and stole the body away' (Matt. 28.13). One suspects that Mark is here being precise in order to refute an earlier version of this kind of calumny, in which it was alleged that a couple of hysterical women had come looking for the body on Sunday morning and simply looked inside the wrong (and therefore empty) tomb.

15

The Ending

I: The Abrupt Ending (Mark 16.1–?)

And when the sabbath was past, Mary Magdalene, and Mary the mother of James, and Salome, bought spices, so that they might go and anoint him. And very early on the first day of the week they went to the tomb when the sun had risen. And they were saying to one another, 'Who will roll away the stone for us from the door of the tomb?' And looking up, they saw that the stone was rolled back – it was very large. And entering the tomb, they saw a young man sitting on the right side, dressed in a white robe; and they were amazed. And he said to them, 'Do not be amazed; you seek Jesus of Nazareth, who was crucified. He has risen, he is not here; see the place where they laid him. But go, tell his disciples and Peter that he is going before you to Galilee; there you will see him, as he told you.' And they went out and fled from the tomb; for trembling and astonishment had come upon them; and they said nothing to anyone, for they were afraid. (16.1–8)

The evidence of our earliest manuscripts makes it clear that the authentic text of the gospel ends here, so that the remaining twelve verses in the traditional text must be by another and later hand. There are those who argue that it was intended to end here, and that the mysterious incompleteness is deliberate. An ending such as the above does have a certain appeal for an age like ours that is loath to seem credulous, and that has in any case been trained by fiction writers to appreciate such incomplete endings on artistic grounds. We are dealing, however, with the first century AD, and the evidence of those times suggests a widely-felt dissatisfaction with the above as the real conclusion to the work. First of all there was the sheer grammatical implausibility of rounding off a full-length prose work with a phrase like 'for they were afraid'. This implausibility does not come over in the English translation, but can very easily be rendered by altering the translation to, 'For they were afraid that ...' The main reason for this feeling of incompleteness seems to reside in the fact that in Greek the word 'for' is enclitic; that is to say, it cannot stand first in any phrase or sentence. It tends therefore to 'hang' and to 'expect'; Greek stylists would have the same misgivings about ending a sentence with it as some English stylists have about ending a sentence with a preposition. And even those English stylists who insist it is perfectly all right to say, 'Who I came to', instead of, 'To whom I came', would probably have misgivings about ending an entire work with this kind of construction.

More important, though, than grammatical considerations is the fact that the work itself seems to bear witness to its own incompleteness. As noted several times before, Mark twice leads us to expect that after Jesus' death he will appear to the disciples 'in Galilee' – once back in 14.28 in the course of the last supper, and once again right here in what is now the second last sentence of the gospel. Surely the work, at least in Mark's intention, was to end with just such an appearance as Matthew's gospel does in fact give. Did he die before completing the work? Has the conclusion simply been lost, accidentally worn or torn away from the 'library' copy from which later scribes had to work? Whatever the reason (which simply has to be guessed) the likelihood is overwhelming that the early church was right to feel that the ending they had was incomplete. Whether they were right to go ahead and add one of their own is of course another matter.

The women who come to the tomb on the morning after the sabbath to complete the burial rites are the same three that Mark has already listed as the most prominent of those 'looking on from afar' at Jesus' death agony in 15.40. Mark offers no explanation of why they needed to do this, but Luke supplies it: the original burial on Friday evening, he suggests, had been hasty and incomplete, being interrupted by the approach of sunset and thus by the beginning of the sabbath (Luke 23.54–24.1). The detail is important, because had the burial been complete the women would not have needed to ask, 'Who will roll away the stone for us from the door of the tomb?'; nor in such circumstances would they have gone into the tomb anyway.

The 'young man sitting on the right side, dressed in a white robe' is clearly intended to be an angel. Why doesn't Mark just say so? Luke also at this point (24.4) talks about 'men' rather than about 'angels' –

for some reason he has two of them, an idea which John's gospel incorporates (20.12). Just as we have noted that both Matthew and Luke seem to have been somewhat embarrassed by Mark's fondness for attributing all the world's woes to demons, it is interesting to note that had Mark known the other two gospels, he would have been equally embarassed by their fondness for angelic appearances. He mentions angels several times (1.13; 8.38; 12.25; 13.27; 13.32) but always as a kind of species in the plural; and though the first of these instances must have involved the solid appearance of angels on earth, Mark seems to avoid actual description of those appearances. In the remaining four instances angels are confined to heaven and the future rather than having anything to do with earth and the present. Matthew on the other hand has a tempestuous angelic appearance at the first mention of the tomb (Matt. 28.2–7) – although all his earlier angelic appearances (confined to the first two chapters) are in dreams; which for the modern reader (almost certainly not, though, by Matthew's intention) conveniently sidesteps the question of whether they actually exist. In contrast to both of these, Luke's first two chapters are a perfect riot of angelic appearances of the most solid and active kind. Why Luke, therefore, should talk about men rather than angels here is genuinely puzzling. There is of course nothing to be said for the suggestion, still quite often put forward, that in Mark's gospel these excited women were in fact talking actually to a young man, and that it was their own suggestibility that transformed him into an angel. We can be certain for instance that Mark himself does not intend to be understood in this sense; and to suggest that he is here revealing the truth without being aware of it is to attribute an unlikely degree of hard historicity to his account.

The young man, therefore, who says to the women, 'Do not be amazed; you seek Jesus of Nazareth, who was crucified ...' is unquestionably an angel. This was no doubt part of the guarantee for the earliest readers of the gospel that the women had not simply mistaken the tomb and, finding it empty, had immediately jumped to an absurd conclusion. (As noted before, one gets the impression from several details in Mark's account that this was the anti-Christian, presumably Jewish, rumour that seems to have been in circulation in his day.) The emphatic statement, 'He has risen; he is not here; see the place where they laid him', seems to point in the same direction. We note that by the time of Matthew's gospel, probably some ten to fifteen years later, the rumour has become rather more crudely slanderous (Matt. 28.11–15). The prophecy of a resurrection appearance to be granted shortly to the disciples if they will gather again in Galilee, which is unfulfilled in the surviving text of Mark but whose fulfilment we find related in Matthew 28.16–20, will be dealt with in more detail later in the chapter.

Perhaps the hardest part of the fragmentary ending to explain is the very last sentence of all: 'and they said nothing to any one, for they were afraid …' The complex problems which it seems to raise, however, will be held over for my later discussion of whether we in fact have a version of Mark's original ending in the present ending of Matthew's gospel.

II: The Shorter Ending

But they reported briefly to Peter and those with him all that they had been told. And after this, Jesus himself sent out by means of them, from east to west, the sacred and imperishable proclamation of eternal salvation.

There is only one surviving manuscript which gives this as the sole conclusion of Mark's gospel; but there are quite a number which include this passage immediately after verse 8, and then continue with what we now know as the longer ending. The evidence therefore suggests three stages on the way to our present text of chapter 16 of Mark. At first the gospel circulated without any ending at all beyond what I have called the abrupt ending, and we still have a few early manuscripts in this form. Nevertheless, at a very early date it was clearly felt that the work was incomplete, and the above ending was suggested as a suitable conclusion. Now we have to start guessing. And the best guess seems to me, not that the above was found unsatisfactory in itself, but that independently of the above someone suggested the longer ending; that for a time both circulated independently, but that the longer ending quickly proved the more popular of the two; and that the transition period is represented by those manuscripts which include *both* endings. How quickly the longer ending established itself is shown by the fact that we find Irenaeus (AD *c.* 130–*c.* 200) quoting it as part of the actual gospel before the end of the second century.

III: The Longer Ending

Now when he rose early on the first day of the week, he appeared first to Mary Magdalene, from whom he had cast out seven demons. She went out and told those who had been with him, as they mourned and wept. But when they heard that he was alive and had been seen by her, they would not believe it.

After this he appeared in another form to two of them, as they were walking into the country. And they went back and told the rest, but they did not believe them.

Afterward he appeared to the eleven themselves as they sat at table; and he upbraided them for their unbelief and hardness of heart, because they had not believed those who saw him after he had risen. And he said to them, 'Go into all the world and preach the gospel to the whole creation. He who believes and is baptized will be saved; but he who does not believe will be condemned. And these signs will accompany those who believe: in my name they will cast out demons; they will speak in new tongues; they will pick up serpents, and if they drink any deadly thing, it will not hurt them; and they will lay their hands on the sick, and they will recover.'

So then the Lord Jesus, after he had spoken to them, was taken up into heaven, and sat down at the right hand of God. And they went forth and preached everywhere, while the Lord worked with them and confirmed the message by the signs that attended it. (16.9–20)

Whoever wrote the shorter ending seems to have had his eye chiefly on Matthew's gospel, which explains why that ending is short: if we remove the nonsense about the guards being bribed by the priests to spread a false rumour, Matthew's account adds very little more to Mark's beyond supplying the prophesied appearance in Galilee. The author of the longer ending, on the other hand, was chiefly looking at Luke, whose final chapter stretches to fifty-three verses as against Mark's eight (and even with completion would have been about fourteen). Rather than simply continue Mark's account, his summary of the resurrection appearances starts again at the beginning of Luke's chapter, creating an odd though commendably honest effect – he gives us good grounds for supposing that he had no intention of trying to deceive anyone. He tells us that Jesus 'appeared first to

Mary Magdalene, from whom he had cast out seven demons'. That last statement is lifted from Luke 8.2, but differs from Luke's account of the resurrection itself which, like Mark, tells us that Jesus first appeared to three women: Mary Magdalene, Joanna (in place of Mark's Salome), and Mary the mother of James. It is very unlikely that Luke knew of Matthew's gospel (or *vice versa*), so that he would have made no connection between Salome and the mother of the sons of Zebedee (Matt. 27.56); he has already mentioned Joanna in connection with Mary Magdalene in the opening verses of chapter 8 (see above), and his mention of her here is quite likely to be no more than the substitution of someone he knew about for someone he didn't. It is in John's gospel (20.11–18) that Jesus first appears to Mary Magdalene alone. Is the author of the longer ending referring to John's gospel? Or is John's gospel referring to the longer ending? Regrettably we have no means of deciding.

The detail that the disciples, when first told about the resurrection, refused to believe it is found only in Luke (24.11), while the reference to his appearing 'in another form to two of them, as they were walking into the country' is clearly a summary of Luke 24.13–35. The next verse, down to 'because they had not believed those who saw him after he had risen', seems to complete the summary of Luke. With verse 15 ('And he said to them, "Go into all the world and preach the gospel ..."') we come to what looks like the longer ending's own version of the conclusion of Matthew.

Thereafter the account goes its own way, and we seem to get a tantalizing glimpse of quite another aspect of early Christianity to the comparatively respectable version that eventually prevailed. 'He who believes and is baptized will be saved.' Believes in what? And will be saved from what? If one looks at the three synoptic gospels, the exhortation to believe takes two very different forms. People who want Jesus to heal them are expected 'to believe' – presumably that Jesus has the power to perform the miracle they ask of him (Matt. 8.13; 9.28; Mark 5.36; 9.23–24; Luke 8.50). It is not obvious that this meaning has any bearing on the passage we are dealing with. But Jesus – and also John the Baptist – are both of them prophets who utter warnings about disaster that threatens people who do not repent of their sins (Matt. 21.25, 32; Mark 1.15; 11.31; Luke 8.12, 13; 20.5), and as prophets they demand to be believed. This meaning *could* provide the explanation here. But there is a third possible meaning, much insisted on by the fourth gospel but otherwise not attested by any authentic passage in the New Testament, which has since become pretty well the exclusive meaning of the word 'belief' in the Christian tradition, and whose early popularity is attested by a spurious verse in Acts (italicized):

> And as they went along the road they came to some water, and the eunuch said, 'See, here is water! What is to prevent my being baptized?' *And Philip said, 'If you believe with all your heart, you may.' And he replied, 'I believe that Jesus Christ is the Son of God.'* (Acts 8.36–37)

I suspect this is already the meaning implied by 'belief' in the present passage (note the connection with baptism, both in the excerpt from Acts above and also in Mark 16.16). I suspect also that a considerable number of readers will share my mystification that this kind of apparently groundless profession of 'belief' should have become so overwhelmingly the dominant use of the term in the tradition.

The signs that will 'accompany those who believe' are above all what prompts me to suggest we have here a glimpse of the less respectable side of early Christianity. To the modern ear they read more like a list of the qualities of a mountebank than those of a disciple. 'Casting out demons' needs no discussion beyond what has already been given. 'They will speak in new tongues': we know from Acts and Paul's epistles that this 'speaking in tongues'[1] was widely practised and highly esteemed among early Christians. Where it derives from, though, is something of a mystery; there are no references to it in any form in any of the gospels, apart from the spurious reference here. 'They will pick up serpents, and if they drink any deadly thing, it will not hurt them': once again we are referred to signs that are not mentioned in the authentic text of any of the four gospels (but see the reference to 'Justus surnamed Barsabas' in the excerpt from Eusebius on page 7), and unlike the previous example we are at a loss to know what to make of them. It is possible, but by no means certain, that we are being referred to Acts 28.1–6, the story of Paul being bitten by a poisonous snake and suffering no harm. However, I cannot quite rid myself of the suspicion (of which the story in Acts may in any case be confirmation, particularly in view of the fact that it is unlikely to be true) that there may have been something like sects of snake-charmers among the early wandering preachers of Christianity; and that either pretending to drink, or actually drinking, known poisons without harmful effect was one of the tricks they used to practise. I imagine a situation not unlike that of spiritualism in the last century, all of whose claims would be dismissed by modern enquiry (despite the fact that some surprisingly intelligent people were impressed with them at the time), but which still presents us with the difficulty of deciding just how much of it was deliberate fraud, how much accidental fraud, how much sincere though groundless belief and (most puzzling of all) the undoubted occasional fraud who nevertheless sincerely believed he was practising fraud in a good cause.

In contrast, the promise that 'they will lay their hands on the sick, and they will recover' goes back not merely to Jesus' original sending out of the apostles from Galilee (Mark 6.7–13), but even earlier than that to Jesus' understanding of his own mission from the very first (Mark 1.21–2.12). With the final paragraph of the excerpt we return once again to Luke, both to the conclusion of the gospel (Luke 24.44–53) and to the beginning of Acts (1.1–11). The last sentence of all is presumably intended as a reference to (rather than a summary of) the whole of the rest of Acts.

IV: Perhaps the Original Ending

Now the eleven disciples went to Galilee, to the mountain to which Jesus had directed them. And when they saw him they worshipped him; but some doubted. And Jesus came and said to them, 'All authority in heaven and on earth has been given to me. Go therefore and make disciples of all nations, baptizing them in the name of the Father and of the Son and of the Holy Spirit, teaching them to observe all that I have commanded you; and lo, I am with you always, to the close of the age.' (Matt. 28.16–20)

Why should anyone think that this was the original conclusion of Mark's gospel, apart from the fact that it fulfills the two prophecies Mark gives us that after Jesus' death he will reveal himself to the disciples in Galilee? This consideration alone would in fact be quite strong, but there are others which strengthen it further. Note, first of all that this is a remarkably *sober* conclusion to Matthew's gospel, in striking contrast to the extravagant impossibilities with which he begins his final chapter. In verse 2–3 an angel appears and lays about him in a way that cannot be ignored. In verse 9, as the women are running from the tomb, they meet the risen Jesus in such solid form that they 'took hold of his feet and worshipped him'. (We can be fairly sure that John 20.17 is his own angry protest at such appalling crudity.) In the above excerpt, however, there is no doubt that we are dealing with a *visionary* appearance ('... but some doubted' – it is amazing to me that Matthew did not spot the implication and remove the phrase altogether, which could have been done without leaving the slightest trace).

But there are also undeniable difficulties for the idea, the most obvious being how Mark got from 'and they said nothing to any one, for they were afraid' to the situation above. Somehow or other they presumably overcame their fear and told the disciples after all. Does Matthew also give us the original Marcan ending when he tells us how the women met Jesus as they were returning to Jerusalem from the tomb, and that this is what changed their outlook? The difficulty with that is that in Matthew the women have no need to change their minds anyway. Compare the two crucial verses:

> And they went out and fled from the tomb; for trembling and astonishment had come upon them; and they said nothing to any one, for they were afraid ... (Mark 16.8)

> So they departed quickly from the tomb with fear and great joy, and ran to tell his disciples. (Matt. 28.8)

There is also the difficulty pointed out above that in Matthew's account the appearance to the women is a 'solid' appearance, whereas the appearance to the disciples is unmistakably a visionary appearance. This is one of the points that to me is persuasive that the ending of Matthew's gospel was also the original ending of Mark's. But the point is destroyed if we then suppose that the appearance to the women described in Matthew 28.9–10 also comes from the original ending of Mark. Unless, of course, Matthew has 'solidified' a resurrection appearance that originally in Mark was as visionary as the end of Matthew's gospel is. But in that case, why didn't Matthew also 'solidify' the concluding appearance? Obviously we cannot answer these questions; we can only point them out. The reader may wish to reject the whole idea that Matthew had the complete version of Mark's gospel – as conventional scholarship has always supposed he did not. He may even reject the idea that there ever was a lost ending of Mark's gospel, as some scholars equally insist. On this question, as on so many others that arise in interpreting all biblical books, we end up recording not so much well-grounded answers as possibilities that have to be born in mind.

V: What Actually Happened?

Not, I suspect for most readers, anything like what the gospels themselves tell us happened; not because we have any kind of 'evidence' that disproves it, but for the kind of considerations which relate to miracles stories generally, and which I have discussed on pages 161–2. There are two possibilities suggested by our present survey which many readers will find tempting as the real explanation of what happened. I noted for instance that underlying Mark's account there seems to be an attempt to refute the suggestion that some grief-stricken, perhaps even grief-crazed, women came to the wrong tomb, found it empty and came to an absurd conclusion. The suggestion will to many readers be more immediately convincing than Mark's refutation of it. Then there is also Luke's telling comment: 'Now it was Mary Magdalene and Joanna and Mary the mother of James and the other women with them who told this to the apostles; but these words seemed to them an idle tale, and they did not believe them' (Luke 24.10–11). Luke's is the most obviously Gentile of the four gospels, and this reads like an attempt on his part to anticipate and refute a suggestion that will immediately have occurred to all Gentile readers of his day – the ancient world (that is to say, up to about thirty years ago) holding a generally dismissive attitude towards female intelligence and stability. To be fair, there is justice in the feminist reply that until very recent times women were rarely admitted to situations in which they could test or exercise their intelligence, and that the characteristics which they typically developed as a result of this oppression were then put forward as the justification for it. But this is a modern view which we must set aside when evaluating the gospel evidence. It is noticeable, and probably also relevant, that in all four gospels the belief that Jesus was risen from the dead arose from the assertions of women.

My own view is that on this point the gospels are probably telling the historic truth. However, we cannot overlook the fact that outside the gospels we have a fifth account of the resurrection appearances which is earlier than any of our gospels and which seems to bear no relation to anything they tell us: there is no mention of women, nor of an empty tomb, nor of anything that we seem meant to interpret as 'solid' appearances. Here it is:

> For I delivered to you as of first importance what I also received, that Christ died for our sins in accordance with the scriptures, that he was buried, that he was raised on the third day in accordance with the scriptures, and that he appeared to Cephas,[2] then to the twelve. Then he appeared to more than five hundred brethren at one time, most of whom are still alive, though some have fallen asleep. Then he appeared to James, then to all the apostles. Last of all, as to one untimely born, he appeared also to me. (I Cor. 15.3–8)

It would be tempting to view this as the 'original' account, and the gospel versions as later miraculous elaborations of an originally non-miraculous narrative. I used to hold such a view myself; but I increasingly suspect that Paul's is the doctored version and that the gospel versions, though they cannot be true, are closer to 'what actually happened' than the above is. First of all there is some indication of manipulating the account in the mention of 'the twelve' (compare 'the eleven disciples' of Matt. 28.16), since the appearance can only have taken place *after* Judas' treachery, but *before* Matthias' election to take his place. Then we should note also that all three synoptic gospels show traces of embarassment about what they tell us. Matthew (28.11–15) is sensitive to current Jewish debunking of Christian claims, and most of his elaborate paraphernalia – the guard, the earthquake and the bribery by the priests (none of which is found in any other account) – seems devised simply to refute the calumny. We have seen that both Mark and Luke are eager to anticipate criticisms that they expect from their readers. It seems easier to me to suppose that Paul has suppressed mention of the women and the empty tomb for similar reasons of embarrassment than that the tradition has invented them.[3] And although it is obvious that descriptions of 'solid' resurrection appearances cannot be true, it is not equally obvious that such descriptions are necessarily later than Paul's account above. It is only too easy to see other motives besides plausibility that Paul might have had for insisting that *all* the resurrection appearances were visions. One cannot overlook, for instance, his own insistence that he too was an apostle (Rom. 1.1; 11.13; I Cor. 1.1; 4.9; 15.9; II Cor. 1.1; Gal. 1.1, 17), and above all his extreme touchiness over the (perfectly true) suggestion that he wasn't really an apostle in the original sense of the term (I Cor. 9.1–2; II Cor. 11.5; 12.11–12; Gal. 1–2). Since his own resurrection appearance had perforce to be admitted to be merely visionary, he had an obvious motive for implying that so must everyone else's have been.

In contrast to the general view of progressive scholarship, therefore, I am inclined to accept the story of the women at the 'empty tomb' as pristine; though I agree with them in holding that the conclusion the women came to, and following them the disciples, cannot be true. Does such a view expose Christianity as a either a delusion or a fraud? Conservative Christians will insist that if such a position is accepted, such a conclusion inevitably follows; but their reasons for doing so are not necessarily any more honest than Paul's were in implying that the early appearances were as visionary as his own. They know from experience that insistence on an 'all or nothing' decision is highly effective in stampeding (sometimes even frightening) unsophisticated hearers into voting for 'all'. But in fact there is neither virtue or good sense in our accepting that an 'all or nothing' choice has to be made. On the one hand Christian claims about the resurrection cannot possibly be true; on the other we have the evidence of two thousand years that the idea of such a resurrection has an overwhelming appeal for a numberless multitude. There are those who would argue that the truth of this second observation is an unanswerable vindication of the very claim we have rejected. That I leave for the reader to decide.

For my part, in a way he himself did not intend, I view Paul's famous dichotomy as relevant to the question:

> Now if Christ is preached as raised from the dead, how can some of you say that there is no resurrection of the dead? But if there is no resurrection, then Christ has not been raised, then our preaching is in vain and your faith is in vain. We are even found to be misrepresenting God, because we testified of God that he raised Christ, whom he did not raise if it is true that the dead are not raised. For if the dead are not raised, then Christ has not been raised, your faith is futile and you are still in your sins. Then those also who have fallen asleep in Christ have perished. If for this life only we have hoped in Christ, we are of all men most to be pitied. (I Cor. 15.12–19)

I have often heard this passage cited as though it proved the reality of 'life after death' from the reality of Jesus' resurrection. In fact Paul is not talking about 'life after death', as Christians have generally understood the idea, at all – nor did he believe in a 'life after death' in that sense. At one time he seems to have held that those who had died had missed out on the resurrection altogether (I Cor. 11.30) as a punishment for their misdeeds, and only those who were still alive at Jesus' return to earth qualified for the blessing of eternal life. But later, as the rest of I Corinthians 15 makes clear (see also I Thess. 4.13–18) Paul's view seems to have been that those who have died are for the moment thoroughly dead, but that when Jesus appears they will be raised to life again. And, however odd and illogical it may seem to modern ears, what he is arguing above is not that the truth of this doctrine is proved by the truth of Jesus' resurrection, but quite the other way round: the truth of Jesus' resurrection is proved by the truth of this doctrine.

Now I probably do not need to point out that the doctrine he holds up as 'proof' that Jesus rose from the dead is not in fact any longer held by any mainstream Christian body, all of whom seem to insist on what Paul denies, that death is an immediate transition from this life into the next. There is a judgment to come, certainly, accompanied by a resurrection of the dead, and that will be 'at the last day'; but in the meantime those who have died have already entered into life, and this more popular doctrine is already explicit in John 11.21–27. The other great difference between Paul's view above and that of traditional Christianity is, as already hinted, that whereas Paul uses *our* resurrection of proof of Jesus' resurrection, the tradition prefers to argue the other way round: we know that we will rise again because we know that Jesus did and this also proves that there is life after death.

I have no wish to dispute the enormous appeal that the idea of life after death has had for any number of societies – not only Christian – and its essential connection in their minds with the whole idea of morality. It is nonsense to suggest, as a matter of plain historic fact, that the idea is no more than a kind of opiate cynically offered by rulers to ease the mental sufferings of the vast majority of their subjects. Individual rulers (notoriously Napoleon) have occasionally taken this view, but the overwhelming impression created by whole centuries of insistence on the belief is that it is by and large sincere. And it is also true that the abandonment of the notion creates huge difficulties for morality – for *any* system of morality – the crux of the problem being that all societies (including those that do not profess any belief in a life after death) think it of the utmost importance to insist that virtue is somehow rewarded and wickedness somehow punished; this despite the fact that no society has ever yet *convincingly* shown that in fact they are. Even the desperate suggestion that 'virtue is its own reward' is no more convincing than any other, and is by far the least appealing. In a stable and benign form of society the problem is not much felt; but in times of cataclysm (such as for instance the second World War) it becomes quite unbearably acute. We read of vast crimes that will never be punished, nor their numberless victims avenged; vast acts of heroism, involving the death or permanent injury and destitution of the hero, that will never be rewarded; huge profits unjustly acquired that remain to be enjoyed by the profiteer; huge sacrifices whose loss will never be made up. Those who forsook their friends and fled are preserved in safety to this day; those whose sense of duty drove them voluntarily to return from a safe distance and sacrifice their lives are buried and forgotten. I do not find the idea of a life after death convincing; but I certainly don't find it frivolous.

Yet we must insist: the fact that we seem so desperately to need such an idea is the strongest possible indication, not that it is true, but that in fact it is unlikely to be. Christians since at least the time of John's gospel have bound up their belief in a life after death with their belief in Jesus' resurrection; and though I do not literally believe in either, this still seems to me to be appropriate. Regardless of whether Jesus rose or not, the resurrection can still be viewed as a symbol of hope, in a situation where at the realistic level there *is* no hope. To me therefore the fact that he did not rise renders the image of his resurrection exactly appropriate to the enormous function that it has to perform.

VI: Postscript

As the Bishop of Durham has recently found to his surprise, the suggestion that the gospel account of the resurrection can not be accepted as history still tends to arouse an angry response from the ordinary churchgoer, despite the fact that any number of professional Christian scholars have for most of this century pretty freely acknowledged this to each other. Such scholars tend to argue that the resurrection must be thought of as a 'spiritual event' which the earliest disciples would have been incapable of understanding themselves, or of relating to others, in any but the physical and material terms in which they in fact describe it. That last part of the argument is undeniable. The modern reader who spends much time in reading the Bible quickly comes to realize that most of the peculiarities of its out-look are down to the fact that with very few exceptions (the author of John's gospel being perhaps the only notable one) those who wrote it belonged to a culture which had only a minimal grasp of abstract thought. It is undoubtedly true, and is a great part of the Bible's attraction, that ideas that we would effortlessly expound in abstract terms have to be rendered by biblical authors by a metaphorical use of concrete terms. If you want a practical illustration of this, look up the words 'hand' and 'arm' in a concordance, and note how very high a proportion of the instances to us describe the abstract notion of 'power'.

Nevertheless, the first part of this scholarly foot-work doesn't quite convince. It certainly doesn't convince most churchgoers, and I don't think it convinces non-churchgoers either. It looks like an attempt to admit on the one hand that the resurrection didn't happen, while at the same time wanting to insist that it did; and it gives very convincing reasons for what it concedes, and no reasons at all for what it insists on. When the scholar admits that historically it didn't happen, we all know pretty well what he means by 'historically', and so on this point we understand what he is saying; but when he goes on to talk about a 'spiritual' event, we have no idea at all what he means by 'spiritual' – and most of us suspect that neither has he. A 'spiritual event' looks to the coldly observing eye like an event that didn't actually happen, though the speaker would like to carry on insisting that it did.

I offer that last sentence initially as a sarcasm, but it can in fact be made the basis of a perfectly serious explanation of the word 'spiritual'; and that is what this postscript is really about. The sort of books I read, I come across the expression pretty often, and over the years I have developed the habit of explaining it to myself – without sarcasm – in much the same way I have outlined it above. I admit it is not how the author himself usually wishes to be understood; but it often makes surprisingly good sense of him, and particularly in view of one's suspicions that he does not wish the word to be precisely understood at all. The word 'spiritual', not only in my personal usage but in most of the contexts in which it occurs, can be taken to mean 'that exists or occurs in human consciousness rather than in the external world'. A 'spiritual being' (such as God, or the gods) is a being that exists in human consciousness, and we have no need to conceive of its existence in any other way than that; a 'spiritual' event is one that is unknown to history but is powerfully present to the minds of human beings (or at any rate of some).[4]

The criticism I anticipate from some readers is that the definition itself is grossly materialistic, and apart from that word 'grossly' I accept that it is. What I suspect lies at the heart of their misgiving is the idea that if 'spiritual beings' and 'spiritual events' exist only in human consciousness, they don't really exist at all. (It is fair to point out, though, that this assumption is even more materialistic than the view being criticized.) A spiritual being in the sense that I have just defined it is after all no different from what atheists have always said it is. This is true; but atheists and believers seem to be united in a common error, in that they both take it for granted that anything that exists or takes place only in human consciousness is thereby proved to be at best an irrelevance, at worst a delusion. It is, however, comparatively easy to demonstrate the reality of spiritual ideas in precisely the sense defined above, which I anticipate that neither party would be ready to dismiss as either irrelevant or illusory. The most obvious of these spiritual ideas is that of justice, which in some form (like the gods) seems to be as old as human society itself.

Initially I expect there will be resistance to the idea that justice is a spiritual notion under the definition given above. Large numbers of philosophers even to this day spend their lives trying to derive principles of justice, if not from the external world as such, at least from some idea of 'the way things are' as distinct from 'the way we would like to see them'. And quite a number of these (though by no means all) also insist there has to be such a thing as absolute justice – 'has to be' because no one has ever yet, even remotely, succeeded in demonstrating that there is. But it makes much better sense of the way we see justice at work if we suppose that it derives, not primarily from any understanding of the way things really are at all, but from our aspirations for the way we would like them to be. We have simply invented the idea, in the belief that a society that accepts such notions will be more like the kind of society we would like to be living in than one that does not. Undoubtedly this idea of justice will be repugnant to a number of readers, who will object that it means that justice can be anything that a sufficient number of us wants it to be, and that is not what they mean by justice at all. I am reminded of an old, and I think foolish, saying: *Fiat justitia, ruat caelum.* Those who disagree with me will be tempted to take this as their banner. It presupposes that we know absolutely and without question what the rules of justice are, that these rules in no way depend on our views of what we would like them to be, and that we must in all circumstances apply the rules regardless of any consequence. Yet if these rules exist externally to ourselves, how do we arrive at our knowledge of them? And those rules that do exist – what purpose are they supposed to serve? Precisely I suggest that of keeping the firmament in place above our heads. And it follows that anything which brings that firmament crashing down upon us by definition cannot be justice.

Let us take a much more recent idea than justice, the idea of human rights. The French claim they invented it at the time of their revolution, the Americans that they invented it during their rebellion against King George, the English that it was the main principal underlying the 'Glorious Revolution'. Overlooking the fact that I too am an Englishman, this last seems to me to be closest to the mark, the true origins being rather earlier than the 1680s, and the idea, though not the name, being evident in the ideology underlying the Great Rebellion of Parliament against King Charles in the 1640s. (To trace it back, though, as far as Magna Charta strikes me as being fanciful.) Whatever the origins they are recent, and we can follow the whole history of the idea from its earliest inception in comparatively modern times right up to the present day. Can it be doubted then that the idea is not any kind of perception of the way things are, certainly not of the way they always have been, but rather a devising of the way that from now on we want them to be? Does anyone think of them as irrelevant or illusory on these grounds? The fact that we have invented them in no way detracts from the extent to which all of us are agreed they must be regarded as *obligatory*. They exist only in human consciousness, yet they undoubtedly do exist and in the modern world not merely invite but actually compel obedience.

The gods of course are no longer obligatory in this sense, which is undoubtedly a disappointment for some. But to insist on thinking of them as beings external to ourselves does nothing to make them so. They have lost their function also of providing any kind of *explanation* for the physical world we live in. Like all other truly spiritual notions, their function now seems to be concerned with the way we want the world to be rather than the way it is. Nor I suspect do most of us have any real hope, as for instance Christian missionaries of the nineteenth century seem to have had, that we can unite the whole world on the basis of a single Christian complex of religious ideas (and this in marked contrast to modern secularism, which seriously does believe that Western notions of justice and human rights are on their way to becoming *universally* obligatory). The gods have also had to adapt themselves to pluralism; whereas in the past they tended to divide up the world into territories, each one ruling his own particular area, increasingly they must be content to assemble voluntary congregations, which any one of them can do in any part of the world. And their saving acts are no longer experienced by whole societies, but only by these voluntary groups of believers. Also the values which any particular deity represents are no longer absolute; but as we have seen, this in no way suggests they are unreal – apart from the sense in which *all* values are unreal.

And yet, however improbable it sounds initially, I suspect we all have gods of a kind, and all believe in saving acts of a kind. The reality of this is obscured by the fact that not everybody's God is a personal God. But we all have some kind of ideals, and longings for some kind of perfection, and some kind of regret that this perfection is for ever beyond human reach. The gods are simply embodiments of these ideals and longings and regrets. And as for their saving acts, though the external world of matter and of history marches on in one direction, doesn't every one of us feel, much of the time quite strongly, that it ought to be marching in quite another. The saving acts of the gods are those events – either unreal interpretations of real events, or quite simply insistence on the truth of events that never happened at all – which reveal to us the direction in which the world *ought* to be moving. And the resurrection of Jesus Christ from the dead is a spiritual event in just this sense.

Notes

Foreword

1. Some readers may be tempted to assume that I am intentionally disparaging the Bible with these comments, but nothing could be further from my mind. I take the view that all possible moral and doctrinal structures always derive, and can only derive, from a skewed response to experience. I would be the last person, for instance, to accuse modern secularism of having no moral views, but the first to insist that those views derive from a radically fictional and unconvincing idea of 'what it means to be a human being'. Ancient paganism, of the sophisticated variety that has come down to us in classical literature, is unusual in the frankness with which authors were prepared to admit that their ideology was purely fictional; and one of the saddest spectacles in history is that of this honest admission being turned into one of the weapons by means of which Christianity overthrew it and replaced it with an essentially fanatical and entirely groundless insistence that its own mythology was true. The insistence also of modern secularism that its doctrines are rooted in some kind of unchanging reality is admittedly less fanatical, but no less groundless and untrue.

2. A good deal of such opposition, I dare say, is less bone-headed than it seems, being no more than a disguised way of saying, 'The work you have produced is not an academic work, and for that reason no academic is ever going to allow that it has merit'. On the other hand I wish to acknowledge that the work has in the end been published as a result of an academic's recommendation, for which I am profoundly grateful.

Introduction

1. It will become obvious as this work proceeds that nothing in any of the four gospels can be taken as the actual words of Jesus himself. Apart from the several decades after Jesus' death during which the gospel material seems to have circulated in oral form, there is the strange fact that though in all probability Jesus himself and all his disciples were monoglot Aramaic speakers, no trace of any gospel material survives in Aramaic (for the problematic *Gospel according to the Hebrews* see the appendix to this chapter), even though the Dead Sea Scrolls are witness to the fact that there was plenty of

enthusiast, half-educated literature (of the kind the gospels themselves can be said to resemble) being produced in Aramaic in
precisely the decades we are talking about (AD 30–70). There are
some indications that Mark himself was an Aramaic speaker and
(though this is much less certain) may himself be the translator into
Greek of some of the material he records; but both Matthew and
Luke seem to have used several other documents in common
besides Mark and all of these were certainly in Greek. No matter
how we may be impressed (I think rightly) by the transparent
'authenticity' of much of the material in the first three gospels we
have to bear in mind that *all* of it has been modified – and to be
frank, quite often distorted – first by two or three decades of oral
transmission, and then by translation.

2. See also Matthew 10.5–42 – where, however, although we have
   lengthy and detailed instructions for such a mission, the mission
   itself is not described. Luke describes a mission of all twelve of the
   apostles together with Jesus himself in 8.1, and then a much larger
   mission of seventy – some texts read seventy-two – 'apostles' in
   10.1–20.

3. It is something of a problem to know what to call the land in which
   Jesus lived. In Old Testament times it was called Canaan: i.e. the
   land of the Canaanites, the nations who had occupied it before the
   originally nomadic Israelites had part infiltrated, part conquered it
   at a time earlier than surviving records allow us to date precisely,
   but probably from about 1,500 BC onwards; thereafter the two
   nations had to some extent shared the territory, though it looks as if
   after 1,000 BC the Canaanites gradually began to disappear or to
   lose their separate identity. The name Canaan as a description of
   the land, had ceased to be appropriate long before Jesus' time. At
   the same time, the other name in historical use, Palestine, does not
   begin to apply until about a hundred years after Jesus' death when,
   in AD 135, the Emperor Hadrian, having quelled the second major
   revolt of the Jews in seventy years, in high-handed fit of exaspera-
   tion renamed the country Syria Palestina (i.e. that part of Syria
   which belongs to the Philistines) and forbade Jews any longer to
   live there. In Jesus' time, in the eyes of the Romans who governed
   the place, the whole country was part of the much larger province
   of Syria. The country itself was divided into three districts: Galilee
   in the north, Samaria in the middle, Judea in the south. There does
   not seem to have been any accepted name for the three districts
   together considered as one country. Another puzzle is why the Jews
   of Judaea (which alone, in their own eyes, was the real land of Jews)
   should have been apparently willing to accept Galileans as Jews
   (though nevertheless regarding them with some contempt) but not
   the Samaritans.

4. Occasionally a saying may have survived without any story context
   at all, as in Acts 20.35, a saying which none of the gospels records.
   One must also bear in mind the possibility that in several instances

the tradition has in fact reinvented a narrative setting for an isolated saying of this kind.

5. Very hard-nosed or sceptical readers will probably need convincing of this. The indications are contained in a number of tiny details, but there are enough of them to create quite a high degree of probability, while the fact that we do have to rely merely on details seems to preclude the likelihood of deliberate fabrication by the tradition. Let me offer a selection.

Mark tells us (3.17) that Jesus had a nickname for James and John – *Boanerges* or 'Sons of Thunder' – but he doesn't tell us why. Luke does not mention the nickname, but he tells us a story (9.51–56) which almost certainly explains it, and which it is hard to see why anyone should have invented. Also in chapter 3 (verse 21) Mark tells us that Jesus' relations made at least one attempt to seize and restrain him by force, reacting to a popular view that he had gone mad; Matthew and Luke understandably suppress the incident.

In Mark 10.17–18 a rich man asks Jesus, 'Good Teacher, what must I do to inherit eternal life?' Jesus begins his reply with, 'Why do you call me good? No one is good but God alone.' Both Matthew and Luke seem to be using Mark as their source for this incident. Luke (18.18–19) makes no change, but Matthew (19.16–17) changes the reply to, 'Why do you ask me about what is good? One there is who is good.' Matthew's obvious embarassment at the implications of Mark's text must have been widely felt, and it is hard to see how Mark's text can ever have been a pure invention of the tradition.

Most interesting of all is the protrayal of Jesus' relations with the Jewish teachers of his day. In Mark's gospel, all contact between Jesus and Judaism is hostile except for one incident related in 12.28–34. In Matthew, the Jew-hater *par excellence*, even this has been altered to make it seem like a hostile exchange (22.34–40). But in Luke's gospel it is a striking feature that Jesus is more than occasionally invited to dine with the local religious leaders (7.36; 11.37 – compare with Mark 7.1–2 and 14.1). It is extremely likely that Luke is telling us the truth, a truth which Mark has already begun to suppress, probably because relations between Jews and Christians had already gone sour in his day.

6. It is an interesting thought that the entire thronology of the Western world depends on this not very dependable assertion of Luke.

7. Jerome tells us that he found a copy of this work in the library at Caesarea, that it was written in Aramaic and in Hebrew script and that he translated it. Despite which the surviving fragments are all in Greek and some scholars frankly doubt not merely whether it ever existed in any other form but even whether Jerome's claim can at all be believed. It is worth remarking on the 'story about a woman who was accused before the Lord of many sins, which the

Gospel according to the Hebrews contains'. This is quite likely to be the story we now find in John 8.2–11. Our earliest and best manuscripts of the gospel do not contain it at all, while some place it after John 7.36, some as a kind of appendix at the end of the gospel, and we sometimes also find it in Luke's gospel immediately before the passion narrative (which starts with chapter 22).

8. Even after Latin ceased to be anybody's mother tongue, probably in the course of the sixth century, it continued for many centuries after that to be the *only* acceptable medium for serious literature in Western Europe. Classicists like to give the impression that only Latin written by the original Latin speakers is 'real' Latin, but this approach falsifies our whole understanding of the language. Until as late as the thirteenth century it simply was not possible to achieve any really serious intellectual – or even to some extent aesthetic – effects in any other language than Latin; to have attempted to conduct a serious argument, for instance, in the vernacular would be like a modern debater trying to express himself solely in the vocabulary and syntax of a working-class dialect. It was the French who first tried to promote their own vernacular as a medium at any rate for literature, which accounts for the extraordinary prestige of the French language throughout Europe until modern times. The classicist view can be *partially* excused by the fact that between the sixth and eighth centuries Latin goes through a very bad patch. But once Charlemagne had put himself forward as patron of the movement to recover as much as could still be recovered of the ancient authors, there is no excuse for regarding the Latin literature of the next five hundred years (at least) as anything but *the* literature of Western culture, and as a most important ingredient of it for several centuries after that. And the invention of printing in the fifteenth century gave yet another boost to the use of Latin as the readiest medium of international communication; which it continued to be in the publishing industry until the early years of the eighteenth century – more than a thousand years after it had ceased to be anybody's mother tongue.

9. It has often been stressed, particularly by liberal theologians, that the gospels were never intended to be read as history. Formally this is true, but in practice the claim is misleading. As a result of the observations contained in the preface to Thucydides' *History of the War between Athens and Sparta* (written towards the end of the fifth century BC) the conventions of writing intelligent history were well understood by sophisticated authors of the first century AD. When we say that the gospels cannot be read as history, we mean that all the gospel writers ignore those conventions, and the gospels themselves could not have been written if they hadn't. On the other hand there is no question but that Matthew, Mark and Luke all believed that what they were writing was true, and that they expected their hearers to do the same. John's gospel seems to be a little more sophisticated and – to be frank – a little disingenous

also: he seems to have intended his unsophisticated readers to assume he believed that what he wrote was true, while leaving enough clues around to suggest to the sophisticated reader that in fact he didn't.

While on the subject, I might as well dispose of another widely-canvassed bit of special pleading. It is often suggested that we must not blame the gospel writers for observing the standards of their own time rather than ours. But the fact is that even by the standards of their own time the gospels would have been dismissed by the educated public as collections of unbelievable nonsense (see for instance Acts 17.32.)

10. It should be noted therefore that the opening chapter of Mark's gospel corresponds to the third chapter of both Matthew and Luke, which renders it very likely (if the material itself did not make the fact plain) that the first two chapters of both these other gospels are essentially legendary in character. This is not an argument that Christmas should be abolished, or the traditional imagery of the virgin birth, but it does seem to me that we should be perfectly frank in admitting that the traditional Christmas is a celebration of legendary and not of historical ideas. To those many Christians (still perhaps the majority) to whom it is obvious that to acknowledge an idea as legendary is the same as to dismiss it as worthless I have little to say, apart from pointing out that such insistence is neither useful nor well-grounded. At the same time, it is perfectly true that theirs is the stance that has always been taken by the acknowledged leaders of the Christian church – and indeed, it may well have been the view of the evangelists themselves.

11. This is normally assumed to be the church at Rome, but the idea should perhaps be treated with caution. The best indication that the claim might be true is the occasional occurrence of trans-literated Latin words in the Greek text. We know that the earliest Christian congregation at Rome was completely Greek speaking for more than a century. (The earliest bishop of Rome who was not a native Greek speaker was Victor I – c.189: the liturgy used by the Roman Christians remained in Greek for a good while after that.) A gospel written in Greek with a sprinkling of strident Latinisms fits these known circumstances fairly well. On the other hand the idea has undoubtedly been helped along by (*a*) the traditional association of the work with Peter and (*b*) the traditional associa-tion of Peter with Rome. On (*a*) see the appendix at the end of section 1; on (*b*) it has already been pointed out that we have no really worthwhile evidence that Peter ever went to Rome.

12. The Greeks, probably because of their high estimation of man's rational faculties (which no other nation before them ever seems to have entertained), tended to look on the material world as a gross clog on man's spiritual and rational nature. It is from this source that Christianity derives its own undoubted hostility to everything physical and material – in direct contrast to the attitude we find to these things throughout the Old Testament.

13. This radical ambiguity can be pinpointed by contrasting 'I and the Father are one' (10.30) with 'the Father is greater than I' (14.28); but these are merely the extreme points of a fluctuating ambiguity that persists throughout the work.

14. 'Haeresis' is a Latin transliteration of a Greek word which originally meant no more than the distinguishing ideas of a philosophical sect – of which there were a very great many in pagan philosophy, each putting forward its own opinions and criticizing those of opponents, to the scandal and disquiet of absolutely nobody. Internal disagreements were equally common in early Christianity, but from the outset the tone of the discussion was vitiated by (*a*) the quite groundless belief that the truth of the question actually mattered, and (*b*) the equally groundless conviction of all parties that they actually knew what that truth was. The long term consequence of this frantic dedication to such groundless claims are perhaps the most notorious blot on the whole history of Western civilization.

15. As I have already made clear in the appendix to section I, my own opinion is that he did. But if so, then the author thought of himself as being specifically *opposed to docetism* ('By this you know the Spirit of God: every spirit [i.e., inspired preacher] which confesses that Jesus Christ has come in the flesh is of God, and every spirit which does not confess Jesus is not of God' – I John 4.2–3; see also II John 7). But this does not automatically mean that the author avoids the charge of docetism as far as the modern reader is concerned. Among traditional Christians, after all, Protestants have tended to accuse Catholics of credulity; but to the modern agnostic,

... Strange all this difference there should be
'Twixt Tweedledum and Tweedledee.

16. Some early manuscripts of Luke's gospel omit verses 43 and 44 from chapter 22. This would normally indicate that these verses are a later addition to the text. As the reader will see, though, from the present discussion, in this instance another explanation readily suggests itself: the passage may in fact have been expunged in some manuscripts by scribes who found its theological implications just too shocking.

17. As the Old Testament now stands, the earliest anointing is that of Aaron and his sons, commanded in Exodus 28.41, 30.30 and 40.13–15, and carried out in Leviticus chapter 8. It is fairly certain however, that although the Pentateuch (the first five books of the Old Testament) contains themes, and even a great deal of actual material, of great antiquity, in its present form it dates from *after* the monarchy. It will be obvious to any one reading these books, particularly the long ceremonial sections scattered through Exodus to Numbers, that they describe the past not so much as it was but as the professional priesthood would like to have imagined it;

scholars plausibly suggest that the impetus to this extended ecc-lesiastical daydreaming was provided by the destruction of the temple in 586 BC, and the wholesale deportation of the priesthood to Babylon at that time, as well as the earlier deportation of 597 BC. We presume (but do not know) that the custom of anointing priests grew up during the later monarchy; the suggestion is even worth bearing in mind that the priests simply usurped the rite once the monarchy had ceased. The earliest description of the making of a priest that seriously interests the historian is that described in Judges 17.5 and 17.12, where in both instances the priest is not anointed at all but simply 'installed'. The Hebrew word for 'con-secrate' means literally to 'fill the hands', and those parts of Leviticus 8 which relate to this theme very probably reflect the reality of ancient pratice.

1. First Appearance (1.1–15)

   1. The Greek translation of the Old Testament, originally made (according to the traditional account) at the instigation of Ptolemy Philadelphus (285–246 BC) who wanted a version of it for his famous library at Alexandria. The Latin word *septuaginta*, from which the traditional name derives, means 'seventy', the tradition being that Ptolemy entrusted seventy (some say seventy-two) scholars with the task. The Alexandrian origin of the work can be accepted, but much of the rest of this account seems fanciful. Internal evidence, for instance, suggests that – like Topsy – the work as a whole just 'growed' without ever being deliberately planned or supervised.

      In New Testament times the Septuagint was *the* Christian Bible, and New Testament quotations from the Old Testament are always in some version of it; so much so that scholarly Jews quickly came to repudiate it and to produce more accurate versions of their own, while deriding the misunderstandings and errors with which the Septuagint undeniably abounds. It needs to be stressed there-fore that the Septuagint was originally a Jewish work, and produced for the use of Jews.

   2. Note that although it is perfectly credible that Jesus inaugurated his ministry with his baptism by John, it is much less clear that he ever intended that the rite should be obligatory on his followers. Whenever he sends the apostles on a mission (see Mark 3.14–15; 6.7–13; also Matt. 10 and Luke 9.1–5) he mentions preaching, healing, even anointing, but never baptism. The only instructions relating to baptism in the synoptic gospels (Mark 16.16; Matt. 28.19) are put into the mouth of the 'risen Lord', which suggests to the less devout mind that the idea arose in the church after Jesus' death.

   3. The Mount Horeb where Moses meets God in Exodus chapter 3, and the Mount Sinai which he ascends to receive the Law in Exodus

chapter 19 onwards are pretty certainly one and the same mountain. The explanation seems to be that the cultural traditions of the northern tribes of Israel had important differences from those of the southern tribes. To the former the sacred mountain was known as Horeb, to the latter as Sinai. The evidence suggests that in historic times neither tradition was any longer aware of the actual identity of their sacred mountain.

4. One of the big differences between the Septuagint and the original Hebrew Old Testament is that the former contains quite a number of books which are not found in the latter. Christians noticed the discrepancy in antiquity, and though there were attempts to 'purify' the Christian Old Testament they came to nothing. It was the Protestant reformers who first insisted that these 'deutero-canonical books' (as they had come to be called) should be excluded. But they still retained the Septuagintal order of the remaining books in preference to that of the Hebrew Bible. It is no more than a happy accident therefore that in Protestant Bibles Malachi appears as the last book in the Old Testament, and the above passage as the concluding passage. But the effect is quite extraordinarily impressive (if also for that very reason a little misleading), and it does not surprise me that recent Catholic translations of the Bible transfer the two books of Maccabees so that they now precede the book of Job; thus Catholics can also now benefit from this 'providential' accident.

5. The relevant references in Mark's gospel are 2.1; 2.15; 7.17; 9.28; 9.33; 10.10, while Matt. 4.13 looks like his own gloss to explain why Jesus, though a native of 'Nazareth', is found living at Capernaum throughout his ministry. Though both are agreed that Nazareth was his birthplace, it is perhaps significant that when Mark tells us that Jesus 'came to his own country'(6.1), he does not otherwise identify the locality; and the same is true of Matthew 13.54.

   In a passage found only in Luke's gospel, which is unmistakably his own version of the Matthew and Mark passages above, he says quite plainly that 'he came to Nazareth, where he had been brought up' (4.16), and later in the same passage he also makes a contrast between Nazareth and Capernaum and – even more to the point – alludes to Jesus' reputation as a miracle worker at Capernaum, even though he never seems to have done anything remarkable at Nazareth. (At this point in Luke's gospel Jesus has not in fact been near Capernaum or done any miracles at all; but this, though an indication of Luke's occasional clumsiness, does not necessarily undermine his testimony.) Thus all three gospel writers are aware of a contrast between Jesus' brilliant reputation at Capernaum and the indifference with which he was regarded 'at home'. Even though I am convinced that Nazareth is a fiction, a reasonable case could still be made for arguing that Jesus was not a native of Capernaum.

On the question of 'the houses' in Mark's gospel, it could well be argued that the house in question is the house of Simon and Andrew mentions in 1.29, and none of the passages listed above – not even 2.1 – make it unambiguously clear that it was Jesus' own house: 'his house' in 2.15 could just as easily be Levi's house. Luke in the parallel passage (1.29) goes out of his way to make it clear that it was in fact Levi's house, but the experienced interpreter of gospel material is always suspicious when a point appears to be emphasized. It is quite possible that Luke, when he came to the passage in Mark, suddenly remembered that Jesus had at some point said 'Foxes have holes, and birds of the air have nests; but the Son of man has nowhere to lay his head' (Matt. 8.20; Luke 9.58), and may have felt obliged to make his story consistent. Mark, on the other hand, does not include the saying.

6. The references are Mark 6.14–16 (= Mat. 14.1–2; Luke 9.7–9); Mark 8.28 (= Matt. 16.14; Luke 9.19). The popular view of who Jesus was is unambiguous, but scholars have questioned whether Herod could have been quite as naive or credulous as that. They suggest that what he really meant was, 'This is the John the Baptist business starting up again', an interpretation which Luke 9.7–9 strongly supports, but perhaps only because the very same point had occurred to Luke himself. His wording is markedly different from that of the other two, who in any case differ significantly from each other: Mark could just about be interpreted in this sophisticated fashion, whereas Matthew seems to take pains to exclude the possibility.

2. 'A Day in the Life of ...' (1.16–30)

1. The main event that gives this impression is Peter's confession that Jesus is the Christ, an impression that is strengthened rather than diminished by Mark's portrayal of him as completely misunderstanding what the Christ is to be like and receiving as a consequence the strongest rebuke that Jesus delivers anywhere in the gospel (Mark 8.27–33). On the other hand, would the disciples have needed to discuss who was the greatest (Mark 9.33) if this was known to be Peter? Also James and John were no doubt sticking their necks out when they suggested to Jesus (Mark 10.35–45) that they should be first and second lieutenant; but I suggest it is improbable, nor does the text at this point in any way imply, that they did this in a deliberate attempt to oust the succession from Peter. What the text does very strongly imply is that at no time was Jesus willing to discuss, much less to settle, the question of which of them was to be leader.

2. One of the more questionable features of the RSV translation of the gospels is its inconsistency in rendering the word 'rabbi'. Anyone looking at the RSV concordance would reasonably conclude that Jesus is frequently addressed by the disciples as 'Rabbi' in John's gospel but never in the other three. This is not in fact the case; Jesus

is occasionally addressed as 'Rabbi' in all four gospels, but for some reason the translators have chosen to translate the word as 'Master' in the synoptic gospels but to transliterate as 'Rabbi' in the fourth. There seems to be no justification for this inconvenient discrepancy.

3. A good illustration of this is the forty days in the wilderness after Jesus' baptism, already discussed in the last chapter. The deliberate echo of Elijah's sojourn in the wilderness may well have been part of Jesus' original intention. But even on this assumption, the intention will have been understood only by Old Testament readers, and have been preserved in the tradition up to Mark's time only through an unbroken series of such readers.

4. In view of the enthusiastic efforts of modern revivalism to reintroduce the notion of possession by demons or unclean spirits into Christianity, it is instructive to analyse the use of the idea by the various gospels. Of the four of them it is only Mark who is wholehearted in his belief in the idea, though in this it is likely that he accurately records the attitude of Jesus himself and of the earliest disciples. In John's gospel, the latest of the four, the whole notion of demon possession has been discarded altogether; the ignorant and hostile crowd occasionally make the groundless accusation that Jesus himself is possessed (7.20; 8.48–52; 10.20–21), but actual cases of demon possession never occur.

But there are clear signs that Matthew also was somewhat embarassed by Mark's uncritical enthusiasm for the notion. He seems very reluctant to talk about 'unclean spirits' altogether. The references in Mark are 1.23–27; 3.11; 3.30; 5.2; 5.8; 5.13; 6.7; 7.25; 9.25; in Matthew this is reduced to 10.1 and 12.43, the second of these being a Q passage where there is an undeniable literary source common to Matthew and Luke (11.24). Even Luke, though much longer than Mark, has reduced the twelve references he found in Mark to six in his own gospel, including the Q reference just noted. Both Matthew and Luke seem ready to accept talk about demons; but again there are signs that initially Matthew may have resisted the idea and then abandoned his resistance as impractical. The three references to demons in Mark 1.32–34 have been reduced to one in Matthew 8.17, while the story of the man in the synagogue has been omitted altogether. If we can detect this kind of intellectual advance in the first century AD, it is a pity we should try to reverse it in the twentieth.

5. It is plausibly suggested, though we have no direct evidence to this effect, that since there are four sabbath days to the month, and the month in question is a lunar month, these four days originally corresponded to the four phases of the moon; and that work was prohibited on these days because they were considered unlucky (compare the *dies nefasti* of the Romans). This would mean that the explanations of the sabbath rest offered by the Old Testament are both of them 'pious errors'. The first and better known, perhaps

because taken up in the New Testament by the author to the Hebrews (4.4), is that God, having created the world in six days, then rested on the seventh (Ex. 20.8–11 referring to Gen. 2.2–3); the second is the suggestion in Deuteronomy (5.12–15) that it is a reminder of Israel's servitude in Egypt, and therefore of God's deliverance of them from it. It is possible that these reinterpretations are attempts to conceal elements of a primitive paganism in the tradition which later orthodoxy disliked; or it may simply be that the true origin of the rest had been forgotten, and these reasons were invented to answer an obvious question.

3. Jesus and the Pharisees (1.40–3.12)

1. 7.36–50 for instance looks like a souped-up version of Mark 14.1–10 which is on a completely different theme. 10.29–37, 15.11–32, 18.9–14 and 19.2–10 are all suspect precisely because so very 'improving'. In 17.11–19 did the Samaritan actually say, 'I'm a Samaritan'?; and if not, how did Jesus know?; which leaves only 7.29–30, 13.28–29, 15.1–10 as likely to be authentic.

2. It is noticeable though, and very curious, that Luke's material deals equally with social and ethnic outcasts, whereas Matthew tends to avoid any mention of the second as being of any interest at all to Jesus, Matthew 8.5–13 (= Luke 7.1–10 plus Luke 13.28–29) being the only exception in the whole of the gospel. In 10.5 Jesus begins his instructions to the missionaries with the words (found nowhere else in any gospel, and directly contradicted, as we have seen, by a great deal in Luke): 'Go nowhere among the Gentiles, and enter no town of the Samaritans, but go rather to the lost sheep of the house of Israel'. However it is by no means impossible that the saying is authentic: as we shall see, we have reason to believe that Jesus did in fact – at least in part – share the prejudice of his fellow-countrymen on the subject of Samaritans. As regards Gentiles, we have only one instance in Mark (7.24–30 = Matthew 15.21–28, excluded by Luke for reasons that will now be obvious) of Jesus ever coming in contact with them. Initially his attitude towards the woman is one of rejection (even more so in Matthew than in Mark); but he changes his mind when she persists – and, as on other occasions, openly admires her persistence.

A more interesting question in some ways is what Matthew himself understood the saying in 10.5 to mean. It is often suggested, though I find the suggestion unbelievable, that Matthew was writing for an exclusively, or at least preponderately, Jewish readership. But as we have already pointed out, particularly with reference to chapter 23, Matthew is the Jew-hater *par excellence* – much more so even than John's gospel. And how could we account for for 27.25 (His blood be on us and on our children) on such a supposition? I suspect the true explanation is that Matthew wanted to emphasize a claim which until very recent times was one of the basic claims of Christianity (and has gone out of fashion, I dare say, only because of the events of the Second World War): that after the resurrection the concept of Israel can no longer be exclusively, or even chiefly, applied to the nation, but from that point on properly belongs to the followers of Jesus regardless of their ethnic origins. This idea is already one of the basic claims of Paul's epistle to the Romans, a work that must be a good ten years earlier even than Mark's gospel. By the time Matthew wrote – no earlier than the seventies, and quite possibly in the eighties – it is hard to believe that there were any congregations anywhere that were preponderately Jewish; and the seething hatred that Jews and Christians typically felt for each other was already at least a generation old.

The contrast between Matthew and Luke on this subject illustrates the difference between them more clearly than any other topic, and is heavily in favour of Luke – not so much as a historian but as a human being. Matthew hates the Jews, but will have no truck with Samaritans and Gentiles either. Luke is emphatic in his openness towards these last, but is also the only one of the four evangelists who goes out of his way to show Jesus as being more than occasionally on friendly terms with the Jewish leaders also: this second aspect, unlike the first, is likely to be authentic history.

3. It must be admitted, on the other hand, that the Vulgate translation is exceedingly inappropriate. The *telonae* of the gospels are quite rightly portrayed as hated and despised; but no one ever despised (though they might sometimes have hated) a *publicanus*, who was invariably a man of considerable wealth and considerable influence. The Roman empire, in some ways like modern British Conservatism was happy to pay out on defence, but apart from that was a firm believer in privatization of public services wherever possible, a belief which extended even to tax-collecting. The senate divided the empire into various districts, and then auctioned the tax revenues of these districts to the highest bidder. It was these bidders who are properly described as *publicani*. As far as the senate was concerned, it was the money they received for the franchise that constituted the revenue; the money the *publicani* actually raised – in amounts of which they were the sole arbiters – was theirs. Naturally they expected to operate at a profit; so that even apart from considerations of paying taxes to a foreign power to help keep them in subjection, the knowledge of how the system worked enormously inflamed the resentment of those at the paying end of it. The *telonae* of the gospels are not themselves *publicani*, but merely the duns, bailiffs and petty clerks responsible for the face-to-face extortion. I presume the reader will not now need any further explanation of why they were so hated and despised.

4. It is quite likely that this assumption was made by the tradition as a whole in the early days, and not just by Mark. The reader may have noticed in the passages quoted on pages 83–4 that the Matthew passage starts: 'Then a blind and dumb demoniac was brought to him'; similarly Luke: 'Now he was casting out a demon that was

dumb.' The suggestion here seems to derive from Q material, and makes the assumption far more explicit than Mark himself ever does.

5. It is clear from the gospels that religious orthodoxy in Jesus' day still held the Old Testament belief that suffering was commonly (though not necessarily invariably) a punishment for sin, and that this was particularly true of bodily affliction. Christians like to claim that Jesus did not share this view, but the evidence as a whole seems to be against them. John's gospel, while less than fully explicit, does to some extent seem to make Jesus question it:

> As he passed by, he saw a man blind from his birth. And his disciples asked him, 'Rabbi, who sinned, this man or his parents, that he was born blind?' Jesus answeried, 'It was not that this man sinned, or his parents, but that the works of God might be made manifest in him'. (John 9.1–3)

The ambiguity here is that although Jesus denies that bodily ailment is a punishment for sin *in this particular case*, even in the fourth gospel we have no clear statement that this was his general view. On the other hand the evidence from the synoptic gospels, which on historical questions is the only evidence worth considering, makes it pretty clear that Jesus did very largely share the orthodox view. The passage (only in Luke) usually cited to prove the contrary in fact does no such thing:

> There were some present at that very time who told him of the Galilaeans whose blood Pilate had mingled with their sacrifices. And he answered them, 'Do you think that these Galilaeans were worse sinners than all the other Galilaeans, because they suffered thus? I tell you, No; but unless you repent you will all likewise perish. Or those eighteen upon whom the tower in Siloam fell and killed them, do you think that they were worse offenders than all the others who dwelt in Jerusalem? I tell you, No; but unless you repent you will all likewise perish,' (Luke 13.1–5)

The references are clearly to two recent disasters of which we have no other record. The second is clear enough, but it might be helpful to some readers to have the first explained. As the appendix will explain, it looks as though 'Galilaeans' here is yet another word for Zealots. In the course of a religious festival (not necessarily in Galilee at all – in fact unlikely to be so, since Galilee was under Herod's and not Pilate's jurisdiction) a political disturbance had arisen – something that was always likely to happen in this part of the world at this time – and the Roman army had forcibly suppressed the disturbance. The popular view would be that those who died must also have been particularly sinful, and were in this way being punished for their sin (see II Macc. 12.39–40); similarly with the victims of the accidental collapse of the tower in Siloam. Jesus' own attitude is perfectly clear (and likely to be authentic):

Yes, they *were* being punished for their sins. But their sins were in fact no worse than yours, so that the same danger hangs over all of you unless you repent.

Although it is not explicitly stated, I have no doubt that in the present passage both Jesus and his hearers share a common assumption that the paralysed man is in the condition he is in as a consequence of sin, and this assumption seems to me to be required to make sense of the passage.

6. In case anyone doubts the possibility of Luke doing anything so obviously inept, let me point out that this is not the only – nor the worst – instance of him doing it. In Luke 16.19–31 we have the parable of Dives and Lazarus, which Luke very obviously interprets as being a parable by Jesus about the proper use of wealth: Dives has misused his wealth, and goes to hell as a result. Without changing a word of what he wrote, a very much more likely interpretation occurs to the modern reader. The story looks much more like an *anti-Christian, Jewish* story whose point is the very good one that if you want to lead a virtuous life, the existing religious tradition already provides you with the means of doing so; and if you find these means insufficient, then there is *nothing* that will be sufficient – not even the resurrection of somebody from the dead.

7. A very good example of this is the New Testament attitude to slavery, and to what we call political injustice generally. Not only are *all* the New Testament authors who ever discuss the subject completely tolerant of slavery, but it never seems even to have occurred to them that the morality of it could be questioned (Ephes. 6.5–9; Col. 3.22–4; I Tim. 6.1–2; Titus 2.9–10; I Peter 1.8–25). On the wider question of political injustice, the New Testament gives the unambiguous instruction, nowhere contradicted, that submission to political authority is an absolute moral requirement (Rom. 13.1–7); and in the only document which ever raises the question of an unjust regime (I Peter) the advice given is that unresisting submission to injustice is positively meritorious. This may not be what our generation wants to hear, but it is undoubtedly what the New Testament actually says.

4. Jesus and the New Israel (3.13–35)

1. In some cases quite literally. The son of Saul who succeeded to his precarious throne after Saul himself and three of his sons were killed in battle on Mount Gilboa (I Sam. 31) is consistently called Ishbosheth in II Sam. chapters 2 to 4; in I Chron. 8.33 and 9.39 we learn that his name was in fact Eshbaal. *Bosheth* is the Hebrew for 'shame'. Similarly in II Samuel there is frequent mention of a surviving son of Jonathan who is there always called Mephibosheth; we learn from I Chron. 8.34 and 9.40 that his real name was Meribael. The work of the Chronicler has largely escaped the censor's blue pencil only because not many people have

ever bothered to read it. Any modern reader now making the attempt will quickly appreciate why.

Most interesting of all is Num. 32.38. Both Nebo and Baal in Baal-meon are the names of pagan deities, and the censor has noted that the names must be changed. But instead of the scribe taking action, he has simply copied down the censor's mark as part of the text!

5. The Teaching of the Kingdom (4.1–34)

1. I refer of course to the recurrent phrase: 'In those days there was no king in Israel; [every man did what was right in his own eyes]' (17.6; 18.1]; [19.1]; 21.25). He means by this that before there was a king there was (*a*) a shocking degree of lawlessness in Israel, as his last five chapters very well illustrate; but also (*b*) that there was a great deal of what later generations would have condemned as idolatry, such as Micah making his own religious images, setting them up in his own chapel and ordaining his own son as priest (17.3–6).
2. An even more blatant instance of this tendency is Matt. 13.24–30 and its crudely allegorical 'explanation' in 13.37–43. The parable itself, even though found only here, is quite likely to be genuine, making the point that this world contains both good and bad and that one can't even be sure which is which. The explanation on the other hand has all the subtlety and artistry of a price-list.

   It is worth commenting also on the curious aspect that though much of Jesus' ministry is supposed to have taken place round the lake of Galilee, the vast majority of the parables are concerned with agriculture and arboriculture, Matt. 13.47–48 (49–50 being once again the shopkeeper's explanation) is the only one concerned with fishing that looks to be genuine. Parables about sheep and the shepherd, a theme which the tenth chapter of John's gospel has made perhaps the most appealing of all Christian imagery, is also scarcely to be found in the synoptics. There are references to 'sheep without a shepherd' (Matt. 9.36 = Mark 6.34), 'the lost sheep of the house of Israel' (Matt. 10.6: 15.24), and 'sheep in the midst of wolves' (Matt. 10.16); but the only parable which looks as though it might be authentic is Luke 15.3–7 (the last verse, though, looks doubtful to me). Apart from the single reference above (6.34), there is no mention of the theme in Mark's gospel.

6. The Healing of the Kingdom (4.35–6.6)

1. Mark says specifically that there were five thousand 'men', and the word he uses (*andres*) must actually mean 'men', and cannot simply mean 'people' (*anthrōpoi*); Matthew sees his opportunity for improving the miracle and adds (Matt. 14.21) 'besides women and children', giving us a likely figure of over ten thousand. But we will set this complication aside.

2. If anyone protests at that, perhaps they should themselves make the experiment of trying to wash someone's feet with their tears and – even more frustrating – to dry them with their hair.

7. The Mission of the Kingdom (6.7–56)

1. Jesus himself never seems to have thought in terms of 'life after death'. *All* the instances in the synoptic gospels where he seems to do so, or is traditionally interpreted as doing so, make better sense (and more plausible history) if they are interpreted as referring to what we should call 'quality of life'. He seems to have believed absolutely literally and in all seriousness that his own sacrificial death would at once inaugurate the new age in which he would immediately return to life and that his followers would never die: hence (at least for his hearers) there was no need of life after death. 'Eternal life', assuming he used the phrase (Mark 10.17 and 10.30), seems to mean not 'life after death', but becoming one of those who from now on were going to live for ever. As we have seen (I Cor. 11.30) in the very early years of Christianity the death of believers before Jesus' return to earth was felt to be a very serious problem.

2. One of the unfortunate consequences of this idea of Jesus having given authority to the apostles is the subsequent development of the idea of there being an 'apostolic succession'. This has been interpreted to mean that not only did Jesus give authority to the apostles (and without it their mission would have been worthless) but the apostles also gave authority to their successors by means of the laying on of hands; and that therefore any parson who has not received this authority is a kind of ecclesiastical free-booter. The best demonstration of the historical worthlessness of such a claim that I know of is Lord Macaulay's review of Gladstone's *The State in its Relations with the Church*. The doctrinal worthlessness needs no other demonstration that the unedifying arguments among Christian churches themselves as to which of them are as it were plugged into the mains, and which of them are operating their own generators without a licence. Most of us in any case would nowadays read Mark 9.38 as a downright refutation of any such idea from Jesus' own mouth.

3. Mark's actual Greek is: *Apelthontes agorasōmen dēnariōn diakosiōn artous* – 'Shall we go and buy loaves for two hundred denarii?' The *denarius* was a Roman coin worth (as its name implies) ten *assess* or four *sestertii*; in these days of sliding values it probably isn't worth being any more precise than that. The RSV at this point talks about 'two hundred denarii worth' and notes that the denarius was a day's wage for a labourer (but relying, I suspect, on Matt. 20.1–16 rather than any precise or scientific evaluation – even for those days a denarius a day sounds to me a bit stingy). Since, as I say, there is little point in being precise about the value, I have preferred English to archaeology and reverted to the traditional 'two hundred pennyworth'.

8. The Kingdom of the Gentiles (7.1–8.10)

1. See Luke 24.52–53; Acts 2.46; 3.1–4.22; 5.12–42. This apparent obsession of the early Christians with the temple, hard to explain in itself, goes a long way to explain some features of the early chapters of Acts which would otherwise be puzzling, the most obvious being the immediate and persistent persecution of the infant church by the Jerusalem priests. The author of Acts tries to give the impression that the motive for this was priestly feelings of guilt over the crime that had been committed in executing Jesus ('We strictly charged you not to teach in his name, yet here you have filled Jerusalem with your teaching and you intend to bring this man's blood upon us' Acts 5.28). But a more plausible reason is the rather simpler one that the disciples were a persistent nuisance in the temple precincts, and one that could not be ignored (And every day in the temple and at home they did not cease teaching and preaching Jesus as the Christ.) It also goes a long way to explain the most puzzling event of all – the martyrdom of Stephen. We have no reason to doubt, for instance, the accuracy of John's gospel: Pilate said to them, 'Take him yourselves and judge him by your own law'. The Jews said to him, 'It is not lawful for us to put any man to death' (John 18.31–32). Although Acts 6.8 and 7 suggest that Stephen delivered his denunciation of the Temple and the Law at a formal trial before the priests, it seems much more likely to me that he met his death at the hands of an enraged mob after uttering these sentiments before all-comers in the temple itself – compare what nearly happens to Paul in Acts 21.27–36.

2. No doubt a large number of these conservatives rejected Christianity altogether when they saw the new direction it was taking. But we know that for about two centuries after Jesus' death there was a 'sect' (this time it is Christian terminology) of Ebionites in Palestine. '... two of their principal tenets were (1) a "reduced" doctrine of the Person of Christ, to the effect, e.g., that Jesus was the human son of Joseph and Mary and that the Holy Spirit in the form of a dove lighted on Him at his baptism, and (2) over-emphasis on the binding character of the Mosaic Law' (*Oxford Dictionary of the Christian Church*, second edition 1974). There can be no doubt that these Ebionites accurately reflect the ideas of the earliest Christians before Stephen/Pauline ideas of universalism overtook the new movement and fundamentally changed its character.

3. This sounds a lot more edifying than it is likely in fact to have been: he means that the audience got carried away, lost all control of itself, and started up a frenzied and unintelligible babbling. 'Speaking in tongues' in the New Testament always describes, just this phenonemon, and it is clear that from earliest days there were some leaders – notably Paul – who were extremely dubious about the value of this particular 'gift' (see particularly I Corinthians 14 on the subject). Nevertheless there are still Christian bodies today who

insist – and it must be admitted on very good scriptural grounds – that this is the only real meaning of the 'gift of the Spirit' in the New Testament, and the only convincing sign that such a gift has been received.

4. Nor has there ever been a convincing suggestion how the numbers five thousand and five loaves relate to Jews, or the number four thousand to Gentiles.

9. The Solving of the Riddle (8.11–9.1)

1. We must also remember that in the days before printing, every single copy of any particular work was an individually produced item. If thirty copies originally circulated at Rome, every one of those copies was different, not only as regards format and punctuation, but also as regards accuracy. All of them contained errors, even the original author's copy (whether written by Mark himself or dictated to a slave); there was no such thing in antiquity as a perfect copy.

2. Although the phrase 'the Pharisees and the Sadducees' sticks in the mind of regular churchgoers, it is to be observed that it is Matthew alone who created this combination. Outside his gospel it occurs only once – and even then not as any kind of formula – in Acts 23.7, Matthew (unlike Luke) specifies that it was 'Pharisees and Sadducees' rather than 'the multitudes' that John the Baptist reviled as 'a brood of vipers', In Mark's gospel Jesus only ever encounters the Sadducees in Jerusalem, and this almost certainly corresponds to fact. Although it is true that in the event it was the Sadducees who brought about his death, it is overwhelmingly likely that had he not bothered them (i.e. by meddling with the temple), they also would not have bothered him. As for Matt. 16.1–4, a real-life Sadducee might well have had difficulty keeping a straight face had he overheard such a dialogue.

3. The evidence suggests that his concept of the Messiah derived from a combination of the ideas of the Son of Man from Daniel chapter 7 and that of the 'Suffering Servant' passages from Isaiah chapters 41–53. To suggest this, however, points to a certain conflict in the evidence; if Jesus identified with these Isaiah chapters, isn't this very considerably at odds with the portrait I have offered of a man who seems to have fought shy of contact with Gentiles, and to have doubted whether his message was really for them at all? I readily admit the contradiction; but after a lot of thought I have concluded that it lies in the evidence itself, and not in my interpretation of it.

4. As mentioned previously, none of the gospels offers any indication that Jesus was ever afflicted himself, or thought that his followers should be afflicted, with the Pauline guilty conscience; but this may be due, at least in part, to a tradition already established by the time Mark wrote of thinking of Jesus as 'sinless'.

5. The usual theory is in fact to attribute 40–55 to Deutero-Isaiah but

I can see no reason why these last two chapters should be included. The crucial point in my view is the occurrence of the word 'servant' in the singular. There are twenty-four occurrences in the Isaiah collection as a whole, twenty of them occurring in chapters 41–53. Since this crucial word does not occur in chapters 54 and 55, I can see no reason for including them as part of Deutero-Isaiah, instead of as part of the remainder of the book. In that case, it could be objected, why not discard chapter 40 as well? I have in fact assumed above that the unified complex of which we are talking really starts with 40.12 with God's majestic description (unparalleled in Old Testament literature) of his own activity in creating and sustaining the universal world. It also needs to be said that we have no real reason for regarding the last thirteen chapters of Isaiah as any sort of unity. But the arguments for regarding 40–53 as a unity are clearly very good indeed.

10. The Road to Jerusalem I (9.2–50)

1. Even Christians themselves would nowadays rather not be reminded, but for most of the church's history the official view of sex was that it is *always* sinful, *even within marriage*. The only circumstance which renders the 'sin' pardonable is the sincere intention to beget a child. Even after such an extreme and hideous notion has long been discarded, its baleful influence is still apparent. It clearly underlies, for instance, the difficulties the Catholic church still has over contraception, and it equally underlies the difficulties all Christian bodies still seem to have over homosexuality.

12. Jesus and Jerusalem (10.46–12.44)

1. Some readers may at some time in their lives have wondered why it is that Matthew's account of the triumphal entry in 21.1–11 seems to make Jesus simultaneously ride *both* an ass *and* its colt. The precise wording of this passage from Zechariah, coupled with Matthew's extraordinary fixation about Old Testament prophecy being fulfilled in the life of Jesus, are jointly responsible for this rather ludicrous image.
2. Very unworldly readers who have actually looked up the passage and are still mystified should be advised that throughout chapter 3 of Ruth the word 'feet' is clearly being used as a euphemism for the genitals.
3. Some Christians like to make a point of the fact that Jesus' summary of the whole duty of man takes the form of two quotations from the Old Testament, and to imply that this somehow 'vindicates' the Old Testament as part of Christian doctrine. I think this approach is a mistake from two points of view. The first is that the Old Testament does not need vindicating in this way. The extreme remoteness with which contemporary Christians tend to

view it is reprehensible in the same way that any other form of
wilful ignorance is reprehensible. But secondly such a reading has
misunderstood the whole point that the scribe is trying to make.
When he asks, 'Which commandment is the first of all?', the
question simply means: 'Which passage from the Torah [in his day,
as in ours, the first five books of the Old Testament] is more
important than any other?' *Any* relevant answer to the question
was bound to be in the form of a quotation from the Torah.

4. I should add that the notorious 'power and glory' clause, which is
   sometimes added in the English prayerbook and sometimes not,
   and tends to be resisted by Roman Catholics as a Protestant
   innovation, is found as an addition to the prayer in some quite early
   texts of Matthew's gospel. The preponderance of the evidence,
   however, does suggest that it is an interpolation rather than being
   integral to the text.

13. The Last Things (13.1–37)

1. It is for this reason that many scholars argue that there cannot
   originally have been any real intention on the part of the author of
   Daniel to deceive, and that the fiction that the work had been
   written four hundred years earlier was no more than a literary
   device, and intended to be immediately recognized as such.

2. As we have seen earlier, it needed no very miraculous vision to
   prophesy this. There is mention of what look like two false
   Messiahs in Acts 5.36–37, and a third in Acts 21.38. It was the
   same kind of Messianism which precipitated the Jewish revolt in AD
   66, culminating in the disaster here prophesied in AD 70. And
   finally, the expulsion of all Jews from Palestine in AD 135 was a
   consequence of the disaster following upon Simon Bar Kochbar's
   claim to be Messiah. False Messiahs were an endemic political
   disorder in the situation of first century Judaea, and no doubt both
   Pilate and the chief priests were prepare to think of Jesus himself as
   just another of them.

14. The Passion Narrative (14.1–15.47)

1. There is no doubt in my mind that Mark intended the whole of
   what we call chapters 14–16 to be one continuous section, and that
   one is falsifying his intention to treat the resurrection as a separate
   section following after the passion and death. It becomes necessary
   to do this, however, not for any theological reason, but simply
   because the apparently lost ending raises questions of a fundamentally different kind from those of the rest of the narrative.

2. The Greek text here talks about *dēnarii*, and the translators have
   followed their usual practice of simply transliterating. I have
   thought it better to revert to the traditional 'pence' of the English
   versions, simply for the sake of euphony.

3. We have no reason to suppose that even Luke thought of 'the

woman of the city' as Mary Magdalene. It looks as though, since her story is the concluding episode of chapter 7, and the first mention of Mary Magdalene is in the opening paragraph of chapter 8, and is accompanied by the description of her as someone 'from whom seven demons had gone out' (Luke 8.2), the tradition (probably assisted by 12.3 of John's gospel) took the concluding episode of chapter 7 as providing the likeliest explanation of the description in chapter 8. But it is extremely unlikely that Luke intended any such connection, and the real meaning of his description of Mary is that she was a cured lunatic rather than a reformed prostitute. Also in view of the fact that Mary Magdalene has played a prominent role in popular ideas about the gospel, it is important to point out that in Mark (and, following him, in Matthew) she is a rather shadowy figure; in neither of these gospels is she ever mentioned until towards the very end of the passion narrative. She is one of the women 'looking on from afar' in Mark 15.40, and one of the two women who witnessed the burial in 15:17, and who were about to anoint the body two days later when they found the tomb empty. The implication of this is undoubtedly that she was close to Jesus, and that she felt his death most deeply. Her prominence in popular tradition is presumably the consequence of an understandable eagerness to explain why that should be so, despite the fact that we know so little about her.

4. Assuming, as I am inclined to, that the incident actually happened, it was this shocking extravagance that originally fixed it in everyone's mind. But naturally as time wore on the shock wore off, and already in the Lucan version the incident has been overdramatized in an attempt to find new reasons for making the scene memorable. In Mark's version the wasteful sacrifice of the precious object is the focus of attention, and the woman simply pours the contents over Jesus' head. By Luke's time this action has lost its power to shock, and both the motive and the manner of the deed have been heavily 'reorchestrated'.

5. I said earlier that Luke's passion narrative was completely independent of the Matthew/Mark version and by and large this is true. But there are passages which provide exceptions to this view, particularly here in the opening episodes. Most of the first thirteen verses of Luke's account for instance are in fact to be classified as P (i.e. too closely resembling Matthew/Mark for the resemblance to be a coincidence). And the second part of Jesus' words over the cup seem to be Q (compare the verse in Matthew but not found in Mark: 'I tell you I shall not drink again of this fruit of the vine until that day when I drink it new with you in my Father's kingdom' (Matt. 26.29). It seems likely that although Matthew follows Mark closely throughout his passion narrative, he also knew of other accounts which by and large he rejected.

6. Earlier in the chapter Jesus has contrasted himself, as the living bread which comes down from heaven, with the heavenly manna

which fed the ancestors of his present hearers in the wilderness. It is these ancestors that are here being referred to as 'the fathers'.

7. Mark describes it simply as 'a place which was called Gethsemane', and in this he is followed by Matthew (26.36). Luke gives no place name as the setting for the arrest apart from the Mount of Olives (Luke 22.39). John gives no place name at all; ('he went forth with his disciples across the Kidron valley, where there was a garden' (John 18.1). It is for this reason the tradition talks about 'the garden of Gethsemane', but even if the conflation is accurate, we should probably think in terms of an area of uncultivated ground which belonged to no one in particular.

8. Matthew's passion narrative is the sole source of one of the most resonent of all the sayings attributed to Jesus: '... all who take the sword will perish by the sword.' The evidence rather suggests that it was originally Matthew's own coining. For once, he gets an alpha.

9. I presume all readers will have noticed that throughout the history of Western depiction of the crucifixion a sheet of paper (originally it was more likely to have been a wooden tablet) is nailed above Jesus' head, with the letters INRI written on it. These derive from John's gospel, where we are told: Pilate also wrote a title and put it on the cross; it read, 'Jesus of Nazareth, the King of the Jews'. Many of the Jews read this title, for the place where Jesus was crucified was near the city; and it was written in Hebrew, in Latin, and in Greek. Artists have tended to ignore the Greek and Hebrew (if the detail is authentic, it would in fact have been Aramaic) and rendered only the Latin. In the Vulgate text the title reads: Iesus Nazarenus, Rex Iudaeorum.

10. All this strongly reinforces the suggestion I made earlier that although Acts 7 tells us that Stephen was condemned by the priestly council to be stoned, it is much more likely that in fact he was stoned by the mob. It is clear, for instance, that Paul would have encountered a similar fate had he not been rescued by the Romans, and that the Romans themselves were very reluctant to agree to his execution on grounds that in their eyes were based on nothing but fanaticism and superstition. And if in Stephen's case it was the council that had authorized his death, why didn't they themselves make sure of Jesus in the same way?

11. This is particularly marked in Matthew's gospel, the only one to contain an account of Pilate washing his hands before the crowd. In the light of recent history, could anything be more chilling:

> So when Pilate saw that he was gaining nothing, but rather that a riot was beginning, he took water and washed his hands before the crowd, saying, 'I am innocent of this [righteous] [man's] blood; see to it yourselves.' And all the people answered, 'His blood be on us and on our children!' (Matt. 27.24–25)

12. Matthew's gospel insists that it was: And they stripped him and put a scarlet robe upon him and plaiting a crown of thorns they put it

on his head, and put a reed in his right hand (Matt. 27.28–29a). For some reason which I cannot fathom the author of John's gospel objects to the reed; he makes no mention of it, and when it comes to the mocking he specifically states that they struck him with their hands (John 19.3).

13. Matthew alters Mark's 'wine mingled with myrrh' to 'wine ... mingled with gall' (Matt. 27.34). His sole reason for doing so seems to be to allow 'prophesy' to influence the course of the crucifixion (see Ps. 69.21 where, though the modern versions seem to agree on translating the first line as 'They gave me poison to eat', the Greek Old Testament, with which the earliest Christians were most familiar, translates as 'They gave me gall to eat'.

15. The Ending (16.1–?)

1. This 'sign' is still practised by enthusiastic revivalist sects today, nor have we any reason to doubt their claim that its manifestation among them is absolutely the same as the way it is described, for instance, by Paul in I Corinthians chapter 14. The claim is convincing precisely because it explains just why Paul in the passage cited is so dubious about this 'sign'. To the detached observer it looks not the least like anything that one would describe as 'speaking with tongues'; it is simply a group of excitable people getting themselves worked up until their exclamations become more and more unintelligible, and end up as pure jibberish. Reading between the lines it is obvious that just the same phenomenon underlies the event described in Acts 2.1–13. At first reading it is a totally miraculous account of how a group of monoglot enthusiasts preached to an assembly of all sorts of languages and were simultaneously understood by each of them in his own tongue. Yet the concluding verse of the narration totally gives the game away: But others mocking, said, 'They are filled with new wine.' As a comment on what we have just been told this is quite unintelligible; as a comment on the scene described in I Corinthians 14 it is only too apt. It is noteworthy also that in the sermon delivered by Peter that immediately follows he makes no reference at all to the supposed miracle, but on the other hand he goes to some lengths to refute the mocking accusation.

2. That is to say, Peter. His real name was Simon, and it seems to have been Jesus who gave him the nick-name Peter. Only Matthew attempts to tell us why, in a passage (Matt. 16.13–20) that is not entirely convincing as history (see the discussion on pages 158–9). The pun that Matthew makes use of is already a Greek pun; what Jesus actually called him was undoubtedly what Paul calls him here, Cephas being close to the Aramaic for rock as Peter is to the Greek for it.

3. We should remember that Paul was a more sophisticated man than any of his fellow Christians; nor have we any reason to doubt that

he could be taken seriously by educated and high-ranking pagans, as we find particularly in the later chapters of Acts, and that he was normally well aware of the different approaches needed in dealing with people of different backgrounds (Act 26.24–26).

4. 'Spiritual values' initially causes difficulty. If we stick to the definition, it is obvious that all values are spiritual, whereas in actual use of the term it is just as obvious they are not. It makes perfect sense to talk about 'material values' as distinct from 'spiritual values', and it is even correct to classify materialism itself as a value. I would like to suggest that 'spiritual values' are values that give a high degree of importance to 'spiritual beings' and 'spiritual events', and 'material values' are values that give a low importance, or no importance at all to such beings and such events. (It clearly will not do to define 'material values' simply as values that give a high degree of importance to the material world; to most of us, anyone who does not do that is more likely to seem insane than merely spiritual.) I don't think this creates any obscurity or ambiguity, or leaves any instances not dealt with.